The Politics of The Mass Media

The Politics of The Mass Media

Calvin F. Exoo

Professor of Government
St. Lawrence University
Canton, New York

WEST PUBLISHING COMPANY
Minneapolis/St. Paul   New York   Los Angeles   San Francisco

Compositor: *Parkwood Composition*
Cover and Text Design: *John Edeen*
Copyediting: *Cheryl Wilms*
Index: *Sandi Schroeder, Schroeder Indexing Service*

Photo Credits
Pages 2, 44, 82, and 138: AP/Wide World Photos; Page 188: Copyright © 1992 Los Angeles Daily News; Page 256: NYT Pictures; Page 300: Kim Newton/Woodfin Camp and Associates; Page 333: Christopher Morrow/ St. Lawrence University

Library of Congress Cataloging-in-Publication Data
Exoo, Calvin F.
   The politics of the mass media / Calvin F. Exoo.
     p.   cm.
   Includes bibliographical references and index.
   ISBN 0-314-02891-9 (alk. paper)
    1. Mass media—Political aspects—United States.   2. United States—Politics and government—1989–1993.   I. Title.
P95.82.U6E95 1994
302.23'0973—dc20
                                  93-34599
                                       CIP

For my roots and branches:
for my dear mother, Bess,
and for my best boys,
Christian Michael and Joshua Joel

Contents

3   Why Is That "The Way It Is"? The Sources of News Bias *83*

4   *A Celluloid Syringe: The Politics and Un-Politics of Hollywood Film*   *139*

Preface

Imagine the condition of men living in a sort of cavernous chamber underground, with an entrance open to the light and a long passage all down the cave. Here they have been from childhood, chained by the leg and also by the neck, so they cannot move and can see only what is in front of them, because the chains will not let them turn their heads. At some distance higher up is the light of a fire burning behind them; and between the prisoners and the fire is a track with a parapet built along it, like the screen at a puppet-show, which hides the performers while they show their puppets over the top. . . . Behind this parapet imagine persons carrying along various artificial objects, including figures of men and animals in wood or stone or other materials, which project above the parapet. Prisoners so confined would have seen nothing of themselves or of one another, except the shadows thrown by the fire-light on the wall of the Cave facing them. . . . Such prisoners would recognize as reality nothing but the shadows of those artificial objects.

—Plato, "The Allegory of the Cave"

Little did Plato know how prescient his parable was. It is almost as if, unwittingly, he had peered into the future and seen that our lives would one day be dominated by a shadow show of flickering images.

Does it stretch the truth to say so? Does Plato's allegory over-state the media's hold on our consciousness? You could, as Casey Stengel used to say, look it up. Here's what you'd find. In the average American household, the television set is on more than seven hours a day. The family of that household will spend about 70 percent of their nonworking, waking evening hours watching it. When asked where they learn about "what's going on in the world," a sizable majority of Americans now answer, "Television."

On a recent weekend, Americans paid $33.4 million to share a single cultural experience—the opening of *Lethal Weapon III*. Before they are through, North Americans will spend over $150 million to see it. In any given year, Americans will make the pilgrimage to their local movie theaters about one billion times. Most of those visits will be to one of only a handful of "blockbuster" movies.

On an average day, the individual American sees about 3,000 ads. By the time of high school graduation, she or he will have spent about one-and-a-half years watching TV commercials.

On another average day, over 152 million Americans—82.1% of the adult population—will flip through a newspaper. By the year 2000, two-thirds of those readers will be perusing a paper owned by one of just ten large newspaper chains. Does Plato's parable exaggerate the media's power? Not by much.

It would seem important then to consider this shadow show. To understand it fully, we need to ask not just *what* the media is and does, but *why*. The latter question is the work of theories. This book considers three. Mainly, we look at mass media through the eyes of cultural hegemony theory. It suggests that those who own or control a society's "idea factories"—like the media—can use them to urge their own ideology on others.

This process may sound simple and straightforward. It is not. It is complex and subtle. So complex it has taken a long time—nearly a century—to evolve. To understand it, we need to examine that evolution. And so, each of our media-industry studies includes a brief history of how that medium came to be what it is.

The process of media hegemony is so subtle that those who produce that hegemony are not, for the most part, consciously trying to. They are just doing their jobs. But written, as it were, into their job descriptions are needs, routines, and values that result in hegemony. Those demands and routines arise mainly from the "commercial imperative"—the media industries' voracious appetite for profit. So this book spends time trying to understand how that imperative shapes the process of making mass media.

Of course, a book about the politics of the media is interested in more than the *process* by which it's made. Ultimately, our interest is in the *product* that emerges from that process. In particular, we'll ask, "What is the political and social message of our mass media? And what effects might that message have on our political life?" Hegemony theory's answer is that the media's message is two-fold.

1. The first message is a massage. With tinsel and glitter, the media divert our attention from the hard work of political and social problems. Of course, when problems go unaddressed, the status quo is maintained, which is just fine with those who are prospering under it, and not so fine for others.

2. When they do talk politics, the media tend to applaud an American Way that may not be the best way for everyone—especially not for working and lower class Americans.

Coming, as it does, from the left side of the idea spectrum, hegemony theory will have to contend with opponents from the right and the center. We meet these opponents briefly and revisit them occasionally to hear this book's perspective—hegemony theory—reply to them.

In the right's corner is the neoconservative theory of the "new class." The media, it argues, are no longer dominated by the "old class" of self-satisfied owners and managers. Today, the process is controlled by a "new class" of dissatisfied anticapitalist liberals. These are the reporters, screenwriters, directors, and producers who actually create the news, movies, and television we see every day. Far from reaffirming the American Way, their constant carping at it has shaken our faith in a system that serves us well, this theory argues.

Our third theory differs from the first two not just in its *position* on the spectrum, but in its *disposition* as well. While the left and the right are critical, the center is sanguine.

Its point is this: mass media, like all forms of popular culture, are popular for a reason. They give the *populus*—the people—what they want. They do this because if they don't, the people will stop reading or watching, and the media will be out of business. That, says this theory, is power to the people—a "cultural democracy." Those who believe it works would argue that when the media praise or blame the system, it probably deserves it.

As later chapters will indicate, I have my doubts about these latter two theories. But there can be little doubt that a quiet coup détat has occurred in American life. We are its willing prisoners. Seeing it clearly and making out its meaning for our politics and society will not be easy. After all, it's dark down here. But it seems important to try.

Acknowledgements

Thank you:

To Sheila Murphy, government department secretary, and to Bonnie Enslow and Laurie Olmstead in the word processing office, for transforming a scrawl that no can read into a text that even a machine can read; and even more, for your infinite patience and unfailing good cheer.

To Clark Baxter, editor at West, for your wisdom, support, and for something any editor of an author like me would need: a really good sense of humor.

To Joe Terry, developmental editor, Amy Gabriel, production assistant, and Liz Heinrichs, promotion manager at West. You're the Dream Team of publishing.

To reviewers of earlier drafts of this book, Susan Behuniak-Long, Le Moyne College; Martin L. Brownstein, Ithaca College; Jeffrey Cohen, University of Houston-Clear Lake; Larry Elowitz, Georgia College; William E. Kelly, Auburn University, Nathan Kingsley, George Washington University; Steffen Schmidt, Iowa State University; and Thomas A. Yantek, Kent State University, for your insights and for your encouragement.

To my colleagues in the government department at St. Lawrence, for showing me, by example, how it should be done.

To friends and family, for knowing what friends and family meant before it became a promotional campaign for a phone company.

To my sons, Josh and Chris, for all the good ideas, and even more, for all the jokes and hugs.

Most of all, to Diane. She knows what for.

News coverage of the Persian Gulf War often featured troops full of gung-ho enthusiasm for a just cause.

Mass Media and
Cultural Hegemony

INTRODUCTION ☆ ☆ ☆ ☆ ☆ ☆ ☆ ☆ ☆ ☆ ☆ ☆ ☆ ☆ ☆

This chapter begins with a case study in selective perception. It looks at the way our mass media—news, ads, prime time TV, and movies—presented the Persian Gulf War. The case study suggests that more was involved than met the media's eye.

The next question is why. Our answer begins with an explication of cultural hegemony theory. The word *hegemony* might be briefly defined as ''domination.'' In this case, domination over our culture—our ways of thinking, believing, and behaving—by capitalism and its ideology. This predominance is achieved, in part, by using our ''socializing'' institutions, i.e., those that help forge our ideas and values. Our look at hegemony theory will focus on the thoughts of one of its pioneers, Antonio Gramsci.

Next we'll try to apply the theory to one of our most important socializing institutions, our mass media. One of Gramsci's central tenets fits the media to a tee. Once it is complete, he said, hegemony is institutionalized, built into the rules and routines of a society's institutions. In the case of the media, the rule that's rigged the game is the commercial imperative—the rule that says the main business of the media is business. This chapter begins the argument that this rule's long-established hold on the media has grown even stronger in recent years.

We then move to the hegemonic message itself: What is this capitalist ideology that supposedly pervades our mass media? And is there evidence of its influence over our thinking?

Once we have answered those questions, it will be time to hear from opposing corners. We begin by introducing neo-conservatism and its theory that the media is dominated by a new class of anti-capitalist liberals. Then this chapter will begin the book's rebuttal to the neoconservative argument.

Having met the left (hegemony theorists) and the right (neo-conservatives), we go next to the center. There we'll meet the theory of the cultural democracy of markets. It argues that the media are controlled neither by a "new class" of anti-capitalist liberals, nor by the "old class" of upper-crust capitalists, but instead by the great middle class of average Americans. Precisely because our media are commercial, this theory argues, their main interest is in pleasing their consumers—the American people. The particular mix of politics and non-politics on display in the media is there because it meets the social and aesthetic needs of its audience, say the cultural democracy theorists. This chapter will begin hegemony theory's rejoinder to them, by raising a couple of questions.

Finally, we'll ask, "So what? Why worry about a hegemonic ideology? Hasn't the dominant 'American way' served us pretty well?" This chapter will raise some doubts. Those, in turn, will raise the question that will occupy us for the rest of this book.

☆ ☆

A Made-for-TV War

At about 3:00 a.m. Middle East time, all hell broke loose in Baghdad. A sky that had gone black was now blazing with tracer fire: like Fourth of July fireworks, or a Christmas tree, reporters said. Ninety minutes before, in the still of a clear desert night, the ground had begun to shake, as a fleet of 2,000 warplanes thundered into the night sky. Over the next 43 days, those planes would drop 88,500 tons of mayhem on Iraqi cities and troops. More than one hundred thousand would die. Desert Shield was now Desert Storm. Now it was war.

Or perhaps it was two wars. The first was the one we saw and heard and read about in our mass media. Then there was another war, one we didn't see or hear much of. And here we see how paradoxical are the politics of perception: each war was a version of the same events, and yet they were very different. Each version called the other a lie, yet neither was untrue.

The following sections will look at three aspects of the "two wars." From two different perspectives, we'll look at the war's rationale, then at the fighting itself, and finally, at the war's conclusion and aftermath.

The Media War: "There Are Things Worth Fighting For"

The media's war was full of high moral purpose, a fight for freedom. In part, this was because the media's war was the president's war, defined for the media by George Bush and his spokesmen. "Our objectives are clear," he said in numerous uncontested sound bites and paragraphs, always near the story's lead, "Saddam Hussein's forces will leave Kuwait, . . . and Kuwait will once again be free." Or, on another occasion, he amplified:

> For two centuries we've done the hard work of freedom. And tonight we lead the world in facing down a threat to decency and humanity. What is at stake is more than one small country. It is a big idea—a new world order where diverse nations are drawn together in common cause to achieve the universal aspirations of mankind: peace and serenity, freedom, and the rule of law. Such is a world worthy of our struggle, and worthy of our nation's interest.[1]

But if George Bush's war was the media's war, it was not only because they quoted him. It was also because the media made the just war their own. "Saddam Hussein . . . cannot have missed the message delivered last night by the waves of bombers and missiles," said the nation's paper of record, on the morning after the first assault. "It is a just message on behalf of honorable goals." [2] And the nation's leading news magazine added, "We knew that madmen still held sway, messianic tyrants riveted by the Nietzschean principle that power is a good in itself. We felt bad for those subjected to such belief, but we felt ourselves immune. We were wrong—and now it again falls to Americans to set matters right. Railing against the truth will not help. The fact is that if the U.S. does not check Saddam, no one else will." [3]

Another War: Selective Outrage; Blood for Oil

Then there was another war. This war was a dubious battle, full of moral ambiguity, mendacity, and hypocrisy. This one was not on the front page or the six o'clock news.

Here as elsewhere the media war was not a falsity, but it was only a half truth. It was true, as the media said, that Saddam Hussein was a brutal dictator. It was also true, though the media mentioned it very rarely, that Saddam Hussein was *our* brutal dictator until he invaded Kuwait.

Throughout the 1980s, as Amnesty International documented Hussein's pioneering efforts in the torture of children, U.S. presidents continued to back him. Iraq became the second largest recipient of U.S. export credits and received "cooperation" from U.S. intelligence agencies. At least 10 American corporations were involved in arming Iraq during the decade, all with the U.S. government's seal of approval.[4] Throughout the decade, the White House unabashedly affirmed this support, arguing that "arming and supplying Iraq was good for American business and American interests in the region."[5]

And it was true, as the media said, that Iraq's invasion of Kuwait violated international law and shed blood. Also true, but unsaid, was the fact the United States had overlooked or condoned or conducted other such invasions.

Turkey took Cyprus; Morocco took the Western Sahara; Indonesia took East Timor. The United States took stock and embraced the aggressors. Casualties were at least a hundred times as high as those inflicted by Iraq. The pattern was so transparent, said one writer, "it's almost unfair to call it hypocrisy."[6] Beneath a rhetoric of rights and law lay a ruthless *realpolitik*, a single-minded pursuit of self-interest. As we shall see, this self interest would become painfully obvious in the war's aftermath. Then, even U.S. rhetoric would abandon the cause of freedom and human rights to embrace a repressive, but U.S.—dominated status quo.

The Media War: Power and Glory

In the media's war, the combat itself was a blaze of glory, full of swashbuckling heroism. In the media war, the allies were "outnumbered and outgunned" as a *New York Times* headline put it. "Basically," General Schwarzkopf told his media war audience, "the problem we were faced with was this: When you looked at the troop members, they really outnumbered us about 3 to 2. In addition, they had a great deal more artillery than we do." [7]

In the face of such odds, only extraordinary bravery and brilliance would do. And the call was answered, the media said, starting with "Stormin' Norman on Top," as *Time* called him, "a passionately engaged leader of considerable talents possessed of a startling, prophetic mind." [8] In the wake of the war, *People* magazine would devote an entire special issue to lionizing such "Heroes of the War."

While stories of derring-do accumulated over the course of the war, the first stories of glory were an expression of aesthetic wonderment, a hymn to the thrilling power of America.

> *The word "beautiful" appeared regularly in U.S. network TV
> coverage of the [first night's] bombing . . . and in the days that
> followed. Tom Brokaw bubbled over with enthusiasm at the
> "threatening beauty of it," and a CNN reporter in Saudi Arabia
> spoke of "the most beautiful sight" of the bombers taking off on
> their missions of glory. As Brent Sadler saw it on ITN, "The night
> sky was filled with the star-spangled display of threatening force."
> Jim Stewart of CBS News referred to "two days of almost pristine
> perfect assaults," and Charles Osgood of CBS found the bombing of
> Iraq "a marvel."* [9]

Newsweek's account of the first bombing began in a similar vein:

> *With the thunderous razzle dazzle of a tomahawk missile launch,
> America unleashed the full fury of modern warfare on the Middle
> East last week. The first assaults were spectacular and terrifying.
> As Baghdad's baffled defenders filled the night sky with futile
> pyrotechnics, the combined forces of Washington's anti-Saddam
> coalition steered their precision-guided munitions into the bunkers
> and command posts of Iraq's outgunned military establishment.*[10]

A few weeks later the *New York Times* wire service extended the theme of power and glory to describe the beginning of the ground war:

> *From the air over the sand-covered Iraqi desert, the scene on
> Monday was one of both majesty and utter menace—more than
> 100,000 American fighting men and their machines . . ."* [11]

Because the "why" of the war was not open to question, combat coverage focused on "how." Besides, these strategies and capacities were, if truth be told, more fun. And so the war became largely a matter of techniques and technologies: war as football, war as Nintendo.

TV screens and news pages were festooned with multi-colored maps diagramming Hail Marys and End-Arounds. "Tale of the tape" charts gave us the spec's on the bionic capacities of Wild Weasels, Ravens, Stealths, Tornadoes, Thunderbolts, Apaches, and a horde of other fearsome wonders.

Reporters watching this wizardry in action described the weapons as something like cyborgs. One reporter described seeing a Tomahawk cruise missile roaring by, turning street corners as it looked for the right address. Another marvelled:

> The pinpoint accuracy of the attacks was spectacular. At a briefing in Saudi Arabia, Air Force Lieutenant General Charles Horner showed videotapes of two laser-guided bombs sailing through the open doors of a bunker in which an Iraqi scud missile was stored.[12]

A premium of this accuracy, at least in the media war, was that more tonnage could be dropped on Baghdad than had been visited on Hiroshima—without causing civilian deaths or damage to non-military targets!

> It seemed effortless, antiseptic and surreal. Casualties were very light, and all the high-tech gadgets in the U.S. arsenal seemed to work with surgical lethality. Like a day at the office, one pilot said. This one's for you, Saddam.[13]

> Bombs and missiles struck . . . targets . . . around and even in the heart of Baghdad—Saddam's presidential palace for one—while apparently doing little damage to civilian lives or property.[14]

Even as the ground war began and ended, there was little loss of life in the media war. A *Time* headline of March 11 crowed, "In a battle for the history books, the allies break the Iraqi army—quickly, totally, and at unbelievably low cost." [15]

There were, of course, Iraqi deaths. But in the media war, we did not see them at all, and heard little about them, and so they were just numbers—regrettable, but unavoidable, numbers.

Another War: Highway to Hell

Unfortunately, the non-media war was not so beautiful, or so antiseptic.

In this other war, 93 percent of the allied bombs dropped were conventional iron bombs. They were not smart, or surgical. In this other war, even smart bombs scored only a 60 on their biggest test. By the Pentagon's own estimates, laser-guided missiles missed their targets 40 percent of the time, sometimes by thousands of feet, leaving homes, shops, hospitals, hotels, and schools in shambles. Former Secretary of the Navy John Lehman estimates "at least 2,000 or 3,000 civilians [were] directly killed by the bombing." [16]

In the other war, the most lethal surgical strikes of all turned out to be those that hit, rather than missed, their "military targets." "In the end, everything is a military asset," and so began the "degrading" and "denial" (to use the military's terms) of water (pumping stations, desalinization plants), transportation (roads, bridges, bus terminals), energy sources (oil refineries, nuclear and electric power plants), and finally, through the embargo left in place after the war, the denial of food and medicine. [17]

In the course of these surgeries, it was not only assets that were degraded and denied. It was life itself. With the denial of water, sewage systems failed; drinking supplies were contaminated; cholera, typhoid, hepatitis, meningitis, and gastroenteritis were epidemic. Hospitals without electricity, water or enough medicine turned away most patients. By May, 55,000 children had died. A Harvard medical team predicted another 170,000 deaths by the end of the year. By October, a follow-up team reported that conditions had improved little, if at all, and predicted tens of thousands of additional deaths among young children.

The cost of food increased by 20 to 60 times its pre-war price. The nearly 90 percent of the Iraqi industrial work force unemployed by the degrading of their factories could not afford it. [18] By the summer their children had stopped growing because of severe malnutrition. [19]

Meanwhile, in the desert, another non-media war was waged. Like the war on the cities, this one was also not so beautiful, or even so heroic as in the media's version. In this war, there were no "battle-harden Iraqi forces" that had us "outgunned and outmanned."

Instead, there were teenage boys in tennis shoes digging holes in the sand, trying to hide from Armageddon. Unprotected by any air defenses, they were "trapped in two dimensions, while their enemies waged war from a third." [20] For 39 days, the skies above them rained "gruesome anti-personnel weapons with names like Adam, Beehive, Bouncing Betty, and 'near-nuclear' explosives such as the fuel air bomb, as well as laser-guided Hellfire missiles and the old standbys, napalm and white phosphorous." [21]

A look at the design of these weapons provides an instructive look at what the media called the "marvel" and "the threatening beauty" of aerial attack:

> The fuel-air bomb ignites a fine spray of fuel above a target. "The resulting 'whoosh' of fire can suck the oxygen from the lungs of all nearby troops, and the powerful concussion from the explosion can obliterate everything in an area the size of two football fields." [22]

> Adam is one of the "so-called bouncing or bounding ordnance systems, designed to detonate at groin level and spray shrapnel at an elevation that is more damaging to vital human organs." Adam, and the other "Bouncing Betty" bombs, hit the ground and then are propelled upward to the most lethal level before they detonate.

> The Beehive, "perhaps the ultimate concept in improved fragmentation . . . spins at high velocity, spitting out 8,800 flechettes—tiny darts with razor edges capable of causing deep wounds."

> White phosphorus howitzer shells spew forth fragments which "can continue to burn hours after they have penetrated a soldier's body, creating deep lesions." [23]

Those who survived this "softening up" might have wished they hadn't. As the ground war began, tanks equipped with tooth-shaped plows bulldozed over their trenches. The tactic was designed to "attrite" large numbers of Iraqis quickly by burying them alive. It succeeded. Because the tanks were impervious to the Iraqis' only weapon—small arms fire—they were helpless to resist the onslaught. "I came through right after the lead company," said Col. Anthony Moreno. "What you saw was a bunch of buried trenches with people's arms and things sticking out of them. . . . For all I know, we could have killed thousands." His estimate was modest. More than 8,000 troops were in the trenches when the assault began. Only 2,000 managed to surrender. As for the rest, "Once we went through there . . . there wasn't anybody left," said Capt. Bernie Williams, who was awarded the Silver Star for his role in the assault. [24]* After a hundred hours of similarly one-sided routs,

---

*This information did not become public until more than six months after the assault. Reporters had been barred from this area of combat—one patch in a pervasive pattern of U.S. censorship. This censorship was one reason—although not the only one—why the media war differed from the non-media war. See Chapter 3 for a further discussion of censorship in the Gulf War.

Iraqi troops by the tens of thousands tried to flee. In military or civilian vehicles or whatever would carry them, they set out, most of them on the main road from Kuwait to Basra.

Quickly, it came to be called the Highway to Hell. The U.S. Air Force was "given the word to work over that entire area, to find anything that was moving and take it out," explained an Army Captain.[25] In four lanes of bumper to bumper traffic, the Iraqis were powerless against the ensuing assault. "It was like shooting fish in a barrel," said one pilot. "They were basically just sitting ducks . . ." said another. "It was just a question of getting back and forth to the carrier to get more bombs." The cluster bombing of the jammed traffic went on for almost 48 hours. Later, a visitor to the scene described it:

> *For a fifty- or sixty-mile stretch from just north of Jahra to the Iraqi border, the road was littered with exploded and roasted vehicles, charred and blown up bodies. The force of the explosions and the heat of the fires had blown most of the clothing off the soldiers, and often too had cooked their remains into wizened, mummified charcoal men. The American warplanes had come in low, fast, and hard. They had saturated the road with cluster bombs, big white pods that open in the air and spray those below with hundreds of bomblets that spew at great velocity thousands of razor-edged little fragments of metal. The explosions had torn tanks and trucks apart . . . and ripped up the men inside into pieces as well. . . .*
>
> *One man had tried to escape to Iraq in a Kawasaki front-end loader. His remaining half-body lay hanging upside down and out of his exposed seat, the left side and bottom blown away to tatters, with the charred leg fully fifteen feet away. Nine men in a slat-sided supply truck were killed and flash burned so swiftly that they remained, naked, skinned, and black wrecks, in the vulnerable positions of the moment of first impact. One body lay face down with his rear high in the air, as if he had been trying to burrow through the truckbed. His legs ended in fluttery charcoaled remnants at mid-thigh. He had a young, pretty face, slightly cherubic, with a pointed little chin, you could still see that even though it was mummified.*
>
> *Some of the American and British soldiers wandering the graveyard joked a bit. "Crispy critters," said one, looking at a group of the incinerated. "Just wasn't them boys' day, was it?" said another. But for the most part, the scene commanded among the visitors a certain sobriety. . . . "Some of these guys weren't but 13, 14 years old," said [a third soldier], in a voice fittingly small.[26]*

The Media War: Happily Ever After

To the media, the war's end was not just a military, but a "moral victory" as the headline of *Time's* lead story called it. Another article in the same issue exulted, "A stunning military triumph gives Americans something to cheer about—and shatters Vietnam's legacy of self-doubt and divisiveness. . . . When the U.S.-led forces raced across Kuwait and Iraq last week . . . they may have defeated not just the Iraqi army but also the more virulent of the ghosts from the Vietnam era: self-doubt, fear of power, divisiveness, a fundamental uncertainty about America's purpose in the world." [27]

Another headline explained why the victory was a moral one, and announced what was to be the overarching theme of media coverage in the coming days: "Kuwait Is Liberated!" The accompanying article drew upon the righteous aura of the civil rights movement for its title: "Free at Last! Free at Last!" Such articles showed and depicted "Ecstatic Kuwaitis" greeting an "allied vanguard with shouts of joy." [28] "Crowds along the way danced and chanted, 'U.S.A.! U.S.A.!' and 'Thank you, thank you!' " [29]

The next six months were a nonstop national revel. There were parades, of course, and rallies, and speeches.

And here is where the entertainment media, which had enlisted early in the war effort, moved to the front.

Already, during the five weeks of combat, entertainment television had "let no opportunity escape to air . . . 'public service' spots. shows like "Entertainment tonight" slipped celebrity war endorsements into at least one ad break every night . . . [local weathermen] could not even mention the wind velocity without informing viewers that 'the flags are showing their colors for the guys and gals over yonder.' Corporate sponsors such as Texaco lost no time getting out special wartime ads featuring . . . voiceovers offering . . . advice on how we can all do our bit for the war effort. . . . Cable companies such as Philadelphia's Greater Media served up their own 'Video Salutes to the Troops in the Gulf.' " [30]

After the war, the networks began rolling out entertainment galas in prime time. ABC presented "Welcome Home, America," in which stars like Lee Greenwood ("God Bless the U.S.A."), Merle Haggard ("The Fightin' Side of Me"), and a host of other stars offered their grateful congratulations. HBO offered "Welcome Home Heroes," headlined by Whitney Houston. The network's full-page ad for the program in *TV Guide* called it "HBO's Most Memorable Event" for "America's Proudest Moment." Even PBS weighed in with "A Musical Tribute," a "Salute to U.S. Persian Gulf Troops."

For those who wanted to rewind the war, each of the major networks offered videotapes with titles like "Desert Triumph" and "How the War Was Won."

For the following fall, ABC readied a made-for-TV movie, "Heroes of Desert Storm." The movie was introduced in prime time, on October 6, 1991, by George Bush. Its script had been approved by the White House. Little wonder.

In this made-for-TV war, GIs, singly or in pairs, and on foot, took on large numbers of the enemy, calling out "way to go, Joe Montana!" or "Touchdown!" as they lobbed grenades and took back Kuwait inch by inch.

The story of the highway of death was told through voiceovers simulating news reports:

> *The Coalition goal of preventing the wholesale looting of Kuwait by retreating Iraqi invaders appears to be working. . . . The order of the day remains not to fire indiscriminately, but to hit only the lead vehicles. The result is a monstrous traffic jam.*

Later, an Army Chaplain is shown conducting individual Muslim funerals for each of the Iraqis who did not survive the traffic jam.

In another scene a brutal Iraqi officer menaces POWs, one of whom gets in his face to say, through clenched teeth, "God Bless America."

Bereaved parents of fallen Americans are consoled by Army Chaplains. A minister eulogizes at the funeral of a young woman soldier, "She lived as a Christian, she died defending her country."

Over shots of GIs returning in triumph to their loved ones and then over a lone GI perched atop a tank, silhouetted against a desert sunrise, the voice of George Bush provides the movie's conclusion: "As President, I can report to the nation that aggression is defeated. The war is over. We're coming home now. Proud. Confident. Heads held high. We are Americans."

Another War:
The Stability of Tyranny

Meanwhile, in the non-media war, the final act of a tragedy was unfolding. Here, the "liberation of Kuwait" seemed more like the replacement of one tyranny by another.

George Bush had promised that "Saddam Hussein's forces will leave Kuwait, and Kuwait will once again be free." He meant, apparently, free to go back to business as usual.

That was a state in which less than one-third of the 2.2 million people who lived and worked in Kuwait before the invasion, enjoyed the rights of citizenship. Even those who did were not free to help choose their civic fate—the Emir had dissolved Kuwait's parliament in 1986. Since that time, he and his royal family had ruled as absolute autocrats.

The freedom Kuwait would once again enjoy was a state in which oil-rich families had imported the poor from Third World Countries to do their manual labor. Many were Palestinian. Tens of thousands of Filipino and Sri Lankan women also worked as domestics. Indentured to this, their only livelihood, they found themselves in a place not known for the liberated condition of its women. Physical abuse of them was not uncommon.

> When foreign workers arrive [in Kuwait], their passports are taken away; they sign documents in Arabic, which they neither speak nor read, and find themselves bound to hard labor for years. Those who refuse to sign are told they must leave at once and pay their own fares home. Some who think that they are going to exercise the professions for which they are qualified find themselves scrubbing floors for half the pay they were promised.

> Foreign workers in the Gulf have no rights and no representation. Their fate is entirely in the hands of the employer and his family. Children are taught to discipline—that is, to insult, pinch, slap and pull the hair of—servants who displease them. . . .

> Now and than the Kuwait Times reported spectacular cases of servants thrown from roof-tops, burnt or blinded or battered to death; the systematic abuse they endured every day was unworthy of remark. . . .[31]

This is the freedom Kuwait enjoyed before, and that George Bush promised "once again." But after the Emir's return, things were less free than ever. Martial law was declared. Palestinians, despised because of PLO support for Hussein, were rounded up by Kuwaiti army troops and by vigilante gangs formed by the Sabah family.

Their treatment, wrote the Executive Director of Middle East Watch, "mirrors that suffered by native Kuwaitis at the hands of Iraqis." His task force concluded that "about 2,000 people have been rounded up arbitrarily since the country's liberation. . . ." Those released gave accounts of "beatings and humiliation, sometimes of unspeakable torture. . . . Dozens have been killed by their Kuwaiti captors, their mutilated bodies dumped on vacant lots and even highways for all to see." [32]

After all the talk about bringing freedom, all the talk about ending "brutality and lawlessness," the pro-democracy and human rights movements in Kuwait had reason to hope for help from the American government. They would have reason to be disappointed. President Bush felt there was "little he [could] do" to urge democratic reform on the Emir.[33] This, after crushing the invader who had crushed the Emir.

As the weight of the contradiction began to make the rhetoric of freedom unsupportable, administration officials simply dropped that rhetoric. And why not? The nation's attention had already moved on. The theme of the war was long since cast, in bronze stars, and hardened: it would always be a fight for freedom.

And so, unabashedly, White House officials began to tell the truth. They explained the failure to push for democratic reform, "The United States does not want to do anything that could destabilize the Kuwaiti government." [34] They explained why democratic reform should not be allowed to "destablize" a cruel autocracy. "By virtue of the military victory, the United States is likely to have more influence" on the Emirates and Princes now under American protection "than any industrial nation has ever exercised." [35] They explained "how they might use their new franchise" for the clear benefit of American business, at a cost to the American consumer. "If crude oil prices plunged, Washington might lean on a reluctant Saudi Arabia to . . . push prices back up . . . high enough to allow American energy companies to make profits." [36]

"The war," they were in effect saying, "was not really about freedom. It was about preserving that corporate American domination that we like to call 'stability.' " The media dutifully recited all this, as if it all made perfect sense, as if "freedom" had somehow flowed into the "stability" of tyranny like rivers to the sea.

A similar logic led to an even crueler outcome in Iraq. Also stirred by the Siren Song of freedom was Iraq's Kurdish minority. The Kurds, having been frequent victims of Saddam Hussein's cruelty, took comfort from the stream of vituperation against the "butcher of Baghdad," and from the promise that "brutality and lawlessness" would not go unchecked. Then, after the cease fire, George Bush explicitly encouraged Iraqis to overthrow Hussein. At that point, the Kurds had almost every reason to expect help from

Washington for their uprising—human rights, freedom, international law and order, democracy—all good reasons to offer the now-
minimal assistance needed to topple Hussein.

Only one reason prevented the aid from coming: the fact that
none of the above reasons mattered much. In the end, what did
matter was an ice-cold calculation. "Whatever the sins of the Iraqi
leader, he offered the West . . . a better hope for his country's stability than did those who have suffered under his repression." [37]
There's that word again, "stability," echoing down the halls of the
history of American empire.

And so, officials openly acknowledged, President Bush "decided to let . . . Saddam Hussein put down rebellions in his country
without American intervention . . . despite reports of atrocities by
Mr. Hussein's forces. The United States, despite its uncontested
control of Iraqi skies, 'has no plans to act on a warning to Iraq not
to use combat helicopters against the insurgents,' " said a senior
official.[38]

The butcher of Baghdad was back in business. Once his helicopters and artillery had prevailed, a rebel spokesman pleaded,
"They are killing any Kurd they see. We are facing a worse genocide
than Halabja," where, in 1988, Iraqi forces had used chemical
weapons to exterminate an estimated 4,000.[39] In Basra, said an
eyewitness, "[Iraqi forces] keep 7,000 prisoners at a university, and
they shoot 50 to 100 every day." [40]

Soon, an estimated 2 million Kurds were refugees. Observers
on the scene described their plight:

> Refugee families are now scattered throughout the snow-covered
> Kurdish mountains, ill-equipped to face the bitterly cold nights. . . .
> Mothers hold babies in their arms, refusing to let go even though
> their children were dead from cold and dehydration. Old men bend
> over in pain from the miles-long trek to sanctuary through snow-
> covered mountains. Children cry out from hunger or from the pain of
> burns caused by napalm dropped by Iraqi troops.[41]

Even as these horrors unfolded, the very media whose job it
was to report them continued to celebrate the might and right of
America and its war. "Victory in the Gulf may not have achieved
all that Americans hoped for, but there are many reasons for glorious—even giddy—celebration," said *Time* as the atrocities spun
giddily on in Kuwait.[42] And as the Kurdish death march dragged
on, the *New York Times* "dismissed the qualms of 'the doubters,'
concluding that Mr. Bush had acted wisely. He 'avoided the quag-
mire and preserved his two triumphs: the extraordinary coopera-

tion among coalition members and the revived self-confidence of Americans,' who 'greeted the . . . cease fire with relief and pride— relief at miraculously few U.S. casualties and pride in the brilliant performance of the allied forces.' " [43]

The Argument in Brief

In the winter of 1991, a war was fought. Or perhaps, it was two wars. One was a fight for freedom; the other, an exercise in naked self-interest. One was heroic, a thrilling show, a high-stakes game, and took no toll. The other was not an epic tale, or a fireworks display, or a game. It was pain and death and disease on an inconceivable scale. One war ended as a great victory, the other, as a great tragedy.

The conclusion to be drawn from this is not that the unreported war was the real war and the media's was spurious, but that both wars happened. The facts of the unreported war occurred. Its inferences were drawn. But curiously, this war was almost completely absent from the mass media. Then again, maybe this absence was not so curious. Maybe, in fact, it was neither an aberration nor an accident.

Indeed, the argument of this book is that the way the media saw the war is its way of seeing all of politics and society. As the war was trivialized, shrunk to the size of a game or a show, so are all social issues. As the war was celebrated, so is all of the American Way.

But why should this be?

The Theory of Cultural Hegemony

Already in 1927, as Antonio Gramsci began his *Prison Notebooks*, the rooftree of history had fallen in upon the notion of "inevitability."* This was what sometimes seemed to be Marx's notion that,

---

*Calvin Exoo, *Democracy Upside Down*, (Westport, CT: Greenwood Publishing Group, Inc., 1987): 5–11; 25–27; 73–101. Excerpts reprinted here, and throughout chapters 2, 3 and 7, by permission of Praeger Publishers, an imprint of Greenwood Publishing Group, Inc., Westport, CT. Reprinted with permission.

inevitably, as a matter of course, working class men and women would see the injustice of modern life, and band together to change that life. But already in 1927, it was clear there was to be no "of course" about history. And so, amid the rubble of the Marxian prediction, Gramsci wondered why not.

The basis for what sometimes seems like cavalier optimism in Marx was his assumption that our culture—ways of thinking, believing, and behaving—are determined by our material circumstances.[44]* Thus, for a while, a property-owning class would be able to command the compliance of working class people, browbeating them with the coercive powers of government and the undeniable demands of making a living. Eventually though, the tensions of working class life—of losing control of the fruits of one's labor, of how one worked, for what—would draw the working class to consciousness of its plight, to resistance and revolt. And, argued many Marxists in the 1920s, wasn't the proof in the historical pudding? Hadn't Marx's scenario just been acted out in Russia?

But as Gramsci looked around him, he saw a Western world very different from Lenin's Russia. There, a state that had lived by the sword died by it—force was undone by force. But here, in the West, nations were stronger than coercion alone could make them; here, they also rested on the consent of the governed. To achieve that consent, the capitalist ruling class had to do more than deploy the police. It had to build and hold the barricades of "civil society,"** all those places where political ideas and instincts are made and remade: the schools, the political parties, the churches, the interest groups. Oh yes, and one more—perhaps the strongest bar-

---

*In fairness, though determinism is certainly on display in some of Marx's writings, the whole body of his work is more balanced. This economism/ inevitabilism becomes categorical only later, in some of Marx's disciples.[45]

**Of Course, Marx himself planted the seedling of this idea, which would grow to challenge both economic determinism and inevitabilism. The most famous passage is from the *German Ideology*: "The class which has the means of material production at its disposal, has control at the same time over the means of mental production, so that . . . the ideas of those who lack the means of mental production are subject to it."[46] The fact that the first two generations of Marx's intellectual progeny never saw *The German Ideology* may well account for their failure to cultivate the notion of ideological hegemony. Gramsci didn't see the book either, but found passages akin to it in Marx's other writings, and took the position that Marx's "genuine doctrine" understood the importance of ideology, and that Marx's frequent stress on the predominance of material over ideological forces were lapses "from his own insight."[47]

ricade of all as the twentieth century reached toward the twenty-first—the mass media.

The flag to be captured on this battleground of civil society is what Gramsci called the "common sense"—the usually uncritical, often unconscious way in which most people perceive the world.[48] It is what we take for granted. Gramsci called the conquest of these heart habits *egemonia,* hegemony.

Hegemony. Domination. It is an old sin, older than the ancient Greeks who first used the term *hegemony.* But Gramsci's understanding of it was new. The Greeks had used the term to describe the military domination of one city-state by another. In Gramsci, hegemony was not military, but cultural, a conquering not of a people's army, but of their hearts and minds.

The great genius of Gramsci's account of this struggle is that it is full of healthy respect for all the combatants, which is not true of some accounts of "false consciousness" that ascribe only self-interest to the dominant and stupidity to the dominated. In Gramsci, to be sure, the common sense does protect ruling class power and privilege. But the propertied class has only succeeded in capturing the common sense by wrapping its ideology around a core of "good sense"—a set of genuinely worthy ideals.*

For example, one might argue that the ideal of freedom, which figures so prominently in the American common sense, is a real *desideratum.* But somehow, propertied-class ideology has conquered that word and wrapped it in a particular meaning (freedom to do as I please with my property, free enterprise, free markets). That meaning, of course, tends to exclude other meanings more favorable to working and lower-class people (freedom from poverty; freedom of a people to choose its civic destiny, even if the choice is to abrogate property).

---

*Is there "good sense" in the dominant ideology? As is often the case, Gramsci is ambiguous here. Clearly good sense involves a philosophical, critical mindset as opposed to an unreflective one.[49] But the conclusions such a mind will come to are not defined in the passages defining "good sense." Abercrombie et al., take the good sense to be only that part of the common sense that opposes the dominant ideology.[50] But Gramsci described his own argument as one that began by trying to find, in his bourgeois adversaries, that which "should be incorporated, if only as a subordinate aspect, in his own construction." [51] And in the passage which most compels a finding of good sense in the dominant ideology, he allows that his own Marxism "presupposes all this cultural past: Renaissance and Reformation, German philosophy and the French Revolution, Calvinism and English classical economics, secular liberalism. . . . The philosophy of *praxis* is the crowning point of this entire movement of intellectual and moral reformation." [52]

Herbert Marcuse put the point this way: in our society, "speech moves in synonyms and tautologies." [53] Words that should begin debates, end them. Words whose meanings should be argued are instead invariably defined by the status quo, where the "haves" have and the ruling class rules. The "free world" is our world, never mind that American workers have long expected to take orders most of their waking lives, at work, while Yugoslav workers ran their own factories, even while they were behind the "Iron Curtain." [54] The "free press" is our press, never mind that it is bound wrist and ankles by commercial imperatives, while news editors in other countries have no commercial overseers (as Chapter 3 will argue). "Success" is commercial success. "The American way" is the capitalists' way. "The good life" is their life. Good words, words whose only limits should be limitless imagination, are, for the moment, bound to the service of one idea, one class. But other meanings remain in them, latent, like the strength of Samson, of Prometheus.

Gramsci's heirs have also added a dose of respect and empathy to the understanding of another form of hegemony. In this form, the media's job is not to indoctrinate people into capitalism but to anesthetize them to its injuries. To carry them away from a world full of poverty, rapacity and indignity, to a realm of undiluted pleasure—a world where laughter and sex and excitement are available at the touch of a button; where the good guys, the ones like us, always win in the end, and find true love; where the endings are always happy.

Again, in theories of "false consciousness," working people's willingness to "buy" this cornucopia offered by the media is viewed derisively—a selling of the birthright of resistance for a bowl of pottage. But this denies the obvious truth: the truth of how hard resistance to injustice is; of how good, really good, the confections of the media do taste; and of what a balm to modern injuries the media's ministering myths can be. " 'False consciousness' always contains its truth," as Todd Gitlin says. "The truth of wish, the truth of illusion that is embraced with a quiet passion made possible, even necessary, by actual frustration and subordination." [55]

For Gramsci, in other words, the capture of the common sense is not a matter of the strong hypodermically injecting their version of the truth into the weak. Human give and take does not work that way. Instead, the common sense is "negotiated by unequal forces in a complex process through which the subordination and resistance of the workers are created and recreated." [56]

Gramsci summarizes his position and hints at its implications in one of the most-quoted passages of the *Prison Notebooks:*

In the East, the State was everything, civil society was primordial and gelatinous; in the West . . . when the State trembled a sturdy structure of civil society was at once revealed. The State was only an outer ditch, behind which there was a powerful system of fortresses and earthworks.[57]

In our time, this system of fortresses and earthworks is to be found in places like Hollywood, Madison Avenue, and Rockefeller Center. From there, the high grounds of the culture, its reach is all but unlimited. Its salvoes of film and news and TV shows and ads have all but completely conquered our culture.

Hegemony and the Media

In case the hegemony thesis has begun to sound like a conspiracy theory, let me quickly add that it is not. Media magnates and managers do not huddle behind closed doors plotting to benight the masses.* Today, hegemony is more complex than that.

Today, it is also more complete than that. Hegemony is now so complete it is built into the very foundation of the mass media—into the imperatives, the norms, and the routines of the business—so that perpetrating hegemony is not deliberately benighting the masses. It is merely doing one's job. In our time, hegemony has become banal.

This was not always the case. In the beginning, these media were not a bundle of unquestioned assumptions, but of unanswered questions. Who would own these new possibilities? What was their function? Who would decide what they would say? By what criteria? The possibilities were endless. Titanic struggles over these issues ensued. As we shall see, in one medium after another,

---

*This statement does not mean that such processes never occur. In the early days, when the media were still contested terrain, corporations did use their ownership and other forms of power to put their politics directly and deliberately into programming. They still do so occasionally, when an employee forgets the rules, and a certain line is crossed. Direct intervention is also necessary in crisis times, when all the rules are once again up for grabs. Chapters 3, 4, and 5 will have more to say about the early days, the employee "lapses," the crisis times, and the attendant interventions. Other writers see direct intervention as the ongoing routine pattern of hegemony. See for example, Parenti,[58] Herman and Chomsky,[59] or recent issues of *Lies of Our Times*.

capitalists emerged victorious. Certainly, their crucial victory was to make the capitalist purpose the media's purpose, that is, to define the media as a commercial enterprise.

With that commercial definition came these commercial imperatives:

1. **Maximize profit.** To do that,

2. **Maximize audience size.** To do that,

3a. **Do not bore the audience.** Entertain it. Avoid the arcana of social issues. Instead, hit their pleasure buttons: laughter, sex, violence, and so on.

3b. **Do not offend your audience.** Do not challenge their common sense. Reaffirm it.

In other words, to make the media commercial was not only to put ultimate power over them in the hands of capitalists. It was also to render their content either apolitical or reaffirmative of the common sense. As we shall see, this was a common sense the business community would be at pains not only to reflect, but to shape, especially in its formative years and in crisis times. Eventually, reaffirming the common sense meant reaffirming the "free enterprise" system and its corollaries.

Apolitical and pro-establishment. An opiate and an ideology in one syringe. What more could a hegemonic class ask for?

Media Hegemony in the 90s: A Turn of the Screw

Recently, the profit motive has tightened its grip on the media business even further. This happened as the media completed a transition foreseen by Thorstein Veblen at the turn of the century. He called it the transition from "industry" to "business." [60]

The founders of the media "industries" were intimately involved in the production of their newspapers, movies, or television programs. They wanted, of course, to make money. But as makers of products, they also indulged themselves in the pride of craftsmen.

This pattern has changed fundamentally in our time, the time of the takeover. Beginning in the 1970s, American corporations were confronted with increased foreign competition. In response, they might have redoubled their efforts to make their own products better. But they chose an easier way; speculative investment instead of productive investment.

One form of this speculation is the takeover. Under this strategy, a company is "acquired." Some divisions are sold to other speculators. Others are shut down, taking advantage of U.S. tax laws allowing companies to profit from the boarding up of productive enterprises, to profit from the creation of unemployment. Still other divisions are retained by the acquiring conglomerate and run, in the new corporate argot, "leaner and meaner."

In one recent three-year period, 12,200 companies, worth almost half a billion dollars, were bought and sold. "The merger-acquisition takeover business amounted to nearly a fifth of the 1986 market value of all traded stocks." Ours had become a "casino" economy.[61]

Among the favorite targets of the acquisition business have been the mass media. Now, NBC is a subsidiary of General Electric; Columbia Pictures belongs to Sony; *Time* magazine is a division of Time-Warner Communications, Inc., and so on.

The CEOs of these sprawling empires have not usually apprenticed in the craft of media production. Their backgrounds are in law, finance, or other non-media businesses. They are not mainly interested in craftsmanship, in quality, or product. They are mainly interested in profit, profit, profit.

They are not preoccupied with profit because they are narrow, greedy people. They are single-minded because they have to be, at this stage of advanced capitalism. For a variety of reasons, investors and stockholders have recently become an ever more fickle crowd.* They demand not just profits, but large profits—larger profits than last year's, larger than the other available opportunities. They do not suffer laggards gladly. Companies that don't produce are abandoned and raided. Today's climate is not one in which to worry about product at the expense of profit. Today, more than ever, profit is the king over television, the movies, and even the news. More than ever, the king's decrees are absolute law. More than ever, the resulting media fare is a toothless politics, a mindless entertainment.

---

*Among the reasons are U.S. tax laws and the computerization of the financial sector, which has made capital "hypermobile."[62]

What Is the Dominant Ideology?
A Catechism

A cultural hegemony argument had better begin with some evidence that there is such a thing; that there is, to begin with, an ideology that best serves the interests of the "house of have," yet is accepted by the "house of want" as well.

Basic, of course, to such an ideology is belief in the economic system under which the haves have and the have nots don't: capitalism. In McClosky and Zaller's concise, comprehensive definition:

> *The values and practices associated with capitalism . . . include private ownership of the means of production, the pursuit of profit by self-interested entrepreneurs, and the right to unlimited gain through economic effort. In its "ideal" formulation, capitalism also stresses competition among producers, a substantial measure of laissez-faire, and market determination of production, distribution, and economic reward. Certain notions from individualist doctrine and the so-called Protestant ethic, such as an emphasis on achievement and hard work, are also widely regarded as part of the capitalist creed.*[63]

The sheer percentage of Americans joined in this litany of capitalism is impressive, as Table 1–1 demonstrates. But even more striking is the fact that assent does not diminish much among working and lower-class Americans, as Table 1–2 indicates. Even those who have not been flattered or blessed by the ideal and the real capitalism nonetheless affirm it.*

Of course, saying only that Americans affirm capitalism oversimplifies a complex people. It says that Americans are "ideologically conservative," which they are. It does not explain Americans' "programmatic liberalism," their support for particular government programs of business regulation, social services, and civil rights.[70]

---

*This pattern grows even more astonishing when compared to the Western European. For example, 68 percent of blue-collar Swedes support equal pay for all occupations; 11 percent of blue-collar Americans support it.[64] It is the European pattern that has prompted Abercrombie and associates to argue that there is no definable "dominant ideology." As is evident from the data presented here, their argument has much more relevance to the European than to the American case.

TABLE 1-1

Support for capitalism and related values among Americans

1. People should place more emphasis on working hard and doing a good job than on what gives them personal satisfaction and pleasure.
   - agree   63%
   - disagree   23
   - unsure   15

2. There is nothing wrong with a man trying to make as much money as he honestly can.
   - agree   95%
   - disagree   5

3. Our freedom depends on the free enterprise system.
   - agree   82%
   - disagree   18

4. Some form of socialism would certainly be better than the system we have now.
   - agree   11%
   - disagree   89

5. Private ownership of property:
   - is as important to a good society as freedom.   87%
   - has often done mankind more harm than good.   4
   - decline to choose.   9

6. The more government regulation there is, the less efficiently companies can operate.
   - agree   65%
   - disagree   22
   - other   13

7. The most important factor in determining who gets ahead is:
   - luck.   8%
   - hard work.   68
   - family background.   24

8. America is the land of opportunity where everyone who works hard can get ahead.
   - agree   70%
   - disagree   30

9. Making incomes more equal means socialism and that deprives people of individual freedoms.
   - agree   74%
   - disagree   26

(continued on next page)

TABLE 1–1 continued

Support for capitalism and related values among Americans

---

10. Incomes cannot be made more equal since people's abilities and talents are unequal.
    - agree   85%
    - disagree   15

Sources: Items 1–6, McClosky and Zaller;[65] item 7, Schlozman and Verba;[66] items 8–10, Kluegel and Smith.[67]

But even this rejection of undiluted laissez faire is no cause for heartburn in the board room. This kind of New Deal liberalism was offered to Americans, and accepted by them, not as the end of capitalism, but as a new beginning; not as a way of destroying entrepreneurialism, but of making it possible. This was to be done by providing a minimum level of regulation for the game's rule-breakers, and welfare services for its blameless losers—just enough, it was hoped, to allow them to get back into the game, which is still capitalism.[71] Thus the finding that Americans are "operationally [New Deal] liberal" and "ideologically conservative [capitalistic]"[72] is not in the least surprising or inconsistent. New Deal liberalism is a perfectly straightforward means to capitalist ends.

The most compelling evidence of this assessment is the fullness with which New Deal liberals sing the anthems of capitalism. "By sizable majorities, they affirm the importance of the free enterprise system, private property, competition, and wages based on achievement rather than need."[73] With only a little less ardor, capitalists have acknowledged their compatibility with New Deal liberalism by embracing some state intervention into the economy. "Unregulated competition, they found, gave rise to a degree of uncertainty that made it difficult to plan their industrial activities efficiently. As a result, some of them . . . demanded that government establish laws and regulatory agencies to . . . help stabilize their markets."[74]

But still more complexity remains to be reckoned with. It is now some sixty years since the New Deal began an epoch of programmatic liberalism. The unfairness it was supposed to address is not a thing of the past. Americans are aware of this. Americans tell pollsters, for example, that in their opinion some have too little,

TABLE 1-2

Support for capitalist individualism, by income and occupational level

	Occupational Level			
	LOW			*HIGH*
	1	*2*	*3*	*4*
1. Hard work is the most important factor in getting ahead. (% agreeing)	67	66	69	70

	Family Income	
	UNDER $6,000	*OVER* 35,000
2. The way property is used should mainly be decided by the:		
• community, since the earth belongs to everyone.	18%	20%
• individuals who own it.	68	60
• decline to choose.	14	20
3. Competition, whether in work, school, or business:		
• is often wasteful and destructive.	9%	12%
• leads to better performance and desire for excellence.	77	73
• decline to choose.	17	15
4. Under a fair economic system:		
• all people would earn about the same.	9%	2%
• people with more ability would earn higher salaries.	76	84
• decline to choose.	17	14

Sources: Items 2–4, McClosky and Zaller;[68] item 1, Schlozman and Verba.[69]

others too much[75] and that life's road is harder for some—for women, for Blacks, for working and lower-class people—than for others.[76]

What is more, Americans seem to have run out of patience with their government's failures. They say they do not trust government to do "what is right," that public officials don't care what ordinary Americans think, and that government is run on behalf of "a few big interests." [77]

At some point, it would seem, Americans would begin to wonder—not only about the repeated failures of particular politicians and programs, but about the system they can't seem to fix.

Unfortunately, that wondering may not get very far. Recent work in social psychology suggests that "people need an explicitly formulated counter-ideology" to effectively critique the dominant ideology.[78] Hegemony theorists' entire argument might be summarized by saying that "an explicitly formulated counter-ideology" is precisely what we Americans won't get from our idea factories. We won't get it, this book in particular argues, from our mass media.

Until we do, we will remain the captive audience to a cave-wall shadow show, groping about—for what? Options we don't know exist. Instincts toward community ("programmatic liberalism"), instincts that we have no words to express or to defend, because only capitalist individualism has been expressed, or defended ("ideological conservatism"). Unformed discontents will continue to fester ("The government is pretty much run by a few big interests looking out for themselves—not for the benefit of all the people"), because the regime, so long unquestioned, now seems beyond question ("Our freedom depends on the free enterprise system"). So it must be the politicians' fault: shift after shift, the train's engineers are blamed, when perhaps we should be asking, "Are we on the right track?" But we cannot ask that. As far as we know, there is only one track.

The Hidden Agenda of Other Values

The supportive relationship of values such as self-reliance and laissez faire to capitalism is clear. Other beliefs, also pervasive in the media, support the established order in ways that are not self-evident. The following sections discuss two such "isms," racism-sexism and what we'll call "Manicheism."

Divided We Fall

Chapters to come will argue that among the attitudes fostered by the media are subtle forms of racism and sexism. What do those attitudes have to do with cultural hegemony? Do they help maintain upper-class power and privilege?

One school of economists has argued that they do.[79] When white males believe that women and blacks are somehow inferior, they are less likely to join with those groups in the common cause of a labor union or political party.

These divisions among workers allow management to usher women and blacks to "their place" in the economy. That place is either in the unemployment line or in the "secondary labor force"— unskilled manual labor for African Americans and other minorities; clerical, retail, teaching-nursing, and peripheral-goods production for women. Once these disempowered groups are segregated into these economic ghettos, wages and benefits there can be limited. Work can be speeded up. Shareholder's dividends can be increased.

The existence of this secondary labor force also limits the concessions made to the primary labor force. If this latter, more advantaged workforce refuses to accept what they're offered, management can turn to the secondary labor force, a "reserve army" of underemployed and underpaid minorities. This readiness to replace a recalcitrant primary workforce can be used as both a bargaining and strikebreaking tool.

And finally, just as women and blacks can be easily brought in to the primary workforce, they can easily be ushered out again, to resume their place in the profit-maximizing scheme of things, once white male workers are brought to heel. No one will object. The myth of inferiority has seen to that.

The Uses of Manicheism

Another belief we'll find popping up in all kinds of media is *Manicheism*. This is the belief that human life is a struggle between good and evil. Conflict, in this view, arises when bad guys make mischief and have to be dealt with by good guys.

Conflict could be seen in other ways. It could be seen as a result of social inequality, or injustice, or ignorance. But the media, later chapters will argue, tend to see conflict in black and white, as bad guys versus good guys.

Manicheism is an indispensable tool for a ruling class. If a society accepts the proposition that a good many of our fellow human beings are inherently bad, then society is ready to deal harshly with these malefactors.

This predisposition makes it much easier to secure the consent of the governed for the repression of dissent. When a threat to the established order breaks out, the producers of our hegemonic shadow shows simply put the familiar mask of the bad guy on the dissidents. At that point, we are not inclined to ask why there is disruption. We know why bad guys disrupt: because they are bad. Our thinking short-circuits before we can ask what the grievances of the dissidents might be.

This pattern is played out on three different stages. The first is in the international arena.

Some observers argue that U.S. foreign policy toward the Third World has been mainly a defense of corporate interests there, "defending the capitalist world from social change—even if the change be peaceful, orderly, *and* democratic." [80] Ordinarily, such a policy would be a hard sell. But it becomes easier if we are predisposed to believe that such countries might be an "evil empire," whose leader is a "little dictator in designer sunglasses," or a "mad dog of the Middle East." Such appeals to our Manichean beliefs have laid the groundwork for recent interventions in Nicaragua, Libya, Panama, Grenada, and the Persian Gulf.

On the domestic front, Manicheism is equally useful. Capitalism has, as we shall see in a few pages, a tendency to produce inequalities. These in turn, may produce unrest among the less equal. They may, for example, refuse to abide by the rules that have, after all, not served them well.

Former Boston Police Commissioner Robert Di Grazia calls the social roots of crime the "dirty little secret" of our era:

> We are not letting the public in on our era's dirty little secret: that those who commit the crime which worries citizens most—violent street crime—are, for the most part, the products of poverty, unemployment, broken homes, rotten education, drug addiction and alcoholism, and other social and economic ills about which the police can do little, if anything.
>
> Rather than speaking up, most of us stand silent and let politicians get away with law and order rhetoric that reinforces the mistaken notion that police—in ever greater numbers and with more gadgetry—can alone control crime. The politicians, of course, end up perpetuating a system by which the rich get richer, the poor get poorer, and crime continues.[81]

Once again, our belief in Manicheism makes that "dirty little secret" much easier to keep. If our world is full of bad guys, we need no search into sociology for the roots of crime.

The most worrisome dissidence of all, of course, is political dissidence—that directed against the system itself. Thanks to the Manichean myth, governments have been able to crush dissident movements without offending public opinion. Once the mask of the bad guy was placed on the Marxist Black Panther party, for example, police agencies had their hunting license. Police harassment of party members began with arrests for minor infractions: loitering, curfew violations, profanity, jaywalking. It escalated to raids on Panther headquarters around the country. In the course of these unprovoked raids, equipment was smashed, thousands of dollars in Panther funds were stolen, and party members were beaten. During one of these, Panther leader Fred Hampton was shot to death in his bed by police. Police were unable to produce evidence that any shots had been fired by Hampton or by any of his associates.[82]

Such are the uses of a Manichean world view. It is a view, later chapters will argue, which the mass media has done its bit to sustain.

Counter-Thesis I:
The "New Class"

Weaving its way through the fabric of this book will be a dialogue between this book's perspective, cultural hegemony theory, and two opinions to the contrary. The first of these comes to us from the school of neoconservatives, who require a word or two of introduction.

Their story begins in the early 1970s. At that moment, American corporations, finding themselves beset by foreign competition and declining profits, decided they were mad as hell and were not going to take it any more. "If," they reasoned, "we are to maintain ourselves in the manner to which we have become accustomed, then we must take a bigger share of what is now a smaller revenue pie. Our workers, consumers, and governments at all levels will have to settle for less: lower wages; fewer benefits; higher prices; lower-quality products; lower environmental, workplace safety, and consumer products safety standards; lower corporate, capital gains, and income taxes for the wealthy; higher taxes for the middle class; less for education, health care, housing. More for the defense of corporate concerns abroad." And so on. Obviously, it would not be easy to insert this proposition into the common sense. But big business was ready to try. *Business Week* sounded the call to arms:

*It will be a hard pill for many Americans to swallow—the idea of
doing with less so that big business can have more. . . . Nothing that
this nation, or any other nation, has done in modern economic
history compares in difficulty with the selling job that now must be
done to make people accept this new reality.*[83]

A massive public relations campaign ensued. Some of its
many prongs will be reviewed in the chapters ahead. One concerns
us here. That is the corporate seeding of the clouds of conservative
scholarship. Over the next decade, big business would pour millions into the endowment of conservative think tanks, university
chairs, academic prizes, research fellowships, journals, and newsletters.[84]

Among the scholarly enterprises so endowed, media studies
were prominent. Institutes like AIM (Accuracy in Media), the American Enterprise Institute, the Center for Media and Public Affairs,
the Media Research Center, the Media Institute; journals like *Public Opinion, Commentary, Public Interest;* and newsletters such as
TV etc, Mediawatch, and *Notable Quotables* were established as
media watchdogs, sicking themselves on any scent of media liberalism and thus, it was hoped, having a chilling effect on it.

The theory these neoconservative critics drew upon was that
of the "new class." It argued that an emerging stratum of anti-
capitalist liberals is now in control of the media and its message.

Unfortunately, this argument is so unlikely that before it is
through, it refutes itself.

Let us begin with the term *anti-capitalist liberal,* which is an
oxymoron. No strain of liberalism has proposed eliminating capitalism, only leavening it with a dash of regulation and welfare services. The conservatives' own data bear this out. In a survey of
media elites designed to show their liberalism, 67 percent rejected
public viewership of large corporations—a fundamental tenet of
anti-capitalists.[85]

But the difficulties with this position amount to more than
the cosmetic problem of verbal imprecision. Ultimately, the very
heart of the argument is clogged with massive internal contradictions. For example, Peter Berger has described the "class interests"
of the new class as follows:

1. Their credentials are mainly educational, and thus they decry
capitalism, which rewards "achievement in economic terms."

2. "A large proportion of this class depends for its livelihood on
government payrolls or subsidies," and thus it has a "vested
interest in the expansion of the welfare state." [86]

At the risk of belaboring the obvious, very few people at work in the American media depend on government payrolls or subsidies. Our media are nearly unique in the extent to which they are privately owned commercial enterprises. Berger acknowledges this, but doggedly infers only that it explains why American media makers are "less to the left than the same class in Western Europe." Never mind that, without a class interest, there is no reason to posit that media creators should be thought of as even a little bit "to the left." Nor that excepting the American media from this class interest, hegemonic as they are over the international media market, is to allow a rather devastating exception to the argument.

What is more, mediacrats are notoriously well rewarded "in economic terms" for their efforts. Now Berger would caution us to focus on media "creatives," not media executives. It is the former, he would argue, who are new class charter members—and who determine the content of the media. I shall challenge the latter assertion in subsequent chapters.

Let me begin with the class placement of media creatives. The fact is that movie studio executives often move from those positions to the "creative end" of the film business—because it pays better.[87] And in television, producers, whom insiders call the "auteurs" of the industry, are typically better paid than network executives. "Even a second string producer or writer can earn two to three times the annual salary of a network program executive."[88] Network television news salaries are now regularly six and seven figures long. Salaries of print journalists in the national press corps are usually a bit less celestial, but not so down-to earth as to make anyone working class.* It is, in short, a little hard to picture this Rolls Royce parade down Rodeo Drive and Park Avenue as the vanguard of the revolution.

But the important point about those who make the media is not that they are conservative, or liberal. The important point, as we shall see in later chapters, is how irrelevant such things are when these people go to work. For there, they are surrounded by a set of rules and routines that say, in innumerable, subtle ways, "Check your politics at the door." This set of routines is pervasive in the media workplace, so pervasive as to constitute an atmosphere as invisible and irresistible as the air. In its now-complete phase, this is how hegemony works.

---

*It is true that salaries among journalists of the sub-national press are often not high. But, contrary to Berger's hypothesis, these newspeople tend to be the most politically conservative members of their profession.[89]

Counter-Thesis II: The Cultural Democracy of Markets

A few pages ago, we learned that Americans sing the anthem of capitalist individualism in unison. But saying this says only that capitalist individualism is a pervasive, prominent ideology. And this book claims there is a dominant ideology, one successfully urged upon one group by another. To get from "prominent" to "dominant," we must contend with a second counter-thesis.

This is the theory of cultural democracy. Its argument is that a culture rooted in commerce, as ours is, is a democratic culture. Commercial mass media, after all, want to make money. To do that, they must generate large audiences. And "a mass medium can only achieve its greatest audience by practicing . . . cultural democracy . . . by giving a majority of the people what they want," says the former president of CBS.[90]

This view is sometimes called the "popular culture" theory, and is often demonstrated by the work of members of the Popular Culture Association:

> If popular culture is a reflection of our society, as indeed it is, then the products it produces can be said to be mirrors of that society. The mirrored images may be somewhat distorted, but the image will be generally accurate. We can know a people by what they consume, and we are what we enjoy![91]

We'll have much to say about this theory in the chapters ahead. Let us begin our reply with a couple of questions:

1. Are some "more equal than others" in the democracy of the marketplace? Equality is one of democracy's defining norms, as in "one person, one vote." But the market's rule is "one dollar, one vote." Those who have dollars to spend—on movie tickets, or on the products of those who sponsor television and newspapers— are the media's electorate. Those who don't, aren't. We shall see some consequences of this truncated electorate in coming chapters.

2. Are trivialized, establishmentarian media really "what the people want"? Opinion polls, as we shall see, suggest otherwise. "Sure," reply the media's apologists, "Americans may say they want more challenging and critical offerings, but what they watch and read is unchallenging and uncritical. What they say is posturing, what they do is preference." Possibly. But these para-doxical Americans are open to a number of interpretations. I will suggest another interpretation in Chapter 5, which asks, "What if we made decisions about our media not as a market, but as a public?" [92]

So What: Why Worry About American Unison?

But surely the analogy to the Gulf War is wrong. While that cru-sade may have been dubious, surely the American experiment is not. While the media's hymns of praise to the War may have shrouded the truth, surely its odes to the American system have not. If the workings of the cultural machine have left us with only one American way, isn't it manifestly the best way? Isn't our lack of ideological debate, in fact, the "genius of American politics," al-lowing us to unite around a healthy pragmatism, to be the nation that works?[93] Hasn't our free enterprise economy made our stan-dard of living the envy of the world?

By some measures, the answer is yes. But then there are some curious anomalies. For example, the United States has tow-ered above the world on measures of wealth for most of the years since World War II. And as one might expect in such a land of plenty, the United States has, for example, more doctors per capita than any other nation on earth. And they are better paid here than anywhere else. But here we find one of those anomalies. Despite all those doctors and dollars, the rate at which babies die is higher in the United States than in Denmark, Belgium, the Netherlands, Norway, Finland, England, and fifteen other countries. Our record for life expectancy of males is no better: the United States trails nineteen other countries—including every industrialized nation on earth. Other measures of the quality of life in areas like housing, nutrition, employment, and occupational health and safety show the United States to be a similarly poor performer. Why?

Obviously, the flow of milk and honey has not reached every-one. Instead, our ethos of self-interest and laissez faire has made us a great nation on another index: inequality. Today, the top 0.5 percent of American families own about half of all corporate stocks and about 35 percent of the nation's total wealth. Meanwhile, about one out of seven Americans is officially classified as living in poverty. (A more realistic definition of poverty would find almost one of every three Americans living in that cold state.) That is far more poverty than is found in most of Western Europe, where capitalist individualism has been, not a civic religion, but one side of a healthy debate. In Sweden, for example, the poorest five percent of the population enjoys a higher standard of living than fully 25 percent of the U.S. population.

In nonresponse, the U.S. has chosen to spend a smaller proportion of national income on social welfare than any other industrialized nation. More than 40 percent of our families living below the poverty line receive no food stamps, Medicaid, housing subsidies, or low-price school lunches. And the social Darwinist argument that this inaction and inequality are the necessary cost of doing business—that our productivity is a function of our inequality—can no longer be sustained. The industrial nations that have outstripped the United States recently in productivity are generally characterized by less income inequality, more progressive tax structures, and more developed welfare systems than our own.[94]

The harvest of our stingy sowing has been bleak indeed: inner city infant mortality and illiteracy rates that would shame a Third World country; chronic high unemployment, unaddressed by government jobs or training programs, carrying mental illness, suicide, alcoholism, divorce, murder, and wife and child abuse in its wake. Eighteen percent of our low-income preschoolers show signs of malnutrition; an estimated 75,000 children have been forced into illegal child labor in the New York City area alone; about 2 million Americans are homeless; about 80,000 are permanently disabled by workplace accidents each year; each year more than 100,000 die of job-related diseases; about 500,000 Americans—most of them poor—are heroin addicts; because of the high rate in low-income areas, death by homicide is eight to nine times more likely in the United States than in other advanced industrial states; one in every 21 young black men is murdered.[95] That, as they say, is life, in "the greatest nation in the only world we know."

At this point, friends of the status quo will object. "Granted, American capitalism has not eradicated poverty. But it is not designed to. It *has* done what it *is* designed, to do—provide prosperity to the vast majority of Americans who are working, and who are middle class." Let's spend a moment with this proposition.

In our free enterprise system, Milton Friedman likes to say, people are "free to choose." Recently, corporate executives have made much use of their freedom, choosing to abandon the American worker and the American middle class. Over the last decade, these corporations have sometimes decided that the land of opportunity is South Korea, Sri Lanka, Hong Kong, Taiwan, Mexico, or Brazil—places where wage rates are a tenth or a fifth of the American average.[96] At other times, the land of opportunity was out of the realm of production altogether, and in the realm of "paper entrepreneurialism" where goods and services are bought and sold instead of made.

Either way, American workplaces were padlocked. Often enough, their failure was not that they weren't profitable, but rather that they weren't *profitable enough* to suit corporations whose only interest was in profit maximization.[97] Nearly a million jobs were lost each year. Most of them were in the unionized, good-paying basic manufacturing sector.[98]

As another profit-maximizing strategy, business began creating other kinds of American jobs. These were in the low-paying, nonunionized service sector.

Even expressed statistically, the consequences of this restructuring are startling. The proportion of "middle wage" American workers has dropped from nearly 90 to less than 50 percent of all year-round, full-time workers. At the same time, the proportion of "low wage"* workers has increased from less than 20 to about 35 percent of the total.

As these changes sweep over them, millions of Americans are losing their hold on middle-class life.

They are losing their hold on medical care. One of every eight Americans now has no health care coverage. One of every five children has none. Most of them are in middle class families. Their health care is worse than that of poor Americans, who are entitled to health care under the Medicaid program.[100]

They are losing their hold on the defining element of middle class membership—home ownership. During the 70s and 80s, as incomes fell and interest rates rose, the down payment on an average starter home rose from 40 to 55 percent of an average young family's income. During the same period, the cost of payments rose from 14 to 33 percent of an average income.

Many homeowners lost hold. In 1982 alone, "200 thousand homes were lost to foreclosure." By the mid-80s, the mortgage-loan delinquency rate was at six percent, the highest level since the 1950s, when recordkeeping began. By the end of the decade, "nearly one homeowner out of every 20 was behind in mortgage payments." [101]

---

*Low wage workers are defined as those year-round, full-time workers whose wages leave them below the federally defined poverty level for a family of four.[99]

And finally, working people are losing hold of the last rung above poverty. This loss has happened most often to those women who are their family's breadwinners. As *Business Week* exulted in 1985, "Just as the shift from high-labor-cost manufacturing to low-labor-cost services was gaining momentum, the influx of women provided a cheap pool of labor." [102] Good for business. Bad for women and their families. Channeled by the millions into low-paying, pink-collar ghettos, they are working hard, only to be poor. Today, two-thirds of all poor adults are women. The poverty rate among black working women is 32 percent. More than one-third of all female-headed households are living in poverty. [103]

And those are just the visible hurts of capitalist individualism. Even more pervasive are the "hidden injuries" of the American way. In free-floating interviews with working class men and women, Sennett and Cobb found themes of "powerlessness and adequacy recur[ring] again and again." [104] How could they not be so obsessed in a land that denies them dignity at every turn? About 40 million Americans have been thrown out of work over the past decade by corporate disinvestment decisions—and often blamed themselves for it. [105] How could they fail to inflict that pain on themselves in a land that demands that each "take responsibility for himself"?

A recent study of mobility in America makes clear that the best way to get ahead is with a head start—"those who do well economically owe almost half of their occupational advantage and 55 to 85 percent of their earnings advantage to family back-ground." [106] But how can those who do not advance respect them-selves in a land where one is expected to "make something of him-self"? How can a man who is bossed have dignity, in a land where he is supposed to "stand on his own feet," "be his own man"? [107] These are the unformed questions of the men and women caught in the contradiction between real life and our cultural mythology.

A Leading Question

In the 1920s, the novelist Henry Miller was working as a personnel manager for the telegraph company in New York City. One day, a company vice president, feeling pleased with his company and his America, suggested to Miller that he write a sort of Horatio Alger book about his employees.

> I thought to myself [said Miller]—I'll give you an Horatio Alger book. ... I saw the army of men, women and children that had passed through my hands, saw them weeping, begging, beseeching,

imploring, cursing, spitting, fuming, threatening. I saw the tracks they left on the highways, lying on the floor of freight trains, the parents in rags, the coal box empty, the sink running over, the walls sweating and between the cold beads of sweat the cockroaches running like mad; I saw them hobbling along like twisted gnomes or falling backwards in the epileptic frenzy. . . . I saw the walls giving way and the pest pouring out like a winged fluid, and the men higher up with their ironclad logic, waiting for it to blow over, waiting for everything to be patched up, waiting, waiting contentedly . . . saying that things were temporarily out of order. I saw the Horatio Alger hero, the dream of a sick America, mounting higher and higher, first messenger, then operator, then manager, then chief, then superintendent, then vice-president, then president, then trust magnate, then beer baron, then Lord of all the Americas, the money god, the god of gods, the clay of clay, nullity on high, zero with ninety-seven thousand decimals fore and aft. . . . I will give you Horatio Alger as he looks the day after the Apocalypse, when all the stink has cleared away.[108]

No, America is no El Dorado. The monotonous ethos of capitalist individualism has not made ours "the best of all possible worlds." And yet, somehow, the alchemists of our mass media have made it seem so. They have made the land of inequality the land of opportunity; the odor of excess, the sweet smell of success; cupidity and rapacity, the American Way.

How?

The answer is a long story. So long, in fact, that it will take the rest of this book to begin to tell it.

References

1. *New York Times,* "Transcript of President Bush's State of the Union Message to Nation," (January 30, 1991): A12.
2. Ibid.: A14.
3. Michael Kramer, "The Moment of Truth," *Time,* (January 21, 1991): 25.
4. Jim Motavalli, "Chomsky's Hidden History of the Persian Gulf Crisis," *In These Times,* (June 1991); Doug Henwood, "War and Commerce," *Lies of Our Times,* (March 1990): 9–10.
5. Jim Motavalli, "Chomsky's Hidden History of the Persian Gulf Crisis."
6. Noam Chomsky, "A Consistent Response to Aggression," *The Progressive,* (March 1991): 22–24.
7. Ellen Ray, "The Killing Deserts," *Lies of Our Times,* (April 1991): 3.

8. Jesse Birnbaum, "Stormin' Norman on Top," *Time*, (February 4, 1991): 28.

9. Edward Herman, "Gulf Speak II," *Z Magazine*, (March 1991): 17.

10. Bill Turque, "Desert Storm," *Newsweek*, (January 28, 1991): 12.

11. *New York Times*, "Huge Armor Movement Both Majestic, Menacing," *Watertown Daily Times*, (February 26, 1991): A1.

12. George J. Church, "The Battle: So Far, So Good," *Time*, (January 28, 1991): 22.

13. Bill Turque, "Desert Storm": 12.

14. George J. Church, "The Battle: So Far, So Good": 22.

15. Ibid.

16. See Holly Sklar, "Buried Stories from Media Gulf," *Z Magazine* (March 1991): 58; Louise Cainkar, "How Paul Lewis Covers Postwar Iraq," *Lies of Our Times*, (July–August 1991): 4.

17. Alexander Cockburn, "The Press and the Just War," *Nation*, (February 18, 1991): 186; Zoltan Grossman, "Ecocide in the Gulf," *Z Magazine*, (March 1991): 26.

18. Louis Cainkar, "How Paul Lewis Covers Postwar Iraq:" 4.

19. Noam Chomsky, "Letter from Lexington," *Lies of Our Times*, (September 1991): 16.

20. Jonathan Schell, quoted in Ellen Ray and William Schaap, "Minefields of Disinformation," *Lies of Our Times*, (March 1991): 5.

21. Ellen Ray, "The Killing Deserts": 3.

22. Ellen Ray and William Schaap, "Minefields of Disinformation": 5.

23. Ellen Ray, "The Killing Deserts": 4.

24. *Newsday*, "Army Claims Iraqi Soldiers Buried Alive," in *Watertown Daily Times*, (September 12, 1991): 1,8.

25. Michael Kelly, "Highway to Hell," *New Republic*, (April 1, 1991): 12.

26. Ibid.: 13–14. Excerpted by permission of THE NEW REPUBLIC, © 1991, The New Republic, Inc.

27. Stanley Cloud, "Exorcising an Old Demon," *Time*, (March 11, 1991): 52.

28. Associated Press, "Kuwaiti's Reclaim Devastated Capital; Citizens Tell of Terror," *Watertown Daily Times*, (February 27, 1991): All.

29. Bruce W. Nelan, "Free at Last! Free at Last!" *Time*, (March 11, 1991): 38.

30. James P. English, "That's Entertainment," *Lies of Our Times*, (April 1991): 5.

31. Germaine Greer, quoted in John R. MacArthur, *Second Front*, (New York: Hill and Wang, 1992): 44–45.

32. Andrew Whitley, "The Dirty War in Kuwait," *New York Times*, (April 2, 1991): 19.

33. Andrew Rosenthal, "Bush Not Pressing Kuwait on Reform," *New York Times*, (March 27, 1991): 1.

34. Ibid.: 8.

35. Louis Uchitelle, "Gulf Victory May Raise U.S. Influence in OPEC," *New York Times*, (March 5, 1991): D1.

36. Ibid.

37. Alan Cowell, "Kurds Assert Few Outside Iraq Wanted Them to Win," *New York Times*, (April 11, 1991): All.

38. Andrew Rosenthal, "U.S., Fearing Iraqi Breakup, Is Said to Rule Out Action to Aid Anti-Hussein Rebels," *New York Times*, (March 27, 1991): 1.

39. Alan Cowell, "Kurds Fall Back from Iraq Forces," *New York Times*, (April 2, 1991): 8.

40. Ibid.: A9.

41. Clyde Haberman, "Six U.S. Planes Begin Airdrops of Relief to Kurds in Iraq," *New York Times*, (April 6, 1991): 1.
42. Nancy Gibbs, "Making Sense of the Storm," *Time*, (June 17, 1991): 23.
43. Noam Chomsky, "Letters from Lexington": 18.
44. Karl Marx, *A Contribution to the Critique of Political Economy*, edited by Maurice Dobb (New York: International Publishers, 1970): Preface.
45. Nicholas Abercrombie, Stephen Hill, and Bryan S. Turner, *The Dominant Ideology Thesis*, (London: George Allen and Unwin, 1980): 9.
46. Karl Marx and Frederich Engels, *The German Ideology*, edited by S. Reyazanskaya, (Moscow: Progress Publishers, 1964): 61.
47. Eugene D. Genovese, "On Antonio Gramsci," *Studies on the Left VII* 1967: 292.
48. Antonio Gramsci, *Selections from the Prison Notebooks*, edited and translated by Quinton Hoare and Geoffrey N. Smith, (New York: International Publishers, 1971): 419.
49. Ibid.: 328.
50. Nicholas Abercrombie, Stephen Hill, and Bryan S. Turner, *The Dominant Ideology Thesis:* 14–15.
51. Antonio Gramsci, *Selections from the Prison Notebooks:* 344.
52. Ibid.: 395.
53. Herbert Marcuse, *One Dimensional Man*, (Boston: Beacon Press, 1964): 88.
54. Carole Pateman, *Participation and Democratic Theory*, (New York: Cambridge University Press, 1970): chapter 5.
55. Todd Gitlin, "Television's Screens: Hegemony in Transition," *American Media and Mass Culture*, edited by Donald Lazere, (Berkeley: University of California Press, 1987): 258.
56. Roger Simon, *Gramsci's Political Thought*, (London: Lawrence and Wishart, 1982): 64.
57. Antonio Gramsci, *Selections from the Prison Notebooks:* 238.
58. Michael Parenti, *Inventing Reality*, (New York: St. Martin's, 1986); and Michael Parenti, *Make-Believe Media*, (New York: St. Martin's, 1992).
59. Edward Herman and Noam Chomsky, *Manufacturing Consent*, (New York, Pantheon, 1988).
60. Thorstein Veblen, *The Theory of Business Enterprise*, (New York: Charles Scribner's Sons, 1904): chapter III.
61. Bennett Harrison and Barry Bluestone, *The Great U-turn*, (New York: Basic Books, 1988): chapter 3.
62. Ibid.: 58.
63. Herbert McClosky and John Zaller, *The American Ethos*, (Cambridge, Mass.: Harvard University Press, 1984): 2.
64. Sidney Verba and Gary R. Owen, *Equality in America*, (Cambridge, Mass.: Harvard University Press, 1985): 255.
65. Herbert McClosky and John Zaller, *The American Ethos:* 108, 120, 133, 135, 140, 152.
66. Kay Schlozman and Sidney Verba, *Injury to Insult*, (Cambridge, Mass.: Harvard University Press, 1979): 107.
67. James R. Kluegel and Eliot R. Smith, *Beliefs About Inequality*, (New York: Aldine De Gruyter, 1986): 44, 106, 107.
68. Herbert McClosky and John Zaller, *The American Ethos*.
69. Kay Schlozman and Sidney Verba, *Injury to Insult:* 109.
70. Herbert McClosky and John Zaller, *The American Ethos:* 272; Lloyd A. Free

and Hadley Cantril, *The Political Beliefs of Americans,* (New York: Simon and Schuster, 1968).

71. Seymour Martin Lipset and William Schneider, *The Confidence Gap.* (New York: The Free Press, 1983): 238.

72. Lloyd A. Free and Hadley Cantril, *The Political Beliefs of Americans,* (New York: Simon and Schuster, 1968); Herbert McClosky and John Zaller, *The American Ethos:* 272.

73. Herbert McClosky and John Zaller, *The American Ethos:* 224; Sidney Verba and Gary R. Owen, *Equality in America:* 72.

74. Herbert McClosky and John Zaller, *The American Ethos:* 149; for further evidence of New Deal liberalism among capitalists, see Thomas R. Dye and L. Harmon Zeigler, *The Irony of Democracy,* (Monterey, Calif.: Brooks-Cole, 1983): 111–113; Robert H. Wiebe, *The Search for Order 1877–1920,* (New York: Hill and Wang, 1967): 297; Gabriel Kolko, *The Triumph of Conservatism,* (London: The Free Press of Glencoe, 1963): 5.

75. James R. Kluegel and Eliot R. Smith, *Beliefs About Inequality:* 120–121.

76. Ibid.: 59.

77. Seymour Martin Lipset and William Schneider, *The Confidence Gap:* 16.

78. James R. Kluegel and Eliot R. Smith, *Beliefs About Inequality:* 292–293.

79. David M. Gordon, Richard Edwards, and Michael Reich, *Segmented Work, Divided Workers,* (Cambridge: Cambridge University Press, 1982): 204–213.

80. Michael Parenti, *Democracy for the Few,* 5th Ed., (New York: St. Martin's, 1988): 95.

81. Ibid.: 137.

82. Edward S. Greenburg, *The American Political System,* 5th ed., (Boston: Scott Foresman, 1989): 72.

83. Peter Dreier, "The Corporate Complaint Against the Media," *American Media and Mass Culture,* edited by Donald Lazere, (New York: Basic Books, 1987): 65.

84. Thomas B. Edsall, *The New Politics of Inequality,* (New York: W. W. Norton, 1984): 117–120.

85. Robert S. Lichter, Stanley Rothman, and Linda Lichter, *The Media Elite,* (New York: Adler and Adler, 1986).

86. Peter L. Berger, *The Capitalist Revolution,* (New York: Basic Books, 1986): 69.

87. Mark Litwak, *Reel Power,* (New York: William Morrow, 1986): 71–2, 195.

88. Richard A. Blum and Richard D. Lindheim, *Primetime,* (New York: Focal Press, 1987): 42.

89. John W. C. Johnstone, Edward Slawski, and William W. Bowman, *The News People,* (Urbana: University of Illinois Press, 1976).

90. David Marc, "Beginning to Begin Again," *Television: The Critical View,* edited by Horace Newcomb, (New York: Oxford University Press, 1987): 358.

91. Michael T. Marsden, Introduction to "Popular Culture and the Teaching of English," *Arizona English Bulletin* 17:3.

92. Todd Gitlin, "Television's Screens: Hegemony in Transition."

93. Daniel Boorstin, *The Genius of American Politics.*

94. Joshua Cohen and Joel Rogers, *On Democracy,* (New York: Penguin Books, 1983): 24; Lester C. Thurow, "A Liberal Looks at Income Distribution," *New York Times,* (August 23, 1981): C3.

95. Philip Mattera, *Prosperity Lost,* (New York: Addison-Wesley, 1990); Joshua Cohen and Joel Rogers, *On Democracy:* chapter 2; Tom Morganthau,

"Homeless in America," *Newsweek,* (January 2, 1984): 20–30; *U.S. News and World Report,* "A Nation Apart," (March 17, 1986): 18–28; Thomas B. Edsall, *The New Politics of Inequality:* 232.

96. Bennett Harrison and Barry Bluestone, *The Great U-Turn:* 32.
97. Ibid.
98. Ibid.: 37.
99. Bennett Harrison and Barry Bluestone, *The Great U-Turn:* 127.
100. Philip Mattera, *Prosperity Lost:* 119.
101. Ibid.: 124–130.
102. Ibid.: 141.
103. Ibid.: 143–4.
104. Richard Sennett and Jonathan Cobb, *The Hidden Injuries of Class,* (New York: Vintage Books, 1973): 41.
105. See Barry Bluestone and Bennett Harrison, *The Deindustrialization of America,* (New York: Basic Books, 1982); Stanley Feldman, "Economic Self Interest and Political Behavior," *American Journal of Political Science* 26 (1982): 446–66.
106. Christopher Jencks et al., *Who Gets Ahead?* (New York: Basic Books, 1979): 81.
107. Richard Sennett and Jonathan Cobb, *The Hidden Injuries of Class:* 33–41.
108. Henry Miller, *Tropic of Cancer,* (New York: Grove Press, 1961): viii–ix. From the book *Tropic of Cancer* by Henry Miller, copyright © 1961 by Henry Miller. Used with the permission of Grove/Atlantic Monthly Press.

The "hoopla" of pseudo-events and photo ops is a prominent part of
political news coverage.

"And That's the Way It Is": The Bias of the News

The basis of our government being the opinion of the people, the very first object should be to keep that right, and were it left to me to decide whether we should have a government without newspapers, or newspapers without a government, I should not hesitate a moment to prefer the latter.

Thomas Jefferson

To be able to see every side of every question;
To be on every side, to be everything, to be nothing long;
To pervert truth, to ride it for a purpose . . .
To sell papers . . .

Edgar Lee Masters, "Editor Whedon"*

---

*Lines from "Editor Whedon" from *Spoon River Anthology* by Edgar Lee Masters. Originally published by the Macmillan Company. Permission by Ellen C. Masters.

INTRODUCTION   ☆ ☆ ☆ ☆ ☆ ☆ ☆ ☆ ☆ ☆ ☆ ☆ ☆ ☆ ☆

This chapter asks, ``What's news?'' We'll begin with the neoconservatives' answer—that peeling back the curtain behind the Great Oz reveals a liberal, blaring liberal bias into the headlines. Close observers of journalists, however, paint a different picture. Theirs is a picture of professionals committed not to a political creed, but to their norm of ``objectivity.'' This impression is confirmed by the best content analyses of news reports, which have found little evidence of the liberal bias neoconservatives describe.

This will bring us to hegemony theorists, who have a different complaint. They see a bias built into the very foundation of the news business—its most basic demands and norms. This structure of the news business will be described in Chapter 3. In this chapter, we look at its results—the ``structural bias'' of the news.

Structural bias has two powerful tendencies. The first is to trivialize the news. Too often, the news is dramatic and spectacular and useless to the citizens who are supposed to be acting on its information. There is no more clear or sorry example of this than what has become of our presidential elections. And so this chapter will pause for a look at that quadrennial extravaganza.

The second tendency of the news is support for the powers that be. We call this tendency ``establishmentarianism.'' We can see this tendency in the criteria used to judge what is ``newsworthy,'' as well as in the routines reporters follow to gather the news. Both these tendencies, hegemony theory argues, help perpetuate power and privilege. The second does so directly, by ``cheerleading for the side that's already won,'' as one writer put it. The first tendency, trivialization, supports the status quo indirectly, by diverting people's attention from serious questions whose answer might be social change.

At this point, we will be ready to meet an objection to hegemony theory's argument. It comes to us from the theorists of ``cultural democracy,'' who argue, once again, that our market-driven media serve us well. Hegemony theory's argument, they say, ignores two redeeming features of the news. First, there is the pride reporters take in telling both sides of the story. Given that, how can the news be monopolized by one establishmentarian point of view? And secondly, there is, in the post-Watergate era, a renewed commitment among journalists to be the ``watchdog of the people''—to be investigative, even adversarial—to ``comfort the afflicted and afflict the comfortable.'' How can hegemony theory explain that? These are good questions. We'll try to answer them.

Finally, we'll ask how the news affects the public mind. The answer, as you might guess, is not good news.

In between these arguments, we'll take a couple of "News Breaks"—one for a whistle-stop tour of campaigns '88 and '92, and another to see how the "watchdog of the people" watched the Iran-Contra scandal.

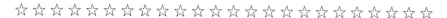

Thesis

Press critics have not been much kinder to his profession than Editor Whedon is in the epigraph to this chapter. The news, they have argued, is neatly tailored to the interests of upper-class Americans. The news is ill-suited to its public trust—keeping the flame of popular control alive with information. In this chapter, we'll examine this bias of the news. In the next, we'll ask how and why it occurs. How does the watchdog of the people become the lapdog of the powerful?

Counter-Thesis: The Usual Definition of Bias

Conventional wisdom has it that the news media are often guilty of partisan bias, favoritism toward one or the other of the mainstream parties or ideologies—Democrats, Republicans, liberals, or conservatives. We might also call this kind of bias "anti-normative," because it violates the norm that the news should be "objective," in other words, evenhanded in the treatment of such parties and points of view. Conventional wisdom also tells us that partisan bias usually points to the left, favoring liberal spokesmen and values. As we shall see, the omnipresence of this "common sense" view has much to do with the ability of corporate money to make its viewpoint common, if not sensible.

Lately, the "liberal bias" argument is most often based on a study sponsored by the corporate neoconservative nexus described in Chapter 1. Not surprisingly, the study purports to show that many journalists describe themselves as "liberals" and give "liberal" responses to multiple-choice opinion questions.* [1] What is more, the journalists interviewed for this study were drawn from the "elite" national press corps, which tends to be the giver of national news to local media as well as to news consumers—the *New York Times, Washington Post,* ABC, NBC, CBS, *Time, Newsweek,* and so on.

Unfortunately for this argument, these are precisely the organizations where personal viewpoint is most sure to be preempted by the cardinal rule of the journalism profession: the norm of objectivity.[3] And this is the bottom line. Repeatedly, the best studies of the content of such prestigious media have found them more or less evenhanded in their treatment of Democrats, Republicans, mainstream liberals, and conservatives,[4] which is not surprising. These organizations are, after all, bearers of a standard to which all journalists aspire.[5]

But perhaps this next point *is* surprising: Scratch the surface of the journalist's "liberalism." Underneath is a consciousness not really liberal, or conservative, but above all, apolitical. Surveys using multiple choice questions, like the study of journalists mentioned above, can determine that respondent A prefers the liberal position on issue 1. Much harder for such surveys to determine is whether respondent A cares much about issue 1. Those of us who have done more open-ended, free-flowing interviews with journalists have been surprised to find that, indeed, they do *not* care much about issue 1, or any others for that matter.[6] David Broder is in an even better position to know about the salience of "isms" for journalists. He has spent a lifetime (or at least, "since the fifth grade") as a journalist, "and for the last thirty years in Washington, where I am part of the largest concentration of reporters in the world." [7] Liberal bias? Broder puts the point this way:

> One reason I am skeptical is that I know how little time reporters
> spend talking among themselves about ideology or policy. The
> barroom debates in press pubs are rarely about American policy in

---

*The phrase "purports to show" refers to criticisms leveled at the methodology that led to this conclusion. Another survey of the Washington press corps found a different result. Of that sample, 58 percent considered themselves either "conservative" or "middle of the road." [2]

> *the Middle East, supply-side economics, or government's role in our*
> *society. We talk about what Clifton Daniel, the former managing*
> *editor of the* New York Times, *called "gossip and maneuver," what*
> *political people are doing to each other. We rehash the day's events*
> *and their possible consequences. Most of all, we love to speculate.*
> *"Why did so-and-so do that?" I don't know why we journalists have*
> *this character failing, but we are not ideologues.*[8]

How strange, that these men and women whose work is so profoundly political should themselves be so profoundly apolitical. Or perhaps we shall see, as the next two chapters unfold, that it is not so strange after all.

But the "liberal bias" position is even more wrong than Broder knows. For in fact, when partisan bias does exist, it is usually conservative. For example, Bagdikian reviewed 84 studies that had found partisan bias in newspapers. In 88 percent of those cases, the bias was "pro-Republican and pro-conservative."[9] By newspeople's own lights, "30 percent of the media for which they are working are right or right leaning, only 12 percent are left or left leaning, and 57 percent are . . . middle of the road."[10]

Repeated surveys of newspaper endorsements have found them overwhelmingly favorable to conservative candidates. For example, in 1984, 394 newspapers endorsed Ronald Reagan's candidacy; 76 endorsed Mondale's.[11] And Bagdikian's review indicates that such editorial page colorations often spill over into the news columns. Based on studies linking endorsements to voting behavior, a third analysis concludes:

> *It would seem that the normal Republican trend of the press is*
> *worth at least a couple of percentage points to the Republican party*
> *nationwide. Humphrey might have defeated Nixon in 1968 for*
> *example, with a more equitable division of newspaper endorsements*
> *between the two major party candidates. . . . For lower offices . . .*
> *one might expect that a newspaper would be more, not less,*
> *influential.*[12]

And while we're on the editorial page, let's note that "the most widely distributed syndicated columnists are conservatives James J. Kilpatrick (514 dailies) and George Will (375) . . . such liberals as Mary McGrory (160) and William Raspberry (150) trail badly."[13] What is worse, with those liberals, the editorial page's map of the political world ends. "Not one nationally syndicated columnist is a socialist, or in European parlance, a 'social democrat.' "[14]

While these findings may seem contradictory to the findings of "no bias" already mentioned, they are not. These latter surveys include small and medium-sized newspapers in the hinterlands, different in key ways from the elite press surveyed in the study referred to earlier. For one thing, journalists in the provinces of pressdom are less liberal than those in the press capitals. A nationwide survey of newspeople, including both groups, found 22 percent of them "leaning to the left"—most of them (18.3 percent) just "a little to the left." Only 3.8 percent would venture "pretty far to the left." On the other hand, a total of 17.9 percent leaned either "a little" or "pretty far" to the right. But the vast majority, 57.5 percent, were comfortably "middle of the road." [15]

But what of that floodgate against partisanship, the journalist's pride of professionalism and objectivity? Again, the hinterland press is different. Here, there is no great prestige to protect; there are no Pulitzers likely to be won, and conservative owners who are not steeped in the norm of objectivity are likely to have a heavier hand in the production of the news. But even here, on the small paper, the force of journalists' values is at work, opposing partisan bias. Because of them, "no executive is willing to risk embarrassment by being accused of open commands to slant a story." [16] So partisan bias occurs in the crevices between the normal and the approved. And evidence suggests that those crevices have grown smaller over time. For example, between the 30s and the 60s, the rate at which newspapers changed their Washington correspondents' stories for political reasons declined. [17]

In the final analysis, the most important truth about partisan bias is not that it is usually conservative, but that it is a red herring: it misleads us away from the real, pervasive bias of the media. The preoccupation of citizens and scholars with partisan bias has focused the curative powers of the people and the profession on the head cold of the media. Meanwhile, below, in its bones, a cancer consumes the news.

What's News? The Structural Bias of the Press

Much more serious than partisan bias, because it is uncountered and therefore pervasive, is the structural bias of the news. Structural bias is that which occurs as a result of the approved routines of newspeople and news organizations, as a result of their system for selecting some kinds of information as news and rejecting other kinds as "not news." Of course newspeople have such a system. After all, there is a whole wild world of facts out there, an infinitude of information, and the journalists' lariat (the newshole) is too small to capture it all.

So the complaint of this chapter is not that the news media have a news-selection system and a resulting structural bias. That is inevitable. The complaint is that the media's bias is hegemonic: it is monolithic and plutocratic. The news outlets offering alternative realities are so few and so obscure* that few Americans ever blinked when Walter Cronkite presumed to say night after night, "And that's the way it is." What is worse, this news monolith was not built by or for ordinary Americans, but by and for an American plutocracy, a wealthy few. This structural bias is the one that will concern us; it is the one in the very foundation of the news. This chapter will describe it: what does it include, what does it exclude? The next chapter will ask, "Why?"

The News Is Trivial

News Criteria: The Rules of Trivial Pursuit

Somehow, the media manage, day in and day out, to refine a rich lode of socio-political information into a high grade of trivia. This process begins with the selection of "stories." A group of newspaper and television editors, asked to describe their criteria for choosing what's news, listed the following:

1. **Proximity.** Or, as Abbie Hoffman once put it, "the headline in the *Daily News* today reads 'BRUNETTE STABBED TO DEATH.' Underneath, in lower case letters '6,000 Killed in Iranian Earthquake' . . . I wonder what color hair they had." [18]

2. **Sensationalism.** ". . . violence, conflict, disaster . . . scandal . . . the kinds of things that excite audiences."

3. **Familiarity.** "News is attractive if it involves familiar situations . . . or pertains to well-known people."

---

*For a look at what else there is besides "all the news that's fit to print," compare coverage of a current event in *Time* or *Newsweek* to coverage in *The National Guardian* or *In These Times*.

4. Timeliness and Novelty. "News must be something that has just occurred and is out of the ordinary." [19]

Notice that "socially significant" is not one of the criteria capable of getting a story past the gatekeepers. Despite Jefferson's fond hope, a story's ability to empower ordinary citizens by teaching them how politics works and how it affects them does not make it "newsworthy."

The fruit of these criteria are the crime, accident, and human interest stories, which often preempt less sensational political stories, even though the latter have more to do with "who gets what" in the lives of news consumers. Of course, crime and human interest events have their own important social stories to tell: violent crime is most often forged in the crucible of lower-class life; white-collar crime is winked at by the penal system, etc. But these are unspectacular stories, and so they are largely untold. Meanwhile, the sensational events produced by these social forces parade across the front page, unconnected to their causes, leaving us with the ignorant impression that they occur randomly, or purely as the result of personal pathology.

This pattern is most extreme on local television news shows, whose "eyewitness" cameras subsist on "action," on spectacle. But the more prestigious network news is not above the temptation to favor exciting pictures over important issues. "[Network] newscasts have gone increasingly for what the industry recognizes as *news that wiggles.* And while they talk about their desire for news in depth, the problem is that the deeper it gets, the less it can wiggle." [20] What kind of news "wiggles"? An NBC cameraman who had covered Vietnam put it plainly; "What the producers want on film is as much blood and violence as we can find. That's the name of the game, and every cameraman knows it." [21] In fact, increasingly those palpitating *pictures* decide what will be *stories,* and not vice versa. The medium decides the message: "On a political campaign, or in any situation, the cameraman comes back with the pictures—and in television to a very large extent you're obligated to write to the pictures, and should write to the pictures," opines Peter Jennings, anchor of ABC's *World News Tonight,* without explaining why.[22]

Nor is the problem limited to television. For example, during a recent four-week period, 48 percent of metro-page stories in the widely respected *Chicago Tribune* were crime, accident, or "human interest" stories. Further subtracting the portion of the two-page metropolitan section that goes to advertising left about two stories per issue devoted to local politics.[23]

Even when important issues are covered, the criterion that insists the news be new has often meant a limited shelf life for even the most urgent ongoing issues. Lipsky and Olson show that news stories about ghetto rioting were fewer and less alarmed in the late 1960s than they had been earlier, giving Americans the impression that the incidents themselves had declined. In fact, the amount of property damage done in ghetto uprisings was three times as great in 1968 as it had been in 1964.[24] In the same way did battlefield stories about Vietnam come to the end of their newsworthiness at ABC News when, in March 1969, the executive producer of that network wrote to his correspondents:

> . . . The time has come to shift some of our focus from the battlefield
> . . . to themes and stories under the general heading: We Are On
> Our Way Out of Vietnam.[25]

Apparently, the novelty of this theme was more compelling than the truth, which was that in March of 1969, we were not on our way out of Vietnam.*

More recently, with the Reagan cutbacks in human services and the recession of the early 80s, the news found the poor. But by 1984, they were no longer new; and so they were not news. "With hunger and homelessness as bad as ever, the media hit upon a new theme: 'economic recovery.' Although the number of Americans living in poverty had increased from twenty-five million to thirty-five million between 1981 and 1985, the media tended to lose interest in the poor."[26]

Elections as Horse Race, Hoopla, and Soap Opera

When important stories do manage to stay in the news, they are often trivialized by being "personalized" and "dramatized."[27] For example, during elections, policy issues become side shows to such center-stage melodramas as these:

1. The "horse race" of preference polls. Who's ahead? Behind? Coming up fast on the outside? By 1988, these questions had become the "computer virus" of campaign coverage. It had "erased" other kinds of coverage (e.g., coverage of what the candi-

---

*The announcement of this theme also had much to do with the ability of political elites to define the truth for the media. More of that to follow.

date said) and replaced that with the horse-race "program": how did what the candidate said *affect his standing in the polls.*

That replacement was made despite the meaninglessness of many polls. The surfeit of polls taken during the pre-primary and early primary season, for example, reflect little more than the fact that voters know nothing about most of the candidates. Yet they are reported as though they are oracles of the people's will. Polls taken after the first of the two parties' nominating conventions, showing its candidate with a "dramatic lead" reflect only the fact that the other party hasn't had its turn.

As former NBC newsman Martin Schram notes, politicians refer to horse race journalism "by a similar term, changing only the second syllable. The politicians have it about right; much of this sort of journalism has to be shoveled rapidly, for it contributes little to the national good and it often cannot stand the test of time without being remembered more for its aroma than its accuracy." [28]

2. The "handicapping" of the race. This coverage takes the crowd "behind the horse race, into the paddocks, the stables, the clubhouse, and the bookie joints." [29] Here, spin doctors, handlers, and press pundits offer us "savvy talk"—the inside dope on campaign tactics and how they're working. After the first Bush-Dukakis debate, for example, reporters talked little about the *substance* of the debate—what the candidates had said and what that meant for the lives of ordinary Americans. Instead, they focused on the *styles,* the tactics of the debate—*how* the candidates had said their piece. Dan Rather asked "a series of pollsters and campaign aides questions such as, 'you're making a George Bush commercial and you're looking for a sound bite. . . . What's his best shot?' " [30]

Handicapping, like horse-race journalism, has become a black hole of campaign coverage. Other coverage, of issues for example, is drawn into the hole—and disappears. Take, for example, coverage of Bill Clinton's speech on the issue of racial division, delivered in the wake of the Los Angeles riots of April 1992. A typical news service story begins with a few sound bites from the speech itself: "Fire bell in the night . . . we must face our fears . . . there is no place to hide." But after a few quick paragraphs of this, the story cuts to the chase: what is the strategy behind the speech, and will it work? For the rest of the story, two-thirds of the total space, we hear "political analysts . . . hotly debate" whether Clinton's gambit will help him "show leadership" or lead him into a "major political trap." [31]

By 1988, the horse race and its handicapping had become "a bigger part of camaign coverage than ever before." Together, they took up almost two-thirds of print-media campaign coverage.[32] In 1992, horse race and handicapping were again off and running. Spurred by a horde of media tracking polls, horse race coverage alone gobbled up 40 percent of network news about the election after October 1. Add to that the 33 pecent of coverage consumed by handicapping stories, and more than two-thirds of all network coverage of the fall campaign is accounted for.[33]

3. The *"soap opera"* of attack, gaffe, and scandal. When elections are not seen as a horse race, they become other kinds of spectacles. Prominent among these are the "Biff!" and "Pow!" of conflict between the candidates: "Brown Rips Clinton With a New Ferocity"; "Bush Steps Up Attacks on Buchanan"; "Democrats Wrangle on TV and in the Street"; "Perot Says He's Victim of Republican Attack Machines"; "Clinton Sets Off Sparks, and Cuomo Fans Flame." Despite all the heat, there is not much light here.

Then there is the spectacle of the gaffe: the verbal misstep that leads, by way of the headlines, to a fall. In 1976, Jimmy Carter said he lusted after women and this indecorous truism somehow became news. In 1980, George Bush was outmaneuvered at the debate table—not by the arguments but by the arrangements—and his *faux pas* found the headlines. In 1992, Dan Quayle's misstep was a misspelling. Hillary Clinton's was a comment that almost cost her the cookie-bakers' vote.

As content analysis makes clear, this lavish attention to the etiquette of the electoral affair comes at the expense, once again, of more serious issues. Thomas Patterson has labeled soap opera stories "media issues." Over 50 percent of these were heavily reported in the year of his study; only 15 percent of policy issues were given heavy coverage.[34]

4. The *"hoopla"* of pseudoevents and photo ops. The last of the media's trivial pursuits is reporters' fascination with meaningless, showy events. George Bush visits a flag factory. Michael Dukakis goes into the tank. Bill Clinton plays the saxophone on the Arsenio Hall Show. George Bush is the starter at the Firecracker 400. In all these cases, our vigilant free press was there, and reported in full the burning truth: it happened; here are some eye-catching pictures to prove it.

All this media trivialization has joined together with the candidates, in recent campaigns, in a symbiotic minuet. Together, they have produced some of the ugliest campaigns and lowest voter turnouts in history.

NEWSBREAK

Scandal in the Headlines

In recent elections, even the heavily covered spectacles of attack and gaffe have been forced off-stage when the third form of soap opera makes its entrance. This is the scandal extravaganza.

It was in the 1988 campaign that the media, with the help of a man from Troublesome Gulch Road, Colorado, would realize the full potential of soap opera coverage.

From the time Gary Hart's dalliance with Donna Rice found the headlines until his erstwhile departure from the presidential race, the scandal consumed 76 percent of all election-related stories in the *New York Times* and *Time* magazine. The story took up 83 percent of election-related front-page or cover stories in those gazettes. All of this left even less room than usual for coverage of policy issues. During this time period, a meager 4 percent of election-related stories concerned themselves with public policy issues.[35]

And what vital information was conveyed to voters by press coverage of this scandal? Instead of meaty issues, the news gave us candy. We learned of Gary Hart's ``longtime friendship with Warren Beatty, an actor with no pretense to celibacy.''[36] In a single issue, *Time* gave us no less than five color photographs of Donna Rice, including a set of three in which she modeled lingerie and swimwear for the edification of voters. We learned that she had dated rock star Don Henley, that she ``was no stranger to the pampered and permissive world of rock stars and multimillionaires. She once dated Prince Albert of Monaco, and was reportedly a guest of Adnan Khashoggi's daughter on his yacht.''[37] We learned how neighbors felt about Gary and Lee's relationship: ``Neighbors said the couple appeared happy when seen around

In 1988, for example, Roger Ailes, the media wizard who gave us the "new Nixon" in '68, was back, this time on the Bush-Quayle team. He read the news media's appetite for drama like a how-to manual, and used it to perfection. "There are three things that get covered," he said, "visuals, attacks and mistakes. You try to avoid mistakes and give them as many attacks and visuals as you can."[41]

town. 'They drive by and everybody waves,' said Mark Volpi, a mason who lives on Troublesome Gulch Road near the Harts' home. . . . Tonda Calvin, owner of Mark Singer's Restaurant in Kittredge, said the Harts 'are real nice people,' and added; 'They come in here for breakfast a lot. They've always been real nice to us and they always tip 20 percent.' "[38]

Having had 1988 as a rehearsal, the media were ready when, in 1992, a woman named Gennifer Flowers claimed to have had a long-time love affair with the front-running Democratic candidate, Bill Clinton. It was an instant "feeding frenzy."[39] In the crucial five weeks surrounding the New Hampshire primary, 63 percent of all election-related stories in *Time* and *Newsweek* magazines were consumed by the Clinton "character" issue. That left room for only three stories concerned with policy issues.

To understand the character "issue," it was important for us to know that Flowers was a blond "sometime cabaret singer" who claimed to have been one of the "cleavage-baring 'Hee-Haw' girls." It was important for us to see large, full-color photos of a mini-skirted Ms. Flowers. We needed to hear reports of late-night phone calls to the Governor's mansion, and of assignations at hotels. We also needed to know that the Clintons "held hands" during a *60 Minutes* interview in which the Governor denied the affair, and that, "at one point, Hillary gently rubbed her husband's back."

The press's own position, expressed in numerous hand-wringing editorials, was that it had a duty to report these stories, however distasteful they might be. The public had a right to know. The public, on the other hand, thought not. Seventy percent of a Yankelovich sample said that candidates' "private behavior should be kept from voters out of respect for privacy."[40]

My own argument is not that the public had no right or need to know about these marital misadventures. It is that we didn't need to learn as much as we did about such soap operas, which pushed the real drama of more vital issues aside.

As it turned out, "avoiding mistakes" meant avoiding almost all unprogrammed statements by the candidate.[42] For all voters knew, this candidate might have been no different from the dupe-president of Kurt Vonnegut's incredibly prescient *Player Piano:* "All the gorgeous dummy had to do was read whatever was handed to him on state occasions . . . to run wisdom from somewhere else through that resonant voicebox and between those even, pearly choppers." [43]

"Attacks and visuals" turned out to mean a campaign of half truth and innuendo, myth and symbol,* all of it scooped up by the press as though it were manna from heaven: Balloons. Dead fish in Boston Harbor. Mr. Bush on stage with a hundred police officers. Willie Horton's glower. More balloons. Bush on stage with a giant flag. Pledge of Allegiance. Card carrying . . . L-word. Another stage, another hundred cops. Bush with children. More flags. Bush with grandchildren. More balloons.[45] After weeks of these photo ops and what one writer has called the "slur *du jour*," Dukakis' lead had disappeared. In the end, voters were angry.[46] Voters voted for a candidate whose policy positions did not match their own.[47] Mostly, voters stayed home.** Bush won. Democracy lost.

Four years later, despite a host of resolutions by reporters to "do better next time," they didn't. In 1992, attacks, mistakes, and visuals once again commanded the media's attention. In addition to the Gennifer Flowers story, leading stories included Bill Clinton's twenty-year-old draft record and tourist's trip to the Soviet Union, George Bush's possible, albeit minor, role in the Reagan-Presidency Iran-Contra scandal, Ross Perot's unsubstantiated charges of Republican dirty tricks, and George Bush's unsubstantiated charge that his dog Millie knew more about foreign policy "than these Bozoes," [Clinton and Gore].

At the end of this trivia orgy, how well-equipped were voters to do their civic duty? One survey asked, by quizzing voters on a series of important, election-related facts. On only two questions did a majority of respondents manage to come up with the correct answer. Those questions were, "Which candidate's family has a dog called Millie?" and "Do you recall which TV character Dan Quayle criticized for setting a poor example of family values?" Overwhelming majorities of voters flunked the rest of the test, including quesitons about Clinton's tax-policy, labor, and environmental records, Bush's budgets and foreign policy positions, about where the

---

*For a more detailed review of the half truths and the whole truth, see Hershey.[44]

**Voter participation nationally was the second lowest of this century. In most northern states, turnout reached its lowest levels in the history of American mass suffrage, dating to the time of Andrew Jackson. In post-election polls, a majority of respondents complained that the news had spent too much time "looking into the candidates' personal lives," and too little time "reporting the candidates' positions on key issues." [48]

candidates' financial contributions came from, and so on. The average pecentage of respondents giving the correct response to non-trivial questions was a woeful 27 percent. This time, Clinton won. Bush finished second. Once again, voters finished last.[49]

News as Fleeting Shadows, Signifying Nothing

In addition to dramatization and personalization, the news trivializes social problems by "fragmenting" them.[50] Lewis Mumford has called ours a world "of broken time and broken attention."[51] The media have done their share of that breaking. Press coverage severs events from their connection with other political events, with theory, and with history. They are signalized, not signified. As a result, they seem to come at us as discrete, random occurrences. Insofar as events are attributed to any causes at all, they are again personalized—left on the doorstep of individuals, not institutions. Attention is turned from deep to surface explanations.

For example, most stories about unemployment are not analyses of an ongoing social problem, but reports of an event, (usually, the release of the latest unemployment figures by the Bureau of Labor Statistics). Recently, journalists have categorized these figures as "alarming-worsening" or "improving-encouraging" (higher or lower than last month's figure). This event is then personalized by relating it to the policies of the incumbent administration. (Critics are quoted as saying high rates prove the President's policies are failing; or White House officials are quoted as saying declining rates prove the policies are working.)

These reports never mention the fact that the United States has been much more "tolerant" of unemployment than most other industrialized Western nations have been. They do not mention the fact that, despite the hype surrounding the most recent "jobs bill," public policy towards unemployment has changed little from one administration to the next since the 1930s. Such observations might in turn lead to broader explanations of American unemployment policy, incorporating history and political theory. For example, unemployment policy might be explained in terms of a historical antipathy to government intervention; or in terms of the political strength of American entrepreneurs, who may find a relatively high unemployment rate to be in their interests; or in terms of the political weakness of the American working class, unorganized as it is by a bona fide working class party; or in terms of the theory of perfect competition and the "invisible hand."

Each of these explanations ties unemployment "events" not only to each other, but also to history, theory, and to other political events, leaving the reader with a sophisticated explanation or set of competing explanations of politics. But they are never offered by the media, and readers are left with the primitive impression that political events are either imposed on us randomly, as if by the gods, or else are influenced mainly by the epic struggles of those Homeric figures, our presidents and congressional leaders.

Recently, researchers have begun measuring the fragmentation of network election coverage in an ingenious way. They have marked the shrinking of the "sound bite"—the time given to candidates to say their piece.

In 1968, nearly one-quarter of all candidate sound bites lasted a minute or more. The average was 42.3 seconds. That is enough time to make at least the rudiments of an argument—some connection between the candidates' position and voters' values. By 1988, the average was down to 8.9 seconds and heading south. By the end of primary season, 1992, it was 7.3 seconds.* That is enough time for a slogan: A "Where's the beef?" or a "Read my lips," or one of the other zingers that substitute for thought in a world of broken attention.

Another way of measuring fragmentation is through "reverse" content analysis of the news—chronicling what's not there. Warren Breed and Herbert Gans, in separate studies, found that precisely those problems and concepts social scientists have often deemed fundamental to understanding society were absent from the news, for example, the concepts of class and power structure, and their uneasy truce with democratic values. One reason for their absence is surely that they *are* chronic, complex problems, tangled thickets, not neatly diced events.[53]

In all of these ways, the news is trivialized. But what does that have to do with hegemony? How does trivializing the news enhance the power of the few? By anesthetizing the many to the central questions of politics: Who does, who should, get what, and how? A people that thinks of politics as parades and personality clashes has no sense that there are "real heads broken in the fustian and

---

*In 1992, CBS News, stung by criticism of the shrinking sound bite, pledged to run no bites of less than 30 seconds. The other networks refused to follow suit. And even CBS' executive producer said, "Frankly we're skeptical whether we can keep it up." His skepticism would turn out to be warranted. Through the general election campaign, the average sound bite on CBS was 8.3 seconds.[52]

the rattle," as the poet Vachel Lindsay put it.[54] Oblivious to the war, ordinary Americans have lost it before it begins, by default. Through the Morphean chemistry of the news, politics itself has become an opiate of the people.

The News Is Establishmentarian

Establishmentarianism in the Values of the News

The structural bias of the news buttresses the status quo indirectly by diverting attention to trivialities and away from questions pregnant with the power to change. But the news also directly supports the establishment, by espousing its values and allowing its press agents to define our problems and monopolize our options. Herbert Gans argues that the "enduring values of the news" include the following characteristics:

Enthnocentrism: Reporting and editorials in the wake of the Nixon resignation, for example, were unabashed odes to the American system, to "the structure unshaken, the genius of American democracy renascent." [55] These bromides are dusted off regularly, and re-used on occasions of national celebration or crisis (e.g., the Constitution's bicentennial, or the Gulf War. For examples from reporting on the Contragate scandal, see p. 73).

Altruistic democracy: This is "an emphasis on . . . the official norms of the American polity . . . derived largely from the Constitution." But this emphasis is a selective one, concerned most with such system-supportive themes as the duties (and sometimes failures) of political leaders (to be selfless, meritocratic) and of citizens (to "participate in democracy"—i.e., endorse the system by voting). "Violations of the civil liberties of radicals and . . . criminals are less newsworthy . . . [as are] economic obstacles to democracy."

Responsible capitalism: This is "an optimistic faith that . . . businessmen . . . will compete with each other in order to create increased prosperity for all, but that they will refrain from unreasonable profits and gross exploitation of workers or

customers."*[56] American news is, of course, "consistently
critical" of socialist economies, including such Western
democratic incarnations as Sweden and France. A recent *Time*
cover story exults, "Free enterprise . . . is the spirit of the age.
Spurred by the economic successes of the U.S., . . . countries
everywhere are taking the fetters off individual initiative and
cutting back the welfare state." Stopping along the way for a
special-section slap at "Europe's Fading Reds," eight pages of
breathless testimony from conservative economists gushingly
conclude: "The most productive figure in history is the individual
trying to improve his status. . . . Countries that want to develop
. . . or stay abreast . . . are finding themselves drawn to free
enterprise, which lets people loose so that they can lose their
economic shackles." [58]

Small-town pastoralism: ". . . may in the end be a surrogate
for a more general value: an underlying respect for tradition of
any kind, . . . valued because it is . . . orderly, and order is a
major enduring news value."

Individualism: "It is no accident that many of the characters in
Kuralt's pastoral features are 'rugged individualists' . . . [The
news assumes that] capitalism enhances this value; socialism
erodes it."

Moderatism: That "which violates the law, the dominant mores,
and enduring values is suspect. . . . Thus, groups which exhibit
what is seen as extreme behavior are criticized . . . through
pejorative adjectives or satirical tone."

The desirability of social order: "The absence of violent or
potentially violent threats to the authority of public officials." As

---

*Conservatives would argue this is just plain false—that the news is really anti-
business. In truth, this enduring value must be modified as follows: journalism's
is an optimistic faith that, *for the most part*, businessmen's activities will serve
us well. As Gans himself argues, the mindset of the journalist is not starry-eyed
about capitalists. But this does not mean they are anti-capitalist; instead, theirs
is the legacy of the Progressive movement of the first three decades of this
century. Basically, the Progressive believes, the systemic ship is sound. But that
does not preclude individual miscreants from taking us off course. The
journalists' job is to blow the bosun's whistle on such malfeasants. Conservatives
confuse this press criticism of irresponsible capitalists with anti-capitalism, but
it is not that. One does not have to think the clergy divine to believe in the
church. And journalists do believe. As the conservatives' own data show, only a
chemical trace of journalists will embrace the "ism" that declares its opposition
to capitalism—socialism.[57]

the flame of ghetto rebellion spread from city to city in the 1960s, for example, some news organizations built a firewall of "advance preparations." They printed "stories pointing out that [their] city planned to treat rioters harshly." They "implied that rioters would most likely be outside agitators" to "increase public support for harsh suppression of dissidents." Once rioting began, there was a "self-imposed blackout of live television and radio coverage" to prevent a "troublesome reaction." [59] Following the assassination of Martin Luther King, Jr., in 1968, "Network tributes to Dr. King were designed to stress peaceful behavior as a genuine tribute" to his memory. Meanwhile, "live camera facilities were set up to permit local mayors throughout the United States [to urge] people to stay calm." [60]

The need for leaders to maintain order: Leaders are "people who, because of their political or managerial skills, or personal attributes which inspire others . . . move into positions of authority. . . . The foremost leader in America is the president, who is viewed as the ultimate protector of order." [61]

But why were these values not discussed under the heading "partisan bias"? Are they not the familiar bleating of the left that the media is conservative? No, these values are not conservative. They are, like the values of the American establishment, centrist.[62] "Extremists" of the right are neglected and derided along with those of the left.[63] Capitalism is approved, but not unfettered capitalism, only "responsible capitalism." Thus, both the left *and* the right are correct when they complain that media bias excludes them. They are wrong only in supposing that what excludes them is a prejudice for the other side; in fact, the media's is a strong prejudice for the center.

Nevertheless, is not a centrist bias an ideological preference, a partisan bias? While you or I might think so, neither the producers nor the consumers of the news would agree. These values are, in fact, so "established," so long unquestioned as to seem unquestionable. To reporters and readers, they are no longer values, they are just "good common sense," and as such do not reflect partisan bias. Jack Newfield, himself a journalist, has presented a list strikingly similar to Gans' and says of it, "I can't think of any . . . correspondent who doesn't share these values. And at the same time, who doesn't insist he is totally objective." [64] As we shall see, several structural imperatives of news production converge to dictate that the news should be exactly this way: common sensible.

Establishmentarian Routine I: Outside the
Mainstream Is Beyond the Pale

So far, support for the establishment has been seen as more or less explicit. But more often, this support is implicit, in the woof and warp of press practice. As a matter of course, for example, "third" parties and candidates are ignored by the news.*[65] So the countervailing, creative thinking of the Citizens, Libertarian, 21st Century, and other "minor parties" has amounted to so much crying in the wilderness, which doesn't carry far these days unless there is a mini-cam around. Apparently, a political idea is not a thing worthy of coverage unless it is attached to a candidate who is, or is fast becoming, a winner. In other words, it is the voter's job to choose which ideas shall be popular, though (s)he has not heard most of them because they are not popular—electoral Catch-22.

Groups or movements with radical views are also customarily left out when the media talk about policy problems and solutions outside of election time. In seven large, high-quality newspapers over a recent twelve-month period, only ten articles appeared that mentioned the nation's most visible radical party.[66]

On those rare occasions when radical groups are covered, they might wish they hadn't been. Coverage fixes on the medium, excluding the message of radical groups. The frightening spectacle of the demonstration, the march, the burning flag is vividly recounted; the reasons for them are not. For example, in the Spring of 1968, students at Columbia University went on strike to protest the University's contributions to the Vietnam war. Michael Klare was head of the research team that uncovered Columbia's ties to the Pentagon. Looking back on it, he would recall ample television coverage of building occupations and police busts. He cannot remember ever "having the chance to tell a television audience about [the University's involvement with] weapons research." [67]

That same year, "The managing editor of the *New York Times* . . . told . . . [an] interviewer that the *Times* gave little coverage to . . . the first woman's antiwar action [the 1968 Jeanette Rankin brigade] because of the size *and because there was not expected to*

---

*The exception was the Ross Perot candidacy of 1992. The media accorded his candidacy instant credibility, and covered it heavily. Why? There were 100 million reasons, and all of them were dollars. The fact that a billionaire could pay his way into the headlines is an exception to the rule that third parties are customarily ignored. It is not, of course, an exception to the rule that the news routine favors established interests, such as billionaires.

be violence. Where a picket line might have been news in 1965, it took tear gas and bloodied heads to make headlines in 1968. . . . The most outrageous, most discordant . . . symbols were the surest to be broadcast—'Viet Cong' flags, burning draft cards and (later) flags and (still later) ROTC buildings." The sorry irony is that radical groups often adopt such spectacular tactics as a last-resort means of being heard. Once they adopt them, they are less likely than ever to be fairly heard, as news coverage depicts them as dangerous to the social fabric, and as unable to win support through the "normal," "democratic" process.[68]

Establishmentarian Routine II: Elites Define the News

While the media force radicals to the fringe of the crowd, spokesmen for the establishment are ensconced at the microphone. One large study of the *Washington Post* and the *New York Times* showed that over sixty percent of their front-page stories came from events such as press conferences, press releases, background briefings, etc., which are staged and managed by elites, usually senior government officials. Needless to say, these officials are usually cast as heroes in their own productions.[69] Although another 25 percent of the sampled stories were attributed to reporters' "enterprise," over 90 percent of those came from interviews, again usually with high-level government officials. None of the 1,146 stories sampled came from research done using books, journals, or statistical data.[70]

Other sources of the news besides high-level government officials also tend to be oracles of the establishment: spokesmen for corporations, for large interest groups, moderate or conservative think-tanks, and from mainstream (not radical) academia.[71] For example, "When journalists look for experts on foreign policy, they rarely go to the Institute for Policy Studies, a well-respected left-oriented think tank." [72] Instead a count of such experts appearing on the "MacNeil-Lehrer News Hour" shows that aside from journalists, "a majority of the participants (54 percent) were present or former government officials, and . . . the next highest category (15.7 percent) was drawn from conservative think tanks."*[73] "Reporters doing stories about the . . . housing crisis or rent control typically go to groups like the National Association of Realtors . . . or the Mortgage Bankers Association of America for statistics and

---

*For a discussion of the growth of these "think tanks," see Chapter 3.

analysis. . . . [Left wing] grassroots groups like . . . National People's Action and left-oriented housing experts . . . are virtually invisible to the national news organs. And the same could be said for any number of issues." [74] In fact, entire shades of the idea spectrum, a whole complex of left wing institutes, foundations, academics, and political organizations are "conspicuously absent from the daily flow of national journalism." [75]

Results of the Routine:
Reality as Elites Define It

The result of this monopoly over the marketplace of ideas is predictable, since "few elites disagree about the essential desirability of the system they control." [76] Gans notes that those "enduring values of the news" described above "coincide almost completely" with the rhetoric of "those public officials who are the journalists' major sources." Gans argues that their "values" enter the news "most pervasively" through official definitions of what is. So, when elites saw the Vietnam War as a "conflict between America and its allies, and a Communist enemy," the news did too. The news might, for a change from time to time, have viewed the war as a struggle against the vestiges of the old colonialism, with the United States entering as a bully of the new colonialism, unwilling to cede Asian markets or raw materials even to the principle of self-determination. But instead, the media referred so regularly to the North Vietnamese and the National Liberation Front as "the enemy," one might have thought "they were the enemy of the news media." [77]

More recently, establishment sources have led the media to a constricted definition of *terrorism*. The dictionary describes that word's meaning as "the political use of intimidation." But the media and its sources have reserved the term for the small-scale desperation of relatively powerless, often anti-U.S. groups like Palestinians. Meanwhile the "wholesale terrorism" of governments that use the torture and murder of untried civilians as instruments of public policy falls under the tepid appellation, "possible violations of human rights." Not just coincidentally, most wholesale terrorists are allies of the United States government.[78]

Small wonder too, that within this category of state violence, some not-so-fine distinctions are drawn by the "experts." Some victims, it would seem, are worthy of our notice, others are not. When a dissident priest was murdered by policemen in Communist Poland, the press was alive with indignation, with the grisly details of the murder, and with the search for responsibility "at the top."

Altogether, the case was accorded over a thousand column inches of space in the *New York Times* and appeared as a story 46 times on CBS News. That is as it should be.

Meanwhile, more than 100 murders of clerics by our friendly neighbors to the south, American client states in Latin America, were scarcely noticed by the news. The *New York Times* gave 72 such murders a sum total of 117 column inches. The stories of these victims did not appear at all on CBS News during the three years its content was monitored. The scant press coverage they did receive tended to provide no wrenching details of the murders, though there were plenty of them. Little indignation was expressed. There were few calls to "get to the top" of the matter.[79] This is not as it should be. It is one thing to be "disappeared" by the death squads of a dictatorship. It is another to be "disappeared" again, this time by the free press of a free society, and the experts it relies on.

But What About . . .?

At this point, two objections urge themselves. First, my argument that the establishment monopolizes the news seems to forget the pride newspeople take in telling "both sides of the story." The phrase itself gives away the feet-of-clay assumption underpinning this practice: it presumes that usually, there are only two important sides to a story.[80] Thus, the "dialectic" of the news consists of counter-balancing elites whose disagreements over means are bounded by a gentlemen's agreement on the ends.

When, for example, conservative and liberal elites clash over foreign policy, the idea that "Marxist" revolutions ought to be discouraged is never in question. Disagreement is restricted to the question of how to discourage them. Debate about the Sandinistas, for example, was limited to this question: Should we wage war on Nicaragua by funding the contras, or limit ourselves to a cold war of words, nerves, and sanctions? While that is not a trivial disagreement, neither is it fundamental. Nor does it begin to suggest the range of intellectually respectable views on the subject. Listening to the "two sides" (both anti-socialist) of this debate, one would never hear from the "other" other side, that:

> . . . *Nicaragua [under the Sandinistas] is more democratic than [U.S.-backed] El Salvador and Guatemala in every non-Orwellian sense of the word; that its government does not murder ordinary citizens on a routine basis as the governments of El Salvador and Guatemala do; that it has carried out socioeconomic reforms important to the*

*majority that the other two governments somehow cannot attempt;
that Nicaragua poses no military threat to its neighbors but has, in
fact, been subjected to continuous attacks by the United States and
its clients and surrogates; and that the U.S. fear of Nicaragua is
based more on its virtues than on its alleged defects."* [81]

Once, during the Reagan years, ABC News exceeded the limits
of this "both sides" protocol by giving a spokesman for the Soviet
Union several minutes of air time to respond to a presidential address on foreign policy. Afterward, chastened by strident criticism
from fellow journalists and administration officials, the network
apologized for providing the time and for not placing the Soviet's
remarks "in context." As Benjamin Bradlee, a dean of American
journalism huffily explained, "There are two sides in a democratic
society. Communism is not a third side."

What is more, the *way* in which the news counterbalances
Democrats vs. Republicans, mainstream liberals vs. conservatives,
and established interest group vs. established interest group further reinforces the status quo. Edward Jay Epstein, who spent six
months observing the "dialectical" procedure at NBC news, describes it as one "in which the correspondent, after reporting the
news happening, juxtaposes a contrasting viewpoint and concludes his synthesis by suggesting that the truth lies somewhere
in between." [82] Such a centrist synthesis is *de rigueur*, even if the
correspondent thinks the facts put the truth on the left or the right.
For example, in the original version of an hour-long NBC documentary on gun control, former correspondent Robert MacNeil
concluded that "it was necessary to restrict the ownership of fire-
arms, and that Congress had not passed such a bill because of the
pressures put on it by the 'well-financed' lobby led by the National
Rifle Association." The network "softened" the documentary and
replaced his conclusion with one (read by MacNeil himself) which
"ran directly contrary to what he apparently believed to be the true
findings of the investigation—that the legislation was . . . fore-
stalled by the gun lobby, not by 'reasonable men' disagreeing on
the 'form' of the law."*[83] What could be nicer for the various estates
than to have the truth automatically located at the epicenter of
their interests?

A second objection to the establishmentarianism thesis points
to that intrepid figure, the investigative journalist. But the structural bias of the news has leashed this "watchdog of the public

---

*For the newspaper equivalent to television's dialectic, called "writing it down the
middle," see Sigal.[84]

interest." Even in investigative journalism, where problems barge into the public consciousness without an introduction from elites, press coverage turns attention from deep to surface explanations, often by personalizing the story: the authorities are to blame; the regime is not questioned. Reporting of the Watergate, Lance, Meese, and Ferraro affairs bruised the heads of the principals involved, but only the heel of the political economy which, it has been ably argued, nurtures such scandals.[85]

How the News Affects the Public

Does the news affect attitudes? Early socialization and voting studies didn't think so. When voting studies found that people's voting intentions changed little over the course of heavily publicized and reported campaigns, they concluded that the media lacked impact.[96] When socialization researchers asked children where they learned about politics, they were much more likely to mention parents or teachers than the media.

Recently, the academic common sense about the media has changed. Since the early studies were done, television has become ubiquitous, and time spent with the mass media has jumped by 40 percent. "On an average day, 80 percent of all Americans are reached by television and newspapers. On a typical evening, the television audience is close to 100 million people, nearly half the entire population." Today, the average American grade-school child spends 27 hours a week in front of the television set—more time than in school.[97] At the same time, the methodology of socialization research has been refined, measuring the sources of direct influence through more precise questions[98] and beginning to measure the enormous indirect influence the media have on children, by way of parents, teachers, and peers.[99] Reassessing the older studies, Neil Hollander has dubbed the media, "the new 'parent.' "[100]

At the same time, voting studies have begun to wonder whether it makes sense to define media influence in terms of changes in the party or candidate preferences of voters, given that the media's "horse race" coverage of the campaign does not provoke evaluations of candidates by voters,[101] and given that the media rarely show a candidate preference when they do discuss the substance of the campaign.[102] In light of this pattern, researchers have begun to ask whether there are tracings on the public mind of the bias the media *does* pervasively display—structural bias.

NEWSBREAK

Investigating Contragate—Front Men and the Real Mr. Big

In the fall of 1986, a Lebanese newspaper reported that the Reagan administration was doing something the President had sworn never to do, and had persuaded allies not to do: negotiate with hostage takers. In fact, U.S. weapons had already been sold to Iran, supposedly in exchange for U.S. hostages. What is more, profits from the arms sale had been diverted to the Nicaraguan Contras, apparently in violation of a Congressional prohibition of aid to that group.

Now the investigative game was afoot. To what door would it lead? Content analysis of Iran-Contra coverage in *Time* magazine and the *New York Times* reveals the following:

1. The role played by the President's men received far more space than the role played by the President. That is partly because, again, those officials being ''covered'' often dictated the coverage. Much of this story's space was based on statements by White House spokesmen and by other minions (mainly Oliver North and John Poindexter) whose professed goal was to protect the President.

2. Their testimony also accounts for the presence of ''regime supportive'' explanations of the affair. These argued for a ''need to expose communism, preserve national credibility, prestige, etc.''

3. When the news did diagnose systemic disorder, which wasn't often, it was always minor—take two small reforms and call me in the morning. For example, one editorial recommended such aspirins as Senate confirmation of the national security adviser, the removal of covert actions from the N.S.C. staff's repertoire, and the placement of such decisions in the hands of the Secretary of State.

4. Most interesting of all about this coverage is not what it said, but what it didn't say. In more than five weeks of news coverage of this event in two of the nation's leading news sources, there appeared not a single allusion to a ''regime

critical'' explanation—i.e., an explanation pointing not to
individuals, but to fundamental features of the system they
serve.

Despite the prominence of such explanations for covert action in the work of political scientists, sociologists, and economists,
and despite their availability in ``alternative press'' coverage of
Iran-Contra,[86] the mainstream news chose not to use them, not
even to mention them.

In fact, the absence of such explanations in the media may
have made it hard to imagine what one might look like. Most point
to the tension between the ideals of democracy and what these
critiques see as the reality of capitalism, i.e., government by and
for the few, especially large corporate capitalism.

The Iran-Contra affair can be seen as a chapter in this story
of propertied-class power. It is a story of the government's campaign to make the Third World safe for corporate capitalism; the
story of 40 years of ``covert actions'' kept secret not so much from
communism as from the democracy that would oppose and end
them.*[87] The father of Iran-Contra himself, Bud McFarlane, spelled
it out in his now famous memo to Oliver North: ``If the world only
knew . . . but they can't know and would complain if they did . . .
such is the state of democracy.''

Americans, his point was, don't understand the way the
world works. They persist in naive affirmation of self-determination,
human rights, compassion, and political equality. That is why the
people must be manipulated and benighted, so that policy makers can attend to business. In the Nicaraguan case, that business
involved ``the potential loss of nearly $10 billion in direct invest-
ment by U.S.-based corporations in Mexico and Central America.
We are talking about more than 1,400 at least partially U.S.-owned
businesses. Over half the top U.S.-based manufacturing companies have Mexican operations.'' [88] While American investments in
Nicaragua itself were not especially large, protecting them, under
the doctrine of ``credibility,'' requires that the United States im-
pose suffering on every emerging socialist government, as an object lesson to its neighbors.[89]

---

*During this period, pollsters consistently reported that majorities of Ameri-
cans opposed aid to the Contras.

> *Ronald Reagan may believe his own ideological rhetoric about the "Soviet Threat" in Central America, but the men behind him—the executives of Citicorp, Exxon, Bank of America, and General Motors—view Central America in terms of dollars and cents. In their minds, Reagan's job is not to save the Central American people from the evils of communism but to save their long-cherished and lucrative base of operations from the Central American people. It is not an issue of East vs. West; it is an issue of popular sovereignty vs. the ability of the transnationals to continue their uninhibited looting of an entire continent. And this is the issue which, in fact, has informed all of U.S. foreign policy for the past four decades.*[90]

But surely the Iranian arms deal, however misguided its means, was pure in its motives. There, "the U.S. government had ... (an) interest in establishing ties to Iran. Few in the U.S. government doubted Iran's strategic importance or the risk of Soviet meddling in the succession crisis that might follow the death of Khomeini."[91]

Can it be doubted that this was in the interest, above all, of American consumers? A brief look at history may help to answer that. In a previous Iranian "succession crisis," it was the United States that meddled, in order to "establish ties to Iran." In 1953, the CIA successfully conspired to overthrow the Iranian Prime Minister, Muhammed Mossadegh. Mossadegh was "neither pro-Soviet nor pro-Communist; his nationalism was single-minded."[92] But he had spearheaded a movement to nationalize Iran's oil fields. In his wake, power was consolidated in the hands of Muhammed Reza Shah Pahlevi, who was "prepared to cooperate with the United States."[93] Not long afterward, the Shah concluded an agreement, midwifed by the American and British governments, with eight multinational oil companies, five of them based in the United States, to develop Iranian oil. "But there was also a more clandestine understanding between the companies." This was a "participant's agreement" to restrict the flow of Iranian oil and so maintain the fixing of the world price. Though the Justice Department argued strenuously that the agreement was an illegal disservice to the consumer, the U.S. government sanctioned the agreement and kept it secret from the Iranian government and the American people.[94]

> Mideast oil, like Central American factories, is called *our* interest in the Third World, but repeatedly, the interest served seems to be *theirs*—that of a privileged, powerful few.
>
> Or at least, so say the regime-critical theorists. For the moment, the point is not that they are right and that other explanations for ethical sloughs are wrong. The point is that the other explanations are, as this content analysis reveals, part of the ''story''—subject to ''investigative journalism.'' But the regime critics are absent; conspicuously, curiously, totally absent from the news.
>
> But the news did not content itself with sins of omission. With Iran-Contra as with Watergate, the system that should, at least occasionally, have been questioned was instead uncritically boosted at every turn. ''It is a uniquely American ritual,'' intoned *Time* as Congressional hearings began. ''A concerned and curious citizenry gathers in an electronic version of a colonial town meeting to watch elected representatives grill government officials, high and low. . . . The viewing can be painful yet mysteriously exhilarating, boring at times yet somehow fascinating. It is an odd self-flagellation, but out of it can emerge a catharsis. The Government's secrets are exposed, its actions explained, condoned or condemned. The issue is faced. The nation moves on.'' [95]

How does the news affect attitudes? Earlier, this chapter asserted that trivialized news makes for a politically anesthetized public. Evidence for that assertion abounds. For example, Patterson found that voters' perceptions of candidates during the 1976 election campaign mirrored the media's odd priorities:

> *Impressions [of the candidates] . . . tended to be stylistic, associated with the candidates' mannerisms and campaign performance. These included thoughts about the candidates' personalities, campaign success and style, and personal backgrounds. People were much less likely to form political impressions, those concerning the candidates' . . . leadership abilities, political backgrounds, and issue positions. . . . No exact coefficient can be attached to the relationship, but there was a remarkable parallel between the themes of . . . news coverage and the impressions people developed.* [103]

The same was true of voters' perceptions of "what was important" during the campaign. "Election news emphasized [what we've
called horse race and hoopla] rather than matters of policy and
leadership, and it was [horse race and hoopla] that dominated people's thoughts. The correlation between journalistic emphasis and
public preoccupation was in fact very high, more than +.85 at
every point once the campaign was under way." [104]

The "garbage in–garbage out" relationship between the news
and the citizen also applies to politics outside the electoral arena.
Doris Graber argues that human beings assimilate information by
fitting it into a preexisting "schema—a cognitive structure consist-
ing of organized knowledge about situations and individuals that
has been abstracted from prior experiences. It is used for processing new information and retrieving stored information." Functions
of schemata include determining "what information will be noticed
. . . and stored, . . ." and making "it possible for people to go beyond the immediate information presented to them and fill in
missing information. This permits making sense from abbreviated
communications." [105] The great commentator on his craft of journalism, Walter Lippman, put it this way: "For the most part we do
not first see, and then define. We define first and then see. In the
great blooming, buzzing confusion of the outer world, we pick out
what our culture has already defined for us, and we tend to perceive that which we have picked out in the form stereotyped for us
by our culture." [106]

Unfortunately, the "socialization of Americans . . . leaves a
number of gaps in the schema structure. These gaps then make it
difficult to focus public attention on some important problems."
For example, there is a "nearly total lack" of understanding about
how public institutions work and a "sparsity" of knowledge about
public policies.[107] The schemata that do exist bespeak a set of
shared stereotypes, often of the civics class storybook variety,
which in turn "means that public political thinking tends to lack
flexibility." [108]

The media share responsibility for this sad state in several
ways. First, fragmented, trivialized news must bear some blame
both for the gaps between schemata and for the froth within them,
because the "media play a significant part in early as well as later
phases of socialization." [109]

Second, the fact of fragmented news combines with the fact
that schematic deficiencies are most egregious among low-status
Americans, meaning that they are least able to perform the functions of schemata. They are least able to "go beyond the immediate

information presented to them and fill in missing information," to make sense out of the "abbreviated communications" of the media. The result is "the knowledge gap," a situation where, as mass media information increases, the high-status, information-rich get richer and the poor stay poor.[110]

This "relative deprivation of knowledge" leads to "relative deprivation of power." For example, because "lower status groups do not know as much at the end of a campaign about the issues and the candidates, they are less able to vote in their own interests and more able to be manipulated by political advertisements."[111] As surely as knowledge is power, so the nescience wrought by the news among low-status Americans is powerlessness.

And third, perhaps most obvious, the media's monolithic "status quo bias," the "deference" paid to the American system has certainly contributed to Americans' uncritical "commonality in thinking."[112]

But perhaps the media's most important effect has to do with the lethal mixture of cynicism and blind faith in American public opinion. We noted earlier the tendency of investigative journalism to scapegoat authorities for problems, absolving the system.* That journalistic voice is eerily echoed in the long-standing tendency of Americans to think politicians are "bumbling or uncaring or corrupt," but to continue to endorse basic institutions.[115] Because "the news media have never given powerless Americans the necessary information to link the ubiquitous rotten apples to the structure of the barrel," discontents have become frustration or resignation instead of demands for useful change.[116]

This then is the news—trivial, anesthetic, establishmentarian; a reverse Robin Hood, robbing power from the poor to give to the rich. As the former editor of the *Los Angeles Times* used to say, "The responsibility of a truly great newspaper [is] to educate the elite and pacify the masses."[117] He may have been joking. But in a twisted way, he was not wrong. How has this come about? How has Jefferson's dream become Editor Whedon's nightmare? Turn the page.

---

*A related phenomenon involves the predominance of "bad news" over "good," including negative reporting of presidential candidates.[113] Conservatives have argued that this produces an anti-system bias. Evidence suggests that first, news about important categories of elites (presidents and congresspersons, for example) is predominantly positive.[114] And secondly, where there is citizen mistrust, it has followed the media's pointing finger—to authorities, *not* to the system.

References

1. Robert Lichter and Stanley Rothman, "Media and Business Elites," *Public Opinion*, (December-January 1982): 42–46; William A. Rusher, *The Coming Battle for the Media*, (New York: William Morrow, 1988).

2. In Mark Hertsgaard, *On Bended Knee*, (New York: Schocken, 1989): 85; for the methodological critique, see Herbert J. Gans, *Deciding What's News*, (New York: Pantheon Books, 1979).

3. Edward Jay Epstein, *News From Nowhere*, (New York: Vintage Books, 1973): 207; Michael J. Robinson, "Just How Liberal Is the News?" *Public Opinion*, (February-March 1983): 55–60.

4. Richard C. Hofstetter, *Bias in the News*, (Columbus: Ohio State University Press, 1976); Austin Ranney and Michael J. Robinson, *The Mass Media in Campaign '84*, (Washington, D.C.: American Enterprise Institute, 1985).

5. John W. C. Johnstone, Edward Slawski, and William W. Bowman. *The News People*, (Urbana: University of Illinois Press, 1976).

6. Edward J. Epstein, *News From Nowhere:* 211–18; Herbert J. Gans, *Deciding What's News:* 211–12; Calvin F. Exoo, "Journalists' Perspectives on the Critique of Political Journalism," (paper presented at the Annual Meeting of the Northeast Political Science Association, 1984).

7. David S. Broder, *Behind the Front Page*, (New York: Simon and Schuster, 1987): 12.

8. Ibid.

9. Ben H. Bagdikian, "The Politics of American Newspapers," *Columbia Journalism Review*, (March-April 1972): 8–13.

10. Doris J. Graber, *Mass Media and American Politics*, 3d ed. (Washington, D.C.: Congressional Quarterly Press, 1989): 63.

11. Nick Thimmesch, "The Editorial Endorsement Game," *Public Opinion*, (October-November 1984): 10–14.

12. Robert S. Erickson, Norman R. Luttbeg, and Kent L. Tedin, *American Public Opinion*, (New York: John Wiley and Sons, 1980): 136.

13. Edwin Diamond, "New Wrinkles on the Permanent Press," *The Mass Media in Campaign '84*, edited by Michael J. Robinson and Austin Ranney (Washington, D.C.: American Enterprise Institute, 1985): 70.

14. Peter Dreier, "The Corporate Complaint Against the Media," *American Media and Mass Culture*, edited by Donald Lazere (Berkeley: University of California Press, 1987): 74.

15. David H. Weaver, Doris A. Graber, Maxwell E. McCombs, and Chaim H. Eyal, *Media Agenda-Setting in a Presidential Election*, (New York: Praeger, 1981): 26.

16. Warren Breed, "Social Control in the Newsroom: A Functional Analysis," *Social Forces*, (Vol. 33, 1955): 327.

17. Ben H. Bagdikian, "The Fruits of Agnewism," *Columbia Journalism Review*, (January-February 1973): 9–23.

18. Quoted in Gaye Tuchman, *Making News*, (New York: the Free Press, 1978): v.

19. Doris J. Graber, *Mass Media and American Politics*, (Washington, D.C.: Congressional Quarterly Press, 1980): 63–65.

20. Martin Schram, *The Great American Video Game*, (New York: William Morrow, 1987): 67–8.

21. Quoted in Edward J. Epstein, *News From Nowhere:* 163.
22. Quoted in Martin Schram, *The Great American Video Game:* 56.
23. Calvin F. Exoo, "Journalists' Perspectives on the Critique of Political Journalism."
24. Michael Lipsky and David J. Olson, "The Processing of Racial Crisis in America," *Politics and Society,* (vol. 6, 1976): 79–103; Edward Jay Epstein, *News From Nowhere:* 23–4.
25. Quoted in Epstein, *News From Nowhere:* 17.
26. Michael Parenti, *Inventing Reality,* (New York: St. Martin's Press, 1986): 11.
27. Terms from Lance Bennett, *News: The Politics of Illusion,* (New York: Longman, 1983): chapter 1.
28. Martin Schram, *The Great American Video Game:* 95.
29. Todd Gitlin, "Blips, Bites and Savvy Talk," *Dissent,* (Winter 1990): 18–26.
30. Ibid.: 37.
31. Knight News Service, "Clinton Urges Racial Harmony," *Watertown Daily Times,* (May 3, 1992): 1.
32. Marjorie R. Hershey, "The Campaign and the Media," *The Election of 1988,* edited by Gerald M. Pomper, (Chatham, N.J.: Chatham House, 1988): 99.
33. *Media Monitor,* "Campaign '92 Topics" (Washington, D.C.: Center for Media and Public Affairs, August-September, 1992): 2; *Media Monitor,* "Election Topics," (October 1992): 3; *Media Monitor,* "Eating Up the Airwaves," (November 1992): 2.
34. Thomas E. Patterson, *The Mass Media Election,* (New York: Praeger, 1980): 36.
35. Diane J. Exoo and Calvin F. Exoo, "News Coverage of Political Ethics: The Muzzled Watchdog," *National Social Science Journal,* (Vol. 3:3, 1990): 19.
36. W. Shapiro, "Fall From Grace," *Time,* (May 18, 1987): 18.
37. Ibid.
38. M. Knudson, "Neighbors Describe Lee Hart as Family's Anchor," *New York Times,* (May 7, 1987): B16.
39. The term is from Larry S. Sabato, *Feeding Frenzy,* (New York: Free Press, 1991).
40. "How the Press Deals with Sleaze," *Time,* (February 10, 1992): 28.
41. Michael Oreskes, "TV's Role in '88: The Medium is the Election," *New York Times,* (October 30, 1988): 1.
42. Marjorie R. Hershey, "The Campaign and the Media": 99.
43. Kurt Vonnegut, *Player Piano,* (New York: Delacorte, 1952): 118–19.
44. Marjorie Hershey, "The Campaign and the Media": 85–7.
45. Form of this recap suggested by Michael Oreskes, "TV's Role in '88": 1,30.
46. R. W. Apple, "From Jersey to Missouri, Voters Are Fed Up," *New York Times,* (October 11, 1988): 1,28.
47. Gerald M. Pomper, "The Presidential Election," *The Election of 1988,* edited by Gerald M. Pomper, (Chatham, N.J.: Chatham House, 1988): 139.
48. Michael Lipton, "T.V. and the Election: America Speaks Out," *TV Guide,* (November 12, 1988): A1-A3.
49. "Issues, Images, Impacts: A Survey of Voters' Knowledge in Campaign '92," (New York: Fairness and Accuracy in Reporting, 1992).
50. Lance Bennett, *News: The Politics of Illusion:* Chapter 1.
51. Quoted in Neil Postman, *Amusing Ourselves to Death,* (New York: Viking, 1985): 69.
52. "Eating Up the Airwaves," in *Media Monitor,* (Washington, D.C.: Center for Media and Public Affairs, November 1992): 2.

53. Herbert Gans, *Deciding What's News:* 23; Warren Breed, "Mass Communication and Sociocultural Integration," *Social Forces,* (vol. 37, 1958): 109–16.

54. Quotation from Vachel Lindsay, "Bryan, Bryan, Bryan, Bryan," in *A Pocket Book of Modern Verse,* edited by Oscar Williams, (New York: Washington Square Press, 1954): 215.

55. *New York Times* editorial, quoted in David L. Paletz and Robert M. Entman, *Media-Power-Politics,* (New York: The Free Press, 1981): 164.

56. Joseph R. Dominick, "Business Coverage in Network Newscasts," *Media Power in Politics,* edited by Doris A. Graber (Washington, D.C.: Congressional Quarterly Press, 1984); William A. Rusher, *The Coming Battle for the Media.*

57. Robert Lichter and Stanley Rothman, "Media and Business Elites": 42–46.

58. John Greenwald, "A New Age of Capitalism," *Time* (July 28, 1986): 39.

59. Doris J. Graber, *Mass Media and American Politics,* 3d ed.: 319–20.

60. Ibid.: 313.

61. Ibid.: 42–63.

62. See James Weinstein, *The Corporate Ideal in the Liberal State,* (Boston: Beacon Press, 1968): chapter 1; Thomas Dye and Harmon Zeigler, *The Irony of Democracy,* (North Scituate, Mass.: Duxbury Press, 1978): 111–13.

63. Pamela J. Shoemaker, "Media Treatment of Deviant Political Groups," *Journalism Quarterly,* (vol. 61, 1974): 66–75, 82.

64. Jack Newfield, "Journalism: Old, New and Corporate," *The Reporter as Artist: A Look at the New Journalism,* edited by Ronald Weber, (New York: Hastings House, 1974): 56.

65. David H. Weaver et al., *Media Agenda-Setting in a Presidential Election:* 83; David L. Paletz and Robert M. Entman, *Media-Power-Politics:* 164; Michael J. Robinson, "Just How Liberal is the News": 58; Michael J. Robinson, "The Media in Campaign '84: Part II, Wingless, Toothless, and Hopeless," *The Mass Media in Campaign '84,* edited by Michael J. Robinson and Austin Ranney, (Washington, D.C..: American Enterprise Institute, 1985): 35.

66. Pamela J. Shoemaker, "Media Treatment of Deviant Political Groups": 68.

67. Todd Gitlin, *The Whole World Is Watching,* (Berkeley: University of California Press, 1980): 193.

68. Ibid.: 182.

69. Leon V. Sigal, *Reporters and Officials,* (Lexington, Mass.: D.C. Heath, 1973): 115–121.

70. Ibid.: 115–21.

71. David L. Paletz and Robert M. Entman, *Media-Power-Politics:* 193.

72. Peter Dreier, "The Corporate Complaint Against the Media": 75.

73. Edward S. Herman and Noam Chomsky, *Manufacturing Consent,* (New York: Pantheon, 1988): 24.

74. Peter Dreier, "The Corporate Complaint Against the Media": 76.

75. Ibid.: 74.

76. David L. Paletz and Robert M. Entman, *Media-Power-Politics:* 23.

77. Herbert J. Gans, *Deciding What's News:* 201; see also Paul Hoch, *The Newspaper Game,* (London: Calder and Bayars, 1974): Chapter 6.

78. Noam Chomsky and Edward S. Herman, *The Political Economy of Human Rights,* vol. 1 (Boston: South End Press, 1979): Chapter 3.

79. Edward S. Herman and Noam Chomsky, *Manufacturing Consent:* Chapter 2.

80. Calvin F. Exoo, "Journalists' Perspectives on the Critique of Political Journalism": 14.

81. Edward S. Herman and Noam Chomsky, *Manufacturing Consent:* xiii.
82. Edward J. Epstein, *News From Nowhere:* 67.
83. Ibid.: 69.
84. Leon V. Sigal, *Reporters and Officials:* 68.
85. David L. Paletz and Robert M. Entman, *Media-Power-Politics:* 158–65; David L. Altheide and Robert P. Snow, *Media Logic,* (Beverly Hills: Sage, 1979); Gaye Tuchman, *Making News:* 87.
86. e.g., Erwin Knoll, Matthew Rothschild, and Linda Rocawich, "Gavel to Grovel: Why the Hearings Failed," *The Progressive,* (September 1987): 14–19; David Conn and Jefferson Morley, "A Guide to Iran-Contra Theories," *Nation,* (August 1, 1987): 1, 88.
87. *New York Times,* "Poll Indicates Drop in Public Support for Contras," (August 7, 1987): 5.
88. Marlene Dixon and Susanne Jonas, eds., *Nicaragua Under Siege* (San Francisco: Synthesis, 1984): 8.
89. Jonathan Schell, *Time of Illusion,* (New York: Knopf, 1975): 113.
90. Marlene Dixon and Susanne Jonas, eds., *Nicaragua Under Siege:* 8.
91. John Tower, Edwin Muskie, and Brent Scowcroft, "The Tower Commission Report," (New York: *The New York Times,* 1987): 19.
92. Barry M. Rubin, *Paved With Good Intentions,* (New York: Oxford University Press, 1980): 59.
93. Gary Sick, *All Fall Down,* (New York: Random House, 1985): 7.
94. Anthony Sampson, *The Seven Sisters,* (New York: Viking, 1975): 128–32.
95. Ed Magnuson, "Hints of Conspiracy," *Time,* (May 11, 1987): 10.
96. Paul Lazarsfeld, Bernard Berelson, and Hazel Gaudet, *The People's Choice,* (New York: Columbia University Press, 1944); Angus Campbell, Philip E. Converse, Warren E. Miller, and Donald Stokes, *The American Voter,* (New York: Wiley, 1960).
97. Doris J. Graber, *Mass Media and American Politics:* 120,122.
98. Gary O. Coldevin, "Internationalism and Mass Communications," *Journalism Quarterly,* (vol. 49, 1972): 365–8.
99. Neil Hollander, "Adolescents and the War: The Sources of Socialization," *Journalism Quarterly,* (vol. 48, 1971): 472–9; Gary O. Coldevin, "Internationalism and Mass Communications": 365–8. John M. Phelan, *Mediaworld,* (New York: Seabury Press, 1977).
100. Neil Hollander, "Adolescents and the War": 472–9.
101. Thomas E. Patterson, *The Mass Media Election:* 89.
102. James B. Lemert, *Does Mass Communication Change Public Opinion After All?* (Chicago: Nelson-Hall, 1981): 60.
103. Thomas E. Patterson, *The Mass Media Election:* 134.
104. Thomas E. Patterson, *The Mass Media Election:* 98; for similar findings, see David H. Weaver et al., *Media Agenda-Setting in a Presidential Election:* 39; Doris J. Graber, *Mass Media and American Politics:* 222–3.
105. Doris J. Graber, *Processing the News,* (New York: Longman, 1984): 23–4.
106. Walter Lippmann, *Public Opinion,* (New York: Harcourt Brace, 1922): 31.
107. Doris J. Graber, *Mass Media and American Politics,* 3d ed.: 208.
108. Ibid.: 207.
109. Ibid.: 206.
110. G. A. Donohue, P. J. Tichenor, and C. N. Olien, "Mass Media and the Knowledge Gap: A Hypothesis Reconsidered," *Communication Research,* (vol. 2, 1975); Doris J. Graber, *Processing the News:* 210.

111. David Moore, "Political Campaigns and the Knowledge Gap Hypothesis," (paper presented at the Annual Meeting of the Northeast Political Science Association, 1982): 9.

112. Doris J. Graber, *Processing the News:* 206.

113. Michael J. Robinson, "A Statesman Is a Dead Politician: Candidate Images on Network News," *What's News?* edited by Elie Abel, (San Francisco: Institute for Contemporary Studies, 1981).

114. Michael B. Grossman and Martha J. Kumar, *Portraying the President,* (Baltimore: Johns Hopkins University Press, 1981); Michael J. Robinson, "Three Faces of Congressional Media," *Media Power in Politics,* edited by Doris J. Graber, (Washington, D.C.: Congressional Quarterly Press, 1984): 217.

115. Seymour M. Lipset and William Schneider, *The Confidence Gap,* (New York: The Free Press, 1983): 384–92.

116. David L. Paletz and Robert M. Entman, *Media-Power-Politics:* 167.

117. David Halberstam, *The Powers That Be,* (New York: Alfred A. Knopf, 1979): 296.

CBS News personnel picket the company's headquarters, protesting drastic staff cuts made in the wake of a takeover of the network by a group of Wall Street investors.

Why Is That "The Way It Is"?
The Sources of News Bias

INTRODUCTION

In Chapter 2, we learned that political news is often trivialized and pro-establishment. In this chapter, we'll ask why.

To answer that, we'll take a tour of six different pressures impinging on the news:

The "Commercial Imperative." At the head of this pack of pressures is the profit motive. We'll discuss why its ''twin commandments'' enjoin precisely the trivial, uncritical news described in Chapter 2. We'll look at why these commandments are more strictly enforced now than ever before, in this age of conglomerate ownership of the news.

Government Pressures. Powerful politicians are not powerless in their dealings with the press. We'll see what weapons are in their arsenal. We'll also begin our study of the Federal Communications Commission. We'll argue that this agency has failed to hand in its assignment, which is to assure a ''wide diversity of antagonistic sources'' in broadcast news.

Pressure from Advertisers and Pressure from Owners.   Next we'll ask whether sponsors, who after all, pay the piper, also call the tune. It stands to reason that they might. It also seems likely that the media's owners might be able to influence the politics of their news. But before owners or sponsors can exercise influence, they'll have to contend with journalists, who believe the news should be ''independent'' of such pressures. We'll watch the intricate tango performed by these contending forces.

Sources of the News.   In this section, we'll begin by looking at the ''Achilles' heel'' of journalism—constraints of time, space, and staff. We'll see how elites have found just the arrows to exploit that Achilles' heel. Those arrows include the public relations industry, with its press releases, photo ops, and pseudo events. They also include the neoconservative blitzkrieg described in Chapter 1. On the news front, that offensive has paratrooped in such ''sources'' as: scholars cultivated in corporate-endowed conservative think tanks, corporate-produced ''video news releases,'' and corporate-executive ''media blitzes.''

The Role of Journalists' Norms.   Why are journalists' norms in a list of pressures that undermine the news' mission? Shouldn't those norms be calling journalists to their mission? Once again, hegemony's power over our idea factories is so complete that it is now built into their very foundations—into the norms, routines, and values of the institution.

We'll look at three of journalism's most important norms—objectivity, common sense, and documentary reporting—and argue that they help turn reporters into stenographers for the establishment.

We'll also observe how a swarm of corporate-sponsored media critics use journalists' norms against journalists—crying ''liberal bias'' like an electroshock whenever a discouraging word is heard about the American Way.

Finally, a historical question will set off another round of our debate between theorists: How did American news come to be what it is?

Popular culture theorists will argue that it happened in the democracy of the marketplace: it was a series of brilliant commercial innovations, which were approved of by the people, were copied by other entrepreneurs, and so became the news as we know it.

Hegemony theorists will reply that the popular culture theory is only half a history. In the other half, elites ''helped'' the people choose commercialized news by making it, in a sense, the only choice.

Throughout the chapter, we'll pause from time to time for a ''News Break.'' We'll revisit some days of rage and change at the *Washington Post*; we'll look in on a bad day at CBS' ''Black Rock''; we'll watch media handlers sell the President; we'll see why the press passed on the S&L story, until it was too late; and we'll watch owners, sponsors, sources, and journalists etch their profiles in cowardice and courage as they face the moment of Joe McCarthy.

Like snow sliding down a slope, gathering itself into an avalanche, a force of little-noticed norms, routines, and institutions has gradually converged to make the news as we know it. To drive rival conceptions so far from the field that we don't know them— or even know of them—until airy trivia and uncritical cant are "all the news that's fit to print." What was behind that force? What were its attendant norms, routines, institutions—the sources of bias in our news?

The Commercial Imperative

"Politics is business," Lincoln Steffens said. "That's what's wrong with it." In fact, he went on, "That's what's the matter with everything." And he included journalism on his list.[1] In our time, much, perhaps most of the bankruptcy in the marketplace of ideas can be traced to a thriving business in the other marketplace.

The "commercial imperative" is, of course, profit. This section will argue that the profit motive is perhaps the basic source of the biases reviewed in Chapter 2. Of the forces converging on a news that is *against* thinking and *for* the way things are, the profit motive is the granddaddy of them all.

Industry to Business: The New Ownership of the News

In fact, Lincoln Steffens, writing in 1904, hadn't seen nothin' yet. The corporate game of "engulf and devour" that began in the 1960s (see Chapter 1) did not overlook the profitable news business.

NEWSBREAK

Things Fall Apart at the *Post*

Kay Graham. Daughter of *Washington Post* owner Eugene Meyer and wife of its dashing, brilliant publisher, Philip Graham. But eventually, it was she who would transform the *Post* from a staid, parochial hometown paper to the rank of second to none.

Then came the pressmen's labor dispute of 1975–76. Kay was the liberal doyenne of the most liberal mainstream newspaper in the country—the paper that had taken on racism, McCarthy, and Watergate. She did not fancy herself an enemy of the working people. But by 1975, the *Post* was part of a conglomerate, 452nd on the *Fortune* list. Though Kay owned the voting stock, Wall Street held the rest, and could vote with its feet. What's more, the *Post's* profit margin was down to 8 and 9 percent of revenue. "Wall Street did not like margins like that, or the kind of management that accepted them." New management people were brought in, people with a reputation for toughness. A reputation, as it turned out, that would be earned.

The *Post* began a move to a more efficient, labor-free printing technology. The pressmen could see the handwriting on the wall: it said their livelihoods were at stake. As contract negotiations neared, the new managers hired an Oklahoma firm that "specialized in helping newspapers to break strikes." At their Oklahoma headquarters—"scab school," the union called it—managers learned how to do the pressmen's jobs. Of course, in this nonnegotiable climate, the strike came. Of course, it was bitter. For the pressmen, a way of life hung in the balance. Before they went out, they wrecked their own presses, the desperate violence of men already beaten.

Today, "there are fifteen dominant companies that have half or more of the daily newspaper business, six in magazines, three in television." [2] Only 14 percent of VHF and 32 percent of UHF radio stations in the one hundred largest national markets remain under control by independents. Only 21 percent of the large-market television stations are independent.

At this writing, for example, NBC is one of the more than one hundred subsidiaries of the General Electric Company. Others

When it was over, the union busted, Kay Graham, who had earlier lived through her husband's suicide, "called the strike the worst thing she had ever been through in her life. It divided the paper, labor from management, reporters from labor, reporter from reporter; finally, it seemed to cut the paper off from its past." But the bottom line was this: profits were up. Wall Street smiled. "There was nothing soft or sentimental about the *Washington Post* Company now."[9]

Inevitably, the new toughness moved from the board room to the press room, and finally, to the news room. Well-respected *Post* reporter Scott Armstrong eventually quit the paper, and he explains why, "I was never unaware at the *Washington Post* that my principal job was to increase the return on investment for the Graham-Meyer family. . . . There was never any question in my mind that if protecting the First Amendment became more expensive than the return on investment, the First Amendment would be the loser." For example, he cites "200 . . . instances when the *Post* was illegally denied access to information and did not challenge the government. That's the way it is at most newspapers. They aren't prepared to go after stories that require a major investment of time. They're oriented toward short-term daily journalism, which—if you read between the lines—means increasing the profit margin."

Now, in the news room too, the bottom line was the bottom line.

Sources: David Halberstam, *The Powers That Be,* (New York: Alfred A. Knopf, 1979); Martin Lee and Norman Solomon, *Unreliable Sources,* (Secaucus, New Jersey: Carol, 1990).

include producers of plastics, financial services, appliances, and aircraft engines. The *Chicago Tribune* is a subsidiary of the Tribune Company, which also owns nine other newspapers, over a dozen radio and TV stations, and more than a dozen companies outside the media field. Time, Inc., itself a conglomerate with assets in excess of $4 billion, has recently merged with Warner Communications, Inc., a giant of the music, TV, and movie industries.[3] To paraphrase Veblen, the news "industry" has become a "business." To paraphrase Lombardi, nowadays, profit isn't everything; it's the only thing.

Gone is the crusading owner-editor. Gone is Hodding Carter, whose valiant little Greenville (Miss.) *Delta Democrat-Times* fought racism in the heart of the South, at the height of its power. Gone is the spirit of Edgar Lee Masters' poetic creation, Carl Hamblin, whose "Press of the *Spoon River Clarion* was smashed, and [he] tarred and feathered" for penning a scathing indictment of American justice on the day Sacco and Vanzetti were executed.

I do not wish to romanticize the editor of yore. After all, gone too is William Loeb, whose scurrilous half-truths wrecked the decent candidacy of at least one decent man.[4] Nor do I wish to indict the editors of today. They are just doing a job—brief links in a chain bigger and stronger than they are. I merely wish to say this: things change. And not always for the better. Gone is the owner-editor who purchased a press because, for better or for worse, he had something to say. Owners nowadays have other goals in mind.

> *Corporations do not purchase . . . newspapers and broadcast stations for sentimental reasons. . . . They buy them as investments that will yield a maximum return as quickly as possible. . . . This . . . is not what media executives talk about in public. But in private they and their acquisition agents are unequivocal. Christopher Shaw, the merger expert . . . speaking at a session of potential media investors . . . said, ". . . no one will buy a 15 percent margin paper without a plan to create a 25 percent [to] 45 percent margin."* [5]

Who are these new owners? The largest (e.g., the three major TV networks, Time, Inc., and the Gannett chain—publisher of *USA Today* and 92 other newspapers) are governed by boards of directors "very similar" to those of large non-media corporations. About two-thirds of those directors are either corporate executives, bankers, or (mainly corporate) lawyers.[6] This is not a group given to sentimentalizing about their companies' obligations to the common good. Indeed, when GE took over NBC and installed one of its corporate lawyers as its president, he firmly declared that the network's overriding responsibility was to "shareholders." At that point, a member of the news division asked whether the network had another responsibility, whether the news was "a public trust." "It isn't a public trust," replied the boss. "I can't understand that concept." [7]

Other media giants (e.g., the *Tribune, Times-Mirror, New York Times,* and *Washington Post* companies) are still controlled by the families whose progenitors built them. And isn't this where the flame is kept? To a greater extent, perhaps. But even here, owners must put a premium on the bottom line. Failure to do so will displease the commercial and investment bankers they rely on for lines of credit and loans. Such failure will also displease the banks and other institutional investors who own 30–45 percent of the stock of such companies.[8] When unhappy, they sell their stock. Its price goes down. So does the family fortune. If the family still refuses to maximize profit, stockholders may turn to takeover marauders who will. Thanks to this new ownership circuitry, the transition is rushing to completion. The transition from "industry" to "business." From passion for product to passion for profit.

The Twin Commandments of Commercial News

But how does the news pursue its passion for profit? In the news business, size of profit is a function of the size and demographic profile of the audience—those readers or viewers who in turn attract advertisers. Fascinatingly, the foremost marketing job of the established media is not what one might think. It is not to attract an audience, but to keep the large, profit-producing one they already have. This is most true of television, whose managers conceive of audience as a river that will continue to flow along one channel unless it is somehow diverted. Thus a "significant portion" of the audience for a network's evening news show is inherited from the local news broadcast which precedes it.*[10]

The analog to "audience flow" in newsprint is the medium's subscribing audience. They constitute more than three-fourths of a newspaper's readership. What is more, they are more affluent than the single-copy reader. This makes them a more desirable audience for advertisers, and thus a more profitable audience for newspapers.[11] The considerable brand loyalty of the newspaper subscriber means that, just as the television station inherits viewers from the previous time slot, so the newspaper inherits its subscribers from year to year, unless the river of readership is diverted.[12]

---

*The fact that local news is often the source of the river of audience flow puts enormous pressure on local news to try to attract, not just maintain an audience. Add to this pressure the fact that its local news show is by far the biggest money maker for the average TV station—generating as much as 50 percent of its annual revenues. Together, these pressures have helped make local news especially susceptible to the influence of "news doctors"—market researchers whose dubious nostrums are described in the following paragraphs.

So the bottom-line question becomes: how to maintain audience flow? Not, the answer begins, by improving editorial content. For example, investing in research or investigative staff will not pay for itself in increased audience. The television viewer, like the newspaper or newsmagazine subscriber, does not see (and so doesn't miss) what news is not there, what news the competition might be offering.[13] In fact, in 98 percent of cities served by a daily newspaper, there's no competition to see: one newspaper enjoys a monopoly on the local news.[14]

Given this reality, Bagdikian argues that news businesses are not just untempted to increase quality. The new, corporate owners are tempted to cut it. "In hundreds of small and medium-sized communities, . . . acquisition of the local paper or television station by a large firm . . . often is followed by drastic cutbacks in staffs." [15] At the TV networks, conglomerate ownership, together with the profit declines that came with competition from cable TV, brought pink slips to thousands of news staffers.[16] The NBC News staff was slashed by 28 percent in just the first round of cuts made by GE. The recession of the 90s brought a second round of layoffs, leaving the news even more "lean and mean." [17] No, quality is not the highway to profit heaven.

Instead, from the Mt. Sinai of audience maintenance come these twin commandments: Thou shalt not bore thine audience. Neither shalt thou offend them. Either sin risks changing the course of the river and tempting the wrath of the profit margin.[18]

How does the news choose to avoid "boring" its audience? Market researchers in this area, called "news doctors," have prescribed a diet very like the sugary pap described in Chapter 2 under the heading "trivialized news." "A new face here, a new set there, here a format, there a helicopter, more crime, less city hall, more local color, more pictures, fewer talking heads, shorter stories, more weather, [more] society and women's sections . . . [in short] the deemphasis of politics in favor of human interest irrelevancies." [19]

How does the news avoid offending its audience? By choosing sources, stories, facts, and themes that do not threaten established cultural values. This includes the kind of sources and themes described in Chapter 1 as "the American unison" and described in Chapter 2 under the heading "establishmentarian news." It excludes almost everything else.[20] Television, journalist Robert MacNeil has written, is a cheering section for the side that has already won.[21]

"Do we question the system?" mused a *Chicago Tribune* editor. "Of course not. If we did, we wouldn't be representative—or read." [22] There, in one basket, are the chicken and the egg. But which is which? Are the dearth and narrowness of ideological debate in the news (the movies, prime time TV, etc.) the effect or the cause of the American consensus? Isn't "being representative" a Catch-22? The popular mind will decide which groups and ideas make the news, but the popular mind knows nothing of a wide range of alternative groups and ideas, because they haven't made the news.

Wires, Affiliates, and Inoffensiveness

The inclination to be inoffensive is reinforced by the seminal role of the wire services in the making of news. These "wholesalers" of news sell their stories of national and international events to news "retailers"—newspapers, television stations, etc., who may not have the staff to cover these events. Small research staffs have forced television networks to rely heavily on the wire services for story ideas and story lines. Seventy percent of the reporting assignments handed out at NBC, for example, came from the wires.[23] Nonnational newspapers, of course, take almost all their national and international news from the wire services.

The audience imperative of these wire services is to please the universe of potential subscribers, huge and diverse in the political leanings of its editors and audiences. Thus, these prime movers of the news are even less likely than other media to engage in interpretive reporting, much less to adopt a controversial story line.[24]

Television networks are also especially wary of controversy. They are like wire services in the sense that they "wholesale" their wares to "retailers"—in this case television stations that "affiliate" with one or the other of the networks. Of course, it is important for network programming to be to affiliates' liking. The larger the number of affiliates a network has, the larger will be its audience share, and the more it can charge advertisers.

What is more, an affiliate has the right, under FCC regulations, to refuse to broadcast any program offered by its network that is not to the station's liking. Such refusal of "clearance" causes ratings and profits to drop. This threat of refused clearance is not hollow. With the explosion of new cable and independent stations (see Chapter 5) has come an explosion in new programming. Much of it is available as well to network affiliates, who are free to air it in lieu of network offerings they don't like.

Who are these affiliates and what do they want? Affiliated stations have been no exception to the conglomeration of the media

NEWSBREAK

Bad Day at Black Rock*

One late November day in 1976, the CBS News team came together to take a long hard look at their own coverage of that fall's election. The transcript of their deliberations, said CBS news president Richard Salant, ''is not going to anybody . . . outside of CBS News.'' That said, there ensued a remarkably candid, and, in the end, poignant introspection.

They talked about ''whether they had been had by the candidates and their strategists, whether they paid too much attention to visuals and cosmetics, too little attention to issues and substance. There were grand resolves pronouced, but the campaign coverage of (the following election) saw only modest changes made.''

Trouble began when well-known print journalist Norman Isaacs, brought in for perspective, suggested the network might have done an in-depth ''campaign and issues'' half-hour each week. Uh oh. It turned out the news team had produced such a thing. But America, like Isaacs, hadn't seen it. For ratings reasons, the network hierarchy had refused to show it during prime time. Instead, they offered it to affiliate stations during ''their'' time, 7:30 p.m. EDT. Where, also for revenue reasons, the affiliates (150 of them) had refused to air it. Isaacs' suggestion touched off a heated exchange between Salant and Walter Cronkite. It provided what might have been the motto for the frustrations of the whole day, and more:

Salant: *Whatever were the limitations,*
                     the constraints, whatever we
                     did wrong . . . I think it's much

---

*''Black Rock'' is the nickname of CBS Inc.'s corporate headquarters in New York.

business. They too have been ingested by giant corporations demanding giant profits. In the country's 100 largest television markets, 80 percent of stations are now conglomerate-owned.[25] As described by one network vice president, "Affiliates tend to be owned too easy for us to take Black Rock as the scapegoat. Sure, it would be nice to have an hour of news (instead of the nightly half hour). It isn't their fault that we don't have it. . . . It would have been nice to get better clearance for our half-hour (specials). It isn't their fault.

Cronkite: Why isn't it? . . . Why do they start us at seven-thirty on Friday night? Now isn't that their fault?

Salant: No.

Cronkite: We selected seven-thirty Friday night?

Salant: Absolutely not. That isn't their fault, Walter. That's the fault of . . . the system.

Cronkite: The what?

Salant: Of the system. The nature of the beast.

At this point, there was a pause, and some clearing of throats, as the men and women assembled pondered the "system" they are part of.

Source: Martin Schram, *The Great American Video Game*, (New York: William Morrow, 1987): 89–90.

by people in another business. . . . Their politics is Republican, their ideas are pragmatic and their preoccupation with return on invested capital and the safety of their [FCC granted] license to broadcast is total." [26] Translation: networks that wish to win new affiliates, keep current ones, and avoid clearance problems would do well to engage in what one network news producer called his "self-censorship" of programming that might threaten the "common sense." [27]

Washington Watches the News

Laissez Faire at the FCC

The most visible governmental influence on the news is the Federal Communications Commission, the federal agency charged with regulating the broadcast industry on behalf of "the public interest." In accord with that mandate, the FCC issued the fairness doctrine in 1949, requiring that when a controversial issue is discussed on television or radio the airing station must present contrasting viewpoints.

While this regulation has made local television news less partisan than local newspapers, it has not variegated the marketplace of ideas. This is mainly because the Commission has allowed television news producers to decide what constitutes a "fair reply." Their decision has involved the constant incantation of the "both sides" litany discussed in Chapter 2: establishment liberal spokesman is countered by establishment conservative spokesman, followed by correspondent concluding that the truth lies somewhere in between. This ritual has indeed warded off the FCC, even though it completely excludes the "contrasting viewpoint" of radicals. No broadcaster's license has ever been revoked for violation of the Fairness Doctrine. In fact, the FCC has actively encouraged these exclusive definitions of "fairness" and of "contrasting viewpoints." "It is not," says the FCC Fairness Primer, "the Commission's intent to make time available to Communists or to the Communist viewpoints." [28]

Recently, a deregulation-minded FCC has tapped what may be the final nail in the coffin of the Fairness Doctrine, declaring it "unconstitutional." Also left to laissez faire by the same merry band of deregulators is the amount of time stations devote to public affairs programming. The FCC has always been one of those agencies indentured to the industry it is supposed to regulate.[29] With these decisions, it has quietly excused itself from even the pretense of performing its mandate—the maintenance of a "wide diversity" of views on the airwaves.

Putting Political Pressure on the Press

A less visible and more sinister source of government pressure comes from the use of official power to pry favorable coverage out of the news media. For example, in 1969, when the news media covered the tide of protest against Richard Nixon's escalation of the air war in Vietnam, the President turned his formidable displeasure on the press. In the fall of 1969, Vice President Spiro Agnew toured the nation, blistering the "liberal bias" of the "effete snobs" who controlled the press. These "nattering nabobs of negativism" were, according to Agnew, using their news coverage of the antiwar demonstrations to purvey their own similar position to the public.[30] Agnew implied that the networks had violated the FCC's fairness requirement and thus should be investigated by the Commission, whose members are selected by presidential appointment. Eventually, the FCC did investigate charges of "news staging" by the networks.

Administration pressure continued with the 1972 filing of an antitrust suit against the three major networks by the Justice Department. Although the Justice Department denied that the suits were politically motivated, broadcasters had good reason to believe other administration spokesmen, who let on that they were. "The administration knew who its . . . enemies were," raged Chuck Colson, media monitor for the White House, in a 1972 phone call to Frank Stanton, president of CBS News. Nixon's team would "bring CBS to its knees on Madison Avenue and Wall Street. The CBS stock was going to collapse. 'We'll break your network,' Stanton heard him say. On he went through a litany of things the Administration was going to do to CBS. . . ."[31]

During this period, news coverage of protest activities declined significantly. In their stead, the networks began to cover a series of support rallies, prayer days, and patriotic demonstrations organized around the country by the White House.[32]

More recently, a *New York Times* staffer reported a massacre implicating the U.S.-backed government of El Salvador. Though his story was later independently corroborated, the reporter was removed from his position after harsh criticism of it by a high-ranking Reagan-administration official. Shortly thereafter, the *Times* hired a new Central American reporter, described as "the best friend the [Reagan-backed] Nicaraguan contras had in American journalism."[33]

But a caveat is in order. While these cases *illustrate* the problem, they may also overstate it. The notion that the press is and should remain "independent" is cherished by press and public alike. It seems to have been a sufficient garlic wreath against all but the most lupine public officials. Thus, although Gans found that journalists believed "themselves to be under frequent pressure," his interviews also suggested that "successful pressure leading to censorship or self-censorship, is rare." [34]

On the other hand, similar reasoning might bring us to an opposite conclusion—that governmental pressure is a *larger* problem than it appears to be. Precisely because independence is a cardinal rule for journalists, surrendering to pressure is a cardinal sin, and the sinner is loath to confess it. [35] It is conceivable that the governmental abuses that have surfaced are only the tip of an iceberg all the more deadly for being mainly submerged.

Government Censorship

Recently, government officials have discovered the most effective means of all of controlling the news. Recent military interventions in Grenada, Panama, and the Persian Gulf gave the government a reason, "military security," for imposing a complete system of censoring the news.

Reporters covering the Gulf War, for example, were allowed to do so only in pools under the supervision of Pentagon press officers. Reporters to be included in a pool were hand-picked by the military. In making their picks, press officers showed a decided preference for "hometown" reporters over members of the national press corps. The former tended to do "softer" pieces—the kind that might talk about how Corporal Diaz from right here in El Paso enjoyed his Thanksgiving Day turkey dinner. In fact, these reporters were imported to the Gulf as part of the Pentagon's "Hometown Media Program." Under its sponsorship, "small-town newspaper and television reporters—especially ones located near military bases—were provided free round-trip transportation on military aircraft to Saudi Arabia, and were encouraged to file upbeat stories for the folks back home." [36]

Soldiers to be interviewed by the press were also hand-picked by press officers. These interviews were monitored. NBC correspondent Gary Matsumoto describes the process of interviewing soldiers from a Patriot missile regiment:

Whenever I began interviewing a soldier, this PAO [press officer] would stand right behind me, stare right into the eyes of the

*[soldier], stretch out a hand holding a cassette recorder, and click it
on in the soldier's face. This was patent intimidation . . . which was
clear from the soldiers' reactions. After virtually every interview, the
soldier would let out a deep breath, turn to the PAO, and ask
[something like], "Can I keep my job?"* [37]

Once stories were drafted, reporters were required to submit
them to the military for review, to determine whether they contained "sensitive information." The changes and embargoes imposed by censors included many made clearly for public relations,
not security, reasons. One *New York Times* reporter, for example,
described a returning unit as "giddy." Military censors changed the
adjective to "proud."

Chris Hedges of the *New York Times* summarized the effects
of this system:

*You never see any problems. You're never allowed to report.
Nothing's ever wrong. The entire war has become videotapes of
planes always hitting their targets like giant Nintendo games and
soldiers up front eating turkey and waving flags and it's all a lie.* [38]

Pressure from Advertisers

Advertising is the *sine qua non* of American news. Between sixty
and eighty percent of newspaper revenue comes from advertising. [39]
Virtually all revenue of over-the-air commercial television comes
from advertising.

Now this dependence on advertising should not be taken, by
itself, to mean control by advertisers of editorial policy. Again, the
norm of independence mitigates advertiser influence. And, one
scholar has argued, the monopoly most newspapers have in their
markets gives them the power to enforce that norm. [40] Indeed, most
business and financial editors insist that they would rebuff editorial suggestions from advertisers. [41]

On the other hand, 22.6 percent of respondents to the same
survey reported that they would "puff up or alter or downgrade"
business stories at the direction of their advertisers. And again, we
might suspect that this figure is depressed somewhat by the reluctance of editors to confess to this professional sin.

The *frequency* of successful influence by advertisers is one of
those questions that is bound to hide from social science. At the
same time, there is another obvious point to be made about ad-

vertiser influence on the news: it does happen. It happens more often in competitive than in noncompetitive markets, more often on small than on larger papers,[42] involving large more often than small advertisers. But it does happen. For example:

1. The president of the Grocery Manufacturers of America crowed of winning editorial support against the late Senator Philip Hart's truth-in-packaging legislation, giving illustrations from eight magazines of his successful message that ". . . the day was here when their editorial department and business department might better understand their interdependency . . . as they affect . . . the advertisers—their bread and butter." Although Senator Hart sent background material to 21 magazines, none covered his efforts. Instead, *Look* managed to find room for an article entitled, "Let's Keep Politics Out of the Pantry," concocted by a food industry spokesman.[43]

2. A former president of CBS News has revealed that the tobacco industry and its ancillaries pressured the network to downplay early news reports of the link between cigarette smoking and lung cancer. For example, Alcoa Aluminum (which supplied aluminum foil for cigarette packages) "dropped its sponsorship of a CBS news and documentary program after the program ran a number of stories that offended Alcoa's customers. The program was gradually shifted from a weekly to a monthly format." [44]

3. "In 1989, U.S. Surgeon General C. Everett Koop angrily alleged that many magazines and newspapers thick with cigarette ads remain unwilling to publish articles on smoking dangers—a charge that received scant media attention." Perhaps *Time* and *Newsweek*, whose cigarette-ad revenues are indeed "massive," were given pause by the cautionary tale of *Mother Jones*. When that magazine ran a series of articles linking cigarettes to 390,000 American deaths each year, tobacco companies pulled their ads. "I think it would be naive to expect publications that take a lot of revenue from the tobacco industry to go after them vigorously," said *TV Guide's* assistant managing editor.[45]

4. When Chicago-based Sears Roebuck was charged by the Federal Trade Commission with widespread advertising deception, the story was big news around the country, but was not news in Sears' home town. Some of the Chicago media did not cover the story at all; others buried it in back pages with fleet mentionings. It is interesting to note that, apparently, Sears did not need to threaten the media to obtain this reticence. This case, like many others under the heading of "pressure," seems to have been a classic "non-decision"—fearing *potential* consequences, the "nondecider" simply fails to do what (s)he normally would.[46]

5. One of television's biggest sponsors, Proctor and Gamble, has instructed its ad agency that "there will be no material on any of our programs which could in any way further the concept of business as cold, ruthless, and lacking in all sentiment or spiritual motivation."[47] And Gulf & Western went one step further, showing that there are teeth behind that sort of admonition. In 1985, the company withdrew its funding from public TV station WNET, because the station showed the documentary "Hungry for Profit," which "contains material critical of multinational corporate activities in the Third World." Though the station, in the words of one official, "did all we could to get the program sanitized," the CEO of Gulf & Western was not satisfied. The program was "anti-business if not anti-American," he charged, and carrying it was not the action "of a friend" of the corporation. Once, WNET might have toyed with the notion that being "American" didn't require that the station be an uncritical "friend" to business. But as the London *Economist* observed, "Most people believe that WNET would not make the same mistake again."[48]

Media Owners and Managers

Is it only coincidence that trivial, establishmentarian news dovetails perfectly with the vested interests of the media's owners and managers? Social science is again hard-pressed to answer that question, partly because owner pressure, like advertiser or official pressure, is a journalistic taboo. Though this has made the *frequency* of this kind of influence hard to establish, the *fact* of it is not. Like advertiser pressure, it happens.[49] On the other hand, the conclusion of several studies has been that, especially in large, "quality" organizations, executive officers intervene only rarely in editorial decisions.[50]

Indirect Influence

But the most sensitive observers of this question have shown us how management *influence* can be a heavy hand even while *inter-*

vention remains a delicate touch. Influence begins with the hiring of editors. "I'm the chief executive. I set policy and I'm not going to surround myself with people who disagree with me," said Otis Chandler of the *Los Angeles Times*.[51] From there, influence is an almost unconscious process of acculturation, as editors learn their limits with the publisher through the sonar of trial and error, as reporters see what is edited from or rewritten in their columns, and especially, as all of them read what is and is not done in their own newspapers.[52]

Turner Catledge, long an editor at the *New York Times*, describes this subtle, powerful process of owner-executive influence, as it flowed through the nervous system of that estimable paper:

> [Owner-publisher] Sulzberger did not want to be an aggressive, dominating publisher, hurling thunderbolts at an awed staff. His style was more reserved, more subtle, and I think more effective. He sought executives who shared his general outlook and he tried, by word and deed, to set a tone for the paper.[53]

For his own part, Catledge received a constant flow of memos from Sulzberger. Perhaps not surprisingly, Catledge felt his boss possessed "unerring good judgment on the big issues." And so, when one of Sulzberger's memos criticized a reporter's work, his editor would often "pass it on to the reporter as my own comment, for insofar as possible I wanted our reporters and editors to go about their work without feeling that the publisher was constantly looking over their shoulders. In truth, however, he was."

In general, Catledge says, his goal was "to make [reporters] do what I wanted done, often by making them think it was what they wanted done." [54]

Sociologist Todd Gitlin, reflecting on these passages, asks, "How could the art of organizing hegemony be more neatly defined?" [55]

Ownership's Interests

What are the interests of the media's owners? For some there may be an ideological ax to grind. Bagdikian guesses that "the chief executive officers of the 29 corporations that control most of what Americans read and see [are] . . . almost without exception . . . conservative Republicans, [who] can, if they wish, use control of their [media] to promote their own corporate values to the exclusion of others." [56] My own guess is that their power is not often used quite so nakedly. But Bagdikian's rejoinder to me is chillingly plausible:

to show that power *is* not used does not show that it *will never* be used. To suppose the latter is "to ignore human nature and . . . ignore history: when central interests are at stake, available power will always be used." [57] In fact, this is precisely Todd Gitlin's point about the 60s—our last moment of regime crisis: the last time "central interests" were at stake, available power *was* used.[58]

At other times owners may be less interested in advancing corporate ideology generally, more interested in the specific political interests of their own company. The General Electric corporation for example, is heavily involved in the politically controversial production of nuclear power and military weapons. In the past, the company has not shied from flexing its power to influence policy makers or public opinion, by endowing think tanks, lobbying, and restricting its advertising dollars to "a program environment that reinforces our corporate messages." [59]

Now GE owns NBC, including its news division. But again, would GE tamper with the Ark of the Covenant—the norm of objectivity—by trying to shape NBC's news about General Electric? It might. Then again, GE might be able to rely on "discretion" (self-censorship) at NBC. In a survey of news editors, 33 percent said they would not "feel free" to carry a news story that might harm their parent company.[60]

Whether it was self-censorship or parent-company censorship, the answer to the question about GE and NBC was not long in coming. It might have been self-imposed. It might have been orders from the top. However it happened, it was censorship. The list of GE scandals NBC has "missed" is devastating. To take just one example:

> A reference to the General Electric Company was surgically removed
> from a report on substandard products before it aired on NBC's
> Today show on November 30, 1989. The report focused on a federal
> investigation of inferior bolts used by GE and other firms in building
> airplanes, bridges, nuclear missile silos and equipment for the NASA
> space program. It said that 60 percent of the 200 billion bolts used
> annually in the U.S. may be faulty.

The censored portion of the broadcast referred to GE's "alarming" use of bolts, one third of which were defective, for the previous eight years. "Peter Kurl, the journalist who produced the segment, called NBC's decision to eliminate references to GE 'insidious.' He cited the chilling effect on a network that is 'overprotective of a corporate owner.' " [61]

But these owner interests, the partisan and the corporate, are antinormative. And again, as such, they must operate in the interstices between the "normal," the approved, the routine. There is, however, a more fundamental owner interest. And it does not have to slip between the cracks of the routine. In fact, it is the routine. Today, ownership's message is all the more powerful because it is mostly coated with the soothing language of journalistic norms. As we shall see, those norms have come, partly through the process of top-down teaching, to enjoin the triviality and establishmentarianism chronicled in Chapter 2. The triviality that sells the owners' papers. The establishmentarianism that maintains their capitalist system. In the end, media owners and managers do not often forcibly inject their interests into the news for a very good and simple reason: they don't have to.

The Sources of the News

Leon Sigal's exhaustive study of news production at the *Washington Post* and the *New York Times* concludes: "News is . . . less a sampling of what is happening in the world than a selection of what officials think—or want the press to report—is happening." [62] Why is that?

Space, Time, Staff: The Achilles' Heel of the Press

As we have already seen, the term "news business" is not a metaphor. Between the lines of every day's news is a profit-loss ledger. This means that every editor's life is a struggle against the commercial elements: space, time, and cost. Daily the newsman must:

1. Fill a "newshole" large enough to carry a heavy load of advertising lineage.
2. Do this with a staff that will not weigh too much on the debit side of the ledger.
3. Do it under deadline.

The result of these imperatives is that management now measures newspaper performance in such terms as "man-hours per news column" and "man-hours per page." [63] The editor under these guns, "knowing that he lacks the manpower even to cover all of Washington, let alone the country . . . tries to . . . cover the key beats," i.e., the highest echelons of officialdom.[64] But perhaps "cover" is too generous a word for what reporters can do while chased by that Fury, the deadline. Even on the highly regarded *Chicago Tribune* most reporters must file at least a story per shift. A busy day on the beat might call for two or three stories. That pace leaves enough time to attend an event, buttonhole two or three "experts" who can be relied on to yield pithy, if predictable, quotations, and file the story. On less well-endowed newspapers, the pace—and the coverage—are worse.[65]

Television news faces these elements, and one more: the additional cost of a film crew severely limits the number of such crews deployed, and so the number of stories that can be covered. The result is: "Camera crews must be assigned to scheduled events that will almost certainly materialize on schedule. . . . Assignment editors therefore tend to give preference to happenings planned in advance for the press." [66]

These limits of TV news became even more acute when the cost-cutting conglomerates took over. Among the cutbacks they imposed were further reductions in the number of camera crews deployed and reductions in the number of longer, more analytical reports. These "provide viewers with more context," but they are more expensive and so they reduce "productivity." [67]

Costs also limit the research facilities available to the journalist. Amazingly, the CBS Evening News had a research staff of one at the time Epstein did his study of the networks. And in the crucial half hour before air time, its research library was closed.[68] Likewise, the national desk of the *Washington Post,* at the time of Sigal's study, had "little research help." [69]

The networks' research staffs were beefed up in later years, but thinned again by conglomerate cutbacks. In the first year of Capital Cities' takeover at ABC, 31 heads rolled in the research department.[70]

The Public Relations Industry: Paris' Arrow Finds Achilles' Heel

The problem with the press' limitations is this: where the fourth estate lacks such resources as time and staff to routinely do extensive research, the other estates, those "covered" by the press, have been happy to fill the breach. In fact, government and corporations have responded to the press' need for an agenda and for information by creating a full-blown industry—the public relations business.

NEWSBREAK

Selling the President; A Study in Symbiosis

Television needs news that is not just dramatic, but *visually* dramatic. News that wiggles. Those pictures that TV news feels obliged to write around, as Peter Jennings told us in Chapter 2.

Here, a White House PR man explains how sensitive his staff tries to be to that need. ''There's a relationship that gets very close. And we do a lot to cooperate with (news staffs). Make their jobs easier.'' And here a CBS news producer acknowledges her appreciation, ''Each advance man knows the question I would ask, 'Is there a prize shot?' . . . And . . . a couple of times that I didn't ask, . . . it was suddenly brought to my attention (by the White House aides) that there was this great high shot. . . . You see, I'm going to protect myself. I'm not compromising myself if I ask if there's a high shot . . . so I work with the advance man. . . . You want to protect yourself (from the competition) so that you have the best picture possible.''[82]

Here's how that waltz between the networks and the advance team played out, on one day during the presidential campaign of 1984.

Six months before July 4, 1984, an advance man scouted the site of the Pepsi Firecracker 400 as a possible presidential ''event'' for that day; the president's image makers saw the race as a door to the hearts of White Southerners, a key to the president's winning coalition in 1980. Successive memos from the advance team shaped this historic occasion:

> President greeting the winning driver . . . would be an
> important gesture . . . so important . . . that (Speedway
> owner) is building a road to facilitate the President's
> departure from the grandstand area following the greeting.
> . . . The President will start the race with a call to ''start your
> engines'' via radio-telephone from Air Force One. . . . While
> in the ''sky suite,'' the President will take part in five minutes
> of a live broadcast going out to 300 radio stations across
> the United States . . . the President will make brief informal
> remarks and present the trophy. ABC will then conduct a
> brief, light, sports-oriented interview with the President in the
> Winner's Circle.

When the big day came other news stories were breaking. Two American journalists had been arrested and detained in the Soviet Union. Jesse Jackson was criticized for proposing a trip to the U.S.S.R. But those stories were given short shrift on the evening news. Instead here is what America saw and heard on its network news, July 4, 1984.

Visual:	(The president is aboard Air Force One, the Commander in Chief on the Fourth of July, a white telephone to his ear.)
Chris Wallace:	*It was one of the most unusual phone calls ever made from Air Force One. The president, eight thousand feet over Virginia, starting the Firecracker Four Hundred stockcar race in Daytona Beach, Florida.*
The President:	*Gentlemen, start your engines.*
Visual:	(The stockcar gentlemen start their engines and roar down the track.)
Chris Wallace:	*By the end he was as involved as everybody else in a close finish. And it turned out the winner, Richard Petty, had organized stockcar drivers backing Mr. Reagan's reelection.*
Visual:	(Petty wins the race; there are shots of the festive Fourth of July crowd, and one of those "heart" signs that says: WE LOVE RON. Blond and attractive Tammy Wynette materializes beside the president; her strong singing voice fills the audio channel as

	she sings ''Stand by Your Man . . .'' She is, indeed, standing by her president as she sings, pressing against the left side of his light sport jacket and blue open-necked sport shirt. As she finishes, she turns his way, presses a bit closer, and, at her initiation, their lips meet in a Firecracker 400 kiss.)
Chris Wallace:	*This afternoon the president went to a picnic at the speedway, where country singer Tammy Wynette sang for him. Mr. Reagan praised the race drivers.*
Visual:	(Reagan is addressing his supporter, Petty, and his fellow drivers.)
The President:	(He has assumed his best aw-shucks, almost embarrassed acting manner, which he does quite well.) *I know how you all feel too, because, ah, I'm in, ah, a little race myself this year.* (The drivers laugh and roar.)

Source: Martin Schram, *The Great American Video Game,* (New York: William Morrow, 1987).

Press agents have been at work since the nineteenth century, but, wrote Edward Bernays, father of the public relations industry, "It was the astounding success of propaganda during the [First World] War which opened the eyes of the intelligent few in all departments of life to the possibilities of regimenting the public mind." [71] Another industry founder, Ivy Lee, described for his employer, John D. Rockefeller, how the business worked in the case of publicizing a Rockefeller gift to a university:

> *In view of the fact that this was not really news, and that the newspaper gave so much attention to it, it would seem that this was wholly due to the manner in which the material was "dressed up" for newspaper consumption. It seems to suggest very considerable possibilities along this line.*[72]

By the mid-twenties, it was estimated that more than half the stories appearing in the *New York Times* originated in the work of press agents. In 1930, political scientist Peter Odegard wrote, "Many reporters today are little more than intellectual mendicants who go from one publicity agent or press bureau to another seeking 'handouts.' " [73]

Today, the public relations army is more formidable than ever. Estimates are that from 30–50 percent of the now-huge White House staff is involved with media relations. The Defense Department alone spends billions of dollars annually on public relations.[74] Its press agents now outnumber Pentagon reporters by a ratio of about four to one.[75] One estimate put the number of *full-time* public relations staffers in just the Air Force at over 1,300. Contrast that with the information services staff at the American Friends Service Committee—one of the largest groups offering a critique of Pentagon PR. AFSC's army numbers eleven.[76] Is it any wonder that over 60 percent of front-page stories in the *Washington Post* and *New York Times* are "inspired" by establishment proceedings, press releases, press conferences, and "non-spontaneous events." [77]

This last category remains one of the most ingenious products of the public relations machine—the pseudoevent. This is a happening staged, usually by elites, to attract the media spotlight and bathe themselves in the warm glow of favorable publicity.[78] It is designed to fit like a glove the media's need for predictable, quickly coverable, dramatic events. For example, in 1969 Richard Nixon moved to stem the adverse publicity flowing from a massive oil spill off the coast of Santa Barbara. After announcing that the situation was under control, Nixon conducted an "inspection tour" of a clean Santa Barbara beach. The news media covered the pseudoevent as news, and did not expose the event's illusory quality: the fact that this stretch of beach had been cleaned especially for this event, while miles of beach on either side "remained hopelessly blackened." [79]

The press did not expose Nixon's five o'clock shadow show for the same reason it rarely reveals how one-sided and self-serving are its sources. To do so would be to "dismantle the news net," [80] in other words, to expose the porousness of that net, calling into question the validity of the news itself, and to untie reporters' relationships with elite sources, those ties that bind the news net together and make what's known as newsgathering possible. [81]

The Journalists Rejoin

But again, journalists will object. Things, they will argue, have changed since Nixon's day. Being led down a primrose path by successive presidents, to Vietnam and Watergate, "exploded" the concept of news. Now, the correspondent's "wrap up" of a pseudoevent is always a nod and a wink about the pseudo-ness of it all. At the Firecracker 400, for example, Sam Donaldson sneered, "Even though the White House maintains this trip was not political, and the taxpayers picked up the bill for it, political overtones were everywhere." [83]

But this is a strange double bind. On one hand, we are told, this is the news. On the other, that this is mere manipulation—an entertaining meringue. (Though often we are told in a wink so quick as to be unnoticeable.) And in the final analysis, who cares? When all the news is so evidently crafted to be an entertaining meringue, why should we object if this particular slice happens to be served up by the president?

The answer is, we won't, as CBS correspondent Leslie Stahl discovered when she put together a six-minute "exposé" of Ronald Reagan's "brilliant . . . orchestration" of television.

To illustrate her point, she replayed four years of vintage Reagan. There he was, "getting the Olympic torch from a runner, greeting wheelchair athletes, . . . senior citizens at their housing project, honoring veterans who landed in Normandy, . . . youths just back from Grenada, . . . hugging Mary Lou Retton . . ." and so on. "Look at the handicapped Olympics," she jabbed, "or the opening ceremony of an old age home. No hint that he tried to cut the budgets for the disabled and for . . . housing for the elderly."

After the broadcast, Stahl waited, worried. The call from the White House came quickly. But it was not what she had expected. "We loved it," said the White House. "You gave us four and a half minutes of great pictures of Ronald Reagan, and that's all the American people see. . . . They don't hear what you're saying if the pictures are saying something different." [84] The medium, he was saying to Stahl, is the message, and the message is entertainment. And you newspeople should know that. After all, you've helped make it so.

Seeding the Clouds of Conservative Sources

Business's neoconservative blitzkrieg (described in Chapter 1), did not neglect the news.

Among other things, its money bought the opinion beyond price—scholarly opinion—and brought it to the newsroom. Corporations did it by endowing "think tanks," thus providing the time, research resources, and collegial setting in which conservative scholars and their words could flourish. For example, the conservative Heritage Foundation, endowed by such corporate champions of free enterprise as Joseph Coors, Richard Mellon Scaife, and William Simon saw its budget grow from about $1 million in 1976 to over $7 million in 1981. Similar growth, sources of support, and ideologies can be found in the Hoover Institution, the American Enterprise Institute, the National Bureau of Economic Research, a large number of smaller academies, a host of endowed university chairs, and a plethora of conservative scholarly journals.[85] The most thoughtful study of the "neoconservatism" springing from the brow of this corporate support describes the process this way:

> Talent is always a scarce resource, and neoconservatives have discovered an old-fashioned means to deal with scarcity—money. Nelson Rockefeller's late Commission on Critical Choices offered [two neoconservative scholars] "$100,000 to obtain on short order fifteen essays analyzing "the ideas and values of human nature inherent in U.S. institutions." As one scholar, accustomed to receiving fees of $75 to $300 from liberal journals . . . remarked of this windfall, "It certainly clears one's calendar and concentrates the mind." [86]

So the first outpost had been taken. The field of public policy was "awash with . . . academic studies" that came to the "right" conclusions (to borrow the language of Dr. Edwin Feulner of the conservative Heritage Foundation). From there, said Dr. Feulner,

likening his task to Proctor & Gamble selling toothpaste, ". . . sell
it and resell it every day by keeping the product fresh in the consumer's mind," by disseminating these conclusions to "thousands
of newspapers," for example.[87]

On the other flanks of this offensive, still other sources were
marshalled. Mobil Oil, for example, began producing its own "documentaries" featuring "journalists" interviewing Mobil executives
and other experts who favor Mobil's policies. Local TV stations can
air these programs *in toto* or break them into interview segments
for use in newscasts. Corporations and other interest groups used
these video news releases (VNR) as a kind of a Stealth bomber of
public relations. Dressed up as objective news and not identified
as PR by the network or station that airs them, they fly into consciousness beneath the viewers' radar of skepticism. All together,
about 4,000 VNRs were made available to newscasters in 1991, up
from around 700 in 1986. Roughly 80 percent of TV news directors
admit they now employ VNRs "at least several times a month" according to a survey by Nielsen media research.[88]

Mobil has also led the way in waging the corporate "media
blitz." Recently, 21 of its executives were dispatched to 21 target
cities, where they appeared on more than 100 talk shows, news
broadcasts, and radio call-in programs, and met with local editors.[89]

Meanwhile, at the other end of the funnel, as we saw in Chapter 2, viewers of the "MacNeil-Lehrer News Hour" heard from the
"experts" on defense issues. Aside from government officials, these
were most often spokespersons for conservative think tanks.[90] And
in general, recent content analysis concludes, "Elite sources still
supply most of the information found in both national and state
newspapers. . . . By the simplest of criteria, . . . newspapers have
failed to live up to the expectations of the media in a pluralistic
democracy." [91]

The Role of Journalists' Norms

So far, this discussion of the sources of bias has been typical of
social science, where too often relationships between human
beings "assume the fantastic shape of relations between things,"
as Marx put it. Journalists are not "things" moved about, insensate
and indifferent, by "social forces," like the pressures listed previ-

ously. Journalists are men and women who can fight back, surrender, or make a truce. In fact, what journalists have done is to forge a philosophy of news and a corresponding casuistry of norms which:

1. Help newsmen to resist the pressures toward antinormative bias (from the particular interests of advertisers, government officials, and media owners). Journalists themselves insist that the main influence on their work is "newsworthiness," i.e., journalistic standards, not the interests of editors or advertisers.[92] And, as we have seen, scholars who have watched journalists work have seen little of such "improper" influence.[93]

2. These norms also dignify the news, and so let newspeople live at peace with the stronger pressures (the commercial imperative and the need to rely on establishment sources as authoritative). In fact, as we shall see, journalists' norms have joined these pressures to produce the structural biases described in Chapter 2. In the next few pages, we'll discuss three of journalists' most important norms, and their effects.

Objectivity

The cornerstone of these journalistic values is, of course, the norm of objectivity. Present in rough form as early as the earliest modern news,[94] the norm was refined in the early decades of this century into a bulwark for an emerging "profession" besieged by charges of crassness and bias. Although the combined critiques of the lost generation[95] and the new journalism[96] have blurred the meaning of objectivity at its edges,* the core of the concept remains pristinely clean and fervently believed by journalists. The job of the newsperson, it professes, is to depict the world's important events, accurately and disinterestedly.[98]

The problem is how to choose unbiased facts when there are none. Given the infinitude of interesting facts, stories, leads,

---

*Disagreement among newspeople centers around the question of whether they should confine themselves to "reporting the facts" or go on to explain those facts. Despite hyperbole about this latter idea "exploding the concept of the news," "interpretive reporting" remains a rather staid concept, based on the objectivity ideal. Interpretation itself, it is believed, can and should be "objective," telling "both sides" of the story.[94]

angles, and sources, and given that liberals, conservatives, and radicals of the right or left will always disagree over which of these facts, etc., are "important" and "newsworthy," the question becomes: How to avoid bias when bias is inevitable? Journalists have responded to this paradox with a set of "rituals"—elaborate contortions designed to soothe the insistent demand for objectivity "almost the way a Mediterranean peasant might wear a clove of garlic around his neck to ward off evil spirits." [99]

This response to one paradox has created another: the norm of objectivity, in the professed service of freeing the people, has in fact helped shackle them to a cave wall shadow show. Included in the objectivity liturgy is the ritualized telling of "both sides" of a story, using "authoritative" sources, i.e., those "in a position to know more than other people." [100] Thus, journalists' norms have helped the Fairness Doctrine give us the form of a debate. At the same time, they join time-cost constraints to give us establishment Tweedledums and Tweedledees as the substance of that debate.

Common Sense

Another norm designed to ward off charges of bias is that facts and stories should comport with "common sense." [101] This "common sense" is much like the one Gramsci described as the assumptions of the hegemonic culture—assumptions so widely held and rarely questioned as to seem less like value choices than like *a priori* judgments. So this "common sense" norm joins with the agenda of elites and the commercial commandment against offending audience to write the status quo in stone.

For example, the truth about massacres and bombings of civilians by American forces in Vietnam went unreported by the establishment press for years, though firsthand reports of these incidents had appeared often in the radical press and even in the mainstream foreign press. These stories were not reported because they were not "consensible," sounding more like "communist propaganda" than like the American G.I. "everyone knows." [102]

This need to partake of the common sense has produced one of the most bizarre behavior patterns outside of zoology: pack journalism. It affects mainly reporters who cover the same beat for rival media. These reporters read one another's work religiously and huddle together at every opportunity to decide what the day's story is, what is the lead, what are the facts, and so on. [103] This herd instinct may be one more reason for the lack of variety at the media bazaar. A recent study found that 71 percent of the stories aired on national television news in a particular week were carried by all three networks.[104] In one recent year, *Time* and *Newsweek* had identical cover subjects about one out of every three weeks.[105]

The need for consensus also makes journalists especially susceptible to what I will call the "conservative fallacy" of any ongoing institution. This is the unremarkable human tendency to accept, for the most part unquestioningly, "the way things are usually done," and to emulate it. Thus, academics teach in the way they were taught, and reporters write in a way they learned by reading their predecessors. For example, when journalists are asked to reflect on the trivialization charge, their responses suggest that their benchmark for answering the question, "How much crime is too much?" or "How deep should analysis go?" is not some external standard such as "numerical predominance of crime over political stories is too much." Instead, the benchmark is "How well are we doing compared with other news media?" [106] If our coverage is not more trivial than theirs, then we are meeting the standard set by the journalistic common sense. United we fall.

Seeing Is Believing What You Are Shown

A third rain dance for objectivity is "documentary reporting." Telling only those stories reporters either witness firsthand or hear from "reliable sources" is supposed to ensure that the news is "the facts," not embellishment or advocacy.[107] But again, the question is "Which facts?" The documentary norm means that the media's need is not only for facts that are dramatic and quickly coverable, but also predictable, so they will be visible to the reporter or to his reliable sources. Thus, this norm helps deliver journalists straight into the hands of press secretaries and pseudoevent stage managers, whose statements and happenings are timed precisely to be predictable and visible to reporters.

Some of the most dramatic stories leading us into the Gulf War were good examples of documentary reporting—and they were also fake.

In one case, a young Kuwaiti refugee identified as "Nayireh" moved the nation when she appeared on the news, testifying of Iraqi atrocities in Kuwait. Iraqi soldiers, she said, had stormed hospitals and torn newborn babies from their incubators, leaving them to die. Thereafter, her story was invoked often by the President, as he urged us to war against the cruel invaders.

Her appearance was the very model of a documentable event. Her testimony was witnessed firsthand by the entire national press corps. It came in a venue fully sanctioned as "reliable"—Congressional hearings. The only trouble was, it was false.

Here is what the press did not know, and so did not report. This "Kuwaiti refugee" was in fact the daughter of the Kuwaiti ambassador to the United States. The public relations firm of Hill and Knowlton, headed by George Bush's former Chief of Staff, had packaged and rehearsed her appearance. Later, Kuwaiti doctors in the hospitals where the "atrocities" supposedly took place would admit that nothing of the kind had occurred.

In this and in numerous other instances, reporters followed the norm of documentation straight down a primrose path to a PR concocted distortion.[108]

Using Journalists' Norms Against Journalists

Earlier, we noted that a corporate-sponsored offensive team of neoconservatives has plunged into the end zone of the news. Meanwhile, a defensive squad has been busy for the same corporate team, red-dogging reporters with charges of "liberal bias." They have made their tackles with a strategic ju-jitsu; using the media's own force against them—using the norm of objectivity to send the press sprawling.

Among these corporate-sponsored defense specialists are:

1. The Media Institute: "The main theme of its corporate-sponsored studies and conferences has been the [alleged] failure of the media to portray business accurately and to give adequate weight to the business point of view* on such subjects as the oil crisis." Its unbiased officers include Herbert Schmertz of the Mobil Oil Corporation and Steven Seekins of the American Medical Association.

---

*I pause for a moment to glance at a daily feature of the *New York Times*, the Business section. In seven pages of today's issue, not a single story appears that could be deemed remotely critical of a business, or of business as such. Instead several stories are downright reverent toward their subjects. Of the many sources quoted, almost all are businessmen. Not one is representative of a consumer-action or public interest group, the kind that have been known to criticize business.

2. Accuracy in Media (AIM): AIM "grew spectacularly in the 1970s. Its annual income rose from $5,000 in 1971 to $1.5 million in the early 1980s, with funding mainly from large corporations and the wealthy heirs and foundations of the corporate system. At least eight separate oil companies were contributors to AIM in the early 1980s, but the wide representation in sponsors from the corporate community is impressive. The function of AIM is to harass the media . . . to follow the corporate agenda and a hard-line, right-wing foreign policy." [109] The "studies" produced by these groups tend to range in quality from the dubious to the ludicrous. [110] Nonetheless, the corporate-sponsored power to cry "bias" to millions seems to have affected journalists and their public. [111]

3. The American Legal Foundation and the Capital Legal Foundation: Two of the meaner linebackers in this league, these foundations specialize in suing the media for libel on behalf of conservatives who have been criticized in the news. Their sponsors are a roundup of the usual suspects. In this case, Richard Mellon Scaife, heir to the Mellon banking fortune and one of the "principal moneybags of the New Right"; the Coors and Fluor families, and the Olin Foundation. [112]

Legal Threats: The Big Chill

In one sense, these legal foundations would not seem to be the most valuable players on the New Right team: i.e., they rarely win these lawsuits. This is because the Supreme Court has set a fairly high standard for proving libel in the case of a "public figure." A low standard, they've reasoned, would have a "chilling effect" on the press's ability to watchdog these trustees of the public interest. So, "upwards of 90 percent of all seriously litigated libel cases never go to trial. . . . Three out of four . . . libel suits were thrown out at the summary judgment stage." [113] Of the handful of libel plaintiffs that make it to trial and win, 70 percent find their libel awards overturned on appeal. [114]

On the other hand, in the legal arena, winning isn't everything. What the New Right realizes is that the mere cost of *defending* themselves against such lawsuits is enough to make the media take a deep breath before criticizing conservatives. The average cost of a libel defense is $150,000 per case, even including those where the suit is dismissed for lack of merit before the trial begins. And what happens when such suits actually go to trial? CBS, for example, spent an estimated $5–10 million successfully defending

NEWSBREAK

Big Chill, Big Bill

Attorney Abrams' advice was one big reason why the Savings and Loan scandal went uncovered by the press until it exploded in crisis. As early as 1986, a reporter named Mike Binstein was convinced that Charles Keating, owner of Lincoln Savings and Loan, was ''cooking the books.'' But Keating had a propensity to sue his detractors, so Binstein's boss, columnist Jack Anderson, refused to break the story. ''My rule was, if someone is litigious, and it will lead to a costly lawsuit, we won't run the stories. I hated every minute of it,'' explained Anderson.

At that point, Binstein shopped his story around to other editors. One article was finally printed in a small circulation magazine covering Keating's home state. The magazine, *Arizona Trend,* was promptly slapped with a $35 million lawsuit, which cost the magazine $150,000 before Keating dropped it. ''That's the terror of the libel suit,'' Binstein says, ''They can make you bleed. The message gets telegraphed to people who cover the S&L industry: if you want to write about Charles Keating and Lincoln, it'll cost you $150,000. That's the admission price.''

As he continued his research, Binstein acquired ''hundreds of pages'' of regulators' documents ''from '86 on that spoke to

itself against a libel suit brought by the Capital Legal Foundation on behalf of Gen. William Westmoreland. This gives new meaning to the term "pyrrhic victory."

Ultimately, of course, the point is to chill the media's willingness to watchdog conservatives. Has it worked? The managing editor of the *Tampa Tribune* admits it has, "We've been a little less aggressive. There are situations we haven't covered that we otherwise might have." [115] Nat Hentoff, a columnist for he *Village Voice,* thinks things have changed more than a little. "[Publishers are] scared. . . . We have at least three or four lawyers who go over much of what appears in the *Voice* every week. . . . I don't think James Madison had in mind that the lawyers should be in the newsroom or in the publisher's office." [116] Attorney Floyd Abrams, who represents many media clients advises, "The ultimate way to avoid the risk is not to write the story." [117] The big chill is on.

how big the problem was, who was going to fail, by name, and how much it was going to cost.'' Among Binstein's documents were the confidential minutes of the now-infamous meeting in which five U.S. senators, all of whom had taken huge contributions from Keating, did their best to intimidate bank regulators investigating the Lincoln S&L.

But once the *Arizona Trend* suit was filed, ''I had AIDS as far as everyone in the business was concerned.'' His stories were rejected by the *New York Times* and the *Los Angeles Times,* among others. ''Intimidation was really the byword here. There was a yellow streak running through journalism.''

Finally, in 1989, the Federal Home Loan Bank Board declared Lincoln Savings and Loan insolvent. Keating was indicted and convicted on charges of fraud. But by that time, the cost of bailing out Lincoln alone had soared to $2.6 billion. It was the most expensive failure in S&L history.

The total cost of bailing out the S&L industry, which had increased steadily while a corrupt Congress and a frightened press refused to act, was now estimated at $500 billion.

Source: Howard Kurtz, ''Asleep at the Switch: How the Media Bungled the Story and Contributed to the S&L Crisis,'' *Washington Post,* National Weekly Edition (December 21–27, 1992): 6–9.

A Brief History of the News

As we have just seen, journalists' norms often fail to contravene pressures toward the structural bias of the news. In fact, Lance Bennett has argued that the coming together of norms and pressures is no accident.[118] These norms were really rationalizations *ex post facto* the commercial construction of the news. But to that, the school of cultural democracy might reply, "So what's the problem?" Again, they might ask, "Doesn't this spectral-sounding 'commercial imperative' really just mean giving the people the news they want? And isn't that what democracy is about?"

Good question. But the answer isn't as self-evident as it might seem. Yes, we are willing to "buy" the news as currently constructed. We do read/watch it *en masse.* But here's a curiosity: We seem to be torn between what we're willing to buy and what we say we want and need. For example, we *watch* the news turn elections into horse race and hoopla, but a plurality of Americans say they think too much time was spent on "daily campaign activities" (hoopla), and a clear majority say they think too little time is spent on issues.[119]

Which raises the question: how would we behave if we were a news public, instead of a news market? What would news be like if we (the people) sat down in direct democracy, and decided on its shape—instead of sitting down as we do in a commercial plebiscite, to ratify a news designed by media moguls?

Stumped? Me too. But here is a tantalizing hint for us: In Western Europe, news is less often a commercial enterprise than is true in the United States. And it is less often trivialized, fragmented, and uniformly centrist than is true here.[120]*

Which in turn raises another question. How did we become a media market and not a media public? Why is U.S. news so uniquely, pervasively commercial?

Within the next few pages, cultural democracy theorists will argue that the United States had a soft spot for commercial news. And it was only a matter of time before media entrepreneurs found that spot.

While I would not disagree, I will add this: at key moments, in crucial ways, noncommercial, public, political news was more than just outsold. It was attacked, tooth and nail, in a fight that was not fair.

All this can best be seen with an eye to history. Without that, the road we have long since taken seems the only way; the themes and assumptions of contemporary journalism seem unquestionable, just good common sense.

We begin our look at abandoned paths and roads not taken in 1833, the year *The New York Sun* signaled the dawn of modern news.

The Entrepreneurs Find Their Mark

Newspapers in existence before 1833 were aimed at either political or mercantile elites. This was partly because of the clumsiness of printing technology, which made the newspapers too expensive for

---

*How long European journalism will remain distinctive is in doubt. Recent trends, especially privatization and conglomerization, have led to an increase in "sensationalist and soft news angles, as practiced by American . . . newspapers."[121]

popular consumption. The "news" of the mercantile paper was mainly marine news—the comings, goings, and cargoes of ships in the local harbor. The political papers were indentured to the parties that subsidized them. These parties seem to have been possessed of the naive notion that the way to win an election was by force of argument, and so their newspapers consisted mainly of political commentary and editorials. Originally these were full of erudition, full of allusions to history, philosophy, and Greek mythology. They talked up to their readers, not down to them. But, eventually, they descended into personalities as Andrew Jackson showed how an *ad hominem* press could be used as a way of tying grass-roots notables into a national party.[122]

The Penny Press and the Wire Services: Depoliticizing the News

But even by the 1830s, capitalism had already carved a niche for a commercial medium. The factory and shop-made goods that had exploded into the economy in the past two decades needed to be marketed, sold—advertised. At the same time, improvements in printing technology, transportation, and literacy levels were making it possible to produce and distribute an advertising medium to a wide audience. The *New York Sun's* achievement was to see this niche and the shape of the medium that would fill it. The *Sun* was hawked by newsboys in the street for a penny a piece. In its advertising, raucous claims for patent medicines and lotteries replaced the staid notices of legal transactions or public sales found in the elite press. But the change reaching farthest—all the way into the VDTs of today's *New York Times*—occurred in the news columns of the penny papers. There, "selling the people replaced telling the people." [123] Human interest stories and melodramatic descriptions of "events" replaced the argument and analysis of the elite press.

Although the norm of objectivity was not born until the 1920s, it too was conceived in the penny press. Its editors proudly trumpeted their "unbound independence" from the patronage-wielding parties, and competed to give "the earliest, the fullest, and most correct intelligence on every local incident." [124] Actually, this "independence from politics" was mainly indifference to it. In its stead, stories of rapes, robberies, suicides, abandoned children left in baskets, and the brawling of drunken sailors were the common fare of most penny papers.

And finally, the penny press prefigured this about modern news: That the real question was not, "What do the people want?" but rather, "What do the people who can afford it want?" James

G. Bennett's *New York Herald* found the answer by stirring financial reporting into his otherwise spicy broth. In doing so, Bennett captured the fancy of the soon-to-be dominant business class and rode with their rise to heady heights of profit and influence.[125]

The success of the penny press was immediately apparent. Within a few months, the *New York Sun* had the largest circulation of any paper in New York City. Within two years, two other papers, one of them Bennett's, had aped its way. Together, the three had a combined circulation twice that of all eleven dailies publishing before the rise of the *Sun*.[126]

The next chapter in the commercial construction of the news was written by the Associated Press. In 1848, a number of newspapers pooled some of their reporters and unfurled the banner of the AP, to provide economical coverage of far-flung events to all of them and to hundreds of other newspaper subscribers over the newly available telegraph wires. In its coverage, the AP eliminated two vestiges of earlier news whose end had begun in the penny papers: partisanship, which would have limited sales to subscribers of varying partisan stripe; and political analysis, which could not be economically transmitted over the wires. These were replaced by the documenting of events whose facts could not be disputed and could be cheaply transmitted on one end of the wire, easily "reconstructed and embellished" on the other.[127]

Yellow and Gray Journalism: Stratifying the News

With the rise, in the 1880s, of department stores and national brand names, advertising became an industry. In turn, so did the monitoring of newspaper circulation. The entrepreneurs who seized this day were the likes of William Randolph Hearst and Joseph Pulitzer, whose "yellow journalism" told in bold face what working class news had become—an extravagant use of illustrations; lurid, multi-column headlines; seductive portraits of the lives of the rich and famous; "women's" pages displaying the allure of being a fashionable consumer; and especially, sensational, often prevaricated "news" of crimes, accidents, scandals, and bizarre or sentimental "human interest."

This formula mesmerized New York's working multitudes, especially that anxious, hopeful 40 percent of the population of foreign birth, to whom Pulitzer's pages were the perfect screen for receiving their projected fears and desires. The *New York World* went from a circulation of 15,000 in 1883, when Pulitzer bought it, to over 250,000 in 1886. His winning formula is one on which

NEWSBREAK

Adolph Ochs

His was an age suspicious of all foreigners, and of Jews in particular. Suspicious of their long hair and beards, strange clothes, radical politics, their un-Christian religion—their un-Americanism.

The reaction of many victims of that xenophobia was a kind
of hostage syndrome—they made a desperate effort to show they
had become what their tormentors wanted them to be.

So it was with Adolph Ochs, who yearned for respectability.
The *New York Times* would be his way of showing people who
mattered that a Jew could be a good American. In it, he wanted
''nothing that would shock or offend or cause controversy . . . as
little partisanship as possible.'' Indeed, he had ''no particular political opinions, other than that America was a good society,''
which made it easy to locate the paper always in the solid center.
It could be liberal, later on, when it was in fashion, but never radical. At the same time, he would offer all he could of real estate,
financial, and market reports, the comings and goings of all store
buyers in the city. And oh yes. The paper was not, at all costs, to
be ''too Jewish.'' The whole package was meant to appeal to
''respected men of finance and state,'' the ''best people,'' the
Gentile gentility.

And it did. Over the next half century, New York papers fell
like battle casualties all around, some with more readers than
Ochs' paper, but the *Times* was invincible. The ''quality'' (read
''riches'') of its readers insured that the great department stores,
the fashion designers and others would pay dearly to reach them.
Until at last the staid, stalwart, respectable *Times* stood alone, *the*
paper of the city's—nay the nation's—educated classes.

Source: David Halberstam, *The Powers That Be,* (New York: Alfred A. Knopf,
1979): 207–212.

today's tabloids, with their own enormous working-class readership, have been unable and unwilling to improve.[128]

But the advertising age also reemphasized that the bottom
line of the news business is not only audience size; it is also

audience demographics. In 1896, Adolph Ochs began to realize the commercial potential of a relatively small but affluent audience when he purchased the *New York Times*. The *Times* pointedly contrasted the coverage of the yellow "freak journals" with its own, which "will not soil the breakfast cloth" and is "all the news that's fit to print," but "not a school for scandal." [129] At the same time, Ochs was shrewd enough to intuit what pollsters later proved: that social and political analysis may bore or offend even educated readers, and that even educated readers are attracted to "human interest" stories.[130] But he began a stress on "decency," and he filled the unspoken demand of classes that saw themselves as "independent and participant" for "accurate, impartial" political information. The resulting fusion was a newspaper that rendered important events in trivialized, establishmentarian terms. It captured the heart of the upscale classes; ever since, the *Times* has been one of the national leaders in advertising lineage and has operated in the red only once since 1895, during the strike of 1962.[131]

But Ochs' coup was not only commercial. It conquered the culture as well. At the same time that he sold his newspaper to affluent New Yorkers, he sold his idea of a newspaper to journalists everywhere. Repeated surveys have shown that, above all other newspapers, journalists read, respect, and try to emulate the *New York Times*.[132]

News in the Age of News Doctors

Following the *New York Times* model, most newspapers reduced their partisanship during the twenties and thirties, but then saw less reason to report politics at all, and coverage of it declined.[133] This tendency has grown worse since that time, as market researchers have honed their polling skills and revealed that human interest stories have "universal appeal," transcending age, class, and gender.[134] In the wake of these findings, even the *New York Times* has increasingly succumbed, not just to trivializing important subjects, but to slighting them. Its 1976 format change reduced coverage of local and national news by 11 and 30 percent, while the number of society and women's pages nearly doubled.[135] At the same time, half of all newspapers of over 100,000 readers and 42 percent of those with 50,000 to 100,000 added lifestyle sections in a single two-year period, 1977–1979.[136]

Finally, in the heat of conglomerization, came the transition from newspaper to "McPaper"—journalism as fast food. This time, the entrepreneur who showed the way was the Gannett Corporation's Allen Neuharth. His *USA Today* quickly grabbed the nation's second largest circulation with its mix of brightly colored graphics, skimpy articles, and expanded sports, weather, and gossip sections.

The industry could hardly wait to follow. Whipped up by newspaper conventions with such themes as, "Keys to Success: Strategies for Newspaper Marketing in the 90s," newspapers added sections on fitness, child-rearing, food, health, pop music, computers, the local nightclub scene, making money, houses, hobbies, pets, shopping malls, and on and on.

This necessitated abolishing some "traditional beats—City Hall, for example." [137]

Walter Lippmann, who defined news as information the citizen could use to take political action, would have trouble finding it in today's newspapers.

News History as Cultural Democracy

This history of the news can be viewed as cultural democracy in action—a series of commercial innovations which, when successful, were copied. The market made the people "free to choose," as Friedman says. And their choices gradually chipped and shaped what we now know as the news out of the marble.

But are we really so shallow as that? Did we really choose a news that is superficial and uncritical? Like lab rats overdoing it on the pleasure button, are we capable, as Neil Postman says, of "amusing ourselves to death"? Part of the answer, probably, is yes.

However, another part, to be explored in the next section, is that elites "helped" the people choose commercialized news by making it, in a sense, the only choice. That is the cultural hegemony answer.

News History as Cultural Hegemony

Is the news what it is because the people wanted it that way, "voted" for it with their quarters at the newsstand? The cultural hegemony theorists have answered no, that Americans were not entirely "free to choose." Let's begin the analysis with an obvious point: If as Will Rogers says, freedom of the press belongs to the fella who owns one, who can afford to own one?

Even by the latter nineteenth century, rapid changes in printing technology were making the news business an expensive one to get into. By the 1920s, city newspapers were selling in the $6–18 million range. By 1945, an analyst noted that "even small-newspaper publishing [was] big business . . . [and] no longer a trade one takes up lightly even if he has substantial cash—or takes up at all if he doesn't." [138]

Since then, as we saw earlier, more and more centralized, conglomerate ownership of the media has given new meaning to the term "big business." So the answer to the question, "Who owns the news" has long been "wealthy people," and lately "big corporations." Not the sort likely to be interested in news that might threaten the system that made them wealthy and big. As I said, an obvious point.

The Rise and Fall of the Radical Press

When leftists did clear that first hurdle and did manage to publish, they found others in their path. By this time, it may come as a surprise to find that there once was a leftist press, and what's more, that it flourished. For example, before 1920, the Socialist Party in this country had "a widespread and vital press" in addition to its "mass support at the polls" and "large following in the trade union movement." [139] J. A. Wayland's socialist *Appeal to Reason* had, in 1902, the fourth largest audience of all weekly newspapers in the country, with 200,000 readers.[140] By 1912, its circulation had more than tripled to 750,000.

Even as late as the 1940s, there remained newspapers sprinkled across the country farther to the left than any major daily is today.[141]

Later, with the resurgence of counterculture in the 1960s, an anti-establishment underground press emerged. Estimates of its readership ranged from 10–20 million.

What became of all these forms of counter-hegemonic news? In striking at these antagonists, elites' ways were Hydra-headed. Some of their tactics were not clever, or subtle, just effective. For example, there was good old-fashioned force. Sometimes the force was legal. "Within five months after [World War I] had been declared, every leading Socialist publication had been suspended form the mails at least once . . . by Postmaster General Albert Beuleson, who used his power under the Espionage Act . . . to destroy political opposition to government policies." Sometimes, it was not so legal. "Socialist papers in dozens of small towns and cities faced the wrath of vigilance committees organized by local chambers of commerce and boards of trade. In Seattle, for example, the *Daily Call* printing plant was smashed by a mob . . . and a few months thereafter the paper ceased publishing." [142]

During the 60s, it was the underground press that came under this fire. "The Washington *Free Press* had been burglarized—by army intelligence, it was later learned. *Nola Express*, the New Orleans paper, was under extensive FBI surveillance. So was *Rat* in New York. During 1969 and 1970, the editor of Miami's *Daily Planet* would be arrested twenty-nine times. He'd win twenty-eight acquittals, but need $93,000 in bond." [143]

A delegate to a Revolutionary Media Conference has given us a sense of what these close encounters of the coercive kind must have felt like:

> At the conference, it was hard to sort out reality from paranoia—until it came charging over the hill. Even as underground-press delegates discussed the impending trial of eight activists indicted for conspiring with intent to riot during the 1968 Democratic convention, squads of shotgun-toting, bulletproof-vested Washtenaw County deputies and Ann Arbor police surrounded the clearing. . . .
>
> "We better sing 'We Shall Overcome' or stand up," Abbie Hoffman said. Police safeties clicked. Trigger fingers trembled. As the women present were lined up and searched, a Rat writer saw "visions of the St. Valentine's Day Massacre." Doors were kicked in, papers taken—and then the police left. "Like a cold-water reality shower," the Rat post-mortem read, "everyone realized how vulnerable we are." [144]

A little less obvious, but no less effective, was the use of money to force the leftist press out of business. Early in the game, the Associated Press secured a near monopoly over the telegraph wires—the new *sine qua non* of news from afar. The AP did it by securing "favorable rates" from Western Union, and denying its own services to any newspaper that contracted with another wire service. As we know from our earlier discussion of the Associated Press, this monopoly meant that the news from afar was mainstream news, "facile, sensational short . . . reports which seldom if ever questioned basic social assumptions." [145]

Another near-monopoly was held by the American News Company, which was in the business of distributing periodicals to newsstands. By 1872, the company owned most of the nation's newsstands, and used its control to "restrict the . . . circulation of . . . radical journals." [146]

More recently, the California state attorney general lodged a $10 million suit against Art Kunkin, publisher of the underground *LA Free Press* for "obstruction of justice." Under the headline, "Narcotics Agents Listed: There Should Be No Secret Police,"

Kunkin had published the names and addresses of eighty California State Bureau of Narcotics agents. Rather than fight for a pro-
hibitively expensive victory, Kunkin settled the case for $10,000.
But afterward, afraid of lawsuits, no Los Angeles printer would let
Kunkin's paper roll off its presses. Not long afterward Kunkin
would lose the *Free Press.* [147]

The fears of those printers were not mere superstition, as the
tale of William Schanen would tell. Schanen was an ordinary,
middle-aged, midwestern small-town newspaperman and print
shop owner, except his was the only print shop "between Iowa City
and Kalamazoo willing to handle underground papers." As he told
Life magazine, "I don't agree with a lot of it, but what are we supposed to do, get rid of everything we don't agree with?" [148]

That innocuous question seemed noxious to local notables in
Schanen's hometown, Port Washington, Wisconsin, who began a
boycott of the three papers he published locally. Eventually, he
would lose two of them. "But a line under the logo of [Schanen's
award winning] *Ozaukee Press* declared it 'the paper that refuses
to die.' It didn't, but Schanen did, of a heart attack, two years after
the boycott began. [149]

But perhaps the most subtle weapon used against the leftist
press was also the most effective. This weapon was the subsidy
that advertising gave the mainstream commercial press. It was a
subsidy not often offered the radical press, and sometimes not accepted when it was offered.

Between 1880 and 1900, advertising went from 40 percent of
newspaper revenues to 55 percent. But from the radical press,
"major advertisers stayed away." Without them, "a radical publisher could have only poverty. . . . Investment in new equipment
would be next to impossible. . . . The difference between modern
and out of date equipment (and . . . the technology of printing was
changing very quickly then) could mean needing five thousand
more subscribers in order to break even." [150] No wonder that radical papers by the hundreds faded like May blossoms.

Commercialism Conquers the News

This brings us to another puzzle: Why was advertising normally
the only subsidy available? In Europe, the norm has often been a
news subsidized by political parties, or by government. Who decreed that it would not be so here?

The failure of a socialist party press has to do, of course, with
the failure of a socialist party in this country. That history is be-

yond the scope of this chapter. But elsewhere, I have made an argument analogous to this section's: For the radical party, as for the radical press, it was not a simple matter of being outsold by the mainstream competition. The left was also out-muscled by capitalists controlling campaign finance, the legal structure of elections, and, among other things, the press.[151]

Which brings us to our last question. Who decreed that the news would be privately owned and commercially sponsored, not publicly owned?*[152]

At one time in our history the previous question was not a strange one. At that time, the commercial media were not so widely viewed as the "American way." In fact, in the early days of radio, there was nearly complete agreement that broadcasting should *not* be a predominantly commercial medium. The conservative Republican President and his Secretary of Commerce, Herbert Hoover, felt that way. Even the National Association of Broadcasters felt that way.[153] At least in theory.

Then reality set in. And as usual, reality trumped theory. It all began in 1927, when Congress established the Federal Radio Commission to regulate the airwaves "in the public interest." Its first job was to allocate limited airwave space among what were already too many (732) existing stations. It was clear that when the music stopped, some stations would be without a chair and out of the game. Which would it be? The existing stations ran the gamut. Sponsored in different ways, their variety seemed exactly the "wide diversity of antagonistic sources" that the public interest required. Less than 100 of them were network-affiliated and most of the independent stations did not sell commercial time, but were sponsored by educational institutions, churches, newspapers, labor unions, and so on. One might suppose that in allocating frequencies, the FRC would have tried to maintain this diversity.

But one would be wrong. As the FRC began its deliberations, commercial broadcasters began a massive campaign, lobbying congressmen to lobby the FRC commissioners. It worked.

When the music stopped, educational radio was a prominent loser. The only such stations given space were handed part-time assignments, often during the daytime, a useless bloc for adult education. Within two years, 33 of them had given up the ghost.

---

*Of course, we do have "public" television and radio. But compared to the efforts made by most governments, ours is an infinitesimal level of public broadcasting. And even these outlets are compromised by their heavy reliance on corporate funding.

NEWSBREAK

Owners, Sponsors, Sources, and Journalists: Profiles in Courage and Cowardice

McCarthy. Now, it is a synonym for demagogue. Red Scare. Witch hunt. But back then . . .

In February 1950, as a freshman senator, he blazed into the national headlines waving a list of ''205 card carrying communists'' he said had ''infiltrated'' the State Department. Aides later bragged that there were in fact no such names on that sheet of paper. But now, the anti-Communist purge which had pre-dated McCarthy began anew. Almost over night McCarthy's public following was huge and ravenous. With that wind at their backs, McCarthy's personal minions were everywhere, circulating ''dog-eared lists'' of suspected ''undesirables'' throughout the bureaucracy. And many were purged—for such subversive activities as opposing nuclear weapons testing, or the Spanish dictator, Franco, or working for ''Negro rights.'' [155] When the carnage was over, this strange fact lingered: never did McCarthy produce the name of a single ''card carrying Communist'' in any government agency.

Where was the watchdog of the people? ''McCarthy was a fascinating example of the weaknesses of traditional journalistic objectivity. He was a senator and thus a great public figure, and reporters could write down what he said, and as long as they spelled his name correctly, they were objective.'' What's more there were precious few ''authoritative sources'' with the courage to contradict McCarthy. For a while, the only ''expert'' on McCarthy's charges was McCarthy. And when, as here, ''the norm of society is corrupted, then objective journalism is corrupted too, for it must not challenge the norm.''

Murrow. The prince of CBS News. The conscience of broadcast journalism. His powerful, heroic broadcasts from London had made him ''perhaps the most admired nonpolitical figure in America.''

Back home, in the early 50s, his *See It Now* series became one of journalism's finest hours—probing, courageous, daring to be controversial. ''Appalled in later years by growing pressure to balance out viewpoints for the sake of an artificial fairness, (he) compared this with balancing the views of Jesus Christ with those of Judas Iscariot.'' As McCarthy raged on, those who knew Murrow began to wonder when the showdown would come.

But even Murrow, respected as he was, had to be wary. CBS was certainly not immune to this plague. It had visited Murrow's own compatriot from the War days, Bill Shirer, himself a star correspondent. Shirer's sponsor and its advertising agent, J. Walter Thompson, ''did not like his politics.'' He was not a militant enough cold warrior. And so eventually, Bill Paley, the chairman of the board of the network told him, ''Your usefulness to CBS is over.''

And so it was not until four years after the reign of terror began that viewers of *See It Now* would see Joseph McCarthy. From this safe distance of forty years, it is amazing that the show provoked a furor at all. Murrow's strategy was not to attack McCarthy, but to put McCarthy on the air—to let McCarthy show the nation what McCarthy was. And Murrow's wrap-up was, given the enormity of his target, temperate, even to a fault.

Nonetheless, the show did make waves. Even before it aired, there was an early warning signal. Network executives refused to advertise the program, despite its obvious momentousness, so Murrow and his producer, Fred Friendly, paid for their own ad. But CBS refused to allow them even to use the network's logo, the CBS eye, in the ad.

For a few days after the show, all was quiet. Too quiet. ''The reason, of course, was that reactions to the show were not yet in and no television executive was about to commit himself before he found out which way the wind was blowing.''

Then, after a few days, Friendly was summoned to the office of Frank Stanton, president of CBS, Bill Paley's right-hand man. It was Stanton who was already engineering a way of measuring audience size that become the ratings system. So it is perhaps predictable that he did not discuss ''the quality of the show, whether it had been bad or good, or needed to be done.''

Instead, he showed Friendly a poll he had commissioned. ''It showed that more people believed in McCarthy than Murrow . . . and that 33 percent . . . felt Murrow was a Communist or a Communist sympathizer.'' Stanton said, cryptically, if rather too dramatically, ''A lot of people think you may have cost us the network.'' Journalist David Halberstam calls the interchange ''an extraordinary insight into the way broadcasting management regarded journalism—not whether it was the right show done in the right way, . . . but what the vote was.''

And so, as these pressures continued, from the audience, from Washington, from the sponsors, from the businessmen on the CBS board, "CBS moved to emasculate Ed Murrow. First to limit the number of *See It Now* shows. Then to control the hour they were shown. Then to change the name. Then to take the show away completely."

As that evening fell on Murrow, he did not go gently into it. By 1958, long after the demise of "See It Now," he hung on at CBS, though he would not be there much longer. Indeed, he did not have long to live. But in 1958, he was still there. In October of that year, he gave a speech to a gathering of news producers and directors. A prophet in his own country, without honor. Or at least without everything but that.

In the tranquillity that was 1958, he must have seemed out of tune. Even by then, his face was drawn and circled by darkness. And in a year before most Americans had even heard of Vietnam, or Watts, or Kent State, he said this:

> And if there are any historians . . . a hundred years from now and there should be preserved the kinescopes of one week for all three networks, they will find recorded, in black and white or color, evidence of decadence, escapism and insulation from the realities of the world in which we live. . . . If we go on as we are then history will take its revenge and retribution will (catch) up with us.

Not long after that, unencouraged to stay, Murrow would leave CBS.

"Up there on the scaffold," a poet said of political martyrs, "you stand . . . and stare, farther than your executioners can see." [156] By 1965, the conscience of broadcast journalism was dead.

Source: David Halberstam, *The Powers That Be,* (New York: Alfred A. Knopf, 1979).

A few years later, political scientist Pendleton Herring summarized the process: "The point seems clear that the Federal Radio Commission has interpreted the concept of public interest so as to favor in actual practice one particular group . . . the commercial broadcasters. [154]

Later, as television developed, the Federal Radio Commission would become the Federal Communications Commission, with a mandate to regulate both media "in the public interest." But the same pressures would be at work. What's more, by that time, the hegemony of commercial broadcasting would be normalized. It would seem "the American way."

Epilogue

Pick up a paper. Turn on the news. What does it say?

> *Fire claimed the life of a west-side woman today . . . on charges of murdering her infant son . . . as the number of Americans living in poverty rose for the third consecutive month. An exuberant President Clinton . . . was submachine-gunned to death during a traffic dispute as his family watched . . . while Dole, who has often joked with reporters about the rivalry in recent weeks . . . was listed in critical condition at St. Luke's hospital in Birmingham . . . where thousands of demonstrators roamed the streets, clashing with riot police, smashing store windows and looting shops . . . of the communist-backed rebel forces . . . many of whom appear to have suffered assaults at the hands of . . . a race too close to call. Reliable sources indicate that despite the nationwide manhunt for . . . a "monstrous act of vicious cowardice, . . ." there was no apparent motive.*

With coffee and toast, we take them in, the banalities of horror. They do not bore us. They do not offend us. They do not enlighten us. And we are here, "as on a darkling plain," surrounded by the incandescent, inconstant light of the news, flashing now upon a murder, now upon a war, now upon a hackneyed explanation, illuminating nothing. Sometimes what we seem to see for a split second is terrifying. Often it is a show, fun to watch, like fireworks. Usually it is reassuring in its sameness. Rarely does it light the depth of our ignorance. News flashes. Signal flares for an army of the night.

References

1. Lincoln Steffens, *The Shame of the Cities,* (New York: Hill and Wang, 1957): 4.

2. Ben H. Bagdikian, *The Media Monopoly*, 2d ed. (Boston: Beacon, 1987): 20.
3. Ibid.: 19–26; Doris J. Graber, *Mass Media and American Politics*, 3d. ed. (Washington, D.C.: Congressional Quarterly Press, 1989): 41–7; Edward S. Herman and Noam Chomsky, *Manufacturing Consent*, (New York: Pantheon, 1988): 3–14; Richard Stevenson, "Not Just Another Charlie Bludhorn," *New York Times*, (June 11, 1989): C1, 9.
4. David S. Broder, *Behind the Front Page*, (New York: Simon and Schuster, 1987).
5. Ben H. Bagdikian, *The Media Monopoly:* 7.
6. Edward S. Herman and Noam Chomsky, *Manufacturing Consent:* 10–11.
7. Ken Auletta, *Three Blind Mice*, (New York: Random House, 1991): 475.
8. Edward S. Herman and Noam Chomsky, *Manufacturing Consent:* 10.
9. David Halberstam, *The Powers That Be*, (New York: Alfred A. Knopf, 1979): 712–16.
10. Edward Jay Epstein, *News From Nowhere*, (New York: Vintage Books, 1973): 93–94.
11. Leo Bogart, *Press and Public: Who Reads What, When, Where, and Why in American Newspapers*, (Hillsdale, N.J.: Lawrence Earlbaum Associates, 1981): 46–7.
12. Lars Engwall. *Newspapers as Organizations*, (Westmead, England: Gower, 1981): 70.
13. Leon V. Sigal, *Reporters and Officials*, (Lexington, Mass.: D.C. Heath, 1973): 10,72; Edward Jay Epstein, *News From Nowhere:* 94–97.
14. Ben H. Bagdikian, *The Media Monopoly:* 9.
15. Ibid.: 7.
16. James Kelly, "Days of Turbulence, Days of Change," *Time*, (March 7, 1987): 62–64; Doris J. Graber, *Mass Media and American Politics*, 3d ed.: 52.
17. Ken Auletta, *Three Blind Mice:* 562.
18. Lance W. Bennett, *Public Opinion in American Politics*, (New York: Harcourt, Brace, Jovanovich, 1980): 307; Doris J. Graber, *Mass Media and American Politics*, (Washington, D.C.: Congressional Quarterly Press, 1980): 62.
19. Lance W. Bennett, *News: The Politics of Illusion*, (New York: Longman, 1983): 72–3; Fred C. Shapiro, "Shrinking The News," *Columbia Journalism Review*, (November-December 1976): 23–7; Fergus M. Bordewich, "Supermarketing the News," *Columbia Journalism Review*, (September-October 1977): 23–36.
20. David L. Paletz and Robert M. Entman, *Media-Power-Politics*, (New York: The Free Press, 1981): 252; Doris J. Graber, *Mass Media and American Politics:* 79.
21. Cited in David Halberstam, *The Powers That Be:* 139.
22. Calvin F. Exoo, "Journalists' Perspectives on the Critique of Political Journalism," (paper presented at the Annual meeting of the Northeast Political Science Association, 1985).
23. Edward Jay Epstein, *News From Nowhere:* 141–43.
24. Robert Semple, "The Necessity of Conventional Journalism: A Blend of the Old and the New," *Liberating the Media*, edited by Charles C. Flippen, (Washington, D.C.: Acropolis Books, 1974): 89; Richard L. Rubin, *Press, Party, and Presidency*, (New York: W. W. Norton, 1981): 63.
25. Ken Auletta, *Three Blind Mice:* 86.
26. Quoted in Edward Jay Epstein, *News From Nowhere:* 56.
27. Ibid.: 57.
28. Ibid.: 64.
29. Doris J. Graber, *Mass Media and American Politics*, 3d ed.: 51; Edward S. Herman and Noam Chomsky, *Manufacturing Consent:* 13.
30. Lance W. Bennett, *News: The Politics of Illusion:* 319.

31. David Halberstam, *The Powers That Be:* 661.
32. Lance Bennett, *Public Opinion in American Politics:* 318–19.
33. Pete Hamill, "Fear and Favor at the *New York Times*," *The Village Voice,* (vol. 30, 1985): 20.
34. Herbert J. Gans, *Deciding What's News,* (New York: Pantheon Books, 1979): 252.
35. Ibid.: 251.
36. John R. MacArthur, *Second Front,* (New York: Hill and Wang, 1992): 169.
37. Ibid.: 171.
38. *Notable Quotables,* (Alexandria, Va.: Media Research Center, February 18, 1991).
39. Jon G. Udell, *The Economics of the American Newspaper,* (New York: Hastings House, 1978): 26, 69; Paul Hoch, *The Newspaper Game,* (London: Calder and Bayars, 1974): 169.
40. John L. Hulteng, *The News Media,* (Englewood Cliffs, N.J.: Prentice-Hall, 1979): 9.
41. Paul Hoch, *The Newspaper Game:* 164.
42. Herbert J. Gans, *Deciding What's News*: 257.
43. Paul Hoch, *The Newspaper Game*: 162.
44. Lance W. Bennett, *Public Opinion in American Politics:* 316.
45. Martin A. Lee and Norman Solomon, "The Buck Comes First," *Dissent,* (Fall 1990): 525.
46. See Peter Bachrach and Morton S. Baratz, *Power and Poverty,* (New York: Oxford University Press, 1970) for an extended discussion of nondecisions; see Paul Hoch, *The Newspaper Game:* 168, for other examples of nondecisions by the news media.
47. Ben H. Bagdikian, *The Media Monopoly:* 160.
48. Edward S. Herman and Noam Chomsky, *Manufacturing Consent:* 17.
49. See Paul Hoch, *The Newspaper Game:* 145, for examples.
50. Herbert J. Gans, *Deciding What's News:* 84; Frank Wolf, *Television Programming for News and Public Affairs,* (New York: Praeger, 1972); Calvin F. Exoo, "Journalists' Perspectives on the Critique of Political Journalism."
51. Quoted in David L. Paletz and Robert M. Entman, *Media-Power-Politics:* 15.
52. Warren Breed, "Social Control in the Newsroom: A Functional Analysis," *Social Forces,* (vol. 33, 1955): 326–35; Lance W. Bennett, *Public Opinion in American Politics:* 238; Gaye Tuchman, "Objectivity as Strategic Ritual: An Examination of Newsmen's Notions of Objectivity," *American Journal of Sociology,* (vol. 77, 1972): 662.
53. Turner Catledge, *My Life and The Times,* (New York: Harper and Row, 1971): 189.
54. Ibid.: 189–90.
55. Todd Gitlin, *The Whole World Is Watching,* (Berkeley: University of California Press, 1980): 39.
56. Ben H. Bagdikian, *The Media Monopoly,* 2d ed.: 6.
57. Ibid.
58. Todd Gitlin, *The Whole World Is Watching:* 274–75.
59. Ben H. Bagdikian, *The Media Monopoly,* 2d ed.: 340; Thomas B. Edsall, *The New Politics of Inequality,* (New York: W. W. Norton, 1984).
60. Ben H. Bagdikian, *The Media Monopoly:* 30.
61. Martin A. Lee and Norman Solomon, *Unreliable Sources:* 78.
62. Leon V. Sigal, *Reporters and Officials:* 188.
63. Jon G. Udell, *The Economics of the American Newspaper,* (New York: Hastings House, 1978): 86.
64. Leon V. Sigal, *Reporters and Officials:* 10–11.

65. Calvin F. Exoo, "Journalists' Perspectives on the Critique of Political Journalism": 11; Leon V. Sigal, *Reporters and Officials:* 10–11.
66. Edward Jay Epstein, *News From Nowhere:* 146.
67. Ken Auletta, *Three Blind Mice:* 344–47.
68. Edward Jay Epstein, *News From Nowhere:* 140.
69. Leon V. Sigal, *Reporters and Officials:* 11.
70. Ken Auletta, *Three Blind Mice:* 130.
71. Quoted in Michael Schudson, *Discovering the News,* (New York: Basic Books, 1978): 14.
72. Ibid.: 138.
73. Ibid.: 144.
74. Lance W. Bennett, *News: The Politics of Illusion:* 41.
75. Leon V. Sigal, *Reporters and Officials:* 54.
76. Edward S. Herman and Noam Chomsky, *Manufacturing Consent:* 20.
77. Leon V. Sigal, *Reporters and Officials:* 121.
78. Daniel Boorstin, *The Image: A Guide to Pseudo-Events In America,* (New York: Atheneum, 1961).
79. Harvey Molotch and Marilyn Lester, "Accidents, Scandals, and Routines: Resources for Insurgent Methodology," *The TV Establishment,* edited by Gaye Tuchman, (Englewood Cliffs, N.J.: Prentice-Hall, 1974).
80. Gaye Tuchman, *Making News,* (New York: The Free Press, 1978): 87.
81. Leon V. Sigal, *Reporters and Officials:* 55.
82. Martin Schram, *The Great American Video Game,* (New York: William Morrow, 1987): 55–6.
83. Ibid.: 44.
84. Ibid.: 24–26.
85. Thomas B. Edsall, *The New Politics of Inequality:* 117–20.
86. Peter Steinfels, *The Neoconservatives,* (New York: Simon and Schuster, 1979): 13.
87. Edward S. Herman and Noam Chomsky, *Manufacturing Consent:* 24.
88. David Lieberman, "Fake News," *TV Guide,* (February 22, 1992): 16, 26.
89. Ronald Berkman and Laura W. Kitch, *Politics in the Media Age,* (New York: McGraw-Hill, 1986): 283–90.
90. Edward S. Herman and Noam Chomsky, *Manufacturing Consent:* 25.
91. Jane O. Brown, Carl R. Bybee, Stanley T. Wearden, and Dulcie M. Stroughn, "Invisible Power: Newspaper News Sources and the Limits of Diversity," *Journalism Quarterly,* (vol. 63, 1987): 53–54.
92. Ruth C. Flegel and Steven H. Chafee, "Influences of Editors, Readers, and Personal Opinions on Reporters": 645–51.
93. Herbert J. Gans, *Deciding What's News:* 84, 252.
94. Michael Schudson, *Discovering the News:* 21.
95. Ibid.: chapter 4.
96. Charles C. Flippen, ed., *Liberating the Media,* (Washington, D.C.: Acropolis Books, 1974): Chapter 1.
97. Lester Markel, "Objective Journalism," *Liberating the Media,* edited by Charles C. Flippen, (Washington, D.C.: Acropolis Books, 1974).
98. John W. C. Johnstone, Edward Slawski, and William W. Bowman, *The News People,* (Urbana, Ill.: University of Illinois Press, 1976): Chapter 1.
99. Gaye Tuchman, "Objectivity as Strategic Ritual": 660; Herbert J. Gans, *Deciding What's News:* 275–6.
100. Gaye Tuchman, "Objectivity as Strategic Ritual": 665–72.
101. Ibid.: 674–75.

102. Leon V. Sigal, *Reporters and Officials:* 40–41.
103. Timothy Crouse, *The Boys on the Bus,* (New York: Random House, 1973).
104. Leo Bogart, *Press and Public:* 176.
105. Paul Hertsgaard, *On Bended Knee,* (New York: Schocken, 1989): 79.
106. Calvin F. Exoo, "Journalists' Perspectives on the Critique of Political Journalism": 9–10.
107. Lance Bennett, *News*: 86.
108. John R. MacArthur, *Second Front: Censorship and Propaganda in the Gulf War,* (New York: Hill and Wang, 1992).
109. Edward S. Herman and Noam Chomsky, *Manufacturing Consent*: 27; for a description of how AIM helped force the Central America reporter referred to earlier from the *Times,* see Louis Wolf, "Accuracy in Media Reunites News and History," *Covert Action Information Bulletin,* (Spring 1984): 26–29.
110. Herbert J. Gans, "Are U.S. Journalists Dangerously Liberal?" *Columbia Journalism Review,* (November-December 1985): 29–33; Edward S. Herman and Noam Chomsky, *Manufacturing Consent:* 321–330.
111. Martin Schram, *The Great American Video Game,* (New York: William Morrow, 1987): 84–87; Doris J. Graber, *Mass Media and American Politics,* 3d ed.
112. Walter Schneir and Miriam Schneir, "Beyond Westmoreland: The Right's Attack on the Press," *Nation,* (March 30, 1985): 361–7.
113. Alexander Stille, "Libel Law Takes on a New Look," *National Law Journal,* (October 24, 1988): 32.
114. Ibid.
115. Quoted in P. Stoler, *The War Against the Press* (1986): 139.
116. Lois Forer, *A Chilling Effect* (1986): 367.
117. Ibid.: 31.
118. Lance W. Bennett, *News:* 78–81.
119. Michael Lipton, "Television Was Too Influential," *TV Guide,* (December 1, 1988): A2.
120. Paul S. Underwood, "Europe and the Middle East," *Global Journalism,* edited by John C. Merrill, (New York: Longman, 1983).
121. Manny Paraschos, "Europe," *Global Journalism,* 2d ed., edited by John C. Merrill, (New York: Longman, 1991): 95.
122. Richard L. Rubin, *Press, Party, and Presidency:* Chapter 1.
123. Ibid.: 82.
124. *New York Transcript,* quoted in Michael Schudson, *Discovering the News:* 23.
125. Ibid.: 50–57.
126. Ibid.: 18.
127. Lance W. Bennett, *News:* 79.
128. Paul Hoch, *The Newspaper Game:* 195; James Curran, Angus Douglas, and Gary Whannel, "The Political Economy of the Human Interest Story," *Newspapers and Democracy,* edited by Anthony Smith (Cambridge, Mass.: MIT Press, 1980): 293.
129. Michael Schudson, *Discovering the News:* 106–20.
130. James Curran, et al., "The Political Economy of the Human Interest Story."
131. Leon V. Sigal, *Reporters and Officials*: 10.
132. e.g., John W. C. Johnstone, et al., *The News People:* 88.
133. Richard L. Rubin, *Press, Party, and Presidency:* 114.
134. James Curran, et al., "The Political Economy of the Human Interest Story": 294.
135. Fred C. Shapiro, "The Shrinking News": 23–27.

136. Leo Bogart, *Press and Public:* 150–51.
137. William B. Blankenburg, "Unbundling the Modern Newspaper," *The Future of News,* edited by Philip Look, Douglas Gomery, and Lawrence W. Lichty, (Baltimore: Johns Hopkins University Press, 1992): 116.
138. Quoted in Edward S. Herman and Noam Chomsky, *Manufacturing Consent:* 335.
139. James Weinstein, *The Decline of Socialism in America, 1912–1925,* (London: Monthly Review Press, 1967): ix.
140. Elliot Shore, *Talkin' Socialism,* (Lawrence: University of Kansas Press, 1988): 106.
141. Peter Dreier, "The Corporate Complaint Against the Media," *American Media and Mass Culture,* edited by Donald Lazere, (Berkeley: University of California Press, 1987): 77.
142. James Weinstein, *The Decline of Socialism in America, 1912–1925:* 90–91.
143. Abe Peck, *Uncovering the Sixties,* (New York: Pantheon, 1985): 185.
144. Ibid.
145. Elliot Shore, *Talkin' Socialism:* 95–6.
146. Ibid., 96.
147. Abe Peck, *Uncovering the Sixties:* 190–91.
148. Ibid.: 191.
149. Ibid.
150. Elliot Shore, *Talkin' Socialism:* 99–102.
151. Calvin F. Exoo, "The Broken Promise of Democracy," *Democracy Upside Down,* edited by Calvin F. Exoo, (New York: Praeger, 1987): Chapter 2.
152. Martin A. Lee and Norman Solomon, "The Buck Comes First": 525–27.
153. Edward S. Herman and Noam Chomsky, *Manufacturing Consent:* 340.
154. Quoted in Erik Barnouw, *A Tower of Babel,* (New York: Oxford University Press, 1966): 219.
155. Erik Barnouw, *The Image Empire,* (New York: Oxford University Press, 1970): 9.
156. Peter Weiss, *Marat/Sade,* (New York: Atheneum, 1968): 22–3.

Thelma and Louise might just have been what many films only claim to be: the most talked-about movie of the year. But was it a feminist film?

A Celluloid Syringe: The Politics and Un-Politics of Hollywood Film

INTRODUCTION ☆ ☆ ☆ ☆ ☆ ☆ ☆ ☆ ☆ ☆ ☆ ☆ ☆ ☆ ☆

This chapter will argue that the Hollywood film industry can be seen as another hegemonic "idea factory," churning out lessons that help upper-class Americans maintain their position. The movies take on this job early in their history, as an antiforeign, antiradical "Americanization" movement helps forge the thinking of the Jewish immigrants who "invented" Hollywood.

The movies' hegemonic role is further supported by the economics of the business. This industry, like the other mass media, has been defined as a commercial enterprise. Now that the industry is owned by conglomerate corporations, it is more purely a commercial enterprise than ever. This in turn dictates that movies cannot be (1) novel, (2) intellectually challenging, or (3) politically objectionable. Instead, the movies must offer (1) escape, (2) reaffirmation of the values that already dominate our thinking, and (3) inclusiveness—a little something for everyone of every persuasion in every film.

Although this formula is the rule in Hollywood, there are, of course, exceptions. Some films aspire to be more. We'll talk about these movies under two headings. First, there are the "quality" films made within the studio system. As their name implies, they can be very good indeed. But as we'll see, they have their political limits. Usually those limits are well within the bounds of what is safe for the system. Then there are the radical films made outside the studio system. Once again, it is economics that dictates their fate: they are few, far between, and rarely seen.

Next we'll look at the style of Hollywood movies—the way they use editing, framing, lighting, camera angles, and so on to tell their tales. We'll see how this "invisible style" invented by Hollywood makes the movies' political argument invisible too—makes it, in other words, unarguable.

Finally, we'll go to the intersection of Hollywood and Washington—where government meets the movies. There we'll see that at crucial moments in the movies' history, the power of the government itself has been invoked to keep this "idea factory" running smoothly—to make sure that a hegemonic product continues to roll off its assembly lines.

"*Ars Gratia Artis*," roars the lion logo of MGM: "Art for Art's Sake." But behind the fine-sounding slogan lies the reality of Hollywood, which is a bit different. To be honest, the logo might read "*Ars Gratia Pecuniae*"—art for money's sake. For in film, as in other media, capitalism has won out. In managing to define film in its own image—as a commercial enterprise—capitalism has made the process and product of Hollywood another instance of cultural hegemony, working in several ways to sustain a status quo that belongs to capitalists.

This is most clear when the movies mount a frontal assault on behalf of capitalist individualism, and that happens often enough. But more often, this medium's tactics are not direct, but diversionary, deflecting our attention away from social and political questions, starving our "sociological imaginations." [1] And of course, it works. A starved imagination is about as unlikely to cause trouble for the status quo as a loyal one.

In this mass medium as in the others, the way hegemony works is complicated. There is no crude conspiracy on the part of movie makers. Once again, hegemony is more complete than that.

It has become so complete that it is now woven into the woof and warp—the imperatives, the norms, and routines—of the movie business.

A Brief History of the Movies

Which is to say, it was not always so. Let us begin with a look at American cinema in its infancy, when it was not at all clear what it might grow up to be. As we shall see, the hand of hegemony was on the cradle early, guiding and shaping the character of the emerging art form.

The low-budget potboilers churned out by a host of independent producers in the early days of film appealed mainly to working class Americans, who, for a nickel, "could be enveloped in a new world, a magical universe of madness and motion."[2] *Survey* magazine, the journal of social work, reported that "in the tenement districts the motion picture has well-nigh driven other forms of entertainment from the field."[3] These silent films, with their accessible mimed interpretations of American life, were especially important to immigrants, who found in them a Rosetta stone to this new culture. In fact, many of the early films were about working-class immigrant life. Some even rendered that life as a challenge to middle-class ideology. In one, scenes of courthouse injustices toward the poor foreshadow the unmasking of blind Lady Justice to reveal an eye fixed on the gold tossed into her scales. In another, a baby grows sick from the impure milk sold in the slums and dies, after his parents fail to raise money from the heartless rich to buy the high-priced pasteurized milk. The comedies of Chaplin and Sennett often feature underdog heroes who prick the pompousness and hypocrisy of middle-class life.[4]

But by the early 1920s, such challenges had begun a fade to black. In that decade, the "Big Five" studios consolidated their oligopoly over the film business, and restricted the movie screen to images of an idealized America, one where "every old glorifying bromide about the country" was affirmed and reaffirmed.[5] How that came about is a crucial chapter in the story of American cultural hegemony.

A recent, acclaimed history of the Jewish immigrants who founded the "Big Five" studios and "invented Hollywood" argues that, "above all things, they wanted to be regarded as Americans, not Jews." [6] Given the America in which they found themselves, that is not hard to understand. For their America was not the great "melting pot" of our mythology, "where all the races of Europe . . . united to build" a new, eclectic culture, "the Republic of Man." [7] No, the new land was not a melting pot, it was a mold—a bed of Procrustes built by the upper-crust northern Europeans who preceded the Jews and other "ethnics" to this country, who held its power, who demanded that newcomers succumb to their mold, and who, in the end, had their way.

What we have called the dominant culture is really the culture of upper-class Anglo-Saxon Protestants, mainly those "Yankees" of New England descent whose "dominion dates from colonial times and whose cultural domination in the U.S. has never been seriously threatened." [8] It was their doctrine of the calling,[9] their Lockian liberalism, their experience on the frontier,[10] and, later, their dominance over the economy that ran as tributaries to the one great river of American social thought: capitalist individualism.

Between 1895 and 1910, a tidal wave of "new" immigration washed over America. Unlike the earlier waves, these immigrants came mainly from southern and eastern Europe. And so, to the Yankee establishment, they were different. They were "foreign." They were suspect. Their religion, their diet, their dress were different.

Their politics was different, too. And this was of particular concern to brahmin WASPs. In the second decade of this century, when socialist party membership reached what was to be its zenith, over half that membership was to be found in the party's foreign-language federations.[11]

This emerging socialism could not be ignored by the elite it challenged so directly, and it was not. The counterattack came with World War I, when all the amorphous xenophobia that began with the new immigration came together in a crucible of fear and patriotic fervor. In the shadow of the war, business and government leaders began to proclaim that diversity was disloyalty. They began to build an unholy trinity of associations in the American mind: foreignness is radicalism is anti-Americanism.

In the presidential campaign of 1916, Theodore Roosevelt made "100-percent Americanism" a major issue in his campaign for the Republican nomination. "Anything less, including any ethnic tie, was 'moral treason.' " Woodrow Wilson went Roosevelt one better. His Democratic platform proclaimed "the indivisibility of the nation" to be "the supreme issue." It denounced alleged "conspiracies" in "the interests of foreign countries," and condemned ethnic associations as "subversive." [12] With the entry of the United

States into the war in 1917, followed by the departure from the war effort of the Soviets after the Revolution, anti-foreignism again resonated with an old companion theme—anti-radicalism. Such critics of the war as the Socialist Party and the Industrial Workers of the World (IWW) quickly found that just beyond the pale of a people whose tolerant talk had come too easily lay a violent intolerance. The backlash against radicals now known as the "Red Scare" focused on the new immigrants, assuming, as had the whole anti-radical tradition, that militant discontent must be a foreign import.[13] In July 1917, the Attorney General of the United States ordered the internment of all German aliens found to be IWW members. Two months later, his Justice Department officers invaded every IWW hall in the United States, seizing natives for trial and aliens of all nationalities for deportation. Also during this period, 23 state governments enacted criminal syndicalism laws under which "a vigorous program of prosecution for [radical] organizational membership or for opinion ensued; in a three-month period the state of Washington convicted eighty-six individuals of membership in the IWW."[14]

Businessmen seized the day in a massive advertising campaign, declaring radicalism and even unions guilty by association with "foreign subversion." Finally, in 1919, Attorney General A. Mitchell Palmer began his blitzkrieg of "Palmer Raids," rounding up thousands of members of the already beaten and balkanized communist parties, separating out the aliens for deportation hearings, often holding them for weeks in overcrowded, unsanitary conditions without preliminary hearings.[15] About a third of them were found guilty and deported, often leaving their families impoverished and ostracized. Their crime was membership in a party whose opinions were not free to be spoken in the land of the free.

While one hand of the American establishment crushed those immigrants who chose the "wrong" path, the other prodded and coaxed the rest to the right course—the way of "Americanization." The Americanization movement was a massive marshalling of the "means of intellectual production" on behalf of one unabashedly stated goal: "[the foreign-born] must be induced to give up the languages, customs and methods of life which they have brought with them across the ocean, and adopt instead the language, habits, and customs of this country . . . the standards and ways of American living."[16]

Participants in this movement included the federal government, most of the state governments, the U.S. Chamber of Commerce, thousands of school systems, thousands of employers, and more than 100 private organizations. Their molding pots included adult education courses in English, patriotism, and "the American Way of Life," the banning of parochial schools and of speaking foreign languages in the public schools, regulation of the home lives of immigrants by social workers, punitive tax and wage rates for aliens not working to become citizens, and surveillance of aliens to prevent strikes and other "disruptive" activities.[17]

The final solution of the Americanization movement came in 1924, with Congressional passage of the national origins formula. The law assigned to each country an immigration quota proportionate to its members among the U.S. population of 1920. The flood of southern and eastern Europeans was now a trickle. Those who had always come to reinvigorate and rebuild immigrant institutions and values came no more. Now it was only a matter of time before those institutions and values would be worn away by the relentless waves of hegemony.

It was in this harsh climate that a handful of immigrant Jews came together in a remote desert outpost of Los Angeles, determined to make themselves respectable Americans. Louis B. Mayer of MGM claimed the Fourth of July as his birthday, having "forgotten" the real date. His children complained of a "childhood dedicated to making the proper impression"—that of a model *American* family—one that would "give the lie to the anti-Semitic stereotype of the Eastern European Jew." [18] He imposed the same requirement on his extended family—his studio. Billy Wilder, then a director at MGM, recalls hearing screaming outside his office window, and looking out to see Mayer holding Mickey Rooney by the lapel. "He says, 'you're Andy Hardy! You're the United States! You're the Stars and Stripes! Behave Yourself! You're a symbol!' " [19]

Carl Laemmle, founder of Universal Pictures, often told his son that as he "walked about [in America], sizing things up, he kept saying to himself, 'I've *got* to be successful. I *must* be successful. I *will* be successful.' " [20]

Of all the realms in which the moguls strove to be in the mainstream, perhaps the most important was politics. "The Hollywood Jews would have done almost anything to disassociate themselves from the old canard that linked Jews to political radicalism." [21] And so Louis B. Mayer would become chairman of the very conservative California Republican Party. Nearly all the other moguls also stayed with the staunchly respectable GOP, even as most other Jewish-Americans aligned themselves with Franklin Roosevelt's New Deal Democracy. When Upton Sinclair ran a serious socialist candidacy for governor of California, the moguls marshalled the full force of their newsreel-making power against him. And finally, when a group of Hollywood writers and directors were accused of being Communists, the moguls cast the fatal stone at them.[22]

But of course, the moguls' most important showcase of respectability was not their families, or their partisan politics, or even their business success. Instead, it was their movies. In these, the moguls could mythologize America, hymn its way of life, and show, for all the world to see, their own patriotism.

Their haloed America included L. B. Mayer's small towns, places where "virtue, . . . the bulwark of family . . . the soundness of tradition . . . America itself" would win in the end.[23] They included the "grand patriotic spectacles" of Adolph Zukor's Paramount, "which treated American history with . . . textbook reverence." [24] They included lavish fantasies of fortune and fashion and the social mobility that placed it all within reach. And they included Warner Brothers' self-reliant men of two-fisted action, whose might made things right.

Each genre was, in its own way, a paean to an American Way not of the moguls' making, a peace offering to the very WASP establishment whose bigotry had made the moguls run. And so these movies—the ones that would define movie making for future generations of film makers—were themselves defined by the Procrustean specifications of the hegemonic class.

Pix as Biz: The Economics of Cinema

But of course, respect was not the only thing the moguls were out to earn. Indeed, the ur-principle of American movies has always been the extent to which they are defined as a commercial enterprise—not as art, not as politics—but as business.

It was true of the moguls' enterprise. It is even more true today, because in our time, movie making has undergone the transition described by Thorstein Veblen as the movement from "industry" to "business." [25] An "industry" is founded by people who have themselves practiced the craft and continue to be involved, even after they've become magnates, in every aspect of production. Jack Warner, for example, began his day scanning scripts, spent his afternoons in projection rooms watching all the unedited footage shot the day before at his studio, and his evenings at previews, sitting next to the film's editor, making changes. "The others, Cohn, Mayer, Zukor, followed similar routines." [26]

These men were interested in making money, to be sure, but as craftsmen, they believed the way to do that was by offering what they thought of as a quality product. Neal Gabler says that Louis B. Mayer, for example, "took his captaincy [of MGM] more as a mandate than an opportunity." "If there is one thing I insist upon," said Mayer, "it is quality."[27] But perhaps this is not surprising. After all, there is more at stake for the founder than profit. Yes, his money is on the line, but his *name* is on the product.

But after the industry proves its profitability, after this generation of founders has passed from the scene, the industry is "acquired" by a purer form of capitalism. By finance capital, as happened to the Hollywood studios in the 30s.[28] Or by conglomerate capital, as has happened to the studios in the 80s and 90s. Today, Columbia is a subsidiary of the SONY Corporation; Paramount Pictures is a child of Paramount Communications, Inc., which also owns Paramount television, Simon & Schuster/Prentice Hall, Madison Square Garden, the New York Knicks and Rangers, and an assortment of TV stations. Recently, Matsushita Electric Industrial Company, an empire of 87 companies in Japan and abroad, glanced down the food chain and gobbled up MCA Inc., itself a conglomerate which owns, among other things, Universal Pictures. In Fall of 1989, MGM/United Artists was acquired by the Quintex Group of Australia. Warner Bros. is now one of the many interests of Time/Warner Communications, Inc., and so on.

Now the "industry" has become a "business." Now its managers, often enough, have no background in the craft of movie production, but have apprenticed in law, other businesses, advertising, market research, or "personal representation."[29] "They are all corporate types," says Jerry Hellman (producer of *Midnight Cowboy*). "You could pick them up and have them run any other business."[30] Even once inside the studio, the surest way up the management ladder is not through the "creative" side of the business, but through the business end of the business. In one recent year, five of the seven major studio heads had been hired, not out of film production, but distribution.[31] "With very few exceptions," says writer-director Nicholas Meyer, "[these executives] know nothing about story-telling, they know nothing about film . . . they're not Jack Warner and Louis B. Mayer."[32]

Now, the passion of the studio head is not for product, but for profit. And indeed, not just any profits will do. Ours is an age of extremely mobile capital. Disinvestment is a constant sword of Damocles over the head of every corporation in the world.[33] It is no longer enough that a business meet its payroll and return something reasonable to its shareholders. In today's all out war for profits, conglomerate corporations normally assign an expected *level of profit* to each division manager.[34] That level must be competitive with all the other available investment opportunities worldwide.

Usually, the level is higher than last year's attainment for the division. This may help to explain the brief tenure—and the mania—characteristic of studio executives. "It's pretty frightening to be an executive today," says producer Edgar Sherick." . . . If you do just a competent job, which is pretty much all you can expect of a human being, you're destined to fail and be fired." [35]

Now some writers have argued that American film making is a battleground between these profit-obsessed studio and network executives, and the product-oriented artists who actually make movies. If so, it is not a fair fight.

In recent years, films distributed by eight major studios have cornered more than 75 percent of overall box office revenue.[36] Though the studios themselves produce only about 60 percent of the pictures they distribute, they bankroll most of them.[37]

This power over whether films are made (financed) and distributed gives the studios Procrustean power over "their" product. "A studio executive, a committee, or research results may alter the script, decide who will star in the picture, select the crew, and even dictate the style of the film. In post-production, the editing, music, and sound track may still be altered by the studio." [38] And that's not all. Studios regularly stipulate the MPPA rating they require (G, PG-13, etc.).[39] They usually insist that a completed film be "in exact accordance with the script" they have approved.[40] Even after the film is in the theatre, the studio can pull it out again, and change it. They have done so often enough. For example, because audiences "rejected . . . downbeat finale[s]" for *Risky Business, First Blood,* and *After Hours,* the studios changed them.[41]

But mostly, the studios do not change the work of filmmakers. Their power is so great, they don't have to. Instead, they employ (or finance) a small, well-known clique of "creatives" who know the dimensions of Procrustes' bed and can be relied upon to "play by the rules"—to anticipate, and then self-censor, to make artistic "nondecisions."

So profit is the king of Hollywood. Product is only an attendant courtier. But how to attend? What is profitable? A film can take many roads to profitability: cable, network, videocassette, foreign markets. But the key stop is the first one, at the box office. If a film is not "boffo at the box-o," the movie will probably be slowed down in these "ancillary markets," and never make it to the heights of profit that major studios insist upon (See Table 4.1). So the fundamental question becomes, "How to get big box office?" As we saw in Chapter 3, the news business has its "ten commandments" of audience attraction. The movie business is no less reverent about profits. Hollywood's commandments are not written on tablets of stone, but they might as well be. As nearly as anything can be in

TABLE 4–1

Top box-office attractions that became top videocassette rentals for 1990

1. Ghost (Paramount)	$94,000,000*
2. Pretty Woman (Buena Vista)	81,903,000
3. Home Alone (20th Century-Fox)	80,000,000
4. Die Hard 2 (20th Century-Fox)	66,500,000
5. Total Recall (Tri-Star)	65,000,000
6. Teenage Mutant Ninja Turtles (New Line)	62,000,000
7. Dick Tracy (Buena Vista)	59,526,000
8. The Hunt for Red October (Paramount)	58,500,000
9. Driving Miss Daisy (continuing 1990 run)	49,500,000
10. Back to the Future, Part III (Universal)	48,951,109

*Figures are total rentals collected by film distributors as of December 31, 1990.

Source: Variety

the city of ephemera, these commandments are immutable. As I recite them, notice how their logic leads to the political implications mentioned earlier. That is, when social and political issues are engaged, the movies will be establishmentarian: the dominant ideology will prevail. But mostly, socio-political issues are not joined. Mostly, the movies are depoliticized, serving as a pleasant, narcotizing diversion from the hard world of social issues and political choices.

Audience Attraction: The Four Commandments of Movie Content

I. Thou Shalt Have No Other Gods Before Thee: The Blockbuster

As the need for a profit has given way to the need for a *big* profit, so the need for *an* audience has become the need for a *big* audience. In fact, a massive audience. The catch is this: the pressing need for audience comes in an era when moviegoers are a more mercurial lot than ever. The America that went to the movies every Saturday night, as faithfully as to church on Sunday morning, is a thing of the past. The average moviegoer now sees only a handful of films each year. The total annual movie audience is now about one-fourth of what it was in the 30s and 40s.[42]

The way out of the catch is thus: If those average moviegoers are all seeing *the same* few films, that is a massive audience, at least per film.

The resulting business logic is this: fewer films, each designed to attract a bigger audience per film, each designed to be a "blockbuster." The total number of films released in recent years is only about one-fourth the total of fifty years ago, but the audience per film is much larger. And so are total earnings, which of course, is the bottom line.[43] In this new era, a few films have truly become *mass* media. In one typical year, a mere 28 films accounted for three-fourths of all box office receipts![44] On a recent weekend, a single blockbuster *(Batman Returns)* drew 50 percent of all moviegoers! Never had so many ceded so much influence to so few.

The quest to make blockbusters reached a fever pitch in Hollywood in the mid-1970s, when "what was thought to be the ceiling on what a movie could earn [was] dramatically broken. *E.T. . . .* grossed an unprecedented $519 million worldwide. *Star Wars* and *The Empire Strikes Back* have together grossed more than $900 million."[45] These were films that "made," not just a year, but a career. They were not just blockbusters, they were cultural events. The lust for more like them has now become the defining logic of the film business. Settling for less is not just unaggressive; it is unacceptable: "If Universal only netted two million dollars off a film," says director Alan Rudolph, "they would be pissed because it wasn't worth the effort."[46]

That is not as illogical as it sounds, for the following reasons:

The massive capital backing which the conglomerates made available to the movie majors carried with it obligations. Shareholders will not invest in stock that fails to produce profits or enhanced capital value at a rate comparable to that of other investment opportunities—and corporations require from time to time to raise capital in order to enter new markets with new products. The inexpensive film, even if as a sleeper it returned unexpected millions on a small investment . . . could not service a major's capital account, though it could provide a pleasant gloss to its accounts. The motion picture industry discovered that its success in raising new capital from the conglomerates meant that the 'event movie'

Puttnam's "Fast Fade" at Coke's Columbia

Louis B. Mayer would have liked David Puttnam. The British-born producer once told an interviewer that he had been ''brought up on American movies;'' that flying into this country for the first time ''was so exciting. I thought, 'Well, that's the place where all these ideas . . . and dreams have been molded. . . .' My sense of the United States was that it was a place where (class antagonism) didn't exist, where there was limitless opportunity, where the notion of what was fair was tremendously important. . . . This is really a wonderful country to a very great extent. The whole middle of this country is an extraordinarily fair and decent place.'' The movies, he went on to say, have a mission beyond just making money. They have an obligation to cull out and reinforce that decency in us. It was a powerful, passionate speech—the kind of speech one of Mayer's own characters might have made, with music swelling in the background.

The new conglomerate owners of Columbia Pictures liked Puttnam too, for a while. These were the chief executives of the Coca-Cola Company, which acquired Columbia in 1981 and made Puttnam its president. Coke's CEO, Roberto Goizueta, himself an immigrant—a refugee in fact from Castro's communism—loved Puttnam's love of the American way. He also liked Puttnam's dislike of the skyrocketing costs studios were paying to ''star'' directors, producers, actors, to their agents and their projects. Best of all, he liked the fact that the movies Puttnam had produced—movies like *The Killing Fields, Chariots of Fire, Midnight Express*—had not just won awards, they had made money.

When Puttnam first met Goizueta at Coca-Cola's Atlanta headquarters, he told his new boss, ''The (movies are) too important an influence . . . to be left *solely* to the tyranny of the box office or reduced to the sum of the lowest common denominator.'' Along with Puttnam's understanding that ''we have a busi-

[author's term for the blockbuster that detonates] had become an essential part of its profit-making programme, for it returned profits of a different order of magnitude.[47]

ness to nurture and build,'' it was a fine-sounding sentiment, and the Coke bosses told Puttnam they appreciated it. What they didn't know was, Puttnam meant what he said.

''The trouble with David is,'' said an executive at another studio, ''he can't seem to separate his personal feelings from the studio's interests.'' Translation: David didn't understand that in Hollywood, the rule is, ''Don't smell 'em, sell 'em.'' ''I have to slog my way through a dozen pieces of crap to get to the stuff I really want to do,'' said the exec, ''but I do it.''

In discussing this sort of problem with his boss, head of Coke's Entertainment Business Sector Fay Vincent, Puttnam confessed, ''I honestly don't care if another studio does better than ours, or if another film opens the same day and out-grosses us. It honestly doesn't bother me.'' Vincent's ''jaw dropped.''

Too often, it seemed to Coke, Puttnam's actions were as strange as his words. Hollywood insiders couldn't believe it, for example, when Puttnam's studio gave radical, rule-breaking black director Spike Lee complete control over $6 million to complete *School Daze* after another studio had pulled the plug on the project.

Within a year, Puttnam was gone. ''While Hollywood is notorious for the revolving doors in its executive suites,'' observed the *Wall Street Journal,* ''Mr. Puttnam's . . . departure marks the shortest tenure of a major studio chief in recent history.'' After he left, the films he had greenlighted went on to earn lots of awards—but only modest profits. In retrospect, Fay Vincent named Puttnam's problem with characteristic understatement: ''I don't think he understood the significance of being part of Coca-Cola.''

Sources: Andrew Yule, *Fast Fade,* (New York: Delacorte, 1989); Bill Moyers, *A World of Ideas,* (New York: Doubleday, 1989).

How to make a blockbuster? Throw in several cups of special effects, a pint of big stars, add well-known director, saturation booking, massive advertising campaign, and stir. These ingredients, of course, cost money. A brief history of movie budgets will illustrate the rising of blockbuster fever. Between 1950 and 1970, the average movie budget only doubled, going from $1 to 2 million. Between 1970 and 1990, that average budget ballooned by more than tenfold. And the result, every now and then, has been the desired blockbuster. Of the top 50 box office hits of all time, forty-two of them were made after 1970, mostly by following the block-buster recipe.[48]

But isn't that, as they say, risky business? Suppose you throw such a $50–100 million filmic party, and nobody comes? The business-like beauty of the blockbuster strategy is that it is not only a potential year-maker, it is also a risk-avoider, not despite its big budgets, but because of them. Their bankable stars, directors, special effects and ad budgets allow the films to be "pre-sold" to exhibitors, cable companies, and distributors to video and foreign markets. When Columbia released *Close Encounters*, for example, "New York City theatres were informed just prior to release that they would have to put up one hundred fifty thousand dollars apiece as a minimum guarantee, although they couldn't even preview the film. . . . Further, the New York theatres had to promise to run the film for three months, and prior to opening had to fork over another two thousand dollars apiece for local advertising and promotion." Exorbitant? Sure. Did they pay it? Based on the film's "blockbuster" director, stars, and budget, they paid.[49]

But these "ingredients," this bigness, speak only to the style of the blockbuster. What is its substance? Here too, the Delphic corporate logic speaks, which brings us to the second commandment.

II. Thou Shalt Not Do the Unpredictable

The hobgoblin of media executives is uncertainty. Currently it costs over $30 million to produce and market the average major studio film. That breathtaking sum is invested in a product no one needs, a product which could go *entirely* unconsumed by the intended market! That's high anxiety.

But that's not all. Nowadays, the film studio is just one subsidiary of a conglomerate corporation, but it is an important subsidiary. Out of its movies may spin other products that carry other subsidiaries to profit—or loss. "For instance, the common notice on a newspaper advertisement for a Warner-distributed film often says, 'Read the Warner paperback,' or 'Sound Track Available on Warner Bros. Records.' Because of these interconnecting distribution chains among [Warner's] subsidiaries, an unsuccessful film can have serious repercussions along a wide section of the entire conglomerate."[50] (See Table 4.2.) That's very high anxiety.

TABLE 4–2

Examples of movie tie-in products marketed by conglomerate subsidiaries

CDs, audiocassettes
Published music
Rock-music videos
TV shows (series, "The Making of . . ." documentaries)
Screenplays
Books ("the making of . . ." books; fotonovels; other spinoffs)
Comic books
Toys
Board games
And, through the company's licensing division, everything else, including
(in the case of *Batman Returns*):
Batman commercials and product tie-ins for Diet Pepsi, McDonald's,
and Choice Hotels
Video games
Trading cards
Back packs
Candy
Clothing
Cereal
Sleeping bags
Lunch boxes
Inflatable pools
Action figures and vehicles
And over 150 other products

The anxious question is, "How to predict the unpredictable?" The obvious answer is, "If it sells, remake it. Nothing succeeds like success."

As a result, says one Hollywood historian, movies are, in the day of the blockbuster, "even more formulaic and conservative . . . than [they were] in the classic Hollywood era." [51] Independent director Jim Jarmusch has refused to work for the major studios, and he explains why: "A script was sent to me that was a teenage sex comedy that sort of summed up Hollywood attitudes for me. There was a cover letter which said, 'We realize this story reads a little like *Risky Business*, but when our rewrite is done it will read much more like *The Graduate*,' which I thought was pretty hilarious. Everything had to be related [to some other film]. The idea of being original is probably terrifying to them." [52]

In Chapter 3, we spoke of the "conservative fallacy." This is the unremarkable human tendency to accept, for the most part unquestioningly, "the way things are usually done around here," and to emulate it. Thus, routines become norms, and "what is" becomes "what ought to be." [53] Hollywood's mania for predictability has made the conservative fallacy more than an inadvertent norm. It is one of the Four Commandments.

But this is conservatism only in the tautological sense that it preserves whatever has gone before. Whether it is conservative in the political sense is an open question until we have seen more of what has gone before, more of "the way things are usually done around here," which brings us to the Third Commandment.

III. Thou Shalt Not Challenge Thine Audience

What are the *thematic* ingredients of a blockbuster? First, it is not intellectually taxing. This is true for a number of reasons. The first is teenagers, whose cognitive development is limited, but whose willingness to attend a blockbuster repeatedly is not. Those repeat attenders helped *Star Wars, Jaws,* and *Batman* redefine the word *profit.*[54]

A second factor in the blockbuster equation is the "family audience." Surveys suggest that the typical family may go to the movies together only a few times each year. But when families go, they go *en masse* and presto: blockbuster. This makes studios keenly interested in the reasons families go to movies, which turn out to be uncomplicated. "For the family audience a major push factor is the need to find something to do which gets children out of the house during their holidays." [55] This explains why so much of Hollywood fare is released for Christmas, summer, and Easter holidays, and well within the ken of the average eight-year-old. Add to the family the box office importance of teenagers (who are of course, not part of their families, at least in public) and the sum is thus: seven of the top grossing films of all time are from the "action-adventure" category, now the definitive genre of the movie business.

Teens and pre-teens are also coveted as the best market for spin-off products. These youngsters showed the way to the pot of profits at the end of the product tie-in rainbow, with their boundless appetite for *Star Wars* toys, books, tapes, tv shows, lunch boxes, and so on. "In fact, . . . George Lucas made most of his many millions not from the film itself but from his sizable take from Star Wars-related . . . tie-ins." [56] In the conglomerate era, when many of these spin-off products—and their profits—can be made "in-house," by other subsidiaries of the parent company, the logic is ever more compelling. If your choice is between making *Batman* or *Crime and Punishment*, suffer the children to come unto you. Quite apart from how these alternatives might fare at the box office, those Raskolnikov action figures just won't test well among the crucial 7–12-year-old focus groups.

A fourth force for simplicity is the studio's marketing department. Perhaps not surprisingly in a world where it is better for films to be gone to than good, the studios' vice president for marketing is now coequal in the hierarchy to the head of production. Few films are made without marketing's approval.[57] This office will insist that story lines be "high concept"—reducible to an immediately appreciable shorthand that can reach out from a newspaper ad or movie preview and "grab" an audience. *Alien* is high concept. It was conceived as "*Jaws* on a spaceship." *Outlands* was "*High Noon* in Outer Space." And *Footloose*: "*Flashdance* in the country." [58]

Unfortunately, real life is not high concept. Neither is a complex socio-political argument, rendered in dramatic form, high concept. These things take a little time to explain. That is why, ordinarily, they do not get on movie screens.

The final reason the blockbuster recipe calls for low-cal ideas is the logic of LCD. While lower-budget films may appeal to a specialized audience, the blockbuster is designed to appeal to *everyone*. Given its budget, it has to: the break-even cost of the average Hollywood film now requires an audience of at least 12 million people. That means an appeal to a people's lowest common denominators. Hollywood is convinced that even smart people may go to a "dumb" movie (if it has plenty of action or sex or special effects), but dumb people won't go to a movie that's too smart for its own good.

IV. Neither Shalt Thou Offend Thine Audience

The next thematic requirement of a blockbuster is that it be unobjectionable. If the blockbuster strategy requires that *everyone* be attracted, *no one* must be repelled by a controversial theme or idea. LCD means LOP (least objectionable programming).

To the senior vice president of the First National Bank of Boston, which works closely with studios in financing films, the point is obvious—a question that answers itself: "Do you want to be an advocate of a cause on the screen, and with your stockholders' money?" [59]

Reinforcing the logic of LCD and LOP is TV. Although box office remains important in determining the post-theatre value of a movie, television quickly became "the single most important factor in the revenues generated by a motion picture." [60] Indeed, a studio like Warner Communications, Inc. (owner of Warner Bros. studio) now sees its main mission as "bringing movies conveniently and economically into the home, allow[ing] the industry to reach the enormous market that rarely, if ever, attends movie theatres." [61] Today, "no film [is] made for the cinema without its producers keeping TV rental in mind." [62] That means being doubly careful not to challenge or offend. As we shall see in Chapter 5, television not only accepted the logic of LCD and LOP. Television invented them. Together, the logic of LCD-LOP-TV means that the movies won't hazard an idea often, and when they do, it will be a bland one. Familiar to all, a threat to none. Any tenet from the dominant ideology will do. That dominant ideology is, after all, exactly what Antonio Gramsci called it. It is our "common sense."

The Formula Film:
Hegemony as Routine

This, then is the economic infrastructure of American film: conglomerate capitalism, blockbuster fever, audience demographics, LCD, LOP, TV, and so on. What superstructure will it allow? To what *product* will this firm foundation of economic *process* lead?

The previous section has already described sins of commission—what *not* to put into the product (the novel, the challenging, the objectionable). But what of sins of omission? What kind of content should not be left out? Here too the oracle of commerce speaks. Its formula commands that movie content must offer three things: escape, affirmation, inclusion.

Escape: An Opiate
in the Celluloid Syringe

"The first principle of Hollywood . . . is that [its fare] must be entertaining. The theory is that people don't go to movies to be educated, enlightened or made better human beings. . . . As Alfred Hitchcock said, 'The cinema is not a slice of life, it's a piece of cake.' Hollywood . . . generally believes that escapist movies are more entertaining than ones that deal with serious subject matter. 'Producers believe . . . movies succeed because they are diverting,' says screenwriting teacher Robert McKee, 'that people just want to check their brains at the door.' " [63]

If Sigmund Freud were to put this point in his own words, he might say that the movies are directed at the id, (the psyche's seeker of bodily pleasure, the source of sensual fantasies) not at the ego (the psyche's thinker about reality) or the superego (the moral sensibility). Freud saw two great instincts toward pleasure emerging from the id: the life wish (mainly the sexual instinct) and the death wish (destructiveness and aggression).[64]

In its effort to appeal to the need for physical pleasure, Hollywood has been Freud's apt pupil. Sex and violence have always been Hollywood's stock in trade, and their prevalence is increasing. "In 1968, 32 percent of pictures were rated G [indicating low levels of sex and violence]. By 1984 that percentage had dropped to a mere 2 percent of the market. During the same time period R-rated films [with their higher levels of sex and violence] grew from 22 to 45 percent of all releases." [65]

One writer has argued that this emphasis on the visceral over the intellectual has recently gone beyond the subject matter of movies, to permeate the *style* of film as well. Style includes editing so fast-paced as to preclude the possibility of thinking about the images as they pass by, leaving us with only "a mesmerizing serial rush." [66] The new style involves music that through the miracle of Dolby systems becomes "a vast and irresistible barrage of synthesized sound, a hyper-rhythmic full-body stimulus" that "thrums and zooms and . . . jangles right on through you, clearing out your head with such efficiency that not only is it impossible to receive ideas but the whole movie, once over, seems to have gone in one ear and out the other—except that it's not just your head that has functioned as a throughway but every vital organ." [67]

More and more, the new style is made up of special effects. Tremendous resources are expended on honing their sophistication, all devoted to moving us beyond thinking, to *feeling* the death-wish thrill as "those razors rake that throat," as the Uzi explodes the head, or the star ship leaps to warp speed. The ad for *Die Hard 2* depicts silhouetted bodies shooting into the sky from an explosion. The caption reads, "Become a Frequent Flier! Die Harder! See It Again!"

More and more, such special effects have graduated from style to substance. More than a way of telling a story, they have become the story. In films like *Indiana Jones and the Last Crusade*, *Terminator II*, *Lethal Weapon III*, *Batman Returns*, and *Jurassic Park*, the "plots" are interstitial pretexts for a series of gut-wrenching stunt spectaculars.[68] Full of sound and fury, signifying nothing.

Affirmation: Ideology in the Celluloid Syringe

No matter how they may try, however, the movies can't be completely devoid of politics. In some sense, the pageant on that screen is meant to stand for human life. Politics and society are part of that life. Unavoidably, the subject will come up.

But not to worry. The subject doesn't have to be completely avoided. The ban on social messages doesn't extend to messages that don't seem to be messages, ones that seem instead to be just "good common sense."

The ideological wolf in the sheep's clothing of common sense. That, of course, is the achievement of the dominant ideology. Its message has always been welcome. After all, it tells us exactly what we want to hear: that what we have always believed in is true, beyond the shadow of a doubt. That what we have never questioned, need not be questioned.

Take the case of the studios' favorite genre, the western. While few "real westerns" are made today, the "disguised western" continues to be Team Hollywood's MVP.[69] A disguised western simply picks up Dodge City's heroes, themes, plots, cliches, and deposits them in Gotham City, Tatueen, or the South Bronx. Together, "westerns" disguised as action-adventure, science fiction, or cop-detective movies represent eight of the top ten box office hits of all time.

What are the politics of this now-definitive genre? Each of these films is a display gallery for the following capitalism-related values.

Individualism and Self-Reliance

"What is the good life?" the philosopher asks, and so begins his argument. Likewise, in answering the question, "What is the good guy?" Hollywood espouses its own philosophy. The fact that the movies' argument is an implicit one may only make it all the more irresistible. We breathe it in, as invisible as air, and as undeniable.

Above all, the good guy is "on his own," self-reliant and self-possessed. The indelible images of the two films that defined the genre are of a cowboy riding off alone into the night, despite a little boy's cries to "come back Shane";* and of Marshall Will Kane standing tall—and alone—in the street at High Noon.

That image continues to course through the veins of all the disguised westerns. It might be a disgusted *Dirty Harry*, alone and throwing away the badge of his societal involvement; or a *Batman*, unable to stay in bed with a new love, getting up to "hang out" by himself; or a John Dunbar, in *Dances With Wolves*, manning the Army's farthest outpost—alone; or a young *Indiana Jones*, peeling off from his boy scout pack to make his first discovery; or the avenging mayhem of the one-man gang—be it Schwarzenegger, Stallone, Swayze, or Seagal.

In the exposition of the classic 50s western, *Shane*, good guy homesteader Joe Starrett tells Shane why he won't hitch the team to the stump he strains to remove by hand: "Sometimes nothin' will do but your own sweat and muscle." As a model of efficiency, the "work smarter, not harder" school could not support it. But of course, this isn't about efficiency, it is about the virtue of self-reliance and its centrality to Hollywood's answer to the question, "What is the good man?"

The "Imperative of Violence" [71]

The medieval followers of Manes conceived of the world as a struggle between light and darkness, good and evil. So, in its own way, do the disguised westerns. Consider the nature of this genre's "bad guys." They are not bad as a function of social forces, or of a

---

*This scene is an intriguing, if inadvertent, parallel to one Max Weber cites as typifying personal relationships under the "Protestant ethic and the spirit of capitalism." The scene is found in Bunyan's Pilgrim's Progress. It is surely one of the most remarkable passages in English literature. "After [Mr. Christian's] call to the celestial city, with his wife and children clinging to him and crying, he stops his ears, and staggers forth across the fields." [70]

A Tour of the Pantheon, Where Our Heroes Explain the Imperative of Violence

Amy Fowler-Kane to Marshall Will Kane (Gary Cooper) in *High Noon:*
You don't have to be a hero for me.

Will Kane:
If you think I want this you're crazy. I've got to . . . (bad guy Frank Miller is) wild and . . . crazy.

★ ★ ★ ★ ★

Detective Masumata to Nick Conklin (Michael Douglas as disguised western hero) in *Black Rain:*
This isn't New York. We have rules here.

Conklin:
Oh, you have rules here, huh? Hey look Pal, I've seen (bad guy) Sato's work, O.K.? He ain't followin' your program!

★ ★ ★ ★ ★

Jennifer Spencer (love interest) to Harry Callahan (Clint Eastwood as disguised-western hero) in *Sudden Impact:*
You're either a cop or Public Enemy #1.

Callahan:
Some people would say both.

Spencer:
Why?

Callahan:
Oh, it's a question of methods. Everybody wants results but nobody wants to do what you have to do to get 'em done.

Spencer:
And you do?

Callahan:
I do what I have to do.

★ ★ ★ ★ ★

Canadian "Mountie" to Eliot Ness (Kevin Costner) in *The Untouchables:*	*Mr. Ness, I do not approve of your methods (use of terror in interrogation).*
Ness:	*Yeah, well you're not from Chicago.*

★ ★ ★ ★ ★

Sam Ketcham (side kick) to Dick Tracy (Warren Beatty) in *Dick Tracy:*	*You can't do this, Tracy. The D. A. will say you're badgering witnesses. . . . It's a gamble, Tracy.*
Tracy:	*I'll tell you what the gamble is: leaving (bad guy) Big Boy on the street.*

★ ★ ★ ★ ★

Vicki Vale to Batman (Michael Keaton) in *Batman:*	*Some people would say you're as dangerous as he (the Joker) is.*
Batman:	*Who says that?*
Vale:	*Let's face it, you're not a very normal guy.*
Batman:	*It's not a normal world out there.*

★ ★ ★ ★ ★

Mr. Nields (bureaucrat) to Oliver North (as himself); referring to deception of Congress and covert arming of terrorists, in the Iran-Contra hearings:	*That's not the way we do things in America, is it?*
Colonel North:	*I think it is very important for the American people to understand that this is a dangerous world, that we live at risk. Covert operations are essential to protecting the country.*

human weakness common to all of us ("there but for the grace of God . . .") No, say the disguised westerns, the bad, to paraphrase Fitzgerald, are different from you and me. They are bad for the sheer incandescent hell of it. They are evil incarnate.

Indeed, so different are these villains from you and me that often they are not recognizably human. They are literally faceless. *Shane's* Wilson and *High Noon's* Frank Miller do not show their faces until the fateful final minutes of their films. Until then, they are the faceless stuff of frightful legends. Even then, Shane's nemesis is shrouded in the chiaroscuro of his black hat. But their faceless inhumanity would look almost benign next to the masked and twisted visages of their successors—Darth Vader, the Joker, and the whole rogues' gallery of *Dick Tracy.*

These villains being the subhuman psychotics that they are, the good guy has "got to do what a man's got to do." Violence is a necessity. Nonviolence is a nonoption, a cloudy-headed fools' paradise. Having watched the quivering, blood-loving, cult-crazed killer of Stallone's *Cobra* take a supermarket full of shoppers hostage, we can only scoff as the civil libertarian police lieutenant* tries to communicate with him via megaphone: "We are willing to talk. There is no more need for violence. There is no way out but talking. Please communicate with us." We know this guy will understand only one thing: the business end of Cobra's pearl handled .38; or in the case of others of his ilk, a magnum, six shooter, laser sword, bull whip, exploding arrow, whatever's handy.

The Role of Women

Of course, the wielders of these weapons are, in the formula film, mainly male. In fact women's inability and reluctance to use violence has traditionally made them second-class citizens in moviedom.

After little Joey and Marian Starrett watch Shane and Joe Sr. dispatch the cattle baron's bullies in a fight, Mrs. Starrett has to upbraid her young son: "That was no place for you, Joey." "It was no place for you either, Marion," Starrett has to gently remind what he calls his "little woman."

Now let us fast-forward, through the decades of women's struggle for full citizenship, to the present. It is remarkable how

---

*Interestingly, the lieutenant's part is played by Andrew Robinson, best known as the quivering, blood-loving, psychotic killer of *Dirty Harry,* a film that helped define the cop movie as disguised western.

little has changed. Oh, sure, Vicki Vale gets to have a career. But when the action starts, her scream is in the passive voice, and she collapses into Batman's rescuing arms.

Of course, things are not *completely* unchanged. They are just *fundamentally* unchanged. In *Aliens* and its sequels, it was a *woman's* knuckles and know-how that prevailed. Similarly, strong women loom large in *Terminator II, Lethal Weapon III*, and *V. I. Warshawski.* In these films and others like them, then, women have achieved equality. But they have done so, I believe, on men's terms, by learning men's lesson—in this case, the art and necessity of violence.*

I suggest that Hollywood will have come a long way (baby), when it celebrates men learning women's lessons: e.g., the futility of violence, the vital importance of nurturing, cooperation, and community.

In fairness, some of these values are on display in a series of recent female bonding movies, e.g., *Steel Magnolias, Terms of Endearment, Crimes of the Heart, Fried Green Tomatoes* and even, in a gender twist, *Three Men and a Baby.* But these movies are a perfectly innocuous brand of feminism. What makes them no threat to capitalist individualism is their resolutely nonpolitical nature. Never is it suggested that this nurturance, this community, should be expanded beyond a personal-sized group. The feminist ethos is no threat as long as its place is in the home.

The Failure of Social Action

As the climax of *High Noon* approaches, a political solution to the town's dilemma is tried—and found wanting. Noon and its train are drawing closer. They carry with them the dreaded Frank Miller, who comes to rejoin his gang, avenge his incarceration at the hands of Marshall Will Kane, and reestablish his reign of terror over the town. It being Sunday, the town's good folk are in church. Kane goes there to ask for their help. Disagreement ensues. The children are dismissed; everyone is given a chance to talk, one at a time. Democracy is in action.

In the ensuing discourse, there is some nobility, some ignobility, some courage, and some cowardice. Finally, one of the town's selectmen speaks. He is a prominent man, a man with a

---

*In several contemporary romantic comedies about women, the men's lesson well
  learned is the art and necessity of business competition. See, e.g., *Working Girl*
  or *Baby Boom.*

Thelma and Louise Go Camping

It might just have been what so many movies claim to be, but aren't: the most talked-about movie of the year.

"Liberating," said women. "Threatening," said men. Unfortunately, the film partook enough of Hollywood formulae that in the end, it was neither of those things.

On one level, this is a film about the oppression of women—about sexual harassment, about domestic servitude, about rape.

These are, among other things, political issues, susceptible to change by social movements. But that of course is not how *Thelma and Louise* sees them. Social movements are not in Hollywood's very brief book of permissible genres. Among those that are in the book is the disguised western/buddy picture. Thelma and Louise is nothing more (or less) than an especially good rendering of that genre.

When Thelma and Louise suffer the film's crucial indignity (the attempted rape of Thelma), it galvanizes them. But again, their action is not political or social. Instead, it is pure, predictable, de-politicized Hollywood: blow away the bad guy; head for the hills.

It is, to be sure, an emotionally appealing formula. Viscerally, the moment Louise shoots the rapist could not have been more satisfying. After his brutal attempt is frustrated by the sound of a pistol cocking in his ear, he begins to abuse both women verbally:

> *I should have gone ahead and f_ _ _ _ _ her.*
>
> *What did you say?*
>
> *I said suck my d_ _ _ .*
>
> *Bang.*

Sitting in the theatre, one could hear—feel—the anger of women venting itself in a victory cry at that moment. Emotionally, it doesn't get any better.

But this film was touted as more than just a feel-good (and then later, feel-bad) movie. It was supposed to be an important film, a milestone in the women's movement. And so we have to ask: what does its message do for women?

Is it really the case that the way to empower women is to allow ourselves to be caught up in the accelerating cycle of violence?

And does the emotional impact of movies like this pump social movements up, or does it let the air out of them—in this way: We are angry about oppression; about rape, or racism, or human rights violations, or some other inhumanity. We go to a movie (like *Thelma and Louise* or *Mississippi Burning* or *Midnight Express*), and we see the oppression acted out, graphically, convincingly. And then we see the bad guy punished—physically, peremptorily—a lesson he'll never forget. Does that satisfying feeling take the edge off our anger—has the movie become a cathartic substitute for doing something about oppression?

The chase motif that follows the shooting is also vintage Hollywood—a feminized *Butch Cassidy and the Sundance Kid,* right up to the apocalyptic freeze-frame ending. These scenes, too, are emotionally satisfying. Now that Thelma and Louise have learned to ``express themselves,'' as they put it, we see them and their relationship grow. They share stories of their oppression. They joke about it. But here too, there are limits. Never, of course, is there any hint that Thelma and Louise could widen the circle of their sisterhood—that sharing just these sorts of stories is the very basis on which the women's movement proceeds.

Butch and Sundance wouldn't be interested. Neither are Thelma and Louise. Hollywood mythic figures, all of them, they must follow the mythic code: you don't join; you don't picket or sit in or march or write letters. You go your own way. You slap leather; you ``drive like hell.''

By the time the movie's over, Hollywood's delivered all it promised, and gotten all it wanted: we did laugh, we did cry, we did kiss six bucks goodbye. What we didn't get, Hollywood never promised: originality, subtlety, dimension, a realistic treatment of what are, after all, real problems.

What a sad commentary on the American movie business it is: in the end, the ``most talked-about movie of the year'' had so little to say.

way about him. By the time he is finished, the townsmen are convinced that for their own and Marshall Kane's sake, they should not stand with Kane but should urge Kane to take his planned retirement forthwith and move on.

We know as well as Kane does that this is wrong. Miller, we've been assured, will follow Kane to the ends of the earth, and come back to terrorize the town.

But Kane does not rejoin to say so. Instead, wordlessly, he leaves the church. Kane, you see, knows that Madison was right: that "men are not angels," and that a charismatic slickster can sway them to pursue a dishonorable self-interest "as if he held the very scepter in his hands." Social discourse is not the answer. The heroic action of individuals is.

The failure of politics is now a ubiquitous theme in this genre. Its main targets are the "suits, politicians, and bureaucrats," "bozoes with big brass nameplates on their desks and asses shaped by the seat of their chairs"; and the courts, where "an eye for an eye means only if you're caught, and even then it's an indefinite postponement and let's settle out of court" (quotations from *Sudden Impact*). "Politics," in the right-wing populism of this genre, consists of faceless elites who don't understand ordinary Americans or their needs.

The "courts" and the "politicians," these arenas of discourse and compromise, turn out to corrupt or fail the natural law that the good guy knows "in his heart." No fewer than four times over the course of the *High Noon* script, Kane or a Kane-figure tells a less exalted mortal, "If you don't know, I can't tell you." The phrase refers to a law that discourse cannot impart, a law that can only be known intuitively—and will be—by good folk.

But what is this heart knowledge that resists being brought to the head? Is it not likely to be that body of "truths" we are told so early, so often, and so reverently that they are dinned deep into us, as part of our "common sense"? If so, then to enjoin action based on what we "know in our hearts," without discourse, without reflection, is to accept unexamined the cant of the dominant tradition.

Formula Film Politics and Public Opinion

Researches into the effects of film content on political attitudes are notable mostly by their absence. This makes the definitive work of Peterson and Thurstone all the more invaluable. They conclude that it is not likely that a single film will cause significant attitude change. However it is likely that repeated versions of the same themes will affect attitudes.[72]

Of course, "repeated versions of the same themes" is exactly the stock in trade of the formula film. This section asks what sort of effects the oft-repeated politics of the formula film might be having on our political attitudes.

But first a warning: we are about to enter the realm of speculation. Please fasten your skepticism. The connections I am about to suggest between movie content and public attitudes have not been tested by social science research, and should be approached with caution.

Nevertheless, it is interesting to see how our peculiar American attitudes pitch and slope in remarkable congruence with our movies' ideology. Is there a connection?

For example, we have watched a hundred Joe Starretts "do the job with their own two hands" forsaking "the easy way out" solely for the sake of virtue. We have watched a thousand Shanes and Will Kanes take care of business while "standing tall," on "their own two feet." After all that, what is our attitude likely to be toward, for example, poverty, toward welfare and its recipients?

For whatever reasons, Americans feel that the main reasons for poverty are the "lack of effort," "thrift," and "ability" of the poor themselves. Far fewer credit such reasons as "failure of private industry to provide enough jobs," or "failure of society to provide good schools for many Americans." [73] Eighty-four percent of Americans endorse the statement, "There are too many people receiving welfare money who should be working." A large majority disagreed with the statement, "We are spending too little money on welfare in this country." [74]

And we have watched a thousand Frank Millers, mean and crazy beyond the reach of reason, much less rehabilitation. Are they in the backs of our minds when we think about the criminal justice system, about the civil rights of the accused versus "law and order," or about prison reform? No doubt for a number of reasons, Americans' support for harsh treatment of criminals is conspicuously strong.[75]

And what is the effect of a Manichean habit of mind on our thinking about international politics? When foreign states do things that seem incomprehensible or wrong to us, we might react by asking what social or cultural forces might be at work there that we need to better understand—not agree with, necessarily—but understand. But instead, we seem to follow the Manichean lead of politicians who attribute the disagreements to the pathology or

A Disguised Western Is Shot in L.A.

"How could it have happened?" asked a stunned prosecutor after the verdicts had been read.

A jury had just found four white police officers "not guilty" of having assaulted black motorist Rodney King.*

The prosecutor couldn't believe the verdicts, because the jury, and the nation, had watched the police commit the assault. A resident of a nearby apartment complex had videotaped the incident. And there it was. For 81 agonizing seconds, we saw the four policemen repeatedly kick and beat with heavy metal batons a prone and evidently helpless man.

How could this strange verdict have happened? The answer is that the verdict was not so strange after all. Indeed, there is no more familiar theme in American culture than the myth used to justify Rodney King's beating.

Defense lawyers referred repeatedly to the "thin blue line" protecting civilized society from "the likes of Rodney King." With his ilk, the implication was, there's no such thing as excessive force. As one officer's attorney put it, "The circumstances here were consistent with the job the man was hired to do. He was part of the line between society and chaos." "Sometimes police work is brutal," said one of the officers in his own testimony. "That's just a fact of life."

venality of our "enemies." The recent dubious battles that killed perhaps thousands in Panama, perhaps a hundred times that many in Iraq, were justified by just such Manichean rhetoric. Perhaps hearing, in this rhetoric, echoes of our heroes' dialogues on the necessity of violence, Americans overwhelmingly supported these adventures.

Formula Film Politics and Public Opinion: A Rejoinder

Movie attitudes and public attitudes—is there a connection? "Of course there is," the school of popular culture would say. "But not

No wonder that was persuasive to the jury. The ``imperative of violence'' is precisely the inexorable logic of every disguised western they had ever seen. Shane and John Wayne, Dirty Harry, Eliot Ness, Batman, Darkman, Dick Tracy, two semesters of the *Terminator* and three of *Lethal Weapon.* One way or another, they all agreed with Stallone's *Cobra,* whose succinct formulation was; ``You're a disease. I'm the cure.'' After the trial, one of the jurors recited the lesson flawlessly: ``They're policemen, they're not angels. They're out there to do a low-down, dirty job.''

Rodney King also brings to the fore why this particular myth has a special place in the pantheon of American culture. Poor and black, Rodney King was on the wrong end of our most acute inequalities. Sooner or later, cruel inequalities will have to be maintained by cruel means, and cruel means will have to be justified.

``How could it happen?'' the prosecutor asked. He had not come to grips with an observation made by John Kennedy:

Sometimes, the enemy of the truth is not the lies we tell ourselves, but the myths.

---

*On one charge—the least serious—against one of the officers, the jury could not reach a verdict. Subsequently, a federal jury found two of the officers guilty of having violated King's civil rights.

the sinister connection Exoo sees. The relationship is not hegemonic, it is democratic. As a commercial medium, the movies had to, and did, give the *people* what *they* wanted."

There is truth in this. But I would add two comments. First, the cultural democracy of the Hollywood studio is a one-party democracy. Yes, moviegoers can "vote" at the box office, and the studios read the "returns" carefully.

But the studios put up the candidates, and they have all been spokesmen of the same centrist party. Precisely because this is a commercial medium, the studios never offered "opposition party candidates" with novel, possibly unpopular "platforms." In a true democracy, we would hear such ideas out. Perhaps, over time, they would grow on us. Perhaps not. But in the "democracy" of the film marketplace, we never knew that they existed.

A further qualification to the culture of democracy thesis is that sometimes, the process was not a democracy at all, not even a one-party democracy. Sometimes, it was aristocracy, as when the WASP establishment had the Hollywood Jews "scared straight" by the Americanization movement. Sometimes, it was good old-fashioned authoritarianism. One such moment came in the 1940s and 50s, when the big stick of state power was used to rout the radicals out of Hollywood, as we shall presently see.

Inclusion: Hollywood's Promiscuous Embrace

Affirmation of the dominant ideology is an important theme in American film, but it is by no means all there is. Indeed, mere affirmation could not, by itself, do hegemony's job. Working class people are not that gullible. They are always in command of their own "good sense," no matter how shrouded in the dominant "common sense" that may be. Among them, shadows of doubt about the prevailing order and their place in it struggle for expression.

In fact, capitalist ideology itself, Gramsci argued, is capitalist self-interest, sugar-coated with "good sense" to help the medicine go down—to make it seem just to the dominant and palatable to the dominated. But this means that within that capsule there are contradictions: Capitalism promises that hard work will let you "provide for your family." But people know that a parent who is always at the office, pursuing that promise, is not providing what a family needs. Capitalism promises freedom. But people who take orders from a boss all day know the difference between that and freedom. And so on.

Enter Hollywood, starring in perhaps her greatest role, that of mythmaker. The job of the myth, the anthropologist Claude Levi-Strauss has argued, is to resolve its culture's contradictions.[76] In non-Hollywood myth, contradictions are often intractable, and resolutions come at a price. For example, the contradiction between Oedipus' moral aspiration and his achievement is "resolved" when he sees his shortcomings—a sight so unbearably painful that he puts out his eyes.

Hollywood heroes don't do that sort of thing. They don't have to, because in Hollywood, cultural dilemmas are not just resolved, they are dissolved.

Take the case of the outstanding dilemma of advanced capitalism, one which has also been a principal preoccupation of Hollywood, the tension between individualism and the need for community and family. In Hollywood, this is no problem: you can eat your cake and have it too. Shane can be that most ruthless of entrepreneurs, the gun for hire, *and* have a meaningful engagement with a family and community, *and* ride off when the excitement's over, looking for further adventures.

Sometimes, the tension is artfully established before it is magically melted away. In *Baby Boom* (or, in *Meet Me in St. Louis*) there is some suspenseful doubt about it for a while, but it turns out you can be a high-powered corporate executive *and* a super-parent and spouse, living in a closely knit small town community. Similarly, in *Pretty Woman*, we learn that you can be a profit-maximizing corporate raider, and a man committed above all to social responsibility and personal relationships.

In that same film, we also discover that social class is no object: you can be a street walker and still expect to marry a *Forbes* 100 polo-crowd guy and live happily ever after. Indeed dissolving such class lines has always been one of Hollywood's favorite tricks, from *It Happened One Night* to *Driving Miss Daisy* and *Far and Away*. Implicitly, the message is, "In America, the land of plenty, you can have it all."

Commercially, the inclusion strategy makes perfect sense. Once these dilemmas are dissolved, happy endings ensue. And happy endings are a key ingredient in the commercial imperative's recipe for escapist entertainment. Directors improvise on the recipe at their peril. A surprising number have suffered the fate of Orson Welles, whose "second movie (*The Magnificent Ambersons*) demonstrated the stark incompatibility of small-town values with those of the modern industrial age. . . . The studio tacked on a wildly inappropriate ending and opened the film as the bottom half of double features. Thereafter, Wells rarely worked in America." [77]

Another commercial asset of dissolving dilemmas is the "promiscuity" of this strategy. Each of these dilemmas is composed of competing political values (individualism versus communalism; egalitarianism versus meritocracy, self-interest versus social responsibility, and so on). Coming down firmly on both sides of these dilemmas makes the movies appealing to viewers of every creed at the same time. Even the left could like *Patton* or *Rambo* as they railed against the establishment. And even in the "anti-war" *Platoon*, Sergeant Elias (Willem Dafoe), the film's Christ-figure, was among other things, a re-enlistee and a well-oiled killing machine.

The effect of embracing both common and good sense themes was to deny "the necessity of choice." [78] This took the inoculating function of film one step further. Where escapism takes us away from politics to a fantasy world, inclusiveness makes a political fantasy of the real world. Where escapism tells us to forget about politics for a while, inclusiveness tells us we can forget about politics permanently. In a land of abundance, there is no need for hard choices.* In a place where virtue and initiative are rewarded, leaders will emerge who embody what we all want and need—left and right, black and white, worker and boss, dove and hawk, all joined together in common purpose. Here, there need be no more "isms," no more issues, no conflict; in short, no politics.

Need I add that once ordinary citizens have agreed that the game is over, elites have won.

"Quality" Film: The Limits of Contest

The blockbuster mentality dominates most of Hollywood's thinking, but not all.

Some films are not wide-open invitations to the omnibus audience, but are instead "targeted" to a particular "market." Unfortunately, most of these silver bullets are even more formulaic and hegemonic than the blockbuster. That is generally true, for example, of such "target" genres as martial arts movies, horror movies, youth movies. Targeted films don't intend to be inclusive. And, depending on their target audience, what they may exclude is any hint of a non-hegemonic theme.

But then there is another kind of film. It is, to be sure, the exception and not the rule. Nonetheless, it is there. It is what some have dubbed "quality" film.

"Quality" media is distinguished by an honest effort to render human life in some of its fullness. At its best, it eschews the formulaic imperatives of escape and affirmation. Among the aspects of humanity included in its wide embrace are political and social questions. I've already argued that formulaic film is often depoliticized. To put that point another way, most movies see only "private troubles," never the "public issues" attached, by a long rope, to those troubles.[80] The "quality" productions see those connections. And often enough, their vision is critical of the way things are and the powers that be. Ecological catastrophe is tied to corporate rapacity *(The China Syndrome)*. The Wall Street creed of

---

*This is also the argument of the anti-socialist "end of ideology" school.[79]

"greed is good" can be bad for working class people *(Wall Street)*. Our justice system is the best that money can buy *(The Verdict)*. Our government is not always of, by, and for the people *(J.F.K.* or *Missing)* And so on.

But there are limits to that criticism. And they are absolute. Ideologically, those limits are well within the bounds of what is safe for capitalism.

Sometimes, the critique the quality films make is liberal: a crusader fights the powers that be, and wins some reform or redress *(Norma Rae, The Verdict, China Syndrome, Country, Born on the Fourth of July,* etc.) The critical message is this: capitalism can and should be regulated and supplemented. But the positive message is this: the system works; work within it. Through it, capitalism *can be* regulated and supplemented, its productive capacity harnessed to provide fairness for all. Together, capitalism and its watchdogs (journalists, public-interest lawyers, union or movement organizers, etc.) are a pretty good team, if not a match made in heaven. In all the above-mentioned films, protagonists triumph not by challenging the system, but by using it. Revolutionary change, they imply, is not necessary for a happy ending.

But more often than they are liberal, or post-liberal,* or any one thing, quality films have mastered the art of being all things. They have mastered the arts of inclusion and reconciliation. Intricately woven into the fabric of whatever critical politics these films may sport are the old reliable fabrics: the dominant and formulaic.

Let us look, for example, at what one writer has called "the last great movie made in Hollywood," Roman Polanski's *Chinatown.* The film is based on a real incident, in which a cabal of Los Angeles' elite conspired to divert the water supply of Owens Valley farmers to irrigate land they had grabbed desert cheap in the San Fernando Valley, thereby multiplying its value.[81] In part then, this is a critical film. In part, it is a story about the kind of selling out of the public interest for private gain that is everywhere in our urban history.

But the very form in which the story is told dilutes the political force of that story, reconciling its critical potential with themes that are safe, familiar, and hegemonic.

The story unravels, not as a community's struggle, but as one man's quest for truth and justice. (Perhaps ninety percent of

---

*See Chapter 5 for a discussion of post-liberalism. Resigned to the death of politics, post-liberals practice "coping." The definitive post-liberal film is *The Big Chill.*

camera time is spent seeing what Jake Gittes sees, or seeing his reactions to it.) The film's final issue is not whether Jake will be able to save L.A. from the cabal, but whether he can save his new-found love from the cabal's leader. Our hero's actions move the film, and those actions are personal, not political. In this way, a political story is personalized, made into a story of individual heroism.

The problem Jake confronts is also depoliticized by being personalized. The villain Jake faces is a daughter-raping murderer. Many American cities have seen their resources plundered, but the men who did it were not daughter-raping murderers, they were upstanding, church-going, family-loving businessmen and politicians. The real villain in these cases was not human evil, but a system that puts its premium on the pursuit of private profit. In this way, what could have been a study of the corruptions implicit in capitalism becomes a Manichean story of a good guy against a bad guy.

Through such an admixture of rebellious and familiar themes, the quality films take an explosive story and defuse it.

These limits of quality films, and indeed, the very existence of such films, are again, part of the logic of audience attraction—i.e., they are good business. Recent years have witnessed a graying of the movie audience. A former president of Universal pictures described this older, more educated and affluent audience this way: "They read reviews. They don't rush out on opening night. And you can't sell a savvy 35-year old with a television commercial. Quality and subject matter become more important." [82]

So realism, dimension, and ideas are "in." But radicalism is out. Whatever else the members of this older, more established, affluent audience may be looking for on the screen, they are not looking for assaults on the system that has served them so well.

The "Language" of Hollywood Film: Medium as Message

Hugo Munsterberg came to America from his native Germany to found a psychology department at Harvard. Oddly enough, what he found himself "mesmerized" by was not our nation's psyche, but our movies.[83] More precisely, he wrote about the "language" of film, the way in which camera work and editing tell their tales. What he began to see was how this language made the message it carried all but unarguable.

"Anticipating the Gestalt psychologists of later years, Munsterberg believed that the coherence humans find in 'reality' is actually imposed on sensory experience by mental configurations." [84] The genius of the "Hollywood style" Munsterberg saw developing was to steal the style of human "mental processes"—our way of imagining—and to project it onto the screen.[85]

For example, if we were to imagine two people conversing, our mind's eye might move from the face of one speaker to the other, as each spoke, and occasionally to an important reaction as one party listens. Hollywood has captured this mental process in its "shot-reverse shot" pattern of camera placement and editing. If we were to imagine one speaker telling the other a vivid story from his past, the image of the two conversing might fade, while our mind's eye conjures those past events. Hollywood's "flashback" technique replicates the process perfectly. If we were to imagine one character surreptitiously poisoning the other's tea while this other momentarily turns his back, our mind might focus on the hand dropping the deadly tablet in and switching the cups.* So does the Hollywood style, as it "privileges" the viewer, by "centering" important information or by using "close-ups."

Because, in these and other ways, the camera and its director "see" in a way that we might see, these filmmakers are invisible to us. Indeed, the Hollywood style is called the "invisible style," or "classical realism." "This is not a writer and director offering their view of reality," the style implies. "This is real." In perfecting this invisible style, Hollywood had achieved the illusionary power described in fiction by Stanislaw Lem as an art form of the future. He called it "the real":

> *"And what is a real?"*
>
> *"A real is . . . a real . . ." she repeated helplessly. "They are . . . stories. It's for watching. . . . A real is artificial, but one can't tell the difference. . . ."*
>
> *My first impression was of sitting near the stage of a theater, or no—on the stage itself, so close were the actors. As though one could reach out and touch them. . . .*

---

*This description is much like a well-known shot from Hitchcock's *The Lady Vanishes.*

> *The real was more than just a film, because whenever I concentrated on some portion of the scene, it grew larger and expanded; in other words, the viewer himself, by his own choice, determined whether he would see a close-up or the whole picture. Meanwhile the proportions of what remained on the periphery of his field of vision underwent no distortion. It was a diabolically clever optical trick producing an illusion of an extraordinarily vivid, an almost magnified reality.*[86]

The ideological effect of this "magnified reality" is powerful indeed. "Under its sponsorship, even the most manufactured narratives came to seem spontaneous and 'real.' "[87] Where the substance of Hollywood movies tells us we *do not* have to make choices (because we can have it all), their *style* adds that we *cannot*: this movie is not an argument, not one of several possible positions, says its style; this is real.

Thus, when the movies affirm dominant myths, all of that ideology, cloaked already in the sheep's clothing of common sense, is doubly disguised by Hollywood's "invisible style."

Radical Film: No Contest

Of course, not all movies are under the thumb of the Hollywood studios. In fact, about 50 percent of the movies in an average year are financed and distributed independently of the studios. It is on this open terrain that countercultural films are made. It is here that taboos are broken, and themes that cannot be spoken, are spoken: Themes such as grassroots radicalism *(Northern Lights)*, worker solidarity, pacifism *(Matewan)*, radical feminism *(Born in Flames)*, and socialism *(Rosa)*.

Never heard of these movies? That is not surprising. Unfortunately, although "many are called" (to be made) "few are chosen" (to be exhibited and seen). These independent releases reap only 10–15 percent of all rental fees paid by exhibitors to producers.

Worse still, most of that 10–15 percent is taken up by *downmarket* "alternatives" to Hollywood fare—porn, slice and dice, martial arts movies and so on.[88]

Why such a paucity of box office for the independents? Why such a plenitude of trash among them? By now it will not be surprising that the answer is, as usual, dollars and cents.

The obvious economic problem faced by a "quality" independent filmmaker is financing. Once the studios have, for all the commercial reasons cited earlier, refused to finance or distribute her
film, an "indie" might turn to the banks. There, he/she won't even
get as far as whether or not the project is commercial. Banks are
not interested in scripts or subject matter. "In twenty-nine years
of banking in this business, I've never once read a script, nor do I
intend to start now," says the executive vice president of the First
National Bank of Boston. That is because "bankers are not investors but are lenders who make loans on proven assets." They want
to know "that the borrower has funding to produce and distribute
ten or twelve films a year, ensuring that a few successful films will
balance the inevitable losses. . . . They insist that borrowers have
secured distribution plans; they demand sufficient financial resources, $100 million to $120 million, to produce and distribute a
line of product." [89] In other words, bank financing is most available
to the studios, who need it least, and least available to the independents, who need it most.

Next our intrepid filmmaker might turn to an independent*
studio or distributor.

> [However,] the independent distributor . . . is usually a company
> with a narrow range of strict requirements, . . . [they] usually go
> after a very specific segment of the population, allowing for even
> less deviation from the formula picture. . . . These independents
> often emphasize a particular genre such as horror or youth pictures,
> and seldom risk making a picture outside the proven formula film.[90]

Altering its formula is even more risky for the independent
studio than for the majors. For the latter, there is a constant flow
of product, and a risk that fails is likely to be offset by some successes. For a small studio, releasing only two or three films each
year, there is little margin for error. The risk that fails can lead
directly to bankruptcy court.[91]

That leaves those independent distributors specializing in
quality films that are too original, too challenging, or too controversial for the studios. But there are few such studios, and many
good filmmakers.

If, when the music stops, our filmmaker is without a chair in
such a studio, she is left to her own devices. This may include

---

*"Independent" here means, of course, independent of the major, conglomerate-
owned studios.

looking for "angels," individual investors who "want to be patrons of certain directors . . . , [or] are interested in a particular subject matter, or bringing movie production to their home state, or learning about a new business, or meeting actresses or whatever." [92] It took director John Sayles and his producers three years to raise the money for *Matewan* from such investors, despite Sayles' record of producing critically acclaimed films that returned investors' money with interest.

Even once our independent film is produced, its travails continue. As we have seen, conglomerization has resulted in vastly increased spending by the major studios on their films. Independents' films, financed on a shoestring, just cannot compete for theater owners' attention with the stars, production values and marketing campaigns of the majors.[93]

The final stop on our dispiriting tour is at the ancillary markets, such as television. As we shall see in Chapter 5, the commercial commandments are even more strictly observed on television than in the movies. HBO's film buyer states succinctly what is surely also the networks' view: "[Independent films] have limited value in relation to a service such as HBO. Our philosophy is to run films with the largest broad appeal." [94]

In short, counter-hegemonic film exists. But it has been pushed to such a periphery that most Americans are unaware of its existence. The force that moved it out of sight was commerce. As with the news, with television, with everything, capitalism has managed to define the movies. It has defined them not as a public good. Not as art. Not as potentially ennobling, edifying, enriching of our public discourse, and therefore worthy of public sponsorship. And so, the independent, critical film, though it may be all those things, will not enjoy much of an audience because it is not the one thing capitalism insists the movies must be: commercial.

Legislating Hegemony: Hollywood Meets Washington

Censorship

In 1915, the Supreme Court came to the dubious conclusion that films were "not to be regarded as organs of public opinion." [95]

In other words, what the movies had to say was not protected by the First Amendment's guarantee of free speech. State, local, and federal government censors "had near life-and-death power over cinematic exhibition." [96] Faced with that threat; with the threat of boycotts by the Roman Catholic church's rating body, the Legion of Decency; and by the xenophobic screed of the "Americanization" movement, Hollywood decided to censor itself.

In the early 1930s, the major studios, organized as the Motion Picture Producers and Distributors of America, established the Production Code Administration. Its job was to enforce what became known as its "Hays Code," named after Will Hayes, president of the MPPDA. Practically all movie scripts required the PCA's approval. Its edicts were absolute. Its Code prescribed in fastidious detail in areas of sex, violence, "morality" generally, and politics.

On this last subject, for example, the Code commanded that:

> *Law . . . shall not be ridiculed, nor shall sympathy be created for its violation. . . . The use of the flag shall be consistently respectful. . . . The courts of the land shall not be presented as unjust. . . . The history, prominent people and citizenry of all nations shall be presented fairly.*[97]

The following letter from the PCA to the producers of a film under review typifies the Administration's willingness to redirect an artistic vision:

> *Scenes 25, 26, and 27: The speeches by 'G' are much too general in that they indicate that all lawyers have to 'betray justice and the law' in order to be successful. All of this should be rewritten to get away from the present flavor.*
>
> *We feel that some punishment should be indicated for the crooked attorney. This might be handled by having the judge in the court indicate that he is going to have this lawyer investigated by the Grand Jury or the Bar Association.*
>
> *In our conference the other day we suggested that since the early portion of the story makes clear that both 'C' and 'B' are unethical in their legal practices, and that the latter as well, is crooked, this material might be objectionable to members of the legal profession.*
>
> *We suggested that the court room scene conclude with a dignified and vigorous condemnation on the part of the court. Upon reading the script we feel that such condemnation is essential.*
>
> *We further suggest that material be injected making it quite clear that 'B' realizes the wrongfulness of his criminal acts, and*

condemns himself for his past misdeeds and regenerates completely.[98]

Hays' office dealt specifically with political radicalism in a 1934 "test case." The film at issue was producer Walter Wanger's *The President Vanishes.* It portrayed the country in the grip of " 'the merchants of death,' munitions manufacturers who are aiming to feather their nests with the profits from a new world war. . . . Congress is befuddled and the president seems ineffectual. The American landscape is littered with a range of xenophobic pressure groups, and the only clear call against these capitalist warmongers comes from—the Communist party!"

Hays demanded a complete rewrite, which washed away the film's anti-capitalism and completely eliminated the role of the Communist party. After this fiasco, "serious films on major political issues were as rare in Hollywood as those dealing with prostitution or drug addiction." [99]

In 1952, governmental censorship, at least, relaxed somewhat. In that year the Supreme Court effectively reversed its earlier position, and formally acknowledged that motion pictures are a "significant medium for the communication of ideas." With that, the Court "read the movies into the First Amendment." [100]

Today, the only grounds on which a film can be legally banned are those of "obscenity," and even that ground has continually shrunk.[101] Legally, heaven knows, anything goes.

Nonetheless, it was not until 1968 that the Motion Picture Association abandoned the Hays Code and adopted a ratings system in its stead. This means that the Code reigned supreme throughout Hollywood's formative "Classic Period," the time that "would establish the definition of the medium itself . . . [and would] set the terms by which all movies, made before or after, would be seen.[102]

What is more, a form of censorship lives on in the MPAA's ratings system. Directors of such recent, politically charged films as *Henry and June; The Cook, the Thief, His Wife and Her Lover, Damage,* and *The Wide Sargasso Sea* have argued that the X (or later, NC-17) rating given their movies by the MPAA "prevents serious adult films from reaching a wider audience." [103] Frequently theater chains are forbidden by their real estate contracts to show NC-17 films in malls, severely limiting their distribution. Many newspapers and magazines will not advertise films rated NC-17, and some of the largest video cassette outlets will not rent or sell them.

As a result, a number of recent films that have tried, without sensationalism, to explore issues of sexuality or violence have been hamstrung by their ratings, and denied the audience they deserve.[104]

Repressing Radicalism

As the Great Depression wore on in the 1930s, the Communist Party enjoyed a resurgence. In Hollywood as elsewhere, a small but significant number of men and women grew disillusioned with a system that could leave so many without means, left the capitalist church, and joined another.

For most of them, violent revolution was not much on their minds. Instead, they fought for the civil rights of the Scottsboro boys; they fought against Spain's fascist dictator, against Hitler's rise in Germany. They fought for what they thought was justice.

But for all their seeming harmlessness, they were avowedly anti-capitalist, which could not go unnoticed. The body that took notice was the House Un-American Activities Committee. As it was reconstituted in 1937, the committee's chairman was Martin Dies, a rabid anti-communist who announced early in his tenure that "rich Jews . . . were planning to seize the government . . . with the aid of . . . Spanish mercenaries routed through Mexico." [105] Despite such lunatic rantings, and despite an "appalling legislative track record, [the committee] was granted remarkably high appropriations by the House of Representatives with little apparent demur." [106]

In 1939, Dies brought his circus to Hollywood, probably at the invitation of studio executives who hoped he would discredit the militant Screen Writers Guild. There to greet Dies when he arrived was a delegation of studio producers, who promised that "if the committee discovered individuals who brought discredit on the industry, 'there will be no attempt to protect those individuals or groups.' " [107]

Witnesses called before the committee had few options, none of them attractive. One could "take the Fifth," appearing to have something to hide, and be placed on a "blacklist" of unemployables. One could take the offensive, as screenwriter John Howard Lawson did, and say:

> I am plastered with mud because I happen to be an American who expresses opinions that the House Un-American Activities Committee does not like. . . .
>
> Why? [Because Committee Chairman] J. Parnell Thomas and the un-American interests he serves . . . [are] conspiring against the

*American way of life. They want to cut living standards, introduce
an economy of poverty, wipe out labor's rights, attack Negroes,
Jews, and other minorities, drive us into a disastrous and
unnecessary war.*

*The struggle between thought-control and freedom of expression is
the struggle between the people and a greedy unpatriotic minority
which hates and fears the people.*[108]

Such "unfriendly" witnesses, refusing to answer the committee's questions about their own politics and those of others, were held in contempt of Congress, and went to prison.

Indeed, the only way witnesses could stave off prison and unemployment was to "crawl through the mud," as actor Larry Parks put it: to denounce communism, renounce any past affiliation with it, and to name friends and colleagues as communists or "sympathizers," thus subjecting them to imprisonment, blacklisting, or the informants' mud.

But the time it was over, 212 writers, directors, actors, producers, and studio workers had been blacklisted. Many more than that were "graylisted." The graylisted were those who could not credibly be accused of communism, but who had dallied with liberal causes. In some ways they were worse off than the blacklisted, whose names, at least, were published, so that they knew where they stood, and what their options were. The graylist was not published. Its victims found themselves in a twilight where, without explanation, the phone stopped ringing. No studio was without a full set of these blacklists and graylists; no studio failed to "honor" these judgments from without; no studio was without its "executive vice president in charge of clearance." [109]

The personal toll the purge took can be measured in broken marriages, broken health, a suicide or two, and other stress-related deaths. Politically, the purge ended the "Popular Front" that had united liberals and radicals in their work for progressive causes. Ended too was the militancy of the Hollywood labor unions.

Artistically, the purge meant the "near-complete exclusion of the poor, workers, blacks, and minorities from the screen. . . . Never daring in the first place, the studios withdrew before the lengthening shadows of HUAC . . . into the dictated confines of patriotic conformity." [110]

Indeed, this "caution" was "probably the effect of the HUAC investigations which lasted longest." [111] Once again, when ordinary means seemed to be losing their grip, capitalism proved itself able to marshal extraordinary means to guarantee its continued hegemony. Hollywood could add this to its already formidable list of reasons for being nothing more, and nothing less, than a celluloid syringe.

Music Up; Fade Out

Welcome to Hollywood. Where all that we behold is reassuring in its sameness. In its innocence of anything unsettling, challenging, radical, offensive. In its relentless simplicity. Where even the outer limits of aesthetic adventure are marked by an equivocal liberalism that is safe. Safe for its audience. Safe for its system.

Welcome to Hollywood. Where speech, as Herbert Marcuse once said of our society, "moves in synonyms and tautologies." [112] Where concepts are defined by their current incarnation in the status quo. Where what will be, what can be, are defined by what is. Where cultural hegemony is thus built into the very definition of institutions. Where "the movies" are defined as what they currently happen to be: as a commercial enterprise, requiring a mass audience, in innocent America. And therefore as inoffensive, happy, simple, safe. Hollywood. Welcome to it.

References

1. C. Wright Mills, *The Sociological Imagination*, (New York: Oxford University Press, 1959).
2. Stuart Ewen and Elizabeth Ewen, *Channels of Desire*, (New York: McGraw Hill, 1982); 87.
3. Ibid.: 86–87.
4. Ibid.: 89–92.
5. Neal Gabler, *An Empire of Their Own*, (New York: Crown, 1988): 6.
6. Ibid.: 2.
7. Israel Zangwill, *The Melting Pot*, (New York: Macmillan, 1909).
8. Milton M. Gordon, *Assimilation in American Life*, (New York: Oxford University Press, 1964): 73.
9. Max Weber, *The Protestant Ethic and the Spirit of Capitalism*. Translated by Talcott Parsons (New York: Charles Scribner's Sons, 1958): 77.
10. Paul Kleppner, "The Politics of Change in the Midwest," (unpublished Ph.D. dissertation, University of Pittsburgh): 537.

11. Charles Leinenweber, "Socialism and Ethnicity," *Failure of a Dream*, edited by John H. M. Laslett and Seymour M. Lipset, (Berkeley: University of California Press, 1984): 261.
12. John F. McClymer, "The Americanization Movement and the Education of the Foreign-Born Adult, 1914–25," *American Education and the European Immigrant*, edited by Bernard J. Weiss, (Urbana: University of Illinois Press, 1982): 97–98.
13. John Higham, *Strangers in the Land*, (New Brunswick, New Jersey: Rutgers University Press, 1955): 219.
14. Ibid.: 227.
15. Ibid.: 230–31.
16. National Americanization Committee Pamphlet, in Gordon, *Assimilation in American Life*: 101.
17. John Higham, *Strangers in the Land:* 9; McClymer, "The Americanization Movement and the Education of the Foreign-Born Adult, 1914–25."
18. Neal Gabler, *An Empire of Their Own:* 241–42.
19. Ibid.: 216.
20. Quoted in Neal Gabler, *An Empire of Their Own:* 47.
21. Ibid.: 320.
22. Ibid.: chapter 11.
23. Ibid.: 119.
24. Ibid.: 204.
25. James Monaco, *American Film Now*, (New York: New American Library, 1984): 31.
26. Neal Gabler, *An Empire of their Own:* 187–88.
27. Ibid.: 111.
28. Richard Maltby, "The Political Economy of Hollywood," *Cinema, Politics, and Society in America*, edited by Philip Davies and Brian Neve, (New York: St. Martin's Press, 1981): 47.
29. Mark Litwak, *Reel Power: The Struggle for Influence and Success in the New Hollywood*, (New York: William Morrow, 1986): 52–56.
30. Ibid.: 96.
31. Suzanne M. Donahue, *American Film Distribution*, (Ann Arbor, Mich.: UMI Research Press, 1987): 192.
32. Quoted in Mark Litwak, *Reel Power:* 96.
33. Barry Bluestone and Bennett Harrison, *The Deindustrialization of America*, (New York: Basic, 1982): 15–19.
34. Ibid.: 151–53.
35. Quoted in Mark Litwak, *Reel Power:* 65.
36. Suzanne M. Donahue, *American Film Distribution:* 189, 278.
37. Philip Davies, "A Growing Independence," *Cinema, Politics, and Society in America*, edited by Philip Davies and Brian Neve, (New York: St. Martin's Press, 1981): 129; Suzanne M. Donahue, *American Film Distribution:* 191.
38. Suzanne M. Donahue, *American Film Distribution:* 196.
39. John Izod, *Hollywood and the Box Office, 1895–1986*, (New York: Columbia University Press, 1988): 108.
40. Suzanne M. Donahue, *American Film Distribution:* 50.
41. Bruce Austin, *Immediate Seating*, (Belmont, Calif.: Wadsworth, 1989): 19–20.
42. Thomas G. Schatz, *Old Hollywood, New Hollywood: Ritual Art, and Industry*, (Ann Arbor, Mich.: UMI Research Press, 1983): 2.
43. Ibid.

44. John Izod, *Hollywood and the Box Office, 1895–1986:* 180.
45. Mark Litwak, *Reel Power:* 89–90.
46. Ibid.: 249.
47. John Izod, *Hollywood and the Box Office, 1895–1986:* 181.
48. Thomas G. Schatz, *Old Hollywood, New Hollywood:* 191–2.
49. Ibid.: 193; John Izod, *Hollywood and the Box Office, 1895–1986:* 192–3; Andrew Yule, *Fast Fade,* (New York: Delacorte, 1989): 185.
50. Robert Gustafson, " 'What's Happening to Our Pix Biz?' From Warner Bros. to Warner Communications, Inc.," *The American Film Industry,* edited by Tino Balio, (Madison, Wis.: University of Wisconsin Press, 1985): 515.
51. Thomas G. Schatz, *Old Hollywood, New Hollywood:* 24.
52. Quoted in Mark Litwak, *Reel Power:* 270.
53. Calvin F. Exoo, ed., *Democracy Upside Down: Public Opinion and Cultural Hegemony in the United States,* (New York: Praeger, 1987): 96.
54. Mark Litwak, *Reel Power:* 113.
55. John Izod, *Hollywood and the Box Office, 1895–1986:* 183.
56. Thomas G. Schatz, *Old Hollywood, New Hollywood:* 194.
57. Mark Litwak, *Reel Power:* 231.
58. Ibid.: 73–4.
59. Quoted in Philip Davies, "A Growing Independence": 132.
60. Robert Gustafson, " 'What's Happening to Our Pix Biz?' ": 582.
61. Warner Communications Industries Annual Report, 1981, in Robert Gustafson, " 'What's Happening to Our Pix Biz?' "
62. John Izod, *Hollywood and the Box Office, 1895–1986:* 169.
63. Quoted in Mark Litwak, *Reel Power:* 102.
64. Calvin Hall, *A Primer of Freudian Psychology,* (New York: New American Library, 1954): 58.
65. Mark Litwak, *Reel Power:* 111.
66. Marc C. Miller, "Hollywood: The Ad," *The Atlantic Monthly,* (April 1990): 51.
67. Ibid.: 52.
68. Ibid.
69. Quoted terms are from Robert Ray, *A Certain Tendency of the Hollywood Cinema,* (Princeton, N.J.: Princeton University Press, 1985): chapter 2.
70. Max Weber, *The Protestant Ethic and the Spirit of Capitalism:* 107.
71. The phrase is from Mark C. Miller, "Hollywood: The Ad": 53.
72. Bruce Austin, *Immediate Seating:* 102.
73. Joe Feagin, *Subordinating the Poor,* (Englewood Cliffs, N.J.: Prentice-Hall, 1975): 97.
74. Ibid.: 103.
75. Thomas Ferguson and Joel Rogers, *Right Turn,* (New York: Hill and Wang, 1986): 18.
76. Claude Levi-Strauss, *The Raw and the Cooked: Introduction to a Science of Mythology: I,* translated by John and Doreen Weightman (New York: Harper and Row, 1975).
77. Robert Ray, *A Certain Tendency of the Hollywood Cinema:* 58.
78. Ibid.: 55.
79. See, for example, Irving Howe, *Politics and the Novel,* (New York: Avon, 1970): 164.
80. Michael Schudson, "The Politics of *Lou Grant*," *Television: The Critical View,* edited by Horace Newcomb, (New York: Oxford Univ. Press, 1987): 102.
81. David Halberstam, *The Powers That Be,* (New York: Alfred A. Knopf, 1979): 115–16.

82. Aljean Harmetz, "The Figures Don't Lie: Hollywood's Audience is Older and Pickier," *New York Times*, (March 6, 1988): C13.
83. Thomas G. Schatz, 1983: 49.
84. Ibid.: 49.
85. Ibid.: 50.
86. Quoted in Robert Ray, *A Certain Tendency of the Hollywood Cinema:* 55.
87. Ibid.
88. Suzanne M. Donahue, *American Film Distribution:* 215, 264.
89. Ibid.: 51.
90. Ibid.: 262.
91. John Izod, *Hollywood and the Box Office, 1895–1986:* 127.
92. John Sayles, *Thinking in Pictures*, (Boston: Houghton-Mifflin, 1987): 40.
93. Suzanne M. Donahue, *American Film Distribution:* 215.
94. Ibid.: 203.
95. *Mutual Film Corporation vs. Ohio*, quoted in Richard S. Randall, "Censorship: From *The Miracle* to *Deep Throat*," *The American Film Industry*, edited by Tino Balio (Madison, WI: University of Wisconsin Press, 1985): 511.
96. Richard S. Randall, "Censorship: From *The Miracle* to *Deep Throat*": 510.
97. Quoted in Ruth A. Inglis, "Self-Regulation in Operation," *The American Film Industry*, edited by Tino Balio, (Madison, WI: University of Wisconsin Press, 1985): 378–383.
98. Ibid.: 399.
99. Richard Koszarski, "Politics and the Movies, or: That's Democracy!" *Culturefront* (Fall 1992): 26–27.
100. Richard S. Randall, "Censorship: From *The Miracle* to *Deep Throat*": 510.
101. Ibid.: 516–23.
102. Robert Ray, *A Certain Tendency of the Hollywood Cinema:* 26.
103. Glenn Collins, "Guidance or Censorship? New Debate on Rating Films," *New York Times*, (April 9, 1990): C11, 17.
104. Ibid.: C17.
105. Neal Gabler, *An Empire of Their Own:* 352.
106. Richard Maltby, "The Political Economy of Hollywood": 78.
107. Quoted in Neal Gabler, *An Empire of Their Own:* 354.
108. Quoted in Larry Ceplair and Steven Englund, *The Inquisition in Hollywood*, (Berkeley: University of California Press, 1983): 284.
109. Ibid.: 388.
110. Ibid.: 422.
111. John Izod, *Hollywood and the Box Office, 1895–1986:* 134.
112. Herbert Marcuse, *One Dimensional Man*, (Boston: Beacon Press, 1964): 88.

Candice Bergen, television's Murphy Brown, thanks then-Vice President Dan Quayle for her Emmy award. Quayle accused the show's makers of being part of a liberal "cultural elite" that flouts American values. This chapter disagrees.

A Shadow Show in Cathode Rays: The Politics of Prime Time

INTRODUCTION ☆ ☆ ☆ ☆ ☆ ☆ ☆ ☆ ☆ ☆ ☆ ☆ ☆ ☆ ☆ ☆

This chapter begins with a debate between this book's perspective, hegemony theory, and its opponents. Marketplace democracy theory begins by arguing that television is "power to the people." It works this way: The television industry watches what the people watch; it gives them more of what they do watch; it cancels what they don't watch.

Hegemony theory replies that the television devised in a marketplace is different from television devised in a public place. The public, at its best, wants to educate and ennoble itself, as well as to entertain. The market wants only to sell. In this sense, the television industry may be giving the people what they want; "but," as one writer put it, "so does the Medellin Cartel." [1]

One important issue in this debate is whether we chose—democratically—to make television a commercial product, instead of a matter of public policy. This chapter reviews the history of that decision. It concludes that the way the choice was made was not democratic, but hegemonic.

Next come the neoconservatives, who argue that the "new class" is hard at work in television too, bringing their anti-capitalist liberalism to our living rooms.

Hegemony theory rejoins that it is not the new class (of writers, directors, etc.) who have power over television. It is the "old class" of business executives who do. For that reason, the new class tends to follow the lead of the old, and their lead takes television from their business imperative (profit) to its conclusion: programs that are inoffensive, unchallenging, and predictable. Along the way, we'll meet the "cast" of the television business, including such characters as networks, producers, affiliates, syndicates, sponsors, the audience, and the FCC. We'll examine the part each plays in this production.

Next we'll turn to the argument that television has changed. Technology—especially the emergence of cable TV—has revolutionized the TV experience, this argument says. No it hasn't, hegemony theory replies. And it won't, for very good reasons—economic reasons, of course.

Once we've reviewed the process that makes television, we will then review the product. We do so under three headings: "situation comedies" and "action-adventure" shows together take up most of prime time. Our third category, "quality television," is the one that television's supporters point to in its defense. We'll explore whether it represents an alternative to the worldview of the other categories.

Finally, we'll look at some of the effects of TV viewing on our thinking.

From time to time along this tour, we'll take a "station break" to hear a story: about what happened when NBC met its new conglomerate owner, GE; about how a show called *An American Dream* became a nightmare; about how the Golden Age of television became the plastic age; and how a show about women became a show about women's bodies.

The Thesis: Television's Power

Picture this: a cave wall shadow show that commands seven hours of the average cave family's attention every day. A show that takes up just under three-fifths of all the evening hours people spend in their caves—one that consumes 72 percent of cave dwellers' non-working, waking evening hours. If we assume that just eight percent of those evening hours must be spent eating, doing home-work, cleaning up the cave, and so on, "We are left with only about 10 percent of people's evening hours that could reasonably be de-voted to [the shadow show] and is not." [2]

Picture such a thing, Plato says. And then he asks, would not such cave dwellers begin to "recognize as reality those artificial shadows?" Thousands of years later, someone bothered to tote up the obvious answer:

> On issue after issue we have found that the assumptions, beliefs, and values of heavy viewers . . . tend to reflect both what things exist and how things work in the television world. [3]

Picture, in other words, Americans of the late 20th century. Shadow-show viewers held not by chains, as in Plato's cave, but by the alluring, prevaricating power of the shadows themselves. An audience restricted not by shackles, but by the fact that others own and shape the shadow show. Viewers benighted not by a physical darkness, but by the delights of a show that shrouds its politics, and so becomes a pleasant, narcotizing diversion from the real world of thorny social problems and choices. A show that is rarely unsettling because it is usually uncritical of the established order of things.

Picture Americans, nightly viewers of a powerful, hegemonic shadow show known as television.

A Counter-Thesis Reconsidered

But let us begin with an opinion to the contrary. It is not easy to dismiss the cry of the TV moguls that this medium is not theirs, but ours—that its message is determined not by an elite, but by the people.

*After all, what is a rating? In the final analysis it is simply a
counting of the votes . . . a system of determining the types of
programs that the people prefer to watch or hear. Those who attack
this concept of counting the votes—or the decisions made in
response to the voting results are saying in effect: Never mind what
the people want. Give them something else."* [4]

*A mass medium can only achieve its great audience by practicing
. . . cultural democracy . . . by giving a majority of the people what
they want.*[5]

And they are hard to rebut. After all, we do watch the stuff.
But here is a paradox. We get up from our watching, to tell pollsters
at our doors that we are less satisfied with watching TV than with
"reading, evenings out, religion, and socializing." We tell them we
don't regard it as "particularly enjoyable" or "necessary to one's
daily life." [6] We also say that we probably spend "too much time"
watching it[7] and that it is not "really worth watching." [8] In fact, we
don't really watch it so much as we just have it on. Researchers
have found that television is a "low involvement" medium, eliciting
a state of "attentional inertia marked by lowered activity in the part
of the brain that processes complex information." [9] Much of the
time it is on, we are not even "low involved." "Over half the time
that families reported viewing, they were actually not viewing—
even though the television might have been on." [10]

What is going on here? An obvious answer is that we're lazy,
and prefer an activity that doesn't require much in the way of brain
waves. But we're also hypocritical, and so we hide our laziness
from the pollster, pretending to prefer Kafka to Cosby.

But there is another possibility. Perhaps this paradox of
watching what we say we don't like is a real ambivalence. Perhaps
we are lazy but we are also sincere when we say we could and
should do better.

That possibility reintroduces a question we have met before:
What would mass media be like if we were related to it as a *public*,
and not as a *market*?[11] What if we (the people) sat down ourselves
to decide what sort of mass media we would have?

Consider, for example, the contrast between U.S. commercial
television and the Western world's publicly owned television. Some
would argue that the latter is better; some would argue that it is
worse. Few would argue that it is not different. A recent survey of
the difference indicates that public, noncommercial television is
more likely to offer "artistic" cultural programming such as

concerts, ballets, and "serious" dramas; less likely to rely on the formulae of past successes; more likely to give serious attention to the life and culture of ethnic minority groups; and less likely to depict violence.[12]

"But," object the marketplace democracy theorists, "commercial TV is just as democratic. There, our 'representatives' (network programmers) are interested above all in the will of the people— what we want is what we get on commercial TV."

In a sense, that is true. But to a curiously considerable extent, network programmers make their decisions apart from the people they "represent." Even network researchers acknowledge that their system of testing pilots on audiences is so unscientific as to be inconclusive. Says Ellen Franklin of ABC, "I don't want to apply what I know from statistics and methodology to that sample because it's nothing. I don't want to start with any kind of assumptions about generalizing to the population." And so, says ABC's former head of comedy development, "I have never seen a case where [pilot] testing has substantially changed anybody's mind." [13]

Instead, in the end, it all comes down to media moguls' market judgments, which they make by conferring with other media moguls. To read the "restless public mood," TV executives pore over *Time, Newsweek, People,* over "what advertisers [are] using to sell soap," and over the movies. Meanwhile, in the network's movie division, an executive finds the inspiration for a TV-movie in a segment of "Real People," or "20-20." [14] And across town, news editors, trying to take the public pulse, also do so by watching other media.[15] Over on Madison Avenue, advertising executives are looking at "other agencies' advertisements, other magazines, and other media." [16] In the end, this "marketplace democracy" turns out to be magnates holding each other's pulses in a strange, seamless circle of elite hegemony.

Who Chose This System?

So far, our colloquy of competing theories has gone like this:

Hegemony Theorists: Television is an instrument of capitalist hegemony. It is, first of all, depoliticized—a pleasant, narcotizing diversion from the real world of social problems and choices. And secondly, it is uncritical—those few political themes that do appear either reinforce or are unthreatening to the capitalist order.

Marketplace Democracy Theorists: Popular culture is popular for a reason: it serves people's real aesthetic, psychic, and political needs. Mass media is mass media because the masses chose it. To gainsay their choice is elitism, pure and simple.

Hegemony Theorists: To the extent that the people "choose" what's on TV, they do so as a reactive market, not as a proactive public. And that distinction is crucial. For it is precisely these definitions—of ourselves as a market, of television as a business—that makes TV so unchallenging and uncritical.

Marketplace Theorists: But didn't the people themselves decide that TV should be commercial—through our democratic politics and free markets?

Hegemony Theorists: Glad you asked that question. Here's the answer.

A Brief History of Broadcasting

Politics did indeed define television, but the process was anything but free or democratic. Instead, the defining moment was a classic instance of plutocratic politics, and of corporate hegemony.

In the fight to define and control broadcasting, capitalism would ultimately score a knockout. But not until the second round. The first round would go not to private profit, but to the "public interest."

The opening bell was rung by Congress, when it passed the Radio Act of 1927. Its immediate objective was to bring order to the Babel of broadcast voices that had filled the hitherto unregulated airwaves. In the process, all parties understood, some voices would be lost. But whose?

The stated purpose of the Act was "to maintain the control of the United States over all [broadcast] channels." The act allowed the use of channels, "but not the ownership thereof," through the granting of government-approved licenses for limited terms, "and no such license shall be construed to create any right, beyond the terms, conditions, and periods of the license." With uncanny foresight, the Act defined radio "as any intelligence, message, signal power, picture or communication of any nature transferred by electrical energy from one point to another without the aid of any wire connecting the points." [17] In this almost inadvertent way did the Act reach into the future and place the as-yet undeveloped television medium under its jurisdiction.

The criterion for granting—or not granting—licenses was to be the "public interest, convenience, or necessity." To put these brave words into deed, the Act created the Federal Radio Commission. Its power—to review license applications and to allocate frequencies—was no less than life or death over every broadcaster in the country. The fight to define broadcasting was on.

In one corner of the ring stood the newly formed National Broadcasting Company (NBC), offspring of a titanic convergence among GE, Westinghouse, their previous child RCA, and AT&T. NBC was the first great linkup of affiliated stations, each receiving their programming over AT&T wires from the network. But the essence of NBC was that its programming was sponsored by advertisers, themselves increasingly large producers of increasingly national brands. On this venture rode the fate of commercial broadcasting. Capitalism's bets were down.

In the opposite corner of the ring stood stations representing the whole wide array of radio's nonprofit possibilities. There were educational stations, many operated by universities, some state-funded. There were stations operated by labor unions, and by self-professed radicals. (WEVD in New York City drew its call letters from the initials of Eugene V. Debs, presidential candidate of the Socialist Party.) Churches and newspapers owned stations; so did the City of New York. A thousand flowers bloomed.

In 1928, the FRC began to clear the air, by ordering 164 stations to "show cause why they should not be abolished." After holding hearings, the commission stripped about half of the 164 of their licenses. The rest survived, but barely, with reduced broadcast time and wattage.

Which voices fell from the air? Which grew stronger? A few years later, Pendelton Herring counted up the casualties in the *Harvard Business Review:* "While talking in terms of the public interest, the Commission actually chose to further the ends of the commercial broadcasters." [18] Of the first twenty-four clear channels created by the FRC, "twenty-one had gone to network stations, with some authorized to use 50,000 watts. . . . Virtually all stations operated by educational channels received part-time assignments, in most cases confined to daytime hours, which many considered useless for adult education. . . . In 1928, twenty-three gave up; in 1929, thirteen more followed." [19]

Those that hung on were sometimes hectored around the radio dial by regulatory torment. " 'For ten years,' wrote Jerome

Davis when the Connecticut State College station finally gave up, 'this station has sought to secure the right to operate a more powerful station and one free from commercial interference. For ten years this college has continued to broadcast programs into whistle-ridden channels, vainly hoping that some provision would be made for state broadcasting needs.' "[20] During that period, the FRC had changed the station's wave length, time-sharing partners or power levels over ten times.

Within a few years, the pattern was set. Broadcasting was a commercial medium and upon that rock was built nearly all that radio and television would become.

"How did this come about?" asked Rousseau, having observed that "Man is born free, but is everywhere in chains." Here's how.

When the Radio Act became law, the commercial broadcast industry quickly created a textbook "iron triangle," an unholy alliance of powerful interest group, Congressional overseers, and regulatory agency. "Probably no quasi-judicial body was ever subject to so much Congressional pressure as the Federal Radio Commission," concluded a Brookings study of this period.[21] Congressmen reinforced their numerous entreaties to the FRC by keeping the commissioners "in a state of uncertainty. . . . Their positions and the life of the commission were determined by Congress for short-term periods. . . . The importance of Congressional assistance in dealing with the FRC became notorious."[22]

If legislators were the first battalion in the corporate offensive, lawyers were the second. The commission was anxious to clear the airwaves quickly, before being caught in a web of injunction. "The avoiding of litigation 'before we could get a system working' became an obsession. 'Personally I can tell you,' Commissioner Caldwell recounted late, 'the Commissioners were more scared than the broadcasters were.' If a station sent a lawyer, or a Congressman interceded, a compromise usually resulted. 'We felt that at that time we did have to make a lot of trades.' "[23]

While that squad of lawyers played defense against the commission, another went on offense against the noncommercial stations. Commercial stations assigned to share time with noncommercials began to harass their "roommates," petitioning the FRC for the full time. Even if such a request was not likely to be granted, hearings would be held, representation would be required, the limited resources of the noncommercials would be stretched—to the breaking point, the commercials hoped.[24]

And finally, best of all, was corporate business' public campaign. 1930 saw the birth of the National Advisory Council on Radio in Education. Funded by John D. Rockefeller, Jr. and the

Carnegie Corp., the Council was dedicated to the proposition that radio's educational mission could best be served by commercial broadcasters, in "cooperation" with educators. At its first meeting, Owen D. Young, godfather of the RCA-NBC family, informed the group "that it was possible for any educational group . . . to obtain all the [NBC] facilities for nationwide broadcasting that it could possibly use, without any expense whatsoever, the sole condition being that the audience must be large." [25] Also on this public stump were the NBC president and vice president, proclaiming the networks "wide open to those who would raise the level of national culture," with "all the place for education that education needs." [26] And so on.

A second prong of the public campaign was NBC itself. The network's birth announcement, made in full-page newspaper ads in 1926, was a model of "corporate responsibility" propaganda. "The purpose of [NBC]," it intoned, "will be to provide the best program available for broadcasting in the United States. . . . We are confident that the new broadcasting company will be an instrument of great public service." [27]

The announcement pointed to NBC's august Advisory Council of "statesmen, churchmen, educators and others [corporate executives] as guardians. of the network's highest aspirations. A Congressional committee was told that appeals could be made to this council 'over the heads of the operating executives.' There is no evidence that this was ever done, but the Advisory Council added to the early aura of splendor surrounding the company." [28]

The announcement, in its heralding of this public service, did not mention private profit or the advertising that would deliver it, though these were of course, the *raison d'etre* of the network.

This reticence was not surprising. Opinion leaders and policy makers alike were outspoken against the idea of "direct advertising" on radio. Even a figure as pro-business as Herbert Hoover would say, in 1924, "If a speech by the President is to be used as the meat in a sandwich of any patent medicine advertisements, there will be no radio left." [29]

And so, in 1928, when a Congressman pointedly asked NBC's president whether there was "direct advertising" in NBC programming, he would reply, "No, . . . these clients neither describe their products or name its price but simply depend on the good-will that results from their contribution of good programs." [30] And for a moment, it was true.

But as commercial radio consolidated its dominance over the airwaves, its colors began to show. By the early 30s, advertising was not only "direct," but "long . . . unrelenting . . . [and]

shoddy."[31] "The total time devoted to news, education, lectures, and religion was 'less than the amount of time absorbed by commercial sales talks.' "[32]

Commercial radio's first smash hit was "Amos 'n Andy," a comedy that showed advertisers the sort of fare that might unite Americans across class lines around their radios. A transplant from the minstrel show stage, "Amos 'n Andy" showed that white Americans from all walks of life loved to laugh at depictions of blacks as lazy, scheming, and stupid. Commercial broadcasting was now afoot, slouching toward the future.

By the time television technology was ready for deployment, the mold was cast: commercial, network broadcasting was the American way. The FRC had a new name (the Federal Communications Commission), but remained on its old leash.

The agency's first woman commissioner proposed, in 1950, that some television channels be reserved for nonprofit, educational stations. By this time, the very idea was a stranger. The networks' *Broadcasting* magazine labelled the idea "illogical if not illegal."[33]

Eventually, Congress did set aside some channels for educational TV. But most of them were not in the VHF range; they were in the useless UHF range. Because the companies that owned the networks and dominated the VHF range also dominated the production of TV sets, they simply refused to equip their models with UHF capacity. UHF stations were left crying in the wilderness for a full decade. Worse still, Congress made no provision for public financing of these public stations.

Nonprofit TV would limp along, underfinanced, for decades. Finally, public TV would come to rely heavily on the same private corporations that dominate commercial television.[34]

In the beginning, TV was, according to corporate proponents, to be a way "to share thought and culture and knowledge, [among] rich as well as poor," the "best in drama, the dance, painting and sculpture," the "biggest classroom the world has ever seen," bringing us closer to "the era when politicians and people met face to face than in many a long decade."[35]

In the end, it was "a glittering toy for an imbecile giant."[36]

In between, there was a contest. And as usual, commerce won. "Thought and culture and knowledge," "the drama and the dance," lost. The "democracy of the marketplace" won. Henceforth the airwaves would be ruled by "what the people would buy." But they would not be ruled by what the people would themselves make of the airwaves, in public policy based on public participation in an ongoing public discourse. In that sense, another, perhaps more authentic kind of democracy lost.

The Political Economy of Television

Industry to Business to Trash TV

In the 1980s, commercial television, like the news media, like the film industry, fulfilled its manifest destiny. Television, too, had made Veblen's passage from "industry to business."*

For example, the General Electric Corporation had jettisoned NBC as part of an antitrust settlement in 1932. In merger-friendly 1986, GE gobbled up NBC once more. Now NBC is part of a conglomerate corporation that makes nuclear missiles, power plants, nuclear reactors, jet engines, electric appliances, and—at the NBC division—dramas and news that might conceivably concern all of the above.

Also in 1986, ABC was acquired by Capital Cities Communications. Its media empire now spans eight local television and 21 radio stations, nine newspapers, Hollywood studios, cable network ESPN and part of Lifetime, 30 magazines, and a publisher of religious material. Like any good conglomerate, Cap Cities' properties are well known for making money, not cultural enrichment. The company's TV stations, for example, have long run "shoot-em-up, sensationalist local newscasts that do for crime and the seven-second soundbite what "Charlie's Angels" do for wet T-shirts." [37]

Our nation's fourth largest network, Fox Broadcasting, is a creation of Rupert Murdoch, whose News Corporation Ltd. "claims more newspaper circulation than any other publisher in the world." [38] Though Murdoch, like the other conglomerates, is widely diversified, he is best known as "the world's principal purveyor of blood and breasts journalism," wares he now plies on the Fox television network. [39]

Like these network "wholesalers" of television, the production and "retail" of TV have also gone from industry to business.

A great deal of this production comes from the television divisions of the big film studios. Columbia, Universal, Paramount, and 20th Century Fox, for example, are all major players. All are now owned in turn by conglomerate corporations—Sony, Matsushita, Paramount Communications (formerly Gulf and Western) and the Murdoch empire, respectively.

---

*Veblen's use of these terms is discussed in Chapters 1 and 4.

Culture Shock as NBC Meets GE

New ownership brought new management to the networks. When GE acquired NBC, the man they tapped to head the network was Bob Wright. Previously he had served GE as corporate lawyer, manager in its plastics and housewares divisions and head of its financial services division. Television? He ``didn't watch much.''

Early in his tenure, Wright held a meeting with a group of 24 field producers, writers, bureau chiefs, and so on from the news division. It was not, as it turned out, a meeting of the minds.

At one point, Larry Grossman, head of the division, rose to ask Wright a question ``on the minds of many in this room . . . 'Is GE running NBC or is NBC running NBC?' ''

``Grossman had obviously hit Wright's hot button. . . . 'GE has a fiduciary responsibility,' '' the president fumed. 'As long as I'm here, NBC has to be sensitive to what GE shareholders think. . . . We're not the Ford Foundation. . . . Ultimately, (this) company has got to recognize we are part of General Electric.' ''

Another member of the audience asked whether there was another side of the coin, besides shareholder responsibility. ``Can you give us GE's view of news?'' he asked. ``Is it a public trust?''

``Well,'' said Wright, ``it isn't a public trust. I can't understand that concept.''

Afterwards, Larry Grossman was disconcerted. ``For a group whose whole being is 'the public trust,' the meeting was 'a real culture shock.' ''

On another occasion, Grossman met with Wright's boss, the CEO of GE, Jack Welch. `` 'The first words out of Jack Welch's mouth when I walked in,' recalls Grossman, 'were this is the greatest day of my life.' Grossman wondered whether one of Welch's children had just done something wonderful, whether he had become a grandfather or acquired a masterpiece. 'Our stock just hit

---

Finally, at the retail level, the ownership of TV stations has also gone conglomerate. Corporate octopi have now enveloped over 80 percent of the TV stations in the 100 largest U.S. markets. By the late 80s:

a new high,' explained Welch. Grossman was stunned. 'I couldn't comprehend his values,' he recalls.''

By the end of their meeting, the incomprehension was mutual. Grossman expressed reluctance to cut the news budget by the amount Welch had asked, fearing it would compromise the product. He then began to excuse himself from the meeting, explaining that he was having dinner with Chief Justice Burger.

> Welch was livid. ''I was ready to fire him right there. That afternoon.'' ''If you don't get your costs in line you won't be having dinners with Justice Burger!'' Welch roared at Grossman, pointing a finger at Grossman's chest. Welch did not let up: ''You're going to do this stuff. You're going to follow our procedures. And if you like seeing Justice Burger you get this thing right. I want it clear you cannot refuse. . . . You work for Bob Wright! You work for GE!''

Before long, Larry Grossman was fired, even though he had made the cuts Welch demanded. His GE-installed replacement was a man who had built himself a successful news business, and whose idea of a good documentary was ''Scared Sexless,'' a piece of sensational fluff that nonetheless captured a thirty share.*

At NBC, the new order had arrived.

---

*A program's ''share'' is the percentage of television sets in use tuned to that program. Ironically, Grossman's replacement, Michael Gartner, would himself resign a few years later under fire for erasing the line between ''info'' and ''tainment.'' His news team, it was revealed, rigged a ''crash test'' of the GM truck said to be likely to explode on impact. Anxious for sensational pictures of such a crash, network producers had incendiary devices installed in the test truck to ensure an explosion.

Source: Ken Auletta, Three Blind Mice, (New York: Random House, 1991).

> Only two of CBS's top fifty stations were privately owned . . . [the new] corporate owners lacked shared history and old loyalties. Run by bottom-line managers, stations were constantly trying to better last year's numbers. "It's commodity trading to us," admitted Martin Pompadur, Chairman of Television Station Partners.[40]

Independent producer Norman Lear once railed against this trend, and against its traveling companion, the changing of focus from product to profit. "It's what we're dying of as a nation," he said. But then in 1985, as a result of its "escalating financial stature," Lear's Embassy Communications was acquired by the Coca-Cola Company.[41]

Now television, like film, like newspapers, has become a business. Now its managers are not the men who built the industry—the Paleys and Sarnoffs—who sometimes fell prey to "attacks of culture." [42] Now the industry's managers need know nothing at all about making television, though they must know a great deal about making money. Now they might be "legal and business school graduates, agents, researchers, broadcast standards executives, management training graduates.[43] Now there are no "attacks of culture."

The networks simply cannot afford them. Not when a single ratings point can, over a season, mean a difference of $90 million to a network.[44] Not when conglomerate executives and stockholders are demanding either higher profits each quarterly report—or network heads on a platter.[45] Not when the now conglomerate-owned affiliate stations, which networks rely on to air network programs, are in turn relying on the networks for their profits—and have more exit options than ever if their exorbitant demands for profits aren't met.[46]

In such a climate, it is not cynical, it is only realistic to say, as one network executive did, "I'm not interested in culture. I'm not interested in pro-social values. I have only one interest. That's whether people watch the program. That's my definition of good, that's my definition of bad." [47]

Counter-Thesis II:
The Wrath of Conservatives

But this time, it is neoconservatives who will object. Network executives may be monomanic about money, but, they argue, TV's auteurs—its writers and producers—are naked (well, since this is television, scantily clad) propagandists for their own anti-capitalist liberalism. And it is their ideology that flows freely into the content of television.[48]

There are at least two difficulties with this position. The first of these has been dealt with in Chapter 1, where we argued that TV's "creatives" have benefited too handsomely from the capitalist system to seriously want to revolutionize it.

But the other problem with this "new class" argument is the most fundamental. The neoconservative diagram of Hollywood's power circuits has its wires crossed. In Hollywood as elsewhere, money talks. As financiers of the product, it is networks—not producers, not writers—who have final say over which glints in the eye will become television programs.

It is networks that have final "approval rights" over actors, directors, writers, and scripts. Even the editing of television goes from the director's cut, to the producer's (right to re-edit), to the network's cut—which is final.[49] As producer Michael Zinberg says, "You work in conjunction with the network because they have scheduling authority. So I can go off and say, 'Hey, I want to make this pilot. . . .' But if it's not something they're going to want to schedule, what the hell do I want to make it for . . . ? The object is to get on the air." [50]

While the Hollywood "hyphenates" (producer-director-writers) might "like a system that provides opportunities to exercise originality [and] social concern . . . they believe that such opportunities have declined over the years." [51]

But in the end, even this picture of an uneven contest seems overdrawn. It emerges from time to time in the trade papers' headlines ("Producer Criticizes Network Censors"), not because it is usual, but because it is unusual. It is worthy of note as a "Man Bites Dog" story. Or more to the point and even less likely, the "Man Bites Hand That Feeds Him" story. The reality, for the most part, is not contest, but comity among creatives and networks. Summarizing surveys of TV producers, writers, and directors, Comstock reports, "What these people had to say about drama and cartoons is strikingly similar to what news personnel . . . have to say about the news—the principal sources for their work are the conventions of the genre in which they work, the expectations of colleagues as to what will succeed and what is worthy, and the demands of the organizations (in this case, the networks) which are their clients." [52]

And why not? A system in which "even a second string producer or writer can earn two to three times the salary of a network program executive," will encourage producer-writers to stay on the team. Indeed, says a former head of programming for NBC, the perks available are not just an encouragement, they are a compulsion:

> It's such a high-profile business and so glamorous. It's like heroin.
> People in the business are junkies. The guys at the networks and
> the studios have all the heroin. But you're so desperate for heroin
> you'll do anything. This desperate need robs you of your courage.[53]

The way to stay on the team, of course, is to be a team player, to get along. Indeed, hyphenates and network execs get along so well that one close observer describes them as "a family," an "old boys' network." [54] It is a network in which producers are themselves often once and future network executives, where writers "normally do what they are told . . . without needing to be told," and where everybody has "master[ed] the unwritten rules and [their] mastery of the game crystallizes the rules, making them harder and faster than they would otherwise be." [55]

Indeed, so clubby is the circle of Hollywood "players" that membership is restricted. "Fully half of prime-time television is scripted by only 10 percent of the Writer's Guild's 3,000 active members." A recent survey of prime time found 75 percent of all its offerings were produced by just ten studios.[56] And it is no accident. This small, inward-turning circle, this chosen few, has made the team by "mastering the rules"—the network's team, the network's game, the network's rules.

So the question that will define television programming becomes, what are those rules? The commercial television game is easy to understand. Just as in the film and news businesses, the goal is to maximize profits by maximizing audience size. And just as the goal is the same as in other mass media, so is the strategy, and so are the consequences for the content of the medium. In the end, we are left with a television world that is largely without politics, without social problems or issues. And when politics does make a brief appearance, it comes not to bury but to praise the capitalist system—the system which, after all, commercial television exists to serve.

The Logic of Broadcasting

From time to time, we are told that technology is about to enrich our lives immeasurably. This is one of those times. The trade journals put it this way:

> *Explosive. That's the only word to describe the changes that have occurred in television during this past decade. . . . Technologies— VCRs and cable television . . . have forever changed the way we use our TV sets. And, indeed, the way we live. . . . Choice. We have a lot more now than we did in 1980.*[57]

*[In response to these technologies], the broadcast networks shifted
. . . from rear guard to avant-garde, rallying behind a banner of
innovation. . . . The most experienced programmer in the business,
Brandon Tartikoff of NBC, supplied the slogan for the revolution:
"Tried and true is dead and buried."* [58]

In a few pages, this chapter will suggest that tried and true is
in fact alive and well. We are no more about to experience trans-
figuration through technology than we were in 1922, when *Good
Housekeeping* promised that broadcasting would "be a sort of pan-
acea to cure all the ills" besetting us.[59] Today, as in 1922, the
potential of technology for human enrichment depends entirely on
who controls it, and for what ends.

We begin, therefore, with the tried and true logic of broadcasting—the one that has dominated television for decades. Afterward, we'll look at the modest alterations of the logic recently
wrought by technology.

In television as in other mass media, the transition from industry to business has changed the need for profits into a demand
for big profits. And so broadcasting's corollary need for an audience
became a need for a mass audience. Ordinarily, a prime time network program drawing "only" 10 million households is on its way
to extinction. Happily (for the networks anyway) producing such
an audience does not require the powerful magic we might imagine.
In fact, that audience is, in a sense, a given—a sort of birthright
bequeathed to television and its major networks by our cultural
history.

It works this way: Every evening at prime time in this country,
a strange thing happens. A vast audience materializes in front of
the nation's TV sets. And here is the strange part: they seem to
materialize not as a function of what is on TV, but as a matter of
course. This thesis is strange enough, in fact, to strain belief. But
evidence for it abounds. Paul Klein, former head of programming
at NBC, found substantiation in the fact that "every day at the
same time the number of TV sets tuned in [holds] remarkably constant." [60] Further evidence comes from viewers' accounts of their
own behavior. For example, only a third report looking at television
listings before deciding to watch. Not surprising, considering that
reasons reported for watching tend to be "nonselective." We watch
not for a specific program, but "to relax," to "pass the time," to "be
entertained." [61] In short, "turning on the set . . . has become . . .
the equivalent of switching on the lights." [62]

What's more, once fixed by the eye of the cathode mesmer, we
tend to be immobilized. Viewers who begin watching a station will

usually stay with that station. Unless offended or bored by what it sees, this "audience flow" will not be diverted.

Todd Gitlin, paraphrasing Klein, puts the point this way: "Viewers do not care much just which shows are plunked in front of them so long as they are [the phrase is Klein's] 'the least objectionable programming.' " [63]

As we are about to see, the logic of least objectionable programming (LOP) explains a good deal of what sometimes seems an inexplicable medium.

The Real Code of Broadcasting

As a show of corporate responsibility, the National Association of Broadcasters has produced a "code" of broadcasting. It is full of pious platitudes that broadcasters are to honor in their programs. But as one might expect from a show of corporate responsibility, a show is all it is. The code is honored mainly in the breach.

Meanwhile, there is another code of broadcasting, this one unwritten. This one's aim is not a false front, but real ratings, and real profits. This one, therefore, is not only honored, it is revered.

The next sections' titles are its bylaws.

Programming Shall Never Offend Its Audience

One obvious way to be "objectionable" is to give offense. The implication for programming is also obvious. As one network executive puts it, "Our goals will be whatever they have to be to avoid being labelled whatever the label may be." [64]

To be a bit more specific, programmers "avoid being labeled" in at least four ways.

First, TV's "wanted ad," like that of the other mass media, usually reads, "No politics need apply." At first blush, that may seem an impossible rule to maintain. After all, politics is about who gets what, and that issue is everywhere in human life.

And yet, TV does manage to dodge that issue, by dodging human life as it is really lived. How? By focusing its attention instead on, well, on . . .

> *Sam drops anchors as a debonair globe trotter aboard a cruise ship,
> where he must capsize the wedding plans of his ex-wife and a
> murderous hood.* ("Quantum Leap")

> *A hard-fought trivia board game ends with a trivial pursuit into the
> hinterlands to verify the answer Georgie gave to the championship
> question.* ("Hearts Afire")

> *A rogue agent who once trained Jonathan to kill mistakenly
> activates Jonathan and three other special agents to murder a
> former Special Forces assassin.* ("Raven")

> *Steve forgets he's dateless when he shines at one of L.A.'s hippest
> venues.* ("Beverly Hills, 90210")

> *Nora is taken hostage in a jail break by a bank robber, a serial
> rapist and a cop killer.* ("Bodies of Evidence")

> *Balki finds a box of money, $50,000 to be exact, and finding the
> rightful owner sends the cousins on a mad dash to a funeral home.*
> ("Perfect Strangers")

These are not real people, with real problems that have real
political implications. These are fantasy people, with fantasy problems in a fantasy land that is devoid of politics. Their function is
spelled out for us in the theme song of a well-known TV soap opera:
"You give my life a hope that's real; 'cause when I'm with you, you
take me away to Another World."

But everyday life is not all that is depoliticized. Television
manages to drain the politics even from those moments when politics is at stage center, in soliloquy. One television writer describes
the process:

> *I was asked to write [an] episode of "The FBI" . . . at about the time
> . . . when four little black girls were killed by a bomb in a
> Birmingham church. . . . The producer checked with the sponsor . . .
> the FBI, [and] the network . . . and reported back that they would be
> delighted to have me write about a church bombing, subject only to
> these stipulations: the church must be in the North, there could be
> no Negroes involved, and the bombing could have nothing at all to
> do with civil rights.*[65]

Such depoliticizing of social problems explains a good deal
about made-for TV movies. These often try for resonance by adopt-
ing current social issues as their subjects. But somehow, their
treatment manages to remove society from these social issues.

So, for example, a movie about AIDS or acquaintance rape or wife abuse will have nothing to do with the politics of those issues. Instead, it will be a story of "one woman's struggle" to "find the courage to reclaim her life," in the words of *TV Guide* blurbs describing recent examples.

But there is one sort of politics, one ideology that is not ideology. It is just "good common sense," and so it is not objectionable. That, of course, is the dominant ideology. Reviewing results of their massive content analysis of TV, Gerbner and associates conclude, "Competition for the largest possible audience . . . means striving for the broadest and most conventional appeals . . . and presenting divergent or deviant images as mostly to be shunned, feared or suppressed." [66]

That means, as our look at programming will show, that television is a house full of all the old familiar faces of liberal capitalist ideology—the "nonpolitical" politics of the American Way.

"But," demand the neoconservatives, "what of the new faces, representing the new class of carping liberals? What of the Maudes, the Mike Stivics, the Julia Sugarbakers, and the Murphy Browns?"

The networks allow them, not for political, but for commercial reasons. They are there, not as leaders of social change, but as followers. Their function is here explained by no less an authority on the commercial needs of television than Jane Fitzgibbon, senior vice president of the research firm of Yankelovich, Skelly & White and consultant to the American Association of Advertising Agencies.

> *Television [she told her clients] must be consistently attuned and alert to life-style changes (this goes for the advertisers as well as the writers), so that it can accurately and responsibly portray them at a point in time when the public will neither be bored because they are too outdated, nor outraged because they are too far out on the fringes. Instead, television's portrayal of societal change can insure that the public be stimulated, informed, sensitized, reassured about what is happening in their own personal lives and the lives of other people in the world at large.*[67]

In this way are social movements housebroken. Only those not "too far out" are presented at all. And even those are rendered as "life style changes." Feminism is not a fundamental challenge to every aspect of patriarchal society; it merely means that Kate and Allie can start their own business if they want to. Lifestyle changes—matters of personal choice in the land of the free-to-choose-which-brand-to-buy. In this way can "the public be . . . re-assured" that the civil rights, feminist, environmental, or peace movements are no threat to the American Way.

Enforcing Inoffensiveness

Inoffensiveness is sacred enough to the networks to have its own in-house temples. These are the networks' broadcast standards departments, which "monitor and control the content of all material, including advertising and programming. The head[s] of [these] department[s] report directly to the president of the network, at a level equal to the head of programming." [68]

Like the enforcers of the movies' "Hays Code," Broadcast Standards is the Inquisition of inoffensiveness, purging scripts of troublesome sex, language, violence, or "unwholesomeness." Following are a few examples of their handiwork.

The NBC Radio and Television Broadcast Standards and Practices manual dictates: "Respect for lawyers, police, teachers and clergy should not be diminished by undue and unnecessary emphasis on unfavorable aspects of members of these professions."*[69] This meant that the pilot script for NBC's "Hill Street Blues" had to be revised. It showed its Officer J. D. LaRue smash open a laundromat coinbox to find a dime for an important phone call. To the writers, "LaRue's transgression was a character point. . . . He was a notorious fuck-up . . . caught . . . in a downward spiral of alcoholism." But Jerome Stanley, head of West Coast Broadcast Standards said, "Absolutely not. We would not permit that kind of wanton disregard for the law on the part of policemen." [70]

Only years later, when videotapes were surreptitiously made showing police savagely beating helpless black men, would television viewers finally discover what "wanton disregard for the law" really meant. Only then would they discover that not all policemen were like television's T. J. Hooker version of our men in blue.

More recently, ABC's "thirtysomething" had that network's standards division "working overtime." "In one episode," says "thirtysomething" producer Marshall Herskovitz, "they deleted a line [about] orgasm after we had agreed to a more acceptable substitute, bleeped a line in which a reprehensible character mentioned his use of an hallucinogenic drug, and forced us to change a speech the network deemed insulting to automobile advertisers." [71]

---

*Note the similarity of this provision to one in the Hays Code discussed in Chapter 4.

And finally, from the "great censors think alike" department: Both CBS and ABC recently refused to air an ad sponsored by the United Auto Workers, because its language was "highly charged" and unfavorable to corporate America.* The kilovolt words in question were:

> *We want to build products Americans can be proud to own. And we've got the skills to do that. But we won't beat the competition if American workers are considered expendable . . . if our good jobs are shipped overseas."* [73]

Inoffensiveness. It is the first of only three precepts in the real code of broadcasting. The second is this:

Television Shall Never Be Anything Less than Entertaining, or Anything More

The injunction against boring one's audience is important to newspaper and film producers. To television producers, it is sacred. Canceling a newspaper subscription is a relatively infrequent occurrence. So is walking out on a movie. But changing a TV channel is not. For that reason, television, to an extent unknown even in film or print journalism, must constantly excite.

And that does not mean, "must excite the Mensa Society." It means, "must excite TV's mass audience." In Chapter 4, we saw how the film industry's need for broad appeal translated into the logic of Lowest Common Denominator. Television, of course, is also no stranger to LCD. Television invented LCD. Its logic, once again, is that smart people may watch a dumb show—if it is viscerally exciting. But dumb people won't watch a show that outsmarts them. And, Hollywood believes, there are a lot of dumb people. So, the syllogism concludes, keep it simple—make TV's excitement physical, not intellectual.

By this time, the corollaries of that theorem will be a familiar parade: Sex. Violence. Escape. High concept. Happy endings. Lotsa

---

*In truth, the facts of this sad story are themselves "unfavorable to corporate America." For the past two decades, U.S. manufacturers have been "disinvesting" from their American factories. Part of their strategy has been to shift operations to Third World labor markets, where the desperately poor will work for a dollar or two per hour. Estimates are that these firms eliminated close to a million American jobs a year.[72]

laughs. To use the hegemony theorists' terms, diversion, anesthetic, opiate.

Interestingly, hegemony theorists are joined in this characterization by television producers themselves, who openly describe their work as deliberate escapism. As former ABC Vice President Bob Shanks says:

> *Comedians and social critics may scoff; we ourselves know life is not like that. So what? People, masses of people, do not watch television to learn what life is like, but to escape it.*[74]

Elaborating, two other TV executive writer-producers suggest that, "Any idea for a series must demonstrate desirability. This means that a concept should answer at least one of the following questions." They list three, the first two of which are:

1. Is the basic storytelling arena interesting? *Is the idea set in a desirable and exotic locale (Hawaii, San Francisco, the Caribbean)? Does it feature interesting occupations (deep-sea diver, astronaut, race-car driver)? Does it have the ability to use unusual and fascinating machinery or technology (special cars, weapons, high-tech equipment)? Does it lend itself to an interesting, visual approach?*

2. Does the concept represent some form of wish fulfillment? *In our contemporary, technological society, there are few places people can turn to satisfy the frustrations of everyday life. Many long-running television series play on this frustration by showing a more comforting world or focusing on a character we would like to believe exists. We might fantasize about the life-style of a character like Magnum, wish for avengers like the A-Team, want to take a cruise on "The Love Boat," and wish to believe in angels like Michael Landon.*[75]

Karl Marx could not have described the tranquilizing function of television better than these captains of the culture industry.

Syndication and Simplicity

In addition to those already mentioned, one more audience consideration leads producers and network executives to avoid making the mind work and instead make the heart race, the belly shake, and the loins ache.

That is the syndication market.

After a program's producers have leased it to a network, usually for two airing dates, it can then be syndicated—released simultaneously to stations in the United States and abroad for additional airings.* Because the network's "license fee" payments will usually not quite cover the cost of producing a program, the syndication market is the brass ring for producers. Only in syndication will the show move from the loss to the profit columns. In fact, because there are few additional costs incurred in syndication, profit there may be enormous. "Magnum, P.I." sold there at about $1 million per episode of almost uncut profit.

What sort of traffic will the syndication market bear? An obvious selling point is several seasons of respectable network ratings. Beyond that, "situation comedies have been the best syndication properties. Their brand of innocuous fun is safe for stations to air at every time of day, or on weekends, making them very desirable and profitable." Industry analysts also say "eight o'clock action shows like 'The A-Team' and 'The Fall Guy' " are good bets. "With their appeal to young people, they can be programmed in the afternoon and early evening hours. Serious drama shows are more difficult syndication sales." [76]

What is more, these shoot-'em-ups also syndicate well in the international market. The subtle cultural and linguistic nuances of a serious drama or sophisticated comedy may be lost in the translation to Swedish or Japanese. But everyone understands a fist fight.

And the importance of this international market looms larger every day. "Overseas program buyers could spend about $3 billion on U.S. TV productions in 1995, up from $1.9 billion [in 1990]." Therefore, says Steven J. Ross, co-chief executive of Time Warner Inc., one of the country's busiest TV studios, "Globalization is basic to everything we do." [77]

High Concept

Another imperative of marketing also conspires to make TV simplistic. This is the requirement that story lines be "high concept"—reducible to an immediately appreciable shorthand—one line that can reach out from a *TV Guide* ad or logline and grab an audience. "Miami Vice" is high concept. Reportedly, it was sold in two words:

---

*Producers can, of course, enter the syndication market without having first leased to a network. Most prefer initial network airings for their shows, in order to get network revenues and the exposure that enhances a show's value in syndication.

"MTV Cops." "Happy Days" is high concept. It was conceived as "a humorous Waltons." [78] Producer Aaron Spelling, apparently more loquacious, needed a whole sentence to sell his idea for "Nightingales" to NBC programming czar Brandon Tartikoff: " 'Student nurses in Dallas in the summer and the air conditioning doesn't work so they sweat a lot,' said Spelling. 'It's a 40 share!' exclaimed Tartikoff. 'Let's do it!' " [79]

Made-for-TV movies are, of course, in particular need of high concept. "If you can't define [a TV movie] in a television log line, how can you get the audience to it?" asks Deanne Barkley, former vice president for movies at NBC and ABC. Because audiences don't know these movies from theatrical runs or previous episodes, "you've only got one shot to get them. . . . It doesn't matter how good it is or bad it is. . . . If you can describe it in one sentence so they know what they're coming to . . . they'll come to it." On the other hand, adds Brandon Stoddard, former movie honcho for ABC, "If you have a movie that takes a long time to explain or . . . is somewhat diffuse, you're going to have a very, very difficult time." [80]

Even once the audience is assembled and the movie begun, high concept remains the rule: "Clear stories that tell viewers instantly whom to care about and root for." Because "industry lore has it that the . . . finger is always poised near the dial, . . . all salient elements have to be established with breathtaking haste. . . . Characters have to be stripped down to unequivocal moral emblems; their troubles spotlit; their traits, like trademarks, leaping off the screen." [81]

But TV movies aren't the only shows in need of "instant clarity." As the race for ratings intensified, so did the race to see who was winning. In 1950, the Nielsen Company took six weeks to deliver program ratings to the networks. Today major-market results arrive over night.

Accordingly, the time given a show to establish its audience appeal has shrunk. In the old days, networks ordered new shows in full-season packages of 39 episodes. That allowed such acquired tastes as "All in the Family" and "Lou Grant" to build their audiences slowly.

Today, some shows are given a trial run of just 4–6 weeks. There is little time for an audience to learn to appreciate subtlety, novelty, or dimension—the stuff of good drama and real life.

Upbeat

One more force for the trivialization of television is the demand that it be relentlessly "upbeat." "Defeat and dreariness are what happen

Bad Dream

It was the demand for upbeat that finally put down a show called "American Dream." Producer Barney Rosenzweig conceived the show, about a blue-collar white ethnic family (the Novaks), who move into the only conveniently located, affordable housing they can find—in an all-black neighborhood. As Rosenzweig described it, "The American dream no longer exists, or is a bare possibility, or may be recapturable. It's a populist kind of picture . . . an opportunity for a guy to see that he's been sold a bill of goods, and he's going to . . . take charge of his own life, . . . and not let the society, not let the bullshit get him down."

Surprisingly, ABC bought the idea. Then, not surprisingly, they began to "flatten" it. "The instructions from ABC were," Rosenzweig recalls, 'Okay now, when you write this, we would like it to be in the idiom of "Eight is Enough" . . . keep it light, keep it gay.' "

Later, Rosenzweig brought the network a pilot script. It showed the family coping with their dilapidated and dirty new house, with one of the children being menaced at school, and with serious conflicts within the family. Rosenzweig was summoned to a meeting with network executives. "They started dumping shit on my head. We had an enormous fight." The network wanted the house "mysteriously fixed up, overnight and without comment, halfway through the pilot." They wanted the Novak children to go to a private school, "as if Danny Novak could afford such a thing." They wanted the family's conflict solved by the end of the pilot.

For subsequent episodes, "they wanted shows that were mini triumphs every week. They wanted a John Wayne ending. And they always wanted the look brighter and brighter. And they also didn't want the show to be shot in the winter in Chicago. They didn't want snow."

to you during the day," says ABC exec Bob Shanks. "At night, in front of the box, most people want to share in victories, associate with winners, be transferred from reality." [82]

This is one reason why TV's characters are disproportionately well to do. Only 1.3 percent of major characters on television are

Rosenzweig's writer, Ronald Cohen, wanted to do an episode in which the father gets fired. ''They said, 'Okay, but you've got to give him a job at the end of the show.' '' And, '' 'What he really should be doing is getting a promotion.' . . . Then I wanted to have him quit over a moral principle. The store that he works for is selling a motorcycle that's not safe, and he quits. 'No, you can't do that either, because then you're portraying American business as unsafe.' '' The network found Cohen's scripts ''horribly depressing,'' ''joyless.'' They said the show ''should be a reinforcement of (the) decision to move to the city; it should be perceived that (the) decision was a winning one. . . . There should be lovely things happening in the city.'' They said, ''Don't be so controversial that the audience feels like we're giving them a civics lesson. . . . Deal with social problems but not in a downbeat or depressing manner.''

Even the physical appearance of the city had to be upbeat. Phone calls to episode directors said, ''Please try to stay away from graffiti on the walls. . . . No garbage cans in the alleys.'' While shooting on location in a real high school gym, a network executive complained, ''The walls are too brown. . . . When I go to the Forum to watch a Lakers game, it's very bright and 'up' and it's a wonderful Technicolor kind of experience.''

After enough of such ''improvements,'' Barney Rosenzweig abandoned the show he had given birth to. Not long after that, Ronald Cohen was fired for continuing to resist network ''suggestions.'' A new, more pliant production and writing team was brought in to ''flatten'' the show.

The following spring, the network finally aired four episodes of ''American Dream.'' Ratings were not high, and it was promptly canceled. ''Another American dream gone astray,'' said Ronald Cohen, still unable to be upbeat.

Source: Todd Gitlin, *Inside Prime Time,* (New York: Pantheon, 1985), chapter 6.

poor, even though 13 percent of the U.S. population is poor. "Blue collar and service work occupies 67 percent of all Americans but only 10 percent of television characters." The plurality of TV workers are "professionals and managers. . . . Blacks on television represent three-fourths and Hispanics one-third of their share of the U.S. population, and a disproportionate number are minor rather than major characters." [83]

Of course, this cavalcade of the comfortable is just one more way of saying that all is well here in El Dorado.

Programming Shall Be Predictable

The final ingredient in the prime time formula rigidifies all the others. That is Hollywood's desperate need for predictability.

Like film moguls, television executives are anxious people. Currently it costs about $1.5 million to produce a one-hour prime time network program. Those seven figures are invested in a product no one needs to consume, a product whose competition is available, literally, at the touch of a button. This makes network executives anxious. They are even more so since they've come to work for conglomerate corporations, whose profit expectations are astronomical. "Nowadays," says producer Norman Lear, "everybody has to have a profit statement this quarter that's better than the last profit statement. That's the social disease of our time." [84]

The anxious question network executives ask themselves is, "How do we predict what audiences will watch?" Like movie makers, TV execs have opted for the obvious answer: what has been watched, will be watched. "Network program heads may give speeches about innovative programming, but they buy just the opposite. . . . Familiar formulas are more saleable than new, untested ideas. New program ideas stand the best chance of interesting buyers only if they are reminiscent of other successes." [85] "I have never been in a TV development meeting," says Michael Kozoll [co-creator of "Hill Street Blues"] "where someone does not ask, 'What's it like?' " [86]

And so TV is the land of the spinoff, the copy, and the rerun. Nancy Signorielli, whose study reviewed over 250 hours of prime time programming in search of diversity, didn't find it. Instead, she concluded, "Life is portrayed across genres in a remarkably consistent way. . . . Programs exhibit an overwhelming degree of similarity on numerous dimensions of program content and characterization." [87]

Perhaps this is just a way of saying that television, only somewhat more than other art forms, draws on its own tradition. But that is a bleak forecast, when we recall that TV's tradition is not Shakespeare and Balzac, or even Capra and Huston. TV's tradition is blandness and fluff, LOP and LCD. For the sake of predictability, that is what will be rerun, spun off, and endlessly copied.

Sponsors

TV viewers are not the only audience programmers must appeal to. Another—at least as important—is the audience that supplies the vast majority of television's revenue: advertisers.

In the prehistory of broadcasting, several schemes for financing the enterprise competed—funding by local governments, by equipment manufacturers, by a tax on radio equipment.

In 1922, AT&T introduced its own plan, a natural extension of its previous business: "Anyone who had a message for the world . . . was to come in and pay their money as they would upon coming into a telephone booth, address the world, and go out." [88] The company called this system "radio telephony" or "toll broadcasting."

Of course, it would turn out that the ones who could afford to send their "message to the world" were corporate advertisers. And so was born the system that would eventually define American broadcasting. AT&T's names for it now seem odd, but also apt. Broadcasting, radio and television, is just as AT&T described it: a "toll call" to America from our corporate establishment.

Because it is they who continue to pay the "toll," it is still their message, even though sponsors are no longer directly in charge of programming production. In 1960, after a series of scandals involving sponsor-produced quiz shows that had been "rigged" to hype ratings, networks took control of scheduling. Now it is they who decide what will be aired and when. But CBS President Frank Stanton immediately reassured his sponsors:

> *Since we are advertiser-supported we must take into account the general objectives and desires of advertisers as a whole. An advertiser has very specific practical objectives in mind. He is spending a very large sum of money—often many millions of dollars—to increase his sales, to strengthen his distribution and to win public favor. And so in dealing with this problem, it seems perfectly obvious that advertisers cannot and should not be forced into programs incompatible with their objectives.*[89]

Stanton even went on to observe that "advertisers and their agents often wanted to 'participate' in the creative process, and he felt they should be allowed to." [90]

And what sort of programming did advertisers finally decide was "compatible with their objectives"? Interestingly, the very

From Golden Age to Plastic Age

Television's early days are sometimes called its Golden Age. The tribute refers mainly to a group of anthology series—Philco Television Playhouse, Kraft Television Theater, Goodyear Television Playhouse. They began as "carte blanche invitations to writers."[91] These writers (among them Paddy Chayefsky, Gore Vidal, Horton Foote, Reginald Rose), given a chance to write whatever inspired them, produced scripts that were indeed inspired. Their words in turn inspired *tour de force* performances from such directors as Arthur Penn, Delbert Mann, and Sidney Lumet, and from actors like Rod Steiger, Paul Newman, Sidney Poitier, Joanne Woodward, and Kim Stanley.

The subjects of their inspiration may seem strange to us now, surrounded as we are by TV subjects that are relentlessly sexy, action-packed, upbeat, and upscale.

What inspired the Golden Age writers was, as Paddy Chayefsky put it, "the marvelous world of the ordinary. . . . There is far more exciting drama in the reasons why a man gets married than in why he murders someone."

And so the subjects of these teleplays were ordinary. They were not especially good looking. (Chayefsky's "Marty" describes himself as a "fat little man" who's tired of asking girls to dance because they usually say no). They are not rich. Their lives play themselves out in working class kitchens, cafes, butcher shops, and dance halls. They are not especially talented. They are not heroic. They are ordinary people, with all of the weakness, hardship, doubt, hope, dignity, and fortitude of ordinary people.

Critics loved these dramas. That is not surprising. But viewers loved them too. Ratings were consistently high.

Another audience, however, did not love the Golden Age. And ultimately, their opinion was decisive.

This decisive audience was advertisers. The reasons for their dislike were "not mysterious," says the definitive historian of the period, and he explains:

catalogue we called the "real broadcasters' code" is exactly what the ad doctor ordered.

Most advertisers were selling magic. Their commercials posed the same problems that Chayefsky's dramas dealt with: people who feared failure in love and in business. But in the commercials there was always a solution as clear-cut as the snap of a finger: the problem could be solved by a new pill, deodorant, toothpaste, shampoo, shaving lotion, hair tonic, car, girdle, coffee, muffin recipe, or floor wax. The solution always had finality.

Chayefsky and other anthology writers took these same problems and made them complicated. (And they were) often convincing—that was the trouble. It made the commercial seem fraudulent.

And then these non-beautiful heroes and heroines—they seemed a form of sabotage, as did the locales. Every manufacturer was trying to "upgrade" American consumers and their buying habits. People were being urged to "move up to Chrysler." Commercials showed cars and muffins and women to make the mouth water. A dazzling decor—in drama or commercial—could show what it meant to rise in the world. But the "marvelous world of the ordinary" seemed to challenge everything that advertising stood for.

Quite aside from the revulsion against lower-level settings and people, advertisers often felt uneasy about political implications. Such settings had a way of bringing economic problems to mind. And some writers kept edging into dangerous areas. (And so, within a year of the anthologies' arrival) sponsors and their agencies began to demand dramatic revisions.[92]

It was not long before the rising stars of this genre migrated to Hollywood, where the death of the old "studio system" seemed to promise artistic freedom. Within a season or two, the Golden Age of television was over.

Usually, sponsors want programming that is upbeat. An advertising agency had to explain this to playwright Elmer Rice after he submitted his "Street Scene" for their assessment.

> *We know of no advertiser or advertising agency of any importance*
> *in this country who would knowingly allow the products which he is*
> *trying to advertise to the public to become associated with the*
> *squalor . . . and general "down" character . . . of "Street Scene." . . .*

> *On the contrary it is the general policy of advertisers to glamorize*
> *their products, the people who buy them, and the whole American*
> *social and economic scene. . . . The American consuming public as*
> *presented by the advertising industry today is middle class, not*
> *lower class; happy in general, not miserable and frustrated.*[93]

Again, intractable problems are at odds with the sponsors' message. When ABC telecast "Roots," the journey of a black family from Africa to emancipation, *Variety* noticed this problem: "It was a bit disconcerting to cut from the anguished screams of a mother whose oldest son had been enslaved to a blurb for Ben Gay, for use 'when pain is at its worst.' "[94]

Usually, sponsors want programming that is unchallenging and inoffensive. For one thing, such shows are thought to make viewers more "receptive" to advertisers, as an ABC vice president for programming explains:

> *Program makers are supposed to devise and produce shows that*
> *will attract mass audiences without unduly offending these*
> *audiences or too deeply moving them emotionally. Such ruffling, it is*
> *thought, will interfere with their ability to receive, recall, and*
> *respond to the commercial message. This programming reality is the*
> *unwritten, unspoken* gemeinschaft *of all professional members of*
> *the television fraternity.*[95]

A second reason not to ruffle viewers is that advertisers are terrified by the prospect of boycotts. Television's steadiest customers are food and drug companies that depend on having their products flow steadily from supermarket shelves. And so, for example, advertisers withdrew from an episode of "thirtysomething" in which two gay men were seen in bed together, talking. ABC announced it would not rerun the episode, and later abandoned the gay storyline, which had earned one of the actors an Emmy nomination. NBC had trouble finding advertisers for even one run of the movie "Roe vs. Wade" because it examined the issue of abortion.[96]

Sponsors like episodic series, governed by the program's predictable formula, not the unpredictable inspirations of writers. They like series where the viewer is invited, week after week, to join a family of charismatic stars, whose warmth may spill over into an association with the product they are "brought to you by." The producers of NBC's highly rated "Cheers" were determined to leave no doubt that their show promised this strange sort of friendship to viewers. So they made their theme song an invitation to get "away from all your troubles . . . to a place where everybody knows your name, and they're always glad you came."

Sometimes the associative leap from stars to sponsors is not left to the viewer to make. Currently, Candice Bergen does commercials for U.S. Sprint, in wardrode and dialogue indistinguishable from those of her series persona Murphy Brown. The ads thus draw on years of our accumulated "friendship" with and knowledge of Murphy as a cut-through-the-hype-to-tell-it-like-it-is character.

Sponsors like their sets and costumes to be upbeat too. To put this point another way, sponsors like shows that are themselves display cases for the good life. Shows that depict these beautiful, charismatic "friends" of ours hip deep in nice things. Indeed, no small part of their attractiveness are the clothes and furnishings of the Huxtables, Sugarbakers, Seavers, Tanners, Banks, Taylors, and so on. In such a program environment, by the time we get to the commercial, its message has become a truism: of course consumer products enhance our pleasure and even our worth.

FCC: The Case of the Muzzled Watchdog

In legal theory at least, there is one more important player in the television game. That is the Federal Communications Commission, the government agency charged with protecting the public's ownership of the broadcast airwaves by seeing to it that programming serves "the public interest, convenience and necessity." But in fact, this player has been relegated to the sidelines by the power of the broadcast industry.

In 1961, newly elected President John Kennedy commissioned a study of the FCC. The unflattering portrait painted by the report surprised no one:

> The Federal Communications Commission presents a somewhat extraordinary spectacle. Despite considerable technical excellence on the part of its staff, the Commission has drifted, vacillated and stalled in almost every major area. It seems incapable of policy planning, of disposing within a reasonable period of time the business before it, of fashioning procedures that are effective to deal with its problems. The available evidence indicates that it, more than any other agency, has been susceptible to ex parte presentations [by the broadcasting industry], and that it has been subservient, far too subservient, to the subcommittees on communications of the Congress and their members.[97]

And that was not just an off year for the FCC. Seventeen years later, a major congressional study came to exactly the same conclusion. "The Commission's principal handicap has been . . . insufficient public representation to offset the assiduous attention paid by commercial interests." [98]

The FCC is a textbook case of a government agency captured by the industry it is supposed to regulate. The process is as easy to describe as it is hard to prevent. First, the broadcast industry pressures the FCC. Then the industry pressures the politicians who oversee the FCC. Then these politicians pressure the FCC. Then the FCC favors the industry over the public interest.

Let's elaborate on this process, one step at a time.

1. The broadcast industry pressures the FCC. The most obvious form of this pressure is the relentless lobbying of the FCC by industry representatives. As President Kennedy's commission reported, "It is the daily machine-gun like impact on both agency and its staff of industry representatives that makes for industry orientation on the part of many agency members, as well as agency staffs." [99]

Everywhere they turn, commissioners come face to face with the industry:

> The opinions and demands of the broadcast industry are expressed through consultative groups (such as joint industry-government committees), interchange of personnel, publication of views in the

> trade press, liaison committees of the Federal Communications Bar
> Association, social contacts and visits to offices of Commissioners,
> informal discussions at state broadcaster and trade association
> meetings, and the formal submission of pleadings and oral
> argument. The Commission is largely dependent for much of its
> information about proposed policies, especially about the impact of
> or potential for technological developments, on industry trade
> associations, the networks, and broadcast licensees.[100]

Given the natural desire for cordial relationships with those
one sees every day, it is not long before this steady relationship
becomes a social relationship:

> Relationships between some [industry retained] Washington lawyers
> and officials of the regulatory agencies can be so intimate they
> embarrass an onlooker. The lawyers and the regulators work
> together in a tight, impenetrable community, where an outsider can't
> understand the language. . . . The lawyers and the regulators play
> together at trade association meetings, over lunch, on the golf
> courses around Washington.[101]

And finally, there is the promise of a future in the company,
for regulators who show sympathy to the TV industry's needs and
objectives. The movement from regulatory agency to regulated industry (and back again) is so common that it is referred to as the
"revolving door." Over the course of a recent fifteen-year period,
one-fourth of FCC commissioners leaving the agency went to work
in the industries they were supposed to have been regulating.[102]

**2. Then the broadcast industry pressures the politicians who
oversee the FCC.** One of the most powerful interest groups in the
country is the National Association of Broadcasters.* The NAB has
the usual panoply of interest group weapons—an annual budget
of over $8 million, a staff of over 150 at work in a $6 million building located just three blocks from the FCC, a Political Action Committee for dispensing campaign contributions.** And then the NAB

---

*It is not, of course, the only lobbyist broadcasters have. Each of the three
networks has its own lobbyists in Washington. There are also separate
associations that serve the particular interests of TV station owners, TV
translator stations, the cable TV industry, UHF TV stations, and so on.[103]

**In addition to these legal means of influence, the broadcast industry has
occasionally bribed FCC personnel. For a recap of several incidents, see
Barnouw.[104]

has one more arrow in its sheaf: air time, the breath of life for politicians.

Since the 1950s, Congress has been operating its own recording studios. Here, members of Congress can cheaply produce flattering audio and video recordings of themselves. These are then mailed to broadcasters as news or public affairs programming. Broadcasters have been happy to air this pseudo-news, as a "courtesy" to Congresspersons. Equally courteous is broadcasters' own news coverage of the local member of Congress. A recent study concludes that "[Congressional] incumbents [whose odds of winning reelection are over 90 percent] receive twice the coverage their challengers get and more positive coverage than challengers or Congress as an institution or the government generally." [105]

3. Then politicians pressure the FCC. For its part, Congress has more than returned the favor. Ernest Hollings, while chair of the Senate Subcommittee on Communications, once said that committee members would "vote anything that the local broadcasters want. . . . Rather than a chairman of a subcommittee, I felt like a foreman of a fixed grand jury." [106]

Congress' part in the regulatory drama is a leading role. Congressional law gave birth to the FCC, and it continues to keep its child in line. "When I was Chairman [of the FCC]," Newton Minow has written, "I heard from Congress about as frequently as television commercials flash across the screen." [107]

Congress can send its message to the FCC over several channels. It can legislate further FCC guidelines, or amend the existing ones. It can expand or contract the FCC's budget. It can investigate the FCC for impropriety—and has frequently done so. Its committees can hold oversight hearings reviewing the administration of its laws by the FCC. Its members can individually communicate their concerns to FCC staff or commissioners. The Senate advises on and exercises veto power over presidential appointments to the Commission.

In sum, Congress has enough influence over its child so that, in the words of the NAB's general counsel, "The FCC will do whatever Congress tells it to, and will not do anything Congress tells it not to do." [108]

And what has Congress told the FCC to do, or not do?

The FCC's most powerful regulatory tool is its power to grant—or withhold—the license to broadcast. Federal law makes clear that the broadcast airwaves belong to the public. Broadcasters may use them only if granted a license by the FCC. The criterion for deciding whether to grant or withhold a license is to be "the public interest, convenience, or necessity." [109]

Or at least, so says the law. In practice, the criteria have been more like "the *broadcaster's* interest, convenience, or necessity." In fact, the FCC has routinely granted license renewal applications, even from mediocre broadcasters.

Then, in 1969, something happened. Inexplicably, and "for the first time in its history, the FCC . . . refused to renew the license to an applicant [WHDH of Boston] that had an 'average' record of performance." Instead the Commission awarded the license to an applicant who might add to the diversity of mass communications in the area.[110]

Public interest groups representing blacks, consumers, and others interested in improving the quality and diversity of television were elated. The broadcast industry was livid.

Immediately a hornet's nest of angry broadcast industry lobbyists swarmed over Capitol Hill. "By the time that the Commission acted on requests for rehearing . . . in the WHDH case, over fifty-five representatives in the House had introduced bills" designed to curb FCC activism.[111]

In response to this industry and Congressional pressure, the FCC muzzled itself. Within a year of its WHDH decision, the commission issued a new policy statement, passed by a vote of 6–1,* saying that licenses would be renewed if a station had "not . . . been characterized by serious deficiencies" and been "substantially attuned to meeting the needs and interests of its area." [113] Passing this relatively easy test would give current license holders preference over rival applicants, no matter what the latter's claims to diversity or quality might be.

Citizens' and minority groups looked to the courts for relief, and got it—temporarily. A federal court ruled that the Commission's policy denied competing applicant groups the equal protection of the laws.

And again, Congress rode to the rescue of the industry, doing by law what the courts said the FCC could not do by administrative fiat. The vote in the House was 379 to 14; in the Senate, 69 to 2.

---

*The lone dissent of Commissioner Nicholas Johnson makes interesting reading:

> The record of Congress and the Commission over the years shows their relative powerlessness to do anything more than spar with America's "other government," represented by the mass media. Effective reform, more and more, rests with self-help measures taken by the public. Recognizing this, the broadcasters now seek to curtail the procedural remedies of the people themselves. The industry's power is such that it will succeed, one way or another. This is sad. Not only can the industry win every ball game, it is now in a position to change the rules.[112]

Even though the bill failed, in a last minute misunderstanding, to become law, the upshot of industry and Congressional pressure remains clear: "Since the WHDH decision, the FCC has not granted a license to a challenger when the incumbent had anything like a record of acceptable past service." [114]

More recently, the FCC has begun to drop even the pretense of regulation. It has discouraged the notion that there is any particular "public interest" at stake in the content of television. As Mark Fowler, Ronald Reagan's FCC chairman put it, it is "time to move away from thinking of broadcasters as trustees . . . television is just another appliance. It's a toaster with pictures." [115]

In accord with this philosophy, the FCC has deregulated the amount of time devoted to advertising, thus increasing the number of commercial minutes per hour. It has lifted guidelines on children's programming, in effect replacing "Captain Kangaroo" with "GI Joe." [116] It has scrapped the requirement that cable services provide public access channels. Also in the trash bin are guidelines that called for five percent of a station's program to be given to news and public affairs. So, on many stations, such programming has already declined; on some, it has disappeared.

"The theory," Fowler summarizes, "is free the businessman; let the businessman react in the marketplace. . . . The free enterprise system has created more wealth for more people in history than any other system. . . . And that is what we are attempting to do in broadcasting, restore free enterprise." [117]

TV Rewired: The Social Circuitry of Cable and VCR

As soon as cable television appeared on the horizon, analysts began to speak of its power as nearly redemptive.

> *An almost religious faith in cable television has sprung up in the United States. It has been taken up by organizations of blacks, of consumers and of educational broadcasters, by the Rand Corporation, the Ford Foundation, the American Civil Liberties Union, the electronics industry, the Americans for Democratic Action, the government of New York City, and—a tentative convert—the Federal Communications Commission. The faith is religious in that it begins with something that was once despised—a crude makeshift way of bringing television to remote areas—and sees it transformed over*

the opposition of powerful enemies into the cure for the ills of modern urban American society. . . . The intriguing thing . . . is that this faith may in no way be misplaced.[118]

Almost twenty years later there is still much talk of technology's promise of salvation. Now it is time to ask whether that promise has been kept.

We begin by looking at what has changed. Technologically much has. Then we proceed to what has not. Culturally, *plus ca change . . .*

Technologically, the changes in television have been phenomenal. Ten years ago, a mere 16.6 million homes—22 percent of the total—had cable television. Today, these electronic umbilicals feed well over 50 million homes—about 56 percent of all TV households.

In 1980, the VCR "didn't exist as a mass market item in the United States." By the 90s, "nearly two-thirds of all . . . TV households own at least one, making it one of the fastest growing consumer products in our history." [119]

In 1982, only one-third of TV homes could "graze" or "channel hop" with the help of remote control. By the 90s, over half could do so.

Surely, observers thought, this revolution in television technology will revolutionize television programming. The exponential increase in channels carried by the cable, the easier access to those channels via remote control, and to any hour of a day's programming via programmable VCR, the store full of movies available on demand to the VCR owner—surely all this was in itself a cornucopia of cultural diversity, wasn't it? What is more, this diversity meant that the networks could no longer oligopolize the audience just by offering "least offensive programming," didn't it? Alas, it wasn't, and it didn't.

Networks: The King Is Dead?

It didn't because, through it all, the networks remained more or less serenely profitable.*

---

*The lone exception was CBS' loss, in 1991, of $85.8 million. But 1991 was exceptional. It was the trough of a deep recession; it was the year of the Gulf War, which by itself may have cost the networks $50 million each in revenue from advertisers unwilling to associate their promise of carefree happiness with coverage of a war. CBS was also paying off the cost of a $3.6 billion investment in sports programming. Remarkably, even in that difficult year, the other networks posted respectable profits: at ABC, $100 million; NBC, $124 million; and Fox, $60 million.

They did so, despite a significant loss to the new technologies of their share of the TV audience. In 1980, the networks still commanded about 85 percent of the prime time viewing audience. By the 90s, that figure was falling toward 60 percent.

But at the same time that network audience share declined, three offsetting trends converged to mean that network revenue did not. The first was an increase in daily television usage per household, from about six and one half hours in 1980, to over seven hours by 1990. The next was an increase in "home TV penetration"—the industry's interesting phrase for the number of households with sets and the number of sets per household. This number of "Nielsen households" has grown by over a third over the last two decades. The third factor was increases in advertising revenue. The price of a minute of advertising time doubled between 1975 and 1985.[120]

More recently, two clouds have appeared in the profit picture. However, it is assumed these will pass. The first was advertising revenue, which fell sharply during the recession of the early 90s. But even this did not entirely undo the earlier gains, and the declines were thought to be temporary.[121]

The second cloud was the people meter. This was a device introduced in 1987 by the networks' ratings accountant, the A. C. Nielsen Co. The people meter replaced the previous measurement system. This had consisted of two samples of TV households, each chosen randomly to represent a more or less accurate picture of all TV households.* The first sample filled out "diaries" of who watched what each day. In the other sample, "audimeters" were attached to household TVs and recorded the times a set was turned on and the channels to which it was tuned.

Diaries, in other words, provided more information than audimeters, but relied on the memories and truthfulness of fallible people.

The people meter was thought to combine the accuracy of audimeters with the detail of diaries. Like the audimeters, the people meter records when sets are on and what they're tuned to. But it also requires family members to "punch in and out" with personal code numbers when they start and stop watching.

The trouble with changing measurement devices is, measurements tend to change with them. In this case, people meters detected a slightly smaller TV audience than diaries had. Networks,

---

*For some doubt about the accuracy of the Nielsen sample, see Gitlin 1985, chapter 3.

of course, cried foul, arguing that viewers were avoiding the complication of "punching in" on the meter. Because the Nielsen Company is paid by the networks, they will likely try to accommodate the network's concerns, probably with a return to multiple measuring instruments that approximately restore the "missing members" of the audience.[122]

But the final, obvious reason the networks remain profitable is that they remain predominant. They are not the only game in town any more. But by a wide margin, they remain the most popular.

Remember, the major networks still capture, on average, about 60 percent of the prime time audience. "The total reach of network TV—95 percent of all viewers tune in to network TV at some time during the week—has not changed in the past 10 years despite smaller audience shares." [123] Compare these figures to cable's—whose network's ratings remain low—averaging less than a 1.0 (i.e., less than one percent of all television households). The broadcast networks claim the largest share even of cable-subscriber viewing—suggesting they will remain predominant even if cable penetration were to proceed much further.[124] Moreover, the demographic profile of the network audience—reflecting its inclination to consume—is more attractive to advertisers than the demographics of the cable audience. And finally, cable television audience growth may have peaked, meaning that network audience losses may have gone as far as they are going.[125]

Ratings for the 1991–92 season seemed to confirm this suspicion. For the first time since the 1976–77 season, broadcast network ratings did not decline, but actually increased to an average 63 percent share of the audience. For the first time since the 1979–80 season, when cable networks' audience measurement began, cable's audience share did not increase, but held steady at an 18 share.[126]

Brand New Technologies, Same Old Audience

The continuing predominance of the networks has much to do with the continuing passivity of the audience, despite the new technologies. Old habits die hard. Even in this age of additional options, only one-third of viewers look at a television guide before viewing. Only one-half of cable subscribers scan channels to select a program, even in the age of remote control.[127] Only 11 percent of viewers flip channels during a program.[128] "There is a general consensus in [the] literature that . . . the net effect of video ownership is only a slight, if any, diminution of live broadcast viewing." [129]

In short, the logic of audience flow remains valid. Most viewers continue to turn on a network channel at the appointed hour, and go with its flow unless diverted by an offensive or boring program. To the extent that this premise of audience flow remains valid, so does its conclusion: the audience-maximizing strategy is still LOP and LCD.

The networks' continued predominance, along with the increases we have discussed—in home penetration, average viewer hours, and ad revenue—have sustained network profits,* despite the significant erosion of audience share.

Sustained profits in turn mean a sustained programming philosophy. With their heads comfortably above water, the networks are not likely to change horses in midstream. With just a few alterations (to be discussed presently), network programming is the same cheap, flashy suit it has always been.**

Long Live the King? The Cable Fable

There is one more reason networks have not met the challenge of cable diversity with network diversity—there hasn't been much cable diversity to challenge the net's.

By the mid-80s, the major cable networks had decided that profits would not be maximized by "narrowcasting"—specialized programming tailored for a particular segment of the audience. So died the dream of early cable supporters—the hope that such segments as ethnic minority groups, the culturally literate, the political left or right, might at last find programming that appreciated

---

*A recent FCC decision promises to further consolidate network profits. The decision will allow networks to own a financial stake in the syndication of their programs, a market estimated at $5 billion annually. As we have already seen, the syndication market tends to require unchallenging fare from those who would produce for it. This development, then, will likely consolidate not only network profits, but network program philosophy as well.

**For a different view, see a recent FCC report that forecasts continuing declines in network audience, and advises networks to be more "distinctive." For a brief period during the early 90s, NBC was thinking along the same lines. The network experimented with "narrowcasting," offering programs that were not for everybody, but were instead tailored especially for younger viewers. Ratings sank like a stone, dropping the network from first to third place in the ratings race. In the wake of the disaster, one industry analyst reported, "All three networks now say they will concentrate on traditional broadcasting with programming that appeals to wide cross-sections of viewers." [130]

their needs. The leading cable industry analysts, Paul Kagan Associates, reported on the trend from a National Cable Television Association annual convention of the mid-80s: "We found little concentration on the narrow programming focus that marked cable's early years. We counted no fewer than nine networks promoting [more broadly cast] directions." [131] Instead, cable stations, like the Big Three networks, found the big money was in *broad*casting. As we saw in Chapter 4, cable's highest-rated network, HBO, has little use for "specialized films." Instead, their philosophy is to run films "with the largest broad appeal." [132]

Likewise are the basic cable networks (TBS, USA), committed to the widecasting strategy of the Big Three. In fact, much of their fare is off-network reruns or cheap imitations of network series.

To the extent that cable has carved a separate niche for itself, it has been "downmarket" from the Big Three.* In search of those viewers willing to swap good taste for a thrill, cable has gone boldly to the frontiers of tastelessness, and discovered the lurid, the lewd, and the ever-more violent.

The Fox Network's "A Current Affair" has brought tabloid journalism to TV, uncovering every titillating bit of the latest rape, murder, or sex scandal.** The syndicated *Hitchhiker* (on HBO and USA) is a torrid sex scene, clad in only the flimsiest of plots, followed by an obligatory "sex kills" ending.

The cornucopia of cable also includes lots of non-network broadcast stations. Without much fanfare, these independents have lately tripled in number—to over 300—and come to prominence on the TV dial. [133] Their most original contribution to our cultural life has been tabloid talk shows. Coming to us via the syndication market are Oprah, Phil, Geraldo, and a host of others,

---

*Cable has produced exceptions to this strategy, some of them notable. Fox's "The Simpsons" is an often-brilliant satire of the standard saccharine sit-com. And Ted Turner has aired a remarkable number of pro-environmental documentaries. In one case, sponsors withdrew their advertising from a "World of Audubon" episode, complaining that it was "anti-business." Turner aired the episode without ads.

**Fox is, of course, not exclusively a "cable network." It owns seven broadcast stations and has another 139 broadcast affiliates. It does, however, owe an important share of its success to cable, for two reasons. First, the network uses cable to reach markets where it has no broadcast affiliates—it has fewer of these than the big three networks. Secondly, most of Fox's affiliates broadcast in the UHF range—that stratosphere above the first thirteen channels, where the air is not dense with viewers. But most cable outlets have found room for a Fox channel on the lower thirteen, considerably enhancing the network's ratings.

each with their armies of alien-spotters, strippers, bigots, biga-mists, witches—what critics call "the freaks of the week." [134]

Cable syndication has also bestowed the mixed blessing of the gamey game show. This genre's trailblazer was "Studs," a show featuring young women with big hair and little skirts directing suggestive double entendres about their dates at the dudes *du jour*. (Example: "He tickled my tongue with his spicy balls of meat," means he made spaghetti for dinner.) Like a Magwah fed after mid-night, *"Studs"* clones were everywhere in no time. "Personals," "A Perfect Score," "Infatuation," "Love At First Sight," each offered only a slightly new twist to the old theme: sex sells.

And finally, what could be more thrilling than the fictional violence of the networks' shoot-em-ups? How about nonfiction vio-lence, graphically recounted and reenacted on "America's Most Wanted"; or real violence, captured on videotape for "Cops" or "American Detective"?

This "reality programming" was so successful, even the Big Three were impressed. Their low production costs and respectable ratings made them some of the most profitable shows on television. And so it was not long before reality programs had become a staple of network fare. [135]

In the end, the visionaries were wrong about cable TV. It was not to be the source of diversity, culture, and politics of all kinds they had hoped for. Meanwhile, advertising and other corporate executives saw something else in cable TV. They saw boundless "opportunities" in the new technology—for selling their products and their way of life. [136]

In the end, it was they who would define this part of the mass culture, as they had done the others.

Quality TV

But let us give credit where it is abundantly due. True, most tele-vision is still the "vast wasteland" FCC Chairman Newton Minow said it was, thirty years ago. But there is also the occasional oa-sis—a show full of heart, humor, wisdom, and passion.

This is what some have dubbed "quality" TV. [137] Its recent re-vival is due to the discovery of the "demographic hit": a show that attracts advertisers not because of the size, but because of the "quality" (age, income, gender, propensity to consume) of its au-dience. [138]

A second factor in the resurgence of quality has been the changing technology we discussed in the previous section. No, it has not revolutionized television, but it has incrementally increased the proportion of quality TV, in the following way. First, cable and the other technologies lowered the average ratings of network programs. Networks learned to live with less. One pair of economists has expressed these reduced network expectations as a lower "threshold of cancellation"—the minimum rating a show needs to stay on the air. In 1971–72, the median average rating for all network shows was 18.7, and a program was on the verge of cancellation with a rating of 17.0 or lower. By 1985–86, average network ratings were down to 14.9, and a show with a rating of 14.8 was likely to be renewed.*[139]

This means that shows no longer have to cast their nets quite so wide as they once did to stay on the air. Now, a show can be viable by capturing just 15 percent of TV homes. This is especially so if that 15 percent happens to have those upscale features so coveted by advertisers.

This "quality" audience is presumed to have a greater tolerance for subtlety and substance. As a result, there is a spot for quality in the prime time lineup.

And what are the politics of quality television? Our earlier discussion of quality film applies here. Like quality film, quality TV is distinguished by an honest effort to render human life in some of its fullness. At its best, it avoids the melodramatic imperatives of good guys, bad guys and happily ever after. It resists the "flattening" formula usually characteristic of Hollywood productions. Unlike formulaic television, quality TV is willing to engage political and social questions.

To put that point another way, ordinary TV sees only "private troubles," never the "public issues" attached, by a long rope, to those troubles.[140] The "quality" productions see those connections. And often enough, their vision is critical of the way things are and the powers that be. Pollution is tied to corporate rapacity. Crime is forged in the crucible of the ghetto. Our justice system is the best that money can buy. And so on.

---

*Since this study was done, network ratings have declined further, to an average of 12.8 for the 1991–92 season, meaning that the threshold of cancellation has probably declined as well. Again, fortunately for the networks, the growth in home penetration and average viewing hours meant that the size of the total audience was larger. Thus, each ratings point, representing one percent of all TV households, equaled a larger number of viewers in the latter period, and was worth more to advertisers. This, together with cost-cutting measures, sustained network profits and allowed them to live with lower ratings.

But there are limits to that criticism. And they are absolute. Ideologically, those limits are well within the bounds of what is safe for capitalism.

Sometimes, the critique made by the quality media is liberal. For example, crusading Ann Kelsey of "L.A. Law" maneuvers cleverly, and succeeds in forcing the stuffy male trustees of an estate to provide aid to the homeless. The critical message is: capitalism can and should be regulated and supplemented. But the positive message is: the system works. Capitalism and its watchdogs (public interest lawyers, journalists, health care specialists, etc.) are a pretty good team, if not a match made in heaven. Ann Kelsey can eat her public interest cake and have her sexy, upscale life-style, too—because her firm's practice is predominantly corporate.

But more often, and more interestingly, the quality media's critique of the status quo is "post liberal." [141] Post-liberalism is neatly summed by Michael Schudson, in his analysis of "Lou Grant": "While private troubles and public issues are related, one has control over the troubles and little leverage with the issues." [142] Stephen Bochco and Michael Kozoll are co-creators of "Hill Street Blues." Bochco has since produced a number of other quality shows, including "L.A. Law." In a poignant and revealing interview, they affirm that post-liberalism is indeed there in their productions, a conscious philosophy. " 'Like a lot of onetime liberals, I think we've gotten to a point where we just throw up our hands and say let's be honest. There's no visible way to change anything anymore . . .' [says Kozoll]. The show carried his own credo, he said, when it settled for coping—active coping, I called it, since I didn't see the show representing defeatism." [143]

That is an intellectual odyssey, I would argue, preordained by the Fates of American cultural hegemony. The journey begins with liberalism. And liberalism fails. But the conservative road is rejected. Most won't retreat from an affirmation of "we" to an absorption with "me"—to "drinking carrot juice in hot tubs" as Kozoll calls it. [144]

So what's left? (No pun intended.) In Western Europe perhaps, one turns left when liberalism reaches a dead end: if patching the system didn't work, perhaps it should be replaced. But in America, the Beautiful, that road is closed. In the first place, the left turn is an option whose name is not spoken by any prominent politicians or journalists, or educators, or even trade unionists. But more to the point of this book, it is not an option to be dallied with by anyone who wants to make his way in the world of mass media. Above all, not there, where the law of profit reigns supreme, benevolent lord over an audience that must not be shocked, bent, stapled, or mutilated by offensive ideas. Even the "quality" audience, with its higher tolerance for realism, dimension, and ideas, has as its defining characteristic, its affluence. Whatever else it may be looking for on the screen, it is not looking for radicalism.

TV Product: The Politics of Formula

There is a spot for quality TV in prime time, but that is all there is. Our earlier discussion of the logic and "real code" of broadcasting suggests that the rest of the prime time lineup will be less concerned with quality, and more concerned with ratings. Having said a few words about the politics of the occasional "quality" offering, we now turn our attention to the staple fare of prime time, the genres that have dominated television's schedule for most of its history—action-adventure and situation comedy.

Where the Action Is

The action-adventure genre is tailor-made to television's needs: it is at once attention-grabbing and unchallenging, guaranteed not to bore or offend. Its structure dovetails perfectly with the message of advertisers, as an advertising consultant explains:

> *"Most people [feel] a great hopelessness . . . about the world's problems. But in [action shows] the good people are rewarded and the bad people are punished. There are no loose ends left. . . . The orderly completion . . . gives the viewer a feeling of security that life itself cannot offer." In [this consultant's] view, this [genre] seemed to serve the same emotional needs as consumer goods, and their alliance was presumably logical.*[145]

By the early 60s, the action genre was already fast becoming programmers' weapon of choice. By the mid-80s, action adventure constituted 45 percent of all prime-time programming. "At 8 p.m., 15 out of 20 programs were action adventures." [146]

And into the 90s, action-adventure maintained its plurality among the genres (see Table 5.1), still accounting for nearly one-

TABLE 5–1

Prime time programming by genre

"Reality" Action-Adventure	9%
*Fictional Action-Adventure	22
Sit-Com	29
Nonviolent Drama	19
News Documentary	6
Sports**/Specials	15

* Figures represent a percentage of all network prime time hours during the week of June 1, 1991.

** The beginning of the NBA Championship series probably inflates this figure.

third of all prime time programming.* But the genre's main ingredient, violence, seemed to be even more pervasive than that, having spilled over into 9 out of every 10 shows telecast in prime time, with an average of eight incidents per hour.[147]

Chapter 4 catalogued the politics of the action adventure film. Those traits apply as well to shoot-em-up film's first cousin, shoot-em-up TV. On TV as in the movies we find the theme of individualism/self-reliance. Sonny Crockett, Lt. Hunter, Jack Killian, the Young Riders, Lt. Ben Carroll, Raven, they are all the sons of Shane and Will Kane and Dirty Harry. All "stand on their own two feet, and go their own way." On TV, too, is film's Manicheism and its corollary—the imperative of violence. "Hunter Is Bait for a Maniac," blairs the *TV Guide* ad copy, as it pictures Hunter doing what a man's gotta do in these circumstances—raising his magnum to a two-fisted readiness. "The Flash," says another ad, "His Justice Is Fast—And Furious." "In a lawless land," argues the blurb for the made-for-TV movie *Badlands Justice*, "it takes a desperado to provide a little law and order."

So it is, content analysis finds, that "the likelihood of a television character falling victim to violence is about 50 times greater than the probability of the average American adult." And because in such a world, you've got to be cruel to be kind, "Stratagems

---

*Adding the "fictional action" and "reality-action" categories gives us 31 percent of a recent week's prime time programming.

either illegal or employing violence constituted more than a third of the means used to achieve goals that in themselves were socially approved. On television, justice and law are not synonymous." [148] "The state in the world of prime time exists mostly to fend off threats to law and order in a mean and dangerous world. Enforcing the law of that world takes nearly three times as many characters as the number of all blue collar and service workers." [149]

As it celebrates these all-American "male" attributes of egoism and violence, television, like film, subordinates women. A study of 555 characters on 80 network shows during the 1989–90 season concluded that "despite some exceptions, women are often still depicted on television as half-clad and half-witted, and needing to be rescued by quick thinking, fully clothed men." [150]

Once again, a perusal of recent network ads quickly illustrates the point. In one, an enraptured, bath-towel-clad Susan Lucci writhes in the embrace of her partner, as the text whispers, "An older woman. A younger man. The possibilities were tantalizing. The reality was deadly." In another, the figure of an attractive woman walks down a dark road, illuminated only by the headlights of the car looming behind her: "There's nothing more deadly than hunting for a killer. Except a killer who comes hunting for you," warns the text. A third asks the burning question, "Why did they do it?" and features three cleavage-baring women explaining why they posed for a men's magazine. An ad for the TV movie *Stranger at My Door* shows an anxious woman and a determined man, and explains their relationship this way: "She didn't know who he was. Where he came from. Why he was there. She only knew . . . He alone could save her life."

The relegation of women goes double for children's TV, which is, "most . . . programmers agree, a boy's world." "It is well known that boys will watch a male lead and not a female lead," says Jeannie Trias, ABC's vice president for children's programs, "But girls are willing to watch a male lead." [151] And so the two top-rated Saturday morning shows are back-to-back episodes of "Teenage Mutant Ninja Turtles," a gang of sai and nunchuck-wielding "heroes in a halfshell." And, adds David Poltrack, senior CBS vice president for research, that which isn't cartoons is "wrestling and kung fu movies," where Manicheism and violence are inviolable orthodoxy. [152]

The most recent innovation in televised violence is in the "reality programming" genre. Shows like "COPS," "Top Cops," "American Detective," "America's Most Wanted," "FBI: The Untold Stories," and "Secret Service" feature a steady diet of action-packed morality plays.

STATION BREAK

A Show About Women, As Told By Men

"Nightingales" was high concept all right. Its premise, as we saw earlier, could be fully rendered in one sentence. "Student nurses in Dallas in the summer and the air conditioning doesn't work so they sweat a lot," was how its producer sold it to NBC. Its appeal was right there, on the surface. The trouble was, there was nothing beneath the surface.

Nevertheless, NBC head of entertainment Brandon Tartikoff was delighted with the project. His only suggestions to the concept's originator, Aaron Spelling, were entirely in keeping with the artistic integrity of Spelling's vision. For example, Tartikoff said, "Have two male nurses in it. It will be like the cock in the hen-house."

On the other hand, Perry Simon, the network's head of Drama Development, was more skeptical of the ideas Spelling had sketched out. He was worried that the characters outlined were not "fresh," that too often the women defined themselves in relation to men. These included characters defined as a "peach-cheeked virgin from a Midwest farm" and another starting over in a new city because she had a "secret child." But Simon's misgivings seemed to miss the point. The project proceeded.

When it came time to audition actresses for the show, Spelling and his team were still on the course his one-sentence sale had set. One by one, actresses read for parts, at ten-minute intervals. After each actress left, the team would evaluate her performance. For example; Traci Lin was "a twenty-year-old with straight blond hair . . . who wore a short white blouse that bared her midriff when she lifted her arms."

When she left the room, Spelling said, . . . "I love this girl Traci! . . . Great transition." Spelling then stood up and, patting the back of his legs, noted, "She has a little"— baby fat. The group was sure that Gail O'Grady—stunning in a tight black leather skirt, black sweater with the sleeves casually rolled up, . . . blond hair combed back with feathered bangs, and prominent breasts—was a contender to play Julie in what they called the bathing suit scene. "I like the hairdo which is today," said Spelling. And, because she was obviously well endowed, Spelling added, ''We don't have to see her in a bathing suit.''

Later, the finalists auditioned again, this time with NBC programmers present. This time, they debated ''which of the two finalists would play Julie, the tease who seduces the doctor in his swimming pool during the bathing suit scene. One faction wanted to go with the better actress, the other with the better body. . . . The body won.''

Finally, the pilot was screened for Bob Wright, GE's president of NBC, and the rest of the network brass. Judging from the audience's reaction, Perry Simon feared that the high concept may have gotten too lowbrow:

> *The audience . . . giggled as the room went dark and a set of drop-dead legs filled the screen, high heels loudly clicking on a marble floor. The good-natured laughter soon turned to snickers when David, the handsome . . . California heartthrob, kisses Becky, the innocent blond from a midwest farm, who announced that she had once been in a convent. . . . They laughed when Dr. Roger Taylor plunged his tongue into the mouth of the student nurse in the bathing-suit scene. They laughed right through David and Becky's third date when he nibbled on her ear, and as his tongue glided up and down her neck.*

''Perry Simon squirmed in his seat and whispered, 'The cat's out of the bag!' '' But after the screening, Wright proclaimed the show '' 'a good idea for us' . . . Wright believed that 'Nightingales' would test well (with sample audiences) and that Tartikoff could resist the criticism of . . . critics. . . . To Wright, whether to air 'Nightingales' was simply a business decision.''

Sure enough, the following season, ''Nightingales'' debuted on NBC. Its first night's ratings were respectable, but they quickly dropped. ''Nurses' associations protested that the series didn't show what nurses actually did but displayed them as sex objects. Parents complained that 'Nightingales' was pornography.'' Within half a season, the show was canceled.

Apparently, the cynic-pundit H. L. Mencken was wrong. Sometimes, you can underestimate the intelligence of the American people.

Source: Ken Auletta, *Three Blind Mice,* (New York: Random House, 1991).

Here we see well-spoken, polite, mainly white policemen explaining the danger to themselves and to the domestic tranquillity of tonight's quarry.

We see the sort of corners street-smart cops need to cut in order to stay on top. "Mind if we come in," they assert after having come in. "Mind if we search," they declare as they begin a search. But then, the camera, which doesn't lie, shows us the natural justice of this constitutionally suspect behavior. We see the disheveled den being searched. We see its unkempt, uncouth, inebriated, often black or Hispanic denizens. And finally—the clincher—we see the drugs or guns that prove their guilt and vindicate the police. If we're lucky, another segment may show a "perp" making a break for it, and there will be a chase and a struggle, again illustrating the peril the police face and their need to use force. The Manichean message is doubly powerful, because it is implicit in actual events we witness, and seeing is believing.

But while it may be true that the camera does not lie, it does leave things out. What is left out by the reality-crime genre's camera is any spark of social imagination. There is no sense here that alcoholism, drug use, and even street crime may be functions of a socially created inequality. As in all Manichean media, there is no sense that crime is anything but the badness of the "bad boys" in "Cops' " theme song.

Make 'Em Laugh

The other twin tower in the landscape of genres is the situation comedy. Sit-coms occupied 29 percent of prime time programming in the week of our survey (see Table 5–1). This genre, together with action-adventure shows, accounted for 60 percent of prime time.

Sit-coms have the same marching orders as the other genres: entertain and don't offend. The easiest way for sit-coms to do that is to press the pleasure buttons (laughter and a little sex), and avoid the hot button of controversy. Again, the networks' advertising in *TV Guide* is revealing:

> *Caution: Repeated exposure to this program may result in fits of uncontrollable laughter.*

> *Only at the Fanelli house can you find so many hunks—and so much hilarity under one roof.*

> *Packed with more laughs than ever.*

Did they or didn't they? And will they do it again? The gang at the bar wonder about Sam and Rebecca.

Just say "I do" to laughs!

Get set to take off laughing!

Final season—don't miss a laugh!

There's a new reason to laugh on Thursday nights!

Laughter is the best medicine, we say: instant relief from a variety of social or personal aches and pains. Sometimes, it is the relief of an opiate, dimming the remembrance of our disease, not pointing us to its cure. That is especially true if the laughter is mindless laughter, as television's tends to be. And of course, a society relentlessly rendered as "happy people with happy problems," is itself an advertisement for the system.

But there is a tension inside TV's mandate. The less offensive programming becomes, the less likely it is to be very entertaining. The best laughs have something to do with our real problems. And so sit-coms sometimes dabble in issues.

Usually, they do so by rooting for the winning side and affirming the dominant ideology. Television's outstanding proponent of the dominant ideology over the past decade has also been television's most watched series—"The Cosby Show."

The Huxtables of the "The Cosby Show" are a typical American family. A gynecologist married to an attorney, living in a fashionable brownstone that is chock full of

> *bright sportswear, plants and paintings, gorgeous bedding, copperware, portable tape players, thick carpeting, . . . and big burnished dressers, tables, couches, chairs and cabinets (Early American yet looking factory-new). . . . In every scene, each character appears in some fresh designer outfit that practically glows with newness, never to be seen a second time. And, like all this pricey clutter, the plots and subplots, the dialogue and even many of the individual shots reflect in some way on consumption as a way of life; Cliff's new juicer is the subject of an entire episode; Cliff does a monologue on his son Theo's costly sweatshirt; Cliff kids daughter Rudy for wearing a dozen necklaces."* [153]

Appearances aside, the Huxtables are also no traitors to their class when it comes to values. In one episode, Rudy is upset because a playmate has called her family "rich." Other parents might duck the issue and offer some mealy-mouthed egalitarianism about being middle class, but not Cliff Huxtable. He tells Rudy that he and his wife have worked hard for what they've got and are proud of their accomplishment. Herbert Spencer could not have said it better.

In another episode, teenage daughter Denise demands to know why she can't use her savings to buy a car, because after all, "It's my money and I can do what I want with it. Are we still in America or what?" This time it's Mama's turn. In high dudgeon, Clare sets Denise straight on what America is all about:

> You're ready to plunge in and buy that car, just like you were with [here she lists previous ill-advised purchases]. And at this point in your life you can do pretty much what you please because you know in the back of your mind we're always there to bail you out. We're your safety net. . . . Well your father and I accept that responsibility because we're your parents. And you'd better remember that young lady, because if you ever take this attitude with us again, you can take whatever is in that bank account of yours and go discover America!

Responsibility. Self-reliance. Deferred gratification. Protestant ethic. Guilt. Patriarchal authority. And, in the end, consumerism. Denise *is* finally allowed to spend some of her money on a car, as long as she saves enough to pay for insurance, gas, and maintenance. Here is the whole catechism of liberal capitalism, summed up in one amazing episode.

In Chapter 4, we met Claude Levy Strauss' notion that mass culture's artifacts—like "Cosby"—perform a mythic function. Generally, myths help to resolve a culture's contradictions, often through painful self-discovery. Hollywood myths dissolve contradictions, often through blithe unawareness.

One of the most blatant contradictions we face is that between our boast of being an equal opportunity society and our underachievement, as one of the most unequal industrialized societies in the world. Generation after generation, one group of Americans is consigned to poverty. Statistically, their chances for upward mobility are lousy. Disproportionately, this class without hope is black.

How palliative, then, for us to be able to tune in to "The Cosby Show." For there we are greeted by a jocular, successful black man, telling us that we *are* an equal opportunity society, that success will still follow hard work and other traditional values as night follows day. "Just look at Cliff," he says implicitly, "he's living proof."

And as if a fictional dissolution of this contradiction weren't enough, Cosby throws in his own real life for good measure. Few actors have been at such pains to identify themselves with their characters as Cosby has. He lists himself in the show's opening credits as "Consultant: Dr. William E. Cosby, Ed.D," by way of saying that Cliff's message is his message, as is Cliff's achievement of the Horatio Alger story. And indeed, Cosby has testified in innumerable interviews about his own journey from rags to riches, about the bedrock values that carried him down that road, and about his identity with Cliff. "Have no doubt about the American Dream," is his tacit message. "Just look at me." And poof, a disturbing contradiction vanishes.

But what of the charge of the right brigade, that sit-coms are a comedic fifth column, riddled with left-wing politics? Table 5.2 lists the titles of all sit-coms aired for at least six episodes in one recent season. For television aficionados, a quick skim through the list is a reminder of how thoroughly apolitical most of these shows are. On only four or five of these 42 programs are political sentiments likely to arise even occasionally. Even then, the "politics" expressed is likely to consist of a Clarence Thomas joke or a Tipper

TABLE 5–2

Network situation comedies aired during a recent season

Roseanne	Empty Nest
Home Improvement	The Wonder Years
Murphy Brown	Doogie Howser, M.D.
Coach	Where I Live
Cheers	The Golden Palace
Full House	Designing Women
Love & War	Mad About You
The Fresh Prince of Bel-Air	Major Dad
Hangin' with Mr. Cooper	Nurses
The Jackie Thomas Show	Bob
Evening Shade	A Different World
Hearts Afire	Delta
Seinfeld	Herman's Head
Blossom	Roc
The Simpsons	The Powers That Be
Wings	Almost Home
Family Matters	Down the Shore
Step By Step	Flying Blind
Getting By	Shaky Ground
Married . . . with Children	Woops!
Martin	Great Scott!

Gore riposte—quickly counterpointed by another view. Rarely is a political or social issue central to a show's story.

But we needn't rely only on our intuitions about TV's politics. Enough systematic content analysis has been done on that issue to confirm our impressions. For example, one recent study of all three networks' scripted shows found that there were indeed very few expressed values having to do with social or political issues. As the study put it, 96.5 percent of all values expressed were "personal." Only 3.5 percent were "citizenship values." [154]

When political values were expressed, it was not in a dissident key. They consisted of "patriotism—love, respect for and loyalty to the United States . . . respect for the U.S. Constitution, the rule of law . . . respect for legitimate authority," and so on.

Indeed, the authors conclude, the personal as well as political values expressed on TV

> *may play an important role in perpetuating established cultural norms. Most important, values observed in this program sample are shown to be "good" not only by their positioning but by their close association with characters representing state authority. Because law enforcement characters are over-represented among characters involved with positive values, displays of positive values are linked strongly and disproportionately with authority and power figures. Such displays help perpetuate the cultural norm that associates goodness and positive values with the state, power, and recognized authority. Television, therefore, not only projects a values system but reinforces the association of such values with mainstream authority institutions.[155]*

Even on those two or three shows where critical thoughts are sometimes expressed, there are limits. CBS's "Major Dad," for example, began as a sort of political *Taming of the Shrew.* Gruff marine Major John MacGillis marries anti-militarist liberal reporter Polly, causing sparks of all kinds to fly. But in the chilly climate of an impending Gulf War, Polly's liberalism "disappeared. The sparks are gone. Polly no longer gives her husband a hard time." The show's executive producer Rick Hawkins explained why: "The network is naturally concerned. This is a half-hour comedy (and a solid success for CBS). They are concerned that we don't offend anybody." And so, as the war began, the network began "taking a much greater interest in 'Major Dad,' with broadcast standards carefully monitoring those scripts that refer to the war." [156]

And finally, we need to ask: even on those two or three shows where rebellious thinking is sometimes allowed out loud, does the medium overpower the message? Writer Larry Gelbart says that when he and his colleagues sat down to make the classic series "M*A*S*H," "We wanted to say that war was futile, to represent it as a failure on everybody's part, that people had to kill each other to make a point." But of course, this had to be said within the conventions of the medium. And so, viewers saw charismatic, attractive stars in madcap or touching situations, muttering hilarious one liners about how war is heck. In the end, actors got fan letters saying, "After watching your show I've decided to sign up." Who could blame them? Not Gelbart himself, who saw how the very forms of the medium could "essentially defeat the original purpose of the series." [157]

Television's Effects

"Will they not take these shadows to be reality?" Plato asks.

For a generation now, the Roper poll has been asking Americans where they learn "what's going on in the world today—from the newspapers or television or talking to people or where?" Since the 1960s, a sizable and growing majority have answered, "television."

We might assume that respondents are referring entirely to news and documentary programs. "But is this likely?" asks Erik Barnouw. After all, he points out, children tend to be almost completely oblivious to news and documentary programming until about halfway through high school. Even then, only about half of them become attuned to it. The rest "remain almost immune to these, sticking with the episodic drama into adult years." In other words,

> Before meaningful involvement in any news programming, a child may have seen ten or twenty or thirty thousand episodes of drama, most of which seem to concern "what's going on in the world today. . . ." The point is that for those growing up today, episodic drama plays a journalistic role for a decade before recognized news media can have an impact. For many it continues to play such a role into adult life, and to prevail over recognized "journalism". . . . Such programming undoubtedly forms patterns of ideas and attitudes about the world. These may later determine what information, from the barrage offered by newscasts, will stick and what will not stick:

> *what will be believed and what not believed. Mental patterns of*
> *"reality," once established, seem to be fortified by selective*
> *perception and retention. On television it is drama, not news*
> *programming, that takes the lead in setting patterns.*[158]

And what lessons about "reality" are learned from this primordial teacher? Given what we now know about what television
beams into viewers' minds, the attitudes that come out are all too
predictable.

First, television's "attachment to the acceptable" has led "blue
collar and other subgroups" to a "middle class perspective. . . .
Class warfare has never been absent from the American experience, and at times . . . it has had a prominent role. However, it has
not been a . . . pervasive condition which Americans have accepted
as a basis for their behavior; television has moved us, if ever so
slightly, away from such a state." [159]

George Gerbner and his associates have dubbed this process
"mainstreaming," a tendency for heavy-TV viewers to be more alike
in their thinking than light viewers.*[160]

One example is the "blurring of class lines and the self-styled
'averaging' of income differences." Low-status respondents were
more likely to call themselves working class—but only if they were
light viewers. Heavy-viewing low-status respondents were more
likely to call themselves "middle class." "The television experience
seems to . . . be an especially powerful deterrent to working class
consciousness." [161]

Heavy-viewers are also more likely to call themselves "moderate" than either conservative or liberal. Among those who call
themselves liberals, heavy viewers are significantly more likely
than light viewers to endorse racial segregation in areas such as
housing, education, and marriage. Heavy-viewing liberals oppose
homosexuality, abortion, and the legalization of marijuana far
more often than light-viewing liberals.

Heavy-viewing liberals are much more rigidly anti-communist
than their light-viewing counterparts, and much more willing to

---

*The goal set by Gerbner and his associates is an ambitious one: to chart the
"general consequences of cumulative exposure to cultural media." Such an
ambitious project is bound to be controversial, and this one has been. A recent
review of the debate concludes, "Although much criticism . . . and many
proposed amendments have been made regarding [Gerbner *et al.*'s] formulation,
a fairly coherent picture has emerged. Numerous null associations have been
reported, but they have not overwhelmed in number the many positive
associations between amount of television viewed and belief or perception in
accord with the demographics or emphases of television." [162]

restrict the freedom of speech of left and right wing nonconformists. And why not? After all, heavy viewers spent four or more hours per day tuned to a medium in which nonconformists have already been silenced.

In other words, television has the power to herd heavy viewers into a docile flock of mainstream middle-class thinkers. Now couple that with the fact that lower-status and black Americans and women are disproportionately likely to be heavy viewers.[163] In fact, a recent Nielsen Media Research study found viewers in black households watching 48 percent more TV than other households—a total of 69 hours and 48 minutes per week.[164]

In other words, those three groups most likely to be disadvantaged by the American socio-economic order are also those most likely to be exposed to a medium of mass socialization that defuses dissent. What ruling class could ask for anything more?

Heavy viewers also "have a keener sense of living in a 'mean world' with greater hazards and insecurities than do comparable groups of light viewers."[165] This is not surprising, given the Manichean assumptions implicit especially in action shows. Nor is it surprising that viewers with a predilection for such shows are significantly more likely to savor "punitive" criminal justice policies.*[166]

Not surprisingly, some of the deepest impressions television makes are made at an impressionable age. "[The] strong impact of the mass media on children's political socialization has been convincingly demonstrated by research. When asked for the sources . . . on which they base their attitudes about such subjects as economic or race problems, or war and patriotism, high school students mention the mass media far more often than their families, friends, teachers, or personal experiences."[168]

And what sort of attitudes might this "new parent," the mass media, be fostering? For example, one study looked at the relationship of TV viewing to sex-role stereotyping among children in grades K–6. "The amount of television viewing was positively associated with stereotyping of both males and females, and

---

*It is interesting to note that researchers have not found these associations between TV viewing and political views among Europeans. They speculate that the difference may come from "the difference between the means and intensity of controls exercised over television in America and in Europe. In America there is a largely market-regulated system in which . . . television comes to control society. On the other hand, in Europe, where there seem to be fewer or no such . . . effects [of TV] as in America, there are effective institutions through which society controls television."[167]

stereotyping tended to increase with age, but decreased among those who were light viewers." [169]

Should we be surprised at this effect of a medium in which, as one massive content analysis put it, "Sex role images over the past 10 or 15 years have been quite stable, traditional, conventional, and supportive of the status quo." [170]

Scholars have paid particular attention to the effects that television's "mean" Manichean world may have on the thinking of children. Separate studies have concluded, "The greater the level of exposure to television violence, the more the children were willing to use violence, to suggest it as a solution to conflict and to perceive it as effective." "Young viewers who watch a lot of television are more likely to agree that it is 'almost always all right to hit someone if you are mad at them for a good reason'. . . . In the realm of television our children are learning that violence and power are synonymous. It is the way you get people to follow your wishes." [171]

Other studies indicate that television brings these lessons to older children as well. Among teenage boys, one study found, there was a positive association between exposure to television violence and "an ideology favoring the use of force." Another found that the viewing of crime shows was associated with reduced support for values associated with civil liberties.

The author of one of the most ambitious studies of the effects of televised violence on children and adults concludes,

> There can no longer be any doubt that heavy exposure to televised violence is one of the causes of aggressive behavior, crime, and violence in society. The evidence comes from both the laboratory and real-life studies. Television violence affects youngsters of all ages, of both genders, at all socio-economic levels, and all levels of intelligence.[172]

In summarizing some of these findings, one writer includes this illustrative colloquy with a young boy:

> "Who would you like to be like when you grow up?"
>
> "I want to be like Rambo because he has a big gun." The child starts to give me the specific name and type, but when I look puzzled, he describes it simply as "a big gun." "And when I grow up, . . . I want to shoot bad guys."
>
> "And what happens to the bad guys you shoot?"

"They die."

"And what happens to you?"

"Nothing," he said, as if in answer to Plato's question.[173]

Coda

In 1907, a man named Lee DeForest patented his "Audion" tube. Unlike Marconi's black box, which communicated through wireless telegraphy, the Audion was capable of voice transmission. "Unwittingly then," DeForest wrote, "had I discovered an Empire of the Air."

It was truer than he knew. Except that, like any good empire, this one had to be more than just discovered. It had to be conquered, control of it taken from the local aboriginals. When that was done, corporations had captured what is perhaps the crucial command center in their fight for cultural hegemony.

References

1. Pete Hamill, "Crack and the Box," *Esquire*, (May 1990): 63–4.
2. Robert T. Bower, *The Changing Television Audience in America*, (New York: Columbia University Press, 1985): 35–6, 86–7; Victor E. Ferrall, "The Impact of Television Deregulation on Private and Public Interests," *Journal of Communications*, (vol. 39, 1, 1989): 8–38.
3. George Gerbner, Larry Gross, Michael Morgan, and Nancy Signorielli, "Charting the Main Stream: Television's Contributions to Political Orientations," *Journal of Communication*, (vol. 32, 2, 1982): 100–127.
4. A. C. Nielsen, quoted in Muriel Cantor, "Audience Control," *Television: The Critical View*, edited by Horace Newcomb, (New York: Oxford University Press, 1987): 365.
5. Former CBS President Frank Stanton in David Marc, "Beginning to Begin Again," *Television: The Critical View*, edited by Horace Newcomb: 35.
6. Daniel Goleman, "How Viewers Grow Addicted to Television," *New York Times*, (October 16, 1990): C1, C8; Farrel Corcoran, "Television as Ideological Apparatus: The Power and the Pleasure," *Television: The Critical View*, edited by Horace Newcomb: 54.
7. Robert T. Bower, *The Changing Television Audience in America*: 31.

8. George Comstock, *Television in America,* (Beverly Hills, Calif.: Sage, 1980).
9. Farrel Corcoran, "Television as Ideological Apparatus": 54.
10. Rick Altman, "Television Sound," *Television: The Critical View,* edited by Horace Newcomb: 569.
11. Todd Gitlin, "Prime Time Ideology: The Hegemonic Process in Television Entertainment," *Television: The Critical View,* edited by Horace Newcomb: 513.
12. Donald R. Brown, "Media Entertainment in the Western World," *Comparative Mass Media Systems,* edited by John Martin and Anja Chaudhary, (White Plains, New York: Longren, 1983).
13. Ibid.: 45; *New York Times,* "The 'Science' of Picking TV Hits: Just Guess," *Watertown Daily Times,* (June 26, 1991): 13.
14. Todd Gitlin, *Inside Prime Time,* (New York: Pantheon, 1985): 163–4, 204.
15. Edward Jay Epstein, *News From Nowhere,* (New York: Vintage, 1973): 150.
16. Michael Schudson, "The Politics of Lou Grant," *Television: The Critical View,* edited by Horace Newcomb, (New York: Oxford University Press, 1987): 85.
17. U.S. House of Representatives, Public Law Number 632 (Washington, D.C.: U.S. Government Printing Office, 69th Congress).
18. Pendleton G. Herring, "Politics and Radio Regulation," *Harvard Business Review,* (January 1935).
19. Erik Barnouw, *A Tower in Babel,* (New York: Oxford University Press, 1966): 260.
20. Ibid.: 260.
21. Lawrence I. Schmeckebier, *The Federal Radio Commission* (Washington: Brookings Institution, 1932): 55.
22. Erik Barnouw, *Tube of Plenty,* (New York: Oxford University Press, 1990): 217. Reprinted by permission of Oxford University Press.
23. Ibid.: 215.
24. Ibid.: 260–61.
25. Ibid.: 262.
26. Ibid.
27. Ibid.: 55.
28. Ibid.: 56.
29. Quoted in *Radio Broadcast,* (Garden City, N.Y.: Doubleday and Page, December, 1924).
30. U.S. Senate, *Federal Radio Commissioners: Hearing Before the Committee on Interstate Commerce,* (Washington, D.C.: U.S. Government Printing Office, 70th Congress, 1st Session, Jan. 6–Feb. 6, 1928): 219.
31. Erik Barnouw, *Tube of Plenty:* 73.
32. Erik Barnouw, *A Tower in Babel:* 239.
33. *Broadcasting,* "Reservation of Channels," (November 10, 1952).
34. Erik Barnouw, *The Sponsor,* (New York: Oxford University Press, 1978): 60–68, 180.
35. Quoted in Barbara Lee, "Taking Television Too Seriously—and Not Seriously Enough," *Meanings of the Medium,* edited by Katherine Henderson and Joseph Mazzeo, (New York: Praeger, 1990): 146–150.
36. William Allen White, quoted in Barbara Lee, "Taking Television Too Seriously—and Not Seriously Enough": 146.
37. Ken Auletta, *Three Blind Mice,* (New York: Random House, 1991): 35.
38. Ben Bagdikian, "The Lords of the Global Village," *The Nation,* (June 12, 1989): 808.
39. Ibid.

40. Ken Auletta, *Three Blind Mice:* 367.
41. Richard A. Blum and Richard D. Lindheim, *Primetime: Network Television Programming,* (New York: Focal Press, 1987): 45.
42. Todd Gitlin, *Inside Prime Time:* 8.
43. Richard A. Blum and Richard D. Lindheim, *Primetime:* 38.
44. Ibid.; David Atkin and Barry Litman, "Network TV Programming: Economics, Audiences, and the Ratings Game, 1971–1986," *Journal of Communication,* (vol. 36, 3, 1986): 38.
45. Todd Gitlin, *Inside Prime Time:* 116, 126.
46. George Comstock, *Television in America,* (Beverly Hills, Calif.: Sage, 1980): 23; Ken Auletta, *Three Blind Mice:* chapter 16.
47. CBS Vice President for television research, in Todd Gitlin, "Prime Time Ideology": 31.
48. See, e.g., Ben Stein, *The View From Sunset Boulevard,* (New York: Basic, 1979): x–xii.
49. Richard A. Blum and Richard D. Lindheim, *Primetime:* 104, 121–24.
50. Todd Gitlin, *Inside Prime Time:* 134.
51. George Comstock, *Television in America:* 24.
52. Ibid.: 73.
53. Brandon Tartikoff, quoted in Ken Auletta, *Three Blind Mice:* 354–55.
54. Producer-Network Executive Ethel Winant, in Todd Gitlin, *Inside Prime Time:* 116.
55. Ibid.: 92, 117.
56. Ibid.: 135, 119.
57. Neil Hickey, "Decade of Change, Decade of Choice," *TV Guide,* (December 9, 1989): 29–34.
58. Bill Carter, "TV's Venturesome Programmers Find It's Lonely Out Front," *New York Times,* (November 19, 1990): C1.
59. Barbara Lee, " Taking Television Too Seriously—and Not Seriously Enough": 146.
60. Todd Gitlin, *Inside Prime Time:* 61.
61. Nancy Signorielli, "Selective Television Viewing: A Limited Possibility," *Journal of Communication,* (vol. 36, 3, 1986): 65.
62. George Comstock, *Television in America:* 38; George Comstock, with Haejung Park, *Television and the American Child:* 112–13.
63. Todd Gitlin, *Inside Prime Time:* 61.
64. George Comstock, *Television in America:* 75.
65. Todd Gitlin, *Inside Prime Time:* 183.
66. George Gerbner et al., "Charting the Mainstream": 105.
67. *Broadcasting,* "Researcher Fitzgibbon Tells AAAA Audience It Will Have to Deal with Changing Social Values," (March 24, 1980): 56–57.
68. Richard A. Blum and Richard D. Lindhiem, *Primetime:* 176.
69. David W. Rintels, "Will Marcus Welby Always Make You Well?" *The Age of Communication,* edited by William Lutz, (Pacific Palisades, Calif.: Goodyear, 1974): 392.
70. Todd Gitlin, *Inside Prime Time:* 288.
71. *TV Guide,* "Producers Angered By ABC Censors," (February 18, 1989): 57.
72. Barry Bluestone and Bennett Harrison, *The Great U-Turn,* (New York: Basic Books, 1988): chapter 2.
73. James Warren, "TV's Expendable Ads," *Chicago Tribune,* (August 5, 1990): 5–2.
74. Bob Shanks, *The Cool Fire,* (New York: Vintage, 1977): 149.

75. Richard A. Blum and Richard D. Lindheim, *Primetime:* 64.
76. Ibid.: 140–141.
77. David Lieberman, "More Action Shows, Fewer Sitcoms—As Networks Aim for New Audiences Overseas," *TV Guide* (May 11–17, 1991): 27–29.
78. Todd Gitlin, *Inside Prime Time:* 76.
79. Ken Auletta, *Three Blind Mice:* 364.
80. Quoted in Todd Gitlin, *Inside Prime Time:* 159, 160.
81. Ibid.: 161–162.
82. Bob Shanks, *The Cool Fire:* 149.
83. George Gerbner et al., "Charting the Main Stream": 105–6.
84. Todd Gitlin, *Inside Prime Time:* 126.
85. Richard A. Blum and Richard D. Lindheim, *Primetime:* 19.
86. Todd Gitlin, *Inside Primetime:* 76.
87. Nancy Signorielli, "Selective Television Viewing": 72, 74.
88. AT&T executive Lloyd Espenschied, quoted in Erik Barnouw, *Tube of Plenty:* 43.
89. Erik Barnouw, *The Sponsor:* 57.
90. Ibid.
91. Erik Barnouw, *Tube of Plenty:* 156.
92. Ibid.: 163.
93. Todd Gitlin, "Prime Time Ideology": 521.
94. Cited in Erik Barnouw, *The Sponsor:* 114.
95. Bob Shanks, *The Cool Fire:* 98.
96. Bill Carter, "Concerns About Content Ready for Prime Time," *New York Times,* (July 25, 1989): C18.
97. James M. Landis, *Report on Regulatory Agencies to the President-Elect.* Print of the Subcommittee on Administrative Practice and Procedure of the Senate Judiciary Committee, (Washington, D.C.: U.S. Government Printing Office, 1960): 53.
98. U.S. House of Representatives, Interstate and Foreign Commerce Committee, Subcommittee on Oversight and Investigation, *Federal Regulation and Regulatory Reform,* (Washington, D.C.: U.S. Government Printing Office, 1976): 2.
99. James M. Landis, *Report on Regulatory Agencies to the President-Elect:* 71.
100. Erwin G. Krasnow, Lawrence D. Longley, and Herbert A. Terry, *The Politics of Broadcast Regulation,* (New York: St. Martin's, 1982): 49.
101. Joseph C. Goulden, *The Superlawyers: The Small and Powerful World of the Great Washington Law Firms,* (New York: Weybright and Talley, 1972): 6.
102. Erwin Krasnow et al, *The Politics of Broadcast Regulation:* 50–51.
103. Ibid.: 53.
104. Erik Barnouw, *Tube of Plenty:* 200, 247, 305.
105. Michael J. Robinson, "Three Faces of Congressional Media," *Media Power in Politics,* edited by Doris A. Graber, (Washington, D.C.: Congressional Quarterly, 1984): 217.
106. Erik Krasnow et al., *The Politics of Broadcast Regulation:* 53.
107. Newton Minnow, *Equal Time: The Private Broadcast and the Public Interest,* (New York: Antheneum, 1964): 36.
108. Paul B. Comstock, quoted in Erwin Krasnow et al., *The Politics of Broadcast Regulation:* 89.
109. Erik Barnouw, *Tube of Plenty:* 58–9.
110. Erwin Krasnow et al., *The Politics of Broadcast Regulation:* 208.
111. Ibid.: 210.

112. Nicholas Johnson, 22 FCC 2d 430 (Washington, D.C.: U.S. Government Printing Office, 1970): 433.
113. Erwin Krasnow et al, *The Politics of Broadcast Regulation:* 214.
114. Ibid.: 231.
115. Mark Fowler, quoted in Tom Engelhardt, "Children's Television: The Shortcake Strategy," *Watching Television,* edited by Todd Gitlin, (New York: Pantheon, 1986): 75–6.
116. Ibid.: 76.
117. Quoted in Victor E. Ferrall, Jr., "The Impact of Television Deregulation on Private and Public Interests": 31.
118. Cited in Thomas Streeter, "The Cable Fable Revisited: Discourse, Policy, and the Making of Cable Television," *Journal of Communication,* (1987).
119. Neil Hickey, "Decade of Change, Decade of Choice": 29.
120. David Atkin and Barry Litman, "Network TV Programming": 38.
121. Bill Carter, "Very Weak Ad Rules Trouble Networks": 562.
122. Randall Rothenberg, "Black Hole in Television," *New York Times,* (October 8, 1990): D1,7.
123. Wayne Walley, "Wounded Networks Go for Jugular," *Advertising Age,* (April 10, 1989): 93.
124. Nancy Signorielli, "Selective Television Viewing": 66.
125. Wayne Walley, "Wounded Networks Go for Jugular": 93.
126. Bill Carter, "The Networks Finally End Their Prime-Time Decline": D7.
127. Nancy Signorielli, "Selective Television Viewing": 65.
128. *Syracuse Post Standard,* "ABC Poll Says Viewers Stick with Programs," (July 22, 1989): B4.
129. Mark Levy, "Why VCRs Aren't Pop-Up Toasters: Issues in Home Video Research," *The VCR Age,* edited by Mark Levy (Newbury Park, Calif.: Sage, 1989): 11.
130. *New York Times,* "FCC Sees Gloom and Doom for T.V. Stations," *Watertown Daily Times,* (June 27, 1991): 17; John J. O'Connor, "Daring to be Different on TV, a Medium Where Safety Thrives," *New York Times,* (April 1, 1993): C17.
131. David Waterman, "The Failure of Cultural Programming on Cable TV: An Economic Intepretation," *Journal of Communication* (vol. 36, 3, 1986): 106.
132. Quoted in Suzanne M. Donahue, *American Film Distribution,* (Ann Arbor, Mich.: UMI Research Press, 1987): 203.
133. Ken Auletta, *Three Blind Mice:* 31.
134. Ibid.: 487.
135. Bill Carter, "Networks, Under Pressure, Seek Viewers on the Cheap," *New York Times,* (December 3, 1990): D8.
136. *Broadcasting,* (March 1976).
137. Jane Feuer, "The *MTM* Style," *Television, The Critical View,* edited by Horace Newcomb (New York: Oxford University Press, 1987).
138. Thomas Schatz, "St. Elsewhere and the Evolution of the Ensemble Series," *Television: The Critical View,* edited by Horace Newcomb: 89.
139. David Atkin and Barry Litman, "Network TV Programming": 45.
140. The point is Schudson's, using the language of C. W. Mills, *The Sociological Imagination,* (New York: Oxford University Press, 1959): 102.
141. The phrase is Todd Gitlin's, *Inside Prime Time:* 308.
142. Michael Shudson, "The Politics of Lou Grant": 103.
143. Todd Gitlin, *Inside Prime Time:* 309–10.
144. Ibid.: 309.

145. Erik Barnouw, *Tube of Plenty:* 261–3.
146. Nancy Signorielli, "Selective Television Viewing": 70.
147. Doris Graber, *Mass Media and American Politics,* (Washington, D.C.: CQ Press, 1989): 176.
148. George Comstock, *Television in America:* 81, 83.
149. George Gerbner et al, "Charting the Main Stream": 106.
150. Andrea A. Adelson, "Study Attacks Women's Roles in T.V." *New York Times,* (November 19, 1990).
151. Bill Carter, "Children's TV, Where Boys Are King," *New York Times,* (May 1, 1991): 1.
152. Ibid.
153. Marc C. Miller, "Prime Time: Deride and Conquer": 208.
154. Gary W. Selnow, "Values in Prime Time Television," *Journal of Communication,* (vol. 40, 2, 1990): 68.
155. Ibid.: 73.
156. Monica Collins, "Humor vs. War: It's a *Major* conflict," *TV Guide,* (February 9–15, 1991): 27.
157. Todd Gitlin, *Inside Prime Time:* 217.
158. Erik Barnouw, *The Sponsor:* 104–5; For more on these patterns of ideas or "Schema," see Doris Graber, *Processing the News,* (New York: Longman, 1984).
159. George Comstock, *Television in America:* 143.
160. George Gerbner et al, "Charting the Main Stream": 109.
161. Ibid.: 110.
162. Robert T. Bower, *The Changing Television Audience in America:* 35.
163. *Watertown Daily Times,* (July 14, 1991): 11.
164. George Gerbner et al., "Charting the Main Stream": 121.
165. Ray Surette, "Television Viewing and Support of Punitive Criminal Justice Policy," *Journalism Quarterly,* (1985): 377.
166. Mallory Wober and Barrie Gunter, *Television and Social Control,* (New York: St. Martin's Press, 1988).
167. George Comstock, with Haejung Park, *Television and the American Child:* 162.
168. Nancy Signorielli, "Television and Conceptions About Sex Roles," *Sex Roles* (vol. 21, May 6, 1989): 341.
169. Neala S. Schwartzberg, "What TV Does to Kids," *Parents,* (June, 1987): 101.
170. Cited in George Comstock, with Haejung Park, *Television and the American Child:* 154.
171. Neala S. Schwartzberg, "What TV Does to Kids": 101–2; see also Surgeon General's Scientific Advisory Committee on Television and Social Behavior, "Television and Growing Up: The Impact of Televised Violence," a Report to the Surgeon General, United States Health Service, (Washington, D.C.: U.S. Government Printing Office, 1972); and George Comstock, *Television in America,* 1st ed.: 99–109.
172. Leonard D. Eron, quoted in Neil Hickey, "How Much Violence?" *TV Guide,* (August 22, 1992): 11.
173. Neala S. Schwartzburg, "What TV Does to Kids."

This GE ad told of how GE was "bring[ing] good things to light" for Eastern Europe after the fall of communism. The real story was a bit more complicated.

Selling Ourselves Short: The Politics of Advertising

INTRODUCTION ☆☆☆☆☆☆☆☆☆☆☆☆☆☆

This chapter applies hegemony theory to the advertising industry. It begins by arguing that advertising occupies a ``privileged'' place in our lives, and that this privilege will not likely be revoked in the age of conglomerate capitalism.

Early on, we'll meet an objection to this argument from one of our counter-theses. This time its cultural democracy theory, asking, ``Doesn't the information provided by ads simply help make the consumer sovereign in the democratic kingdom of the marketplace?''

Once again, a good question. In reply, hegemony theory will break the question down into two others and ask:

1. *Whether a consumer's ``life style'' is indeed ``what the people want,'' or whether other options were foreclosed.* To answer that, we'll take one more of our forays into history. As you might have guessed, we'll find that, indeed, other options were foreclosed. Then we'll ask,

2. *``What do ads do—provide useful information, or something else?''* We'll see that, in fact, the ad industry has made a

deliberate decision to shun the rational, information-based pitch in favor of the following kinds of appeals:

a. *Selling therapy.* Like any revolution, the capitalist revolution of this century brought wrenching changes to Americans' lives. Ironically, advertising decided to prescribe capitalism's own products as the therapy for the injuries wrought by capitalism: for the loss of community, autonomy, craftsmanship, nature. You name it, the ad industry has its cure.

b. *Selling America.* Advertisers learned early that patriotism sells. Of course, the America celebrated in these ads is not just anyone's idealized America; it is capitalism's idealized America: the land of the free to choose what product to buy.

c. *Selling sexism.* Advertisers also learned the selling advantage of portraying women in "their place," that is, in subordinate positions, doing domestic chores, or making themselves "beautiful." On the other hand, the ad industry has also begun to include themes from the women's liberation movement in its appeals. Once again, however, the ad industry gives us capitalism's peculiar form of women's lib, promising liberation not through political struggle, but through consumption.

d. *Selling the "Good Life":* Advertising, of course, has its own answer to the philosopher's question, "What is the good life?" By their lights, it is one in which products confer upon us prestige, power, sex, love, indeed, "complete satisfaction."

Before we leave product advertising's appeals, let's note that all of them, in one way or another, are hegemonic messages. They either reaffirm capitalist values, or they divert attention away from politics as a possible answer to some of life's problems.

Next we are ready to discuss advertising's effects. These, we'll suggest, are not trivial, as we might expect from an industry that spends $130 billion per year to influence people's thinking.

Then we'll take a long look at the advertising of politicians. We'll see why politicians came to the same conclusion product advertisers did: sell the image, not the substance. We'll review content analyses of political advertising, as well as recent examples of the state of the art.

Next we'll ask how politicians get away with campaigns of smoke and mirrors—are voters fools? The answer is no, but voters can be fooled, because of the nature of human language. To make this argument, we'll draw on some of the ideas of language philosopher Ludwig Wittgenstein.

Finally, we'll look at the increasing power of corporations to sell their political agenda through advertising. This is advertising as "grass-roots lobbyist." We'll see it at work on Op-ed pages and on television, and we'll see how effective it was in several recent referendum campaigns.

Along our way, we'll pause for three "Commercial Breaks." One looks at how GE used the coming of freedom to Eastern Europe in a commercial, and how it used Eastern Europe in real life. Another looks at how admakers used nostalgia and myth to sell "The Man from Hope." The third uncovers the subtle use of racism in a famous political ad.

☆ ☆

Everywhere You Look: The Ubiquity of Advertising

Advertising is a "privileged" form of discourse.[1] It is accorded a special place in our lives. And that place is, well, everywhere.

An overstatement? Try these numbers on for size: The average American sees about 3,000 ads per day. By the time of high school graduation, he or she has already watched 350 thousand television commercials, and has spent about one-and-a-half years of a still-young life doing so. Each year we spend over $130 billion on advertising in the United States alone. Worldwide, the total spent on marketing (advertising plus packaging-design, sales promotions, etc.) is $620 billion—or $120 for every man, woman, and child in the world.[2]

Those numbers are staggering. And they are not likely to get smaller, given the fact that business is business. Here is why: The business of advertising agencies is, of course, to sell things. As we shall see, they are good at what they do. And of all the things they sell, the most important is—themselves. The ad industry, together with the mass media, are "promoters of promotion." "Advertising agents [are] not only men of confidence: they [are] confidence men. Their livelihood depend[s] on selling to business the idea that advertising [is] an effective marketing tool."[3]

Indeed, as the demands of that "livelihood" grow more pressing than ever, so does the ad industry's need to sell itself. For the ad business, like the other communications media, has now observed Veblen's Law and gone from industry to business. The largest ad agencies have now been acquired by multinational, conglomerate corporations. For example, BBDO Worldwide, (the world's seventh largest agency), together with DDB Needham Worldwide (the 13th largest) are now divisions of Omnicom, a company whose name is not mere braggadocio. Perhaps the two most venerable names in advertising, J. Walter Thompson and Ogilvy and Mather, are now subsumed under the less venerable but more heavily capitalized WPP.

The executives of these conglomerates are not necessarily masters of the craft. They are necessarily businessmen and women. The head of the world's largest agency conglomerate, WPP, has "never written an ad in his life and [has] no desire to do so." [4] Likewise, at the third largest advertising conglomerate, Interpublic, the CEO's office "talks to Wall Street, finances acquisitions, handles all the legal affairs," and so on—but does not make ads. Instead, the office "sets financial targets for each agency [owned by the company] and rewards them accordingly. Interpublic . . . serves as a model for [the other advertising conglomerates]." [5]

In short, what might once have been the industry's concern with product has now given way to a businesslike obsession with profit.

And how to maximize profit? Convince business to make and air and print more and more ads. The volume of ads actually pumped out to the public is particularly important, since 30 percent of billing is on commission. Under this system, the agency is not paid on a cost plus profit basis. Instead agencies are paid a percentage of what the advertiser paid the media to display their message: more display, more income. In short, the advertising business is more determined than ever to maintain its omnipresence in our lives.

Fortunately (for them), their job of selling themselves is not hard. The multinational corporations who hire agencies to advertise their wares are already sold on advertising. Indeed, they are chemically dependent on it. As usual, Erik Barnouw puts it best:

> Business spokesmen often pay lip service to "market forces."
> Orthodox economic theory pictures a need or demand over which the entrepreneur has no control but which he seeks to satisfy by what he produces. But this picture, while it seems to survive in college textbooks and may apply in small businesses—especially local or

regional businesses—is obsolete for the large corporations that dominate [advertising]. Of the top 100 network sponsors of 1975, 81 were multinational corporations. Some have supply sources, manufacturing operations, and markets spanning several continents. Their global deployment holds potential for enormous power and profit—and disasters. With assembly lines dependent on distant suppliers, scattered labor forces, complex webs of regulations and levies, and ultimately on wide merchandising operations, they feel they cannot leave themselves at the mercy of "market forces." Such companies, to ward off governmental interference, may invoke classic economic doctrine, but meanwhile their total effort is toward control—of supply at one end, demand at the other.

To manufacture a product without at the same time manufacturing a demand has become unthinkable. Today the manufacture of demand means, for most large companies, television—its commercials as well as other program elements. The growing scale of mass production has inevitably made advertising more crucial.[6]

In sum, there are huge, multinational corporations who wish to see demand "manufactured." There is a huge, multinational advertising industry anxious to do it for them. Together, they will see to it that the argument of advertising retains its privileged, prominent place in our lives.

Advertising, Hegemony, and Cultural Democracy

In previous chapters, the point was this: Built into the very definition of our mass media is a hegemonic outcome. Defining the news, film, and television as commercial enterprises has resulted in an anesthetizing, uncritical media message.

But when it comes to advertising, that point seems self-evident. It is hardly worth remarking that advertising is uncritical of capitalism, or that the solutions it offers to life's problems do not point us toward fundamental social change. Indeed, criticizing ads for espousing "materialism" is "somewhat akin to criticizing a football player for aggressiveness."[7]

"And the criticism is not just obvious," add the free market theorists, "it is inconclusive. What if ads do encourage purchases?

Aren't they just providing additional information, which consumers can take—or leave—as they like? And doesn't additional information make those consumers all the more sovereign in the democratic kingdom of the marketplace?"

What is wrong with helping to give Americans what they so clearly want, asks the Dean of the advertising profession: "Left-wing economists hold that advertising tempts people to squander money on things they don't need. Who are these elitists to decide what you need? Do you *need* a dishwasher? Do you *need* a deodorant? Do you *need* a trip to Rome? I feel no qualms of conscience about persuading you that you do. What the Calvinistic dons don't seem to know is that buying things can be one of life's more innocent pleasures, whether you need them or not." [8]

These are good questions. Let's pursue them. Let's ask:

1. Whether a consumer's "life style" is indeed "what the people want," or whether other options were foreclosed. As usual, history will tell us something about that.

2. What ads do. Do they provide us with useful information about products we may be interested in, or do they do something else?

3. What are the effects of this $100 billion a year argument on the nation's thinking?

The Re-Education of America: A Brief History of Advertising

Consumerism did not become the American way of life without a struggle. Other ways of life stood in its way, "like Indians on the frontiers of . . . development," in Stuart Ewen's powerful phrase.[9] For several decades prior to the 1920s, Americans turned down consumerism's offer. During this time, productive capacity increased by "quanta" but consumption increased only by "droplets." [10]

This reluctance of turn of the century Americans to be consumers is not surprising, given the values that held sway among them. Even the Protestant ethic that Max Weber associated with the "spirit of capitalism" was not interested in consuming its profits. Quite the contrary. To the Protestant mind, the hallmark of the elect was the prosperity brought about by reinvestment and accumulation, which were permitted in turn by a sober, even ascetic life style.[11]

The New England Yankees who fostered this Protestant ethic were crucially important as culture shapers. Indeed, a definitive work on American ethnicity argues that their cultural "dominion dates from colonial times and [their] domination . . . has never been seriously threatened." [12]

But of course they were not all there was to American culture. A second great wave of immigration followed these Protestant founders, bearing its own values. Each year between 1895 and 1910, about 1 million of these "new immigrants" washed on to these shores. Most of them were Catholic, or Orthodox; over three-fourths came from southern and eastern Europe. Most were of peasant background. The culture they carried with them was just as antithetical to consumerism as the asceticism of their Protestant predecessors.

The fixity of the peasant's legal and economic life, together with Catholic doctrine, caused the southern European to respect those who could "endure and be reconciled." [13] The peasant understood himself as in "the inscrutable world of an unfathomable God," [14] where the human lot is not to exert himself against fate, but to "remain in the state in which we are placed," as the Catholic Bible still translates I Corinthians 7:17.*

And so, for the new immigrant, the "loyal dutiful man" was the one faithful to tradition and family; the one who remained in the household, returning his paycheck to *paterfamilias;* or who at least remained in the neighborhood, a solid rock of "reciprocal goodness" in the network of family, friends, and neighbors. He was the one whose head was not so turned by *hubris* as to try to accumulate more wealth for himself than was enough for a gift to the church. To such a man or woman, capitalism's "idea of success was itself strange; to thrust oneself above one's station in life called for harsh competitive qualities the peasant had always despised." [16]

Together, this exceptionally religious American people had ample reason to affirm, in the words of their dominant religion, that "self-indulgence is the opposite of the spirit. . . . When self-indulgence is at work, the results are obvious: fornication, gross

---

*Max Weber, whose account of Protestant-Catholic cultural differences is still the most erudite, points out that Luther retranslated this verse (somewhat redundantly): "Let each man remain in that calling to which he was called." [15]

indecency, and sexual irresponsibility; idolatry and sorcery; feuds and wrangling, jealousy, bad temper, and quarrels; disagreements, factions, envy; drunkenness, orgies, and similar things . . . if he sows in the field of self-indulgence, he will get a harvest of corruption (Galatians 5:17–23; 6:8).*

All of this asceticism and humility was, of course, bad for business. The emerging capacity for mass production was no good to the profit margin unless there was also mass consumption.

And so industry set out to reeducate America; to substitute, for the book of Galatians, a new curriculum of consumption. The tutor of choice was, of course, the advertising industry.

Just as the captains of industry were pondering this problem of reluctant consumption, a problem of production arose. The final arrival, at about this time, of industrial capitalism was not warmly received by what had been an agrarian and artisan workforce. The "machine in the garden" came as a shock to workers' autonomy, to their status, to the very rhythms of their lives.[17] They resisted, both individually, on the job, and collectively, with unionization and strikes. But it was their political reaction that was the most dangerous of all to capitalism. Increasingly, workers' recourse was to socialist politics.

Capitalism's reply to anti-capitalist politics was, as we saw in Chapter 4, swift and unsparing. Suspected radicals were fired, jailed, beaten, deported.

And reeducated. Leading industrialists of the '20s understood that violent repression was only a temporary solution. They concluded (just as Gramsci would late in this decade) that the long-term solution was cultural conquest—conquest of the common sense. If, they reasoned, a worker could be persuaded "to conceive of himself primarily as a consumer of mass-produced goods, rather than as a producer, a unionist, an Anarchist . . . or whatever . . . two benefits would accrue to the corporate economy: a tractable and . . . nonrevolutionary workforce and increasingly dependable mass consumption." [18]

In the words of a leading advocate of consumerism, department store magnate Edward Filene, "When something wrong is happening," [e.g., a strike or the election of a socialist?] businessmen must "direct their energies" toward assuaging dissatisfaction.

---

*Of course, many more tributaries fed the national culture. Some lent themselves more easily to consumerism than the religious traditions we have just reviewed. One more that did not was agrarian republicanism, whose Levellor brand of democracy would not have fancied the badges of status that consumer products so often hold themselves to be.

At the same time, he added, we must demand "the abandonment of all class thinking." [19]

Again, the designated tutor was the advertising industry. It would take, Filene and other prescient businessmen knew, a lot to get the job done. It would require some of the best literary and artistic imaginations of the time. It would require some of the best minds of the newly emerging sciences of human engineering—also known, when not in corporate service, as the social sciences. And so it was that such titans of the psychology profession as Walter Dill Scott (later president of Northwestern University), John B. Watson (dean of American behaviorism), and Floyd Allport ended up on the payrolls of ad agencies. Soon *Business Week* could write of the "torrid love affair" between advertising and psychology.[20]

These human engineers, together with their cohorts, the ad-men themselves, the mass media, and the billions and billions of corporate dollars that animated all of them, seem to have succeeded. They seem to have persuaded Americans to think of themselves as consumers often, and seldom as unionists, socialists, Democrats, Christians, or whatever.[21]

How did they do it? What appeals were strong enough to reeducate America?

Lessons of the Advertising Academy

The appeals of ads are many, reflecting the rich imaginations of their makers. In this section, we review just a few of the more common and effective themes deployed. As we do so, we may note that advertising, like the other mass media, performs the two jobs of hegemony.

1. It diverts attention away from politics as a possible answer to some of life's problems.

2. It reaffirms dominant values when it does allude to political or social issues.

Information and Irrationality

"Do ads provide us with information, or something else?" we promised to ask ourselves.

In general, the ad industry's strategy has been to focus less and less on the strengths of the product, and more and more on the weaknesses of the consumer. One content analysis of magazine ads has watched the fading of "rational" appeals. These were "ads in which reasoned argument based on product qualities, price, comparison with other products, description or demonstration of benefits, and utility are dominant preoccupations. Rational appeals decline fairly steadily, appearing in 27 percent of ads in the 1910–20 period, but only in 14 percent by the 1970s." [22]

So pronounced is this trend that one can "read" it in the very layout of ads. During the same period, the percentage of ads' space devoted to the main medium of rational appeal—words—declines by almost 25 percent. Meanwhile, nonrational, visual material gobbled up space. By the 70s, the "dominant field of representation" was pictures—not even of the product itself—but of the ambiance surrounding the product. [23]

There were several reasons for this shift. The first was the aforementioned psychologists, many of whom saw humans as motored by nonrational, even unconscious forces. They saw also that the onslaught of industrial capitalism had sent much into retreat. As old values and habits retrenched, people's self-conceptions, their very "souls" (to use an ad psychologist's term) were also dislocated. [24] Here was the perfect opening into the consumer-to-be for that newlywed couple, advertising and psychology: advertising would be therapy for the discomfited. [25] The products of the very capitalism that had caused these anxious disorders would now be offered as their cure.

There is another good reason for not emphasizing the facts that might sell the product. Often enough, there are no such facts, as admen are the first to acknowledge. "Our problem is," says legendary adman Rosser Reeves, "a client comes into my office and throws two newly minted half dollars onto my desk and says, 'Mine is the one on the left. You prove it's better.' " [26]

As the consumerist moment matured, so did this dilemma. As consumption increased, brands proliferated. [27] Among many of these different brands of the same product, there is no significant difference. "Detergents are largely the same. Toothpastes are largely the same. Most beer drinkers cannot tell their own brand from a rival in blind taste tests. Most cigarette smokers cannot tell one brand from another within a range of the same type of cigarette." [28]

In this situation, information won't help sell the product. What will help, says a new consensus among admakers, is "brand image." [29] "If products do not differ materially, they may nonetheless . . . be made to differ in *attributed* qualities, or image."

If consumers believe a product to be distinctive, this belief in itself may become a product attribute. If, thanks in large part to effective advertising, Campbell's "MM-mmm Good" soup takes on the image of wholesomeness more than other soups . . . or if people regard Marlboro as a "real man's cigarette," then the product has a distinctive brand image.[30]

This is no less than magic. The power to build, not just a car, but excitement; the power to make the skies friendly; the power to make a carbonated beverage that is more than just a beverage—it is *the real thing*, a Platonic ideal. Or at least, the power to make it seem so. This is the power of "brand image," of advertising.

Anthropologists tell us that cultures invoke magic when they have trouble resolving their anxieties.[31] Let's talk about those anxieties.

Capitalism and Its Discontents: Ads as Therapy

As we saw earlier, advertising decided to use the dislocations of capitalism to its own advantage. Here is how ads prescribed consumption as the therapy for four of those dislocations.

For the Loss of Community

In a simpler time, relationships were informal and multifaceted. But in the factory and the city that grew with capitalism, encounters were not only more formal, they were more judgmental. Efficiency would be served.

If this alienation from others was painful, if being judged was intimidating, advertising had its balm. Roland Marchand calls it "the parable of the first impression." The cold, judgmental eyes of strangers were not to be feared, if one carried the right talisman— the right scent, the right clothes, the right clear smile. But beware, the parables warned; the converse was also true.

In one early ad published by the Association of American Soap and Glycerine producers, a rumpled, nail-biting young man withers under the critical gaze of the crisp, stern man seated across the desk. "He had to fight himself so hard," the text moans, "He didn't put it over."

Yes, he was his own worst enemy. His appearance was against him and he knew it. Oh why had he neglected the bath that morning,

*the shave, the change of linen? Under the other fellow's gaze it was
hard to forget that cheap feeling.*

*There's self-respect in soap and water. The clean-cut chap can look
any man in the face and tell him the facts—for when you're clean,
your appearance fights for you.*[32]

In our time, allegories of judgment still abound. A young businessman has bought the wrong computer system and is dressed
down by a co-worker ("No—you listen! These are facts!") The grainy
black and white film and tight knot of discordant noise heighten
our anxiety. But another, who has bought the right system, gets
not just approval, but affection, an arm around the shoulder from
the boss.

Indeed, "so prevalent" has this therapy for alienation become,
that it is now "nearly impossible to find a bank, a supermarket,
drug chain, auto repair business, or hardware store that [doesn't]
'care.' "[33]

What these institutions care about, of course, is profit. But
that merely reminds us of the unshakable reality of capitalism, and
our anxiety. To dispel it, we need a good incantation ("We do it all
for you." "We're on your side." "We're all connected.") Pure magic.

For the Loss of Dignity

Likewise, if capitalism had put the "machine in the garden" of the
workplace, advertising could remove it.[34] Once, the workplace had
been a small shop, perhaps located in the home, where a craftsman
or small group of them would fashion the shoes or carriages or
farm implements their neighbors could not do without. Then came
life in the factory. It was dark, impersonal, dull, debilitating, demanding, and dangerous. Recalcitrant workers were beaten.

Advertising had a sweeping solution: "obliterate the factory."
Warned Helen Woodward, "the leading woman copywriter of the
1920s,"

*If you are advertising any product, never see the factory in which it
was made. . . . Don't watch the people at work. . . . Because, you
see, when you know the truth about anything, the real inner truth—
it is very hard to write the surface fluff that sells.*[35]

In our time, advertising has occasionally ventured back into
the factory, not to represent it, but to romanticize it. It may be that
this has become possible as more of the work force is employed in

the service-delivery sector, and unaware of what factories are really like.

In these ads, Coors Beer is not made in a noisy factory, where men do stultifying, mechanical labor, but in a quiet, old world setting, where *meister* brewers assay the quality of hops with a learned olfactory sense handed down through generations. Bartles & Jaymes Wine Cooler does not come from Gallo Bros. Winery, one of the most fractious workplaces in the country, where workers have complained of being carelessly poisoned by pesticides. Instead, it comes from those two delightful bumpkins who sit on their back porch somewhere in the Midwest, and never forget to thank us for our support. Or at least, so it is in the magical world of advertising.

For the Loss of Tranquillity

Was consumerism consuming nature, laying waste to open spaces, tranquillity, resources? Advertising could restore them. Marchand calls this one the "Parable of Civilization Redeemed." The price, said these ads, of "civilization" (advanced capitalism) was "noisy, crowded streets. Dust and gas-ridden air. Machine made speed. Strain. Nervous tension." But be not afraid of the "progress" that brought these unfortunate side effects. For that same progress is the bearer of our redemption in the form of Squibb's vitamins, General Foods' cereals, Tareyton cigarettes, and even the local Scripps-Howard newspaper that crusaded for a public park and so said "STAND BACK CITY . . . GIVE THEM AIR!" [36]

Today, there is scarcely a product that is not "pure . . . all natural . . . nature's own . . . the natural way." And this is true, if it means that natural resources were consumed to produce these products. "In fact, Americans—scarcely 5 percent of the world's population—are consuming the globe's resources at a rate approximating that of the rest of the world combined." [37]

This greenwashing of environmental devastation often comes in the form of "institutional advertising"—advertising, not a product, but the company that sells it. A *Greenpeace* reporter recently described some of the pitches used:

> *Supermarket chains that refuse to stop selling pesticide-dusted grapes are trying to promote themselves as environmentally correct because their pickle jars are reusable. An oil company is forced by federal regulations to put a few bucks into preserving wildlife habitat, so it spends 10 times that much to buy newspaper ads patting itself on the back for obeying the law.*

*I learned all of this at the 43rd annual convention of the Public
Relations Society of America (PRSA), which met in New York City
last November. The theme of the 1990 convention was "Our World
in Transition," but when I looked through the program for the first
time I thought it was How to Make Your Corporation Look Like a
Friend to the Planet While Reaping Billions in the International
Waste Trade. And they're getting away with it.*[38]

For the Loss of Autonomy

And finally, if capitalism had shorn work of its autonomy, advertising could help. If the worker had declined from an independent
yeoman to a corporate toady memorizing the IBM dress code, advertising had a salve for that wound.

A man, for example, can still be a man, even in a time of corporate hierarchy, if he buys right. He can still be *independent*:
"There are some things a man will not relinquish." (Like his Tretorn
tennis shoes.) He can still be *free*: "Dress easy, get away from it all
and let Tom Sawyer paint the fence. Because man was meant to
fly, we gave him wings" (on his Alexander Julian sunglasses). He
can still be *adventurous*: KL Homme cologne is "for the man who
lives on the edge." With New Man sportswear, "Life is more adventurous."

Even in the hierarchical workplace, the lion's den of potential
indignity, one can fend off the worst of these with the right suit.
"The Right Suit can't guarantee he'll see it your way. The wrong
suit could mean not seeing him at all." And outside the workplace,
one can still be powerful: "Pure shape. Pure power. Pure Z." "[Con-
quest Tsi] doesn't take any [Japanese characters] from anyone. It
won't stand for any guff from 300 ZX. Or RX-7." [39]

But wait a minute. Is this really plausible? Can advertising
and the products it sells really stand in for a loss of intimacy, dignity, tranquillity, autonomy?

The answer, of course, is no. But they can seem to. For example, in a series of poignant and revealing interviews conducted
by Richard Sennett and Jonathan Cobb, working class men and
women have described some of the "hidden injuries" of their subordinate status. Sometimes, their thoughts showed how "posses-
sions can appear to make up for a feeling of personal powerlessness." Asked why he didn't drive a cheaper car, one respondent
explained, "Because . . . you got plenty of power. In that little car
of yours (the interviewer's Volkswagen station wagon) you got no
control, you gonna get pushed around on the road." [40] Presto,
chango. A car becomes a vehicle for dignity and power, in a life
that may lack these things. Pure magic.

Advertising America

"It was the astounding success of propaganda during the war," wrote Edward Bernays, father of the public relations industry, "which opened the eyes of the intelligent few in all departments of life to the possibilities of regimenting the public mind." [41]

This war propaganda, said its coordinator, George Creel, was "so distinctly in the nature of the advertising campaign . . . that we turned almost instinctively to the advertising profession for advice and assistance." [42]

The war-supportive copy these admen wrote for Creel's Committee on Public Information was in fact so warmly received by the public that it quickly spilled over into their corporate advertising. For example:

> *Ivory soap follows the flag. Wherever Americans go, it is "among those present." Ivory is as unchangeable a part of American life as the practice of cleanliness itself. Ivory Soap is, in fact, the very joy of life itself to Our Boys when they are relieved from the front lines for rest, recreation, and a bath.*[43]

Patriotism, the "intelligent few" had learned, was a big seller. It is a lesson the ad industry has not forgotten. Because it seems so commonplace to us, it took a British ad executive to notice how often "America" appears in our advertising.[44]

> *America shops for values at Sears . . . America is turning Seven-Up . . . [Coca Cola's] Look up, America, . . . Merrill Lynch Is Bullish on America . . . [and, tunefully] This Land Is Your Land [for United Airlines] . . . Good Morning America, How Are Ya [for Oldsmobile] . . . The Pride Is Back, Born in America [for Chrysler-Plymouth] . . . Listen to the Heartbeat of America [for Chevrolet].*

In case we should miss the point of the text, these ads are replete with visual icons of America: (small town barber shops, boys playing baseball, pickup trucks, and endlessly, cowboys). They are perhaps, one more therapy for a sense of community lost to the hurly-burly of competitive capitalism.[45]

But by the 80s, advertisers were demonstrating how easily a surfeit of patriotism can easily become jingoism. As the Iranian hostage crisis wore on, tough-guy spokesmen like Johnny Cash and Frank Sinatra stared into the camera on behalf of the Chrysler Corporation and said, "America's not going to be pushed around

Bringing Light to the Benighted

Another visionary of freedom for Eastern Europe is General Electric Corporation, as a lavishly produced 1990 commercial explained. The ad described the corporation's 1989 purchase of Tungsram Co. Ltd., Hungary's largest light bulb maker, in this way:

> The spot opens in fading sunlight, as the camera sweeps over the Danube River separating Buda and Pest, the Hungarian capital's two districts. As the strains of a "Hungarian Rhapsody" by Liszt play, gradually building, a young man says in accented English: "Freedom's all that matters. Freedom is everything."

> As the sun sinks, the camera zips between scenes of people lighting candles and smiling. "There's a new light shining over Eastern Europe," says the announcer, who proceeds to explain briefly the G.E..-Tungsram arrangement.

> More Hungarians are seen: working in their offices, meeting in the Tungsram factory, congregating in groups, marching over a bridge. Their faces glow. "Everything is changing,"

anymore." A little later, Tri-State Oldsmobile dealers would point out that American men are taller than Japanese men: "That's why our car is built for our size families, not theirs." And New York Pontiac dealers ran an ad referring to Mitsubishi Estate's purchase of Rockefeller Center, site of the city's annually erected Christmas tree. "A futurologist says glumly, 'It's December, and the whole family's going to see the big Christmas tree at Hirohito Center.' After a pause, he adds, 'Go on. Keep on buying Japanese cars.' " [46]

Then, as Stalinism crumbled in Eastern Europe, advertising exploited the obvious, equating freedom with capitalism. An elderly woman in a babushka is now free to visit the United States. She rides a bus down an American street, and is free to get off and choose—Kentucky Fried Chicken.

one woman says. Another adds, ''I'm so happy.'' The candles reappear, but they are increasingly interspersed with electric lights switching on, illuminating museums, monuments, a ballet and a waltz party.

The camera freezes on a little girl lighting one last candle as the company's 11-year-old corporate slogan appears on screen: ''G.E. We bring good things to life.'' [47]

What the ad did not mention are what the *Economist* calls the ''real reasons'' for the investment: ''To stop Tungsram from undercutting GE in the American market'' and to acquire Tungsram's toehold in the Western European market—a toehold GE's own products had been unable to secure.[48] The glowing commercial also forgot to mention the more than 5,000 Tungsram employees quickly ''let go'' by GE. These layoffs were not necessary to make Tungsram profitable—apparently, it was in the black before the layoffs. But at GE, mere profits won't do. Only mega-profits will suffice. And so the layoffs were a step GE ''has had to take . . . to make Tungsram a *more* profitable company *in line with its other operations.''* [49] Hungarians of course, would have to deal with the layoffs, while GE took the profits. The ad chose to summarize much of this activity by saying, ''At GE we are proud to play even a small part in helping the Hungarian people build what promises to be a truly brilliant future.''

A Woman's Place Is in the Ad

Commercial media, I've argued, are hegemonic media. Their goal is to offend no one, to appeal to everyone. To do that, they draw from a common sense that is itself largely built and backed by dominant groups—the owners of the nation's idea factories.* This common sense is not necessarily good to, or for, subordinate groups.

---

*This paragraph implies that corporate capitalism may have some material interest in the subordination of women. For this argument, see Chapter 1, or Barrett[50] or Sargent.[51]

So it is with women in the most commercial medium of all—commercials. A typical article in an advertisers' trade journal makes the point clear: "Extremely liberal [women's] lifestyle themes" can go "beyond what is acceptable to a majority of subjects." As a corollary, the authors add, "the gender of the model chosen should match the image of the product held by users." [52]

Advertisers didn't need to be told. They have studiously avoided "extremely liberal lifestyle themes" and they have "matched" common gender images in three basic ways:

1. By placing women in subordinate positions and roles.

2. By portraying domestic chores as women's work.

3. By demanding that women devote a substantial part of their time and effort to being "beautiful."

Sometimes, ads' subordination of women is subtle, unspoken. Nonetheless, Erving Goffman's insightful eye has managed to see it.

Goffman finds that advertisements are highly ritualized versions of the parent-child relationship, with women treated largely as children. For example, women's hands are usually portrayed just caressing or barely touching an object, as though they were not in full control of it, whereas men's hands are shown strongly grasping and manipulating objects.

Persons on beds and floors are obviously positioned lower than those sitting or standing. People lying down are also in a poor position to defend themselves and thus are at the mercy of others. Lying down is also, of course, a "conventionalized expression of sexual availability." Goffman's sample of ads shows women and children on beds and floors much more than men are. In addition, he contends, women are shown "drifting away" mentally while under the physical "protection" of a male, as if his strength and alertness were enough for two. Women are also shown in a childish finger to mouth pose. Further, when men and women are shown in physical contact, the woman "snuggles" into the man in the same way that children solicit protection and comfort from their mothers. Goffman asks what such portrayals say about the relative social positions of men and women, and he highlights the question by suggesting that we try to imagine a reversal in the positions of the male and female models.[53]

Sometimes, the relegation of women to "their place" is not so subtle. In a recent sample of TV ads, 75 percent of domestic commodities were modeled by women.[54]

Sometimes, the subordination of women may seem like their idealization, which may be why it is so seductive—to women as well as men. A content analysis of high-circulation women's magazines found their advertising preoccupied with "the beauty role: the importance of appearing attractive in public, of maintaining standards, of encouraging male attention." [55]

Another content analysis found that 55.4 percent of all ads in two American women's magazines were for "personal beauty" products. Interestingly, such ads appeared "almost twice as frequently in the U.S. magazines as in . . . British [women's] magazines." [56]

The implicit demand that women focus *that much* attention on being attractive to men is, in itself, demeaning. But the tone of many of these ads makes them even more so. Women are "scolded for their failings, for their ignorance and their sloth . . . for not carrying out to the full the expectations of the beauty role. They are, in brief, kept in the position of the child." [57] The tone of these little scoldings can range from insinuation ("Shouldn't you take care of your nails as well as you take care of your skin?") to thinly veiled disgust ("Now, anyone still missing out on body lotion has no excuse.")

The uncommodified woman is so unacceptable, the message is, that no less than a complete "makeover" will do:

> *From unnoticed . . . before, to unforgettable. The beautiful, believable transformation.*
>
> *A realistic change for the better. The opportunity to rethink ourselves within the context of our own lives and emerge with a renewed and glowing sense of self.*
>
> *[Before]: "I really needed help in every direction . . . my hair's in bad condition and my makeup needs updating."*
>
> *[After]: "Thanks for giving me my confidence back."* [58]

Are women buying this? At least in a literal sense, they are. Women spend more than $1 million each year on cosmetic products that are often uncomfortable and bad for their health. Chances are, they have also bought some of the pitches used to sell those products. Chances are, they may have absorbed the assumption that one of their most important roles in life is to be attractive to men, and that they can't even do that without "putting on appearances" supplied by the cosmetics and fashion industries.

That, of course, is a heartbreaking self-assessment. Perhaps it is also movement-breaking. If subordinated groups, such as women, think little of themselves, they are all the more likely to accept their subordination.

"But," say the popular culture theorists, "the ad industry is just one more of those 'giving the people what they want.' Now that women have begun to want liberation, advertising gives it to them." [59]

The truth is, one doesn't have to look hard to see reflections of the women's movement in advertising. They are there, for example, in these tributes celebrating female qualities *other than* physical attractiveness and mop mastery:

> *You're tough, you're smart, you're driven. . . . You go from day to night without missing a beat. You've become the person you were meant to be. You've come into your own. . . . She's accomplished and fulfilled. She's determined and enterprising. . . . She's attentive and thoughtful. . . . A woman has crossed the Atlantic single-handed by sail, has conquered Himalayan peaks, has soared to outer space itself. . . . She's always in control over the situation. . . . Her presence is commanding. . . . When a four inch balance beam is the only thing between me and the floor, I can't afford any distractions.*[60]

I have two reservations about such contributions to the women's movement. First, an obvious point. Notice that this is a capitalist version of liberation. According to it, the way to end domination is to begin dominating, to be "tough . . . driven . . . in control . . . commanding." This ignores a very rich vein of feminist theory that argues the right way to liberate women is to end this crippling cycle of domination and subordination.[61]

A second reservation, related to the first, is that advertising offers us a completely depoliticized women's lib. This quickly becomes clear if we look beyond the hook lines cited above, to their tag lines:

> *You're tough, you're smart, you're driven. You've become the person you were meant to be. You've come into your own. . . . In colors for your eyes, lips, cheeks and nails. Charles of the Ritz.*

> *She's always in control over the situation . . . in slick, sensuous Sweet Nothings.*

> *Her presence is commanding . . . in elegant Chantilly.*

The real women's movement offers liberation through struggle, through the hard work of making common cause. Madison Avenue's women's movement is not just different, it is diversionary. It calls women away from struggle, to an easier way, promising liberation through consumption.

To depoliticize women's struggle in this way is to cheapen it. It perverts and debases the contribution of the women on the movement's front lines. It denies the pain and forecloses the options of all those women whose lingerie or perfume have failed to protect them from a pervasive pattern of harassment, assaults, and discrimination.*

Advertising as an Ideology

Michael Schudson has summarized much of advertising's meaning in one term. It is, he says, *capitalist realism.*[62] The term alludes to the form of art prescribed by the Soviet Communist Party in the 1930s, which was called "socialist realism." The term implies that Madison Avenue's artists and writers, like Soviets under Stalinism, are not free to say whatever they please. Instead, their basic message, their ideology if you will, is prescribed. For Soviet artists, the prescription was, "romanticize Soviet socialism." On Madison Avenue, the prescription is, "romanticize American consumerism."

But isn't "capitalist realism" just a clever way of saying that ads try to make products appealing? Isn't it too much to claim that advertising is an ideology?

Political philosophers, tapping into the well-spring of a full-blown ideology, have long asked, "What is the good life?" Advertising, of course, has its own answer to that question. Indeed, making that answer now consumes the industry. From the moment psychologists told advertisers to turn their attention away from the product and focus instead on human fantasies and insecurities,

---

*For a content analysis of how advertising has treated another subordinate group, African Americans, see Humphrey and Schuman.[63] Briefly, their argument is that since consumers are mostly and disproportionately white, ads depict blacks as whites would like to see them. What that turns out to be (as admakers see it) is: (a) innocuous (e.g., often as children, under the protection of white adults), (b) equal in the workplace, (c) not there: not there in close social contact, residential integration, and especially in interracial sexual relationships. In short, once again, for commercial reasons, ads play a hegemonic role. Black problems are denied, and so is access to white social life.

"the Good Life replace[d] the Good Product as the salable commodity." [64]

Is the good life (the philosophers ask) a life devoted to God, to justice, to art, to knowledge? No, says the full force of the $130 billion-a-year ad industry. The good life is one replete with clothes and cars and VCRs, CDs, RVs, and PCs—"Toys and trains and videogames" and many, many more things. In short, the consumer's life style is the good life. It is the pathway to complete satisfaction. This message is implicit in almost every ad we see.

It is certainly there in the ads that "glory in privilege." [65] "Capitalism," its critics cry "is not economic democracy; it's plutocracy." These ads agree, and celebrate the fact, promising what John Berger calls that "solitary form of reassurance . . . the happiness of being envied." [66]

> *Society, by Burberry's—you were born to it (shows succession of women in places identified as "Carlton Hotel, Cannes"; "Royal Opera House, Covent Garden, London"; "Royal Ascot Races, England.")*
>
> *Jean d'Aveze . . . part of the lifestyle of a certain genre of woman, whose breeding shows by the way she takes care of herself.*
>
> *Often a woman is judged by her possessions. . . . Carry a Whiting and Davis. Few possessions speak so well of you.*
>
> *Recognizing style as the requisite for membership, discerning men prefer the natural shoulder styling of Racquet Club. Meticulously tailored in pure wool, each suit and sportcoat is the ultimate expression of the clubman's classic good taste.*

The ultimate extension of this marketing strategy is designer clothing. Not everyone can afford to wear it. And so its logos and initials are prominently displayed. Like the badges of a bygone aristocracy, they serve to announce the wearer as a member of a privileged class. This, it is implied, is a worthy aspiration. It is the Good Life.

The ideology of the Good Life is implicit in all those ads that promise sex and power and love and happiness through consumption.

> *Cole-Hahn footware: Beauty captivates.*
>
> *A single whiff of Joy turns a rich man into a generous man.*
>
> *They can't stay away from Mr. J.*

Infinity . . . A sense of well being and control that is rare enough in life, much less cars.

Oscar de la Renta. Experience the power of femininity.

Ruffles. A fragrance to love and be loved in.

Red for men. Pure attraction (shows man being mauled by a woman).

You always feel perfect in Navy.

The ideology of the Good Life is even there in those ads that promise nothing, but threaten much. These are the ads that "deal in open sores. . . . Fear. Greed. Anger. Hostility. You name the dwarfs and we play on every one," as an adman once colorfully described them.[67] For these ads are parables of the Bad Life that will attend the failure to consume. And so these ads too hold the promise of the Good Life, that with consumption "one will belong rather than be excluded, one will have happiness rather than misery, good rather than evil, life rather than death."[68]

Has it worked? Has advertising's ideology conquered the common sense? Ask yourself this: What comes to mind when someone, in the course of common parlance, uses the term "the Good Life"?

Sold: Advertising's Effects

"Ours is the first age in which many thousands of the best-trained minds have made it a full-time business to get inside the collective public mind . . . to get inside in order to manipulate, exploit, and control."[69] So wrote Marshall McLuhan, in 1951. By the 90s, advertising dollars had enlisted, not just good minds, but state of the art cinematographers, editors, choreographers, and musicians. Hollywood directors like Michael Cimino, Alan Parker, Adrian Lyne, Tony and Ridley Scott were moving back and forth between what the latter Scott called "thirty seconds for the money and ninety minutes for the ego."[70] The Cola Wars alone brought viewers a roster of celebrities reading "like the lineup in a game of superstar tug of war": Michael J. Fox, Madonna, Patrick Swayze, Robert Palmer, Michael Jordan, Bo Jackson, Don Johnson, Wayne Gretzky, George Michael, to name a few. Pepsi paid Michael Jackson and Madonna more than $5 million each for appearing in a few minutes worth of advertising. The same amount of money is now lavished on some commercials as on the average half hour of prime time programming. "Wretched excess," one producer of commercials calls it.[71]

It is not hard to imagine that all this may have some effect. Unfortunately, such effects are hard to measure, which is not to say we can ignore the issue of effects. After all, as Richard Pollay has wryly observed, "Many of the most important aspects of life elude simple measurement. Indeed, measurability may be highly correlated with triviality." [72]

With this disclaimer as prologue, let's proceed to a few speculations about advertising's social effects.* We might begin by speculating that advertising has no effects. After all, we know what advertising is up to. We're smart enough to know that Pontiac doesn't really build excitement, just cars. We don't really believe we can "be like Mike" (Jordan) by drinking Gatorade.

True enough.** At the same time, some research suggests that advertising may be effective in spite of—or even because of—our discounting. Herbert Krugman of General Electric Research suggests that "the special power of television [commercials]" is that "we take them to be trivial or transparent or both. . . . Precisely this attitude enables the ad to be successful. Were consumers convinced of the importance of ads, they would bring into play an array of 'perceptual defenses' . . . Instead, even as we ignore or discount ads, they are engaging us in 'low involvement learning' . . . In such learning, people are not 'persuaded' of something. . . . But there is a kind of 'sleeper' effect." [75]

---

*Because our focus is on the cultural effects of advertising, we can note two other effects only in passing. The first is on price levels. Would-be competitors of large corporations might be able to match the giants in quality and price, but cannot match the massive advertising budgets that now create brand loyalty. The cost of this advertising is passed on to consumers, raising prices by about 15 percent in heavily advertising, noncompetitive industries.[73]

A second effect that cannot go unmentioned is on the biosphere. Advertising conditions us to want—like Breathless Mahoney—more, more, more. But how much more can the biosphere take and give? Already, we sense there are limits; limits to its resources; to its ozone layer; to its capacity to absorb pollutants and sustain life. Already we sense that in this mania for more, "man is among the endangered species." [74]

**Though the Michael Jordan ads raise the troublesome issue of whether kids know that ads are often fibbing. For evidence that they may not, see Barnouw.[76]

Also replying to those who would minimize advertising's effects is Philip Gold, who warns us against the fallacy of composition—"attributing to an aggregate the characteristics or effects of its parts." For example, "an individual ad, whatever its style or effectiveness, is rarely regarded as an intrinsically significant part of the universe." From this "admittedly correct perception" some might infer that "advertising as an aggregate" has little impact. "Not so," says Gold. "For nearly a century now, the whole has been rather more than the sum of its parts." [77]

Many of advertising's alleged social effects fit under the umbrella of the phrase, the "impoverishment of the self." This means two things.

The first is that advertising renders the self inadequate. As we have seen, psychologists moved advertising's focus from "quality product" to "inadequate consumer." In the latter ads, humankind, once thought of as the crown of God's creation, was rendered "hardly viable" without products to cure its woeful inadequacies: "bad breath, enlarged nose pores, corned feet," yellow teeth, dry hair, dry skin, cellulite, on and on in an endless indictment of the uncommodified self. [78]

A second meaning of "impoverished self" is "incomplete self." Advertising is interested only in part of us. It is anxious to have us get to know what Ewen has called the "commodity self," that part of us that can enjoy and express itself through consumer goods. [79]

But given ads' single-minded attention to making this introduction, other introductions are left unmade. There is, for example, no introduction to the political self, that part of us capable of understanding the self as a part of concentric communities, capable of enjoying and expressing itself through politics. Nor is there any introduction to the religious self, the artistic self, the intellectual self, and so on.

The obvious answer to this complaint is that those other introductions are for others to make. They are not advertising's job. True enough. But recall here that advertising has a privileged place in our lives. When advertising's answer to the question "Who am I?" arrives 3,000 times a day, while other answers rarely get through, which answer will be heard? Eventually, which will be remembered? Which believed?

Finally, it is alleged, advertising has impoverished our culture, by impoverishing our language. As one critic put it,

Poetic language is used so constantly and relentlessly for the
purpose of salesmanship that it has become almost impossible to

say anything with enthusiasm or joy or conviction without running into the danger of sounding as if you were selling something.[80]

Advertisers know this, and so they have taken the logical next step. Having co-opted sincerity, passion, poetry and all but used them up, advertising now co-opts "cynicism itself, in a manner evocative of *Julius Caesar*: 'But when I tell him he hates flatterers, he says he does, being then most flattered.' "[81]

So here's Joe Isuzu, reminding us, in effect, that we mistrust salesmen. And we say we do, being then most flattered—and most trusting of the subtext. Or MTV, always a hop ahead of the hip, saying with a nod and a wink, "MTV. Everyone else is lying scum."

Political Advertising

By 1961, Daniel Boorstin could say, "It is not only advertising which has become a tissue of contrivance and illusion." In our time, it is also politics. Like other advertising, political advertising manages to soothe our anxieties without speaking to their sources. It substitutes "words [and images] that work" for policies that don't.[82]

As in other media, the rules of political advertising include:

1. **Don't challenge your audience by questioning the common sense.** Reaffirm the foundation myths of the American Way.

2. **Don't bore your audience with arcane political argument.** In fact, don't bother them with any political argument. Instead, let them eat frosting: entertainment, laughter, and especially, therapy for their anxiety about the problems you won't address.

How did politics come to this? Other institutions of mass communications behave this way, we've argued, because capitalists succeeded in defining them as *commercial* enterprises—interested in selling themselves by whatever means necessary. To sell yourself, the logic of commerce goes, don't challenge and don't bore your audience.

Political communication has gone through an analogous development. In politics, too, capitalists have succeeded in defining the enterprise as one of selling the candidates—by whatever means necessary.

This salesmanship is not the only way of defining politics, even in the television age. Just as it is not inevitable that the news, or film, or television should be commercial, so it is not inevitable that politics should be commercialized. In Western Europe, the goal has not been so exclusively to make a sale. At least a coequal goal has been educating the polity about the party's principles.*[83] There are, for example, working-class parties dedicated to working-class principles.

Not so in the United States. Here, an upper class dismantled the organized campaign for working-class principles. They did so in at least three ways:**

1. They destroyed political party organizations. Now political parties do not "put up" candidates. Candidates, and their financiers, put themselves up. And who holds them responsible for upholding their parties' principles? No one does.

2. They constructed a campaign finance system requiring massive contributions from wealthy interest groups and individuals.

3. They excused a sizable percentage of working and lower-class voters from the electorate.

We are now left with this: Individual candidates, beholden not to a party ideology, but to fat-cat financiers, appealing to a disproportionately middle-and upper-class electorate.

In this environment, a politician might be forgiven for avoiding the mysterious realm of issues and principles, especially ones that challenge the capitalist common sense.

Mr. Smith Goes to Madison Avenue

By the 1950s, as this process was maturing, politicians were introduced to the advertising industry. Of course, the meeting of

---

*It may be objected that European politics has recently become more commercialized. Interestingly, Europeans do not see this as the inevitable modernization of politics, but as a lamentable "Americanization."

**How they did so is a much larger story than this abbreviated version can tell with any detail or substantiation. For the uncondensed version, see Exoo.[84]

The Man from Hope

In 1992, the Bill Clinton team took the feel-good campaign a step further. If Reagan could bypass the usual political consultants and go to Madison Avenue, Clinton would go all the way to Hollywood. There he found a team of television producers to create ''The Man from Hope,'' a portrait-in-video of the candidate, shown first at the Democratic National Nominating Convention. Brief segements of the video later appeared as spot ads over the course of the campaign, and finally a longer version was aired on the night before election day. Here is some of what it had to say:

Sound	*Snapshots interspersed with narrator*
Bill Clinton: ''I was born in a little town called Hope, Arkansas, three months after my father died. I remember sitting in that old two-story house where I lived with my grandparents, and going to my grandpa's grocery store with that big jar of Jackson cookies that were there on the shelf. It was a wonderful little small town; it seemed like everybody knew everybody else.''	Hope, Arkansas, railroad station. Interior of grocery store. Parade on Main Street. Downtown cafe.
Roger Clinton: ''Religion was really important and church-going was important in our family. Bill loved singing the hymns and the gospel music. And even today it's an extremely significant part of his life. . . .''	Snapshots of older brother Bill with arm around Roger.

Bill Clinton: (Describes meeting John F. Kennedy as part of Boys' Nation program): ``I remember thinking what an incredible country this was that a boy like me who came from a little town in Arkansas, who had no money and no political position would be given the opportunity to meet the President. . . .''

John F. Kennedy, addressing Boys' Nation delegates, moves into crowd, shakes hands with young Bill Clinton.

Bill Clinton: ``I was there when Chelsea was born. It was the most incredible thing I've ever been through. . . .''

Snapshots of Bill Clinton rocking, kissing baby Chelsea.

Chelsea Clinton: ``Sometimes my dad, to make me laugh, makes funny faces, and when I was little, when I would squeeze his nose he would talk in a really weird voice. And when I play softball, sometimes he'll embarrass me by jumping up and down and yelling and waving his arms. And sometimes he'll come over and talk to me during the game, but that's O.K. What I'd like America to know about my mother and father is that they're great people.

Bill pitching softball to Chelsea. Bill, Hillary, and Chelsea together in hammock, laughing.

Bill Clinton: ``Sometimes, late at night on the campaign plane, I'll look out the window and think how far I am from that little town in Arkansas. And yet in many ways, I know that all I am or ever will be came from there. A place and time where nobody locked their doors at night. Where

Campaign plane, flying through an evening sky. Teenage Bill, diving into local swimming hole on a summer day. Children coming out of a school. Parade on Main Street, Bill dancing with Chelsea; dancing with Hillary.

everybody showed up for a parade on Main Street, and kids like me could dream of being part of something bigger than themselves. . . . I still believe these things are possible. I still believe in the promise of America. And I still believe in a place called Hope.

Shaking hands with Kennedy. Railroad station that says, ``Hope.''

★ ★ ★ ★ ★

commercialized politicians and an industry devoted to merchandising was love at first sight.

It is also no wonder that the offspring of this marriage was an increasingly issueless politics. For at about the time the party and its issue positions became irrelevant, advertising was taking its turn from information to image. And so "the world of political advertising absorbed its commercial counterpart and became as one. A common thread was that . . . facts . . . could not compete with evocative imagery. The key was experience, or how does purchasing the product make me feel, as in the Toyota ad; 'Oohh, what a feeling! Toyota.' "[85]

Some have argued that this shift was innocuous, or even healthy. It shifted attention, they say, from issues that often bore voters, to the candidate's character, which is also important.[86] Ray Price, media handler and packager of the "new Nixon," disagrees. In a 1968 internal memo to campaign staff, he explains:

> We have to be very clear on this point: that the response is to the image, not to the man. . . . *It's not what's there that counts, it's what's projected—and, carrying it one step further, it's not what* he *projects but rather what the voter receives. It's not the man we have to change, but rather the received impression. And this impression often depends more on the medium and its use than it does on the candidate himself.*[87]

Today, the medium of choice for conveying what Price calls "the image, not the man" is television. The major product of candidate advertisers is the television commercial. The decline of political discourse in the Madison Avenue Age is so clear that it can be quantified. "Where half hour speeches were the norm [for commercials] in 1952, five minute segments were the politician's preference in 1956 and 1960." [88] In 30 minutes, a candidate can make an argument, from rationale right down to specific policy proposals, with plenty of evidence sprinkled throughout. In five minutes, one can at least make the rudiments of an argument. But "by the 1970s sixty and thirty second spot ads had become the political mainstay." [89] In that time, there is time for a snappy slogan, a catchy jingle, and a few iconic pictures.

Indeed, the most careful survey of these "spots" concludes that most of them are "carbon copies" of "the parade of symbols, flashing photographs, and easy-whistling music" used in product advertising."*[90] More recent studies suggest that issue content has continued to wane as advertising's influence waxes. Lately, only about 15 percent of ads "reveal a candidate issue position that could be called specific." [94]

That figure has been reduced even further since the stunning success of Ronald Reagan's 1984 advertising. Prepared by a "Madison Avenue all-star team," the commercials used "poignant music and soft, sun-dappled scenes of life in a small town as a way of conveying what Reagan had done for America. Footage of the candidate himself was in the same genial, nonspecific mold. The makers of the ads quite openly modeled them on successful campaigns for companies, such as Pepsi-Cola and McDonald's, that felt that identifying themselves with a happy America was more effective than making specific claims about their products." [95]

---

*The authors' more widely cited finding is that many political commercials do "contain substantial information." [91] Two caveats are in order here. First, their survey was of the 1972 presidential campaign, an unusually programmatic one by recent standards.[92] But more importantly, the finding that some commercials articulated candidates' issue positions was based on an extravagantly generous definition of "issue stand." For example, The Nixon campaign most frequently communicated four "issue stands":

—Richard Nixon favored honoring our commitments to other nations.
—Richard Nixon had done an effective job of handling China.
—Richard Nixon had done an effective job of handling Russia.
—Richard Nixon did not favor spending less money on the military.[93]

But surely an "issue stand" is not something about which everyone agrees (like "honoring our commitments to other nations"), and is something that advocates or opposes a policy proposal (unlike "he did an effective job . . ."). By these criteria, the first three statements listed above fail to be "issue stands."

Such sleight of hand may have contributed to the strange divorce of politics from politics observed during the Reagan years: voters voting for a president whose policies they did not support.[96]

Negative Ads: "Make 'Em Feel Bad"

In 1988, too, the winning formula contained plenty of sun-dappled lawns, filled this time with George Bush's benignancy, grandchildren, and puppies. But this time, there was something added. Reagan's team had brought one of the basic strategies of modern, nonrational advertising to a new state of the art. That was, quite simply, "Make 'em feel good" about your candidate. The Bush team discovered the other side of the strategic coin: "Make 'em feel bad" about the alternative.

Or, as one advertising scholar put it, "buy me and you will overcome the anxieties I have just reminded you about."[97] Over an undertone of discordant music, or a dead musicless background, harsh grainy film or "dead" (still) shots show pictures of the "other" candidate or of the damage he has done, described for us by a harsh or derisive voice. One by one, the Bush team made Michael Dukakis all our worst nightmares. In "Boston Harbor," he was an environmental disaster ("and now he says he wants to do for America what he's done for Massachusetts.") In "Dukakis Furlough Programs" he was squishy soft on the criminal violence that seems to lurk around every corner. In "The Tank," he was unilaterally disarming us while riding around in a tank looking like Atom Ant, goofily oblivious, it seemed, to the military dangers all around us.

But is negative advertising really an appeal to irrationality? Often enough, the voiceovers in these ads are a steady stream of factual information. Bush's "Dukakis Furlough Program," for example, provided the following data:

> [Dukakis'] revolving door prison policy gave weekend furloughs to first-degree murderers not eligible for parole. While out, many committed other crimes like kidnapping and rape. Many are still at large. And Michael Dukakis says he wants to do for America what he's done for Massachusetts. America can't afford that risk.

What could be nonrational about a recitation of facts? Two aspects of negative advertising suggest that there is less here than meets the eye. The first is the slipperiness of their "facts"—half

Racism on Furlough

One student of political ads suggests that the Senate campaigns of Jesse Helms are a "how to" of racist attacks. Lesson number one of the Helms primer is, "Use symbols appropriate to the visual media, rather than words, which have specific, identifiable meanings." In other words, make your racist attack sound like it might be something else. (This is what the folks who brought us Iranscam called "plausible deniability.")

Fellow Carolinian Lee Atwater "read" Helms' "book," and took its lessons to the presidential campaign he managed for George Bush.

Critics charged that "Dukakis Furlough Program" was part of an appeal to racial anxiety. The Bush team's denial was plausible. The ad's text never mentions race, and only two of the dozen or so prisoners depicted as filing out through "Dukakis'" revolving door are Black. One is seen only briefly.

But look again. Through nearly the entire chilling 20 seconds the prisoners are on screen, one prisoner is at the center of the frame. He is the one in the revolving door at the outset. In slow motion, he is the one we see emerge in the middle of the pack. The terrifying picture dissolves as he moves off center, out into the streets. He is the one who is black.

truths that are less than no truth. The "Furlough" ad, for example, failed to mention that the Massachusetts program was a creation of a Republican predecessor, and that Dukakis had discontinued part of it; failed to mention that the crime rate in Massachusetts had dropped sharply since Dukakis' election; failed to mention that many states have furlough programs; failed to mention that under the federal furlough program administered, ultimately, by the Reagan-Bush administration, a released prisoner had raped and murdered a mother of two. Strangest of all, the ad neglected to mention that these issues were largely irrelevant to the presidential contest, since crime control is mainly the responsibility of state and local governments.

This ad was not designed to promote *thinking*, but *feeling*. Its appeal was not to ideas, but to anxieties—including that most irrational, vicious anxiety, racial fear (see inset). And content analysis suggests that irrationality goes for most negative advertising.[98]

This last point brings us to another way negative ads "act suspicious." A fair percentage of them confer guilt by association on an opponent. "Frequently," the opponent is pictured with someone voters despise in a "dead shot, . . . etched in black and white." Fully one-fifth of these despised human symbols "represent economic and social minority groups." [99] Willie Horton may have been the MVP of the '88 election, as George Bush's campaign manager called him. But he was not the only guy on the team of racist negative totems.

Another classic example of the guilt-by-association genre was made for the '92 campaign by Floyd Brown, the man responsible for the most overtly racist Willie Horton ads. This time, the candidate associating with the wrong kind of people was Bill Clinton, who said, the voiceover explained, "he'll appoint Mario Cuomo . . . [shown in a dead shot, looking very much like the Italian-American he is proud to be] to the Supreme Court." Also, the ad charged, "Clinton wants to make Washington, D.C., a state, and that'll make Jesse Jackson [another dead shot] a U.S. Senator." Just what was wrong with that, the ad did not say. Perhaps the pictures of these men were meant to be explanation enough.

Are Voters Fools?

How do politicians get away with avoiding the issues? How do they generate warmth without light? Are voters fools? The answer is no, but they can sometimes be fooled, in part by the elusive nature of human language. That will be easier to understand if we borrow a few concepts from the school of "ordinary language" philosophy. This school calls communications that help us understand our real relationship to the world "reality representation." In politics, reality representation involves talk about the little issues that comprise the big issue: who gets what and how.

Intuitively, we often assume that reality representation is the main, or even the only, function of language. That is why we are surprised that there can be so much talk, such convincing talk, with so little political reality to it. But in fact, reality representation is only one among many of what Ludwig Wittgenstein called the "language games" we play, only one of the functions served by language.[100]

Another, which politicians have made increasing use of, is the "mythic nation" game, which serves our need for social location and adjustment—our need to feel that we belong somewhere.[101] In this game, politicians invoke the cherished symbols—history and values—that we share as Americans. Because we share them, affirming the speaker's incantation affirms, for each of us, that we belong in this society and culture. Intuitively, we know when we are in this mode of discourse, and we ask no more of it than that it fulfill its function.

So, for example, one of Ronald Reagan's 1984 commercials was thought to be highly effective, though it didn't say much about anything, and least of all about the issues. Indeed, there were no words at all, only Lee Greenwood singing, as photographic icons of America flashed by:

Sound *(Lee Greenwood singing)*	**Visuals**
From the lakes of Minnesota,	Sunrise over a lake.
To the hills of Tennessee,	Farm.
Across the plains of Texas,	Amish buggy.
From sea to shining sea,	Farmers in cowboy hats.
From Detroit down to Houston,	Children playing.
And New York to L.A.,	Touch-football players.
Well there's pride in every American heart	More cowboys.
And it's time we stand and say,	Ronald Reagan.
That I'm proud to be an American,	Children praying.
Where at least I know I'm free,	Flag.
And I won't forget the men who died,	Boy saying Pledge of Allegiance
Who gave that right to me,	Ronald Reagan at Arlington.
And I'll gladly stand up next to you,	Country church.
And defend Her still today,	Statue of Liberty.
Cause there ain't no doubt I love this land,	Ronald Reagan, smiling, in jean jacket.
God Bless the USA.	

The audience knew, of course, that this ad was not playing the "reality representation game," where the critical questions of "reality testing" are appropriate. Instead, sensing the mythic nation mode, the audience could relax, suspend its disbelief, and bask in the warm glow of belonging—a glow that radiated not only from, but back to, its source, Ronald Reagan.

The success of negative ads is even easier to explain. Here the question is, why do voters seem to believe a pack of vicious distortions? The "Furlough" ad, for example, was rebutted by press criticism and by a Dukakis counter-commercial. Still the slung mud stuck. Why?

Admakers, ever alert to the scent of an open sore, have found one in the body politic. The public has grown mistrustful, even cynical, about a wide range of institutions, including government and politics.[102] Their mood has the public nodding in agreement as soon as aspersions are cast, and shaking their heads at the denials, which must be a lie. "In short, negative messages were believed to rate highly [with advertisers] because of existing predispositions." [103]

It is little wonder that admakers discovered this cynicism. Critics charge that advertising played no small part in creating it. Once again, voters are not fools, but they can be made fools of, and they have been. They have responded as people will when they are bested by swindlers—with inarticulate rage. The number of Americans agreeing with such statements as "What you think doesn't count very much any more," and "The government is pretty much run by a few big interests looking out for themselves," and "I don't think public officials care what people like me think," has more than doubled since the 60s. These are now acceded to by a majority.[104] These alienated Americans come disproportionately from "the lower end of the socio-economic spectrum, among persons with a grade school education, and those who think of themselves as 'average working class.' " [105] Much of their frustration proceeds, as might be imagined, from the failure of candidates to take clear and different stands on the urgent issues that have arisen in recent decades.[106]

Instead, their campaigns, taking a leaf from advertising textbooks, have given us slogans and images. Now, as our cynicism begins to match theirs, political advertisers pander to that as well, with the half-truth and innuendo of the negative campaign.

Advertising as Grass-roots Lobbying

In any given issue, *Time* magazine is likely to carry an ad sponsored by the Mobil Oil Corporation. That is hardly worthy of note. Except that this ad is not selling Mobil's oil or gasoline; it is selling Mobil's politics.

It is estimated that corporations now spend well over $1 billion a year on political advertising. The message of this advertising is, of course, that what's good for corporate America is good for America: "The most consistent theme . . . has been a sustained attack on the use of government money and regulation to solve social problems." [107] Mobil, for example, now spends about $30 million a year on "public affairs." One of the things its money buys is a regularly appearing column on the editorial pages of the *New York Times*, the *Washington Post*, the *Chicago Tribune*, *Time* magazine, and six other leading national news publications. [108] While these op-eds are aimed at opinion leaders, "Observations," another Mobil-produced column, is aimed at a popular audience. It reaches 80 million adult readers in Sunday newspaper supplements every other week. The Mobil vice president in charge of lobbying the public points proudly to surveys showing that people exposed to the column "have a greater affinity for the free-market economy . . . than those with similar . . . characteristics who are not exposed." [109] Mobil also produces television commercials, often dressed to look like news programs and aired during local newscasts, as well as half-hour "documentaries" featuring "journalists" interviewing Mobil executives and other experts who favor Mobil's policies. Local stations can air these programs *in toto* or break them into interview segments for use in newscasts.

Mobil is not an exception; it is just part of the large corporate movement to rewrite the rule. For example, "with an annual budget of only $2 million" the corporate-funded Advertising Council places about $500 million worth of free "public service announcements" on radio, television, newspapers, magazines, and buses each year. [110] Sometimes these messages are naked ideology: "Today the research efforts of U.S. industry are actually lagging because of costly government regulations and discouraging taxation," warns one. [111] Usually, they are more subtle—and insidious—defining, for example, pollution as a function of the lassitude of litterbugs, not of corporations. [112]

Needless to say, the Advertising Council's imprimatur is not available to all public service groups. "Some are rejected on the ground that they are 'controversial.' " For example, "the Washington-based Center for Growth Alternatives, suggesting a campaign on the theme, 'We can't grow on like this,' . . . received no encouragement." [113]

Meanwhile, an "educational" campaign backed by the Commerce Department, urging the public to send for a pamphlet on

"The American Economic System" did not seem controversial to the Ad Council, which created and ran the ads. It did seem controversial to Representative Ben Rosenthal, who complained that the project "took $239,000 earmarked for the creation of jobs" and gave the money to the Advertising Council to produce a pro-corporate, anti-labor "economic understanding booklet." [114]

The potential effectiveness of corporate political advertising is written on the wall by several recent studies. The first was of a range of referendum campaigns. On an average, business outspent the public interest groups that opposed them in these campaigns by a ratio of 27 to 1. Of the 14 campaigns studied, business prevailed in all but three.[115] A second study looked specifically at the results of ballot initiatives dealing with returnable beverage containers and nuclear power. On average, bottle bill advocates spent $50,500 to advertise their position. Corporate opponents spent an average of $950,750. The ratio of corporate to public interest spending in the nuclear referenda was, on average, $231,000 to $1,275,000. "Although causality is difficult to determine, these expenditures no doubt played some role in shifting public opinion." [116] That conclusion is buttressed from several directions. First, opinion shifted markedly, in a pro-corporate direction, over the course of these campaigns. In Colorado, for example, initial support for a bottle bill of 74 percent eventually sank to 31 percent. Secondly, "Post-election polls consistently revealed that opponents of the bills used the precise wording of the corporate ad campaigns to explain their opposition." [117]

Corporations, of course, explained that they were just exercising their right of freedom of speech, which they share with every other citizen. But, as attorney Charles Rembar pointed out, "If I speak through a bullhorn while you speak through a kazoo, you have no freedom of speech." [118]

Coda

We began with questions.

Is consumerism the choice of a cultural democracy, is it "what the people wanted"? Certainly, it was not so to begin with. At first, the products were there but the demand was not. Demand—consumerism—had to be created. Other "isms"—Puritan asceticism, Catholic fatalism and humility, republican egalitarianism—had to be overcome. Then the advertising industry began its relentless, ubiquitous, seductive campaign. Finally, from the privileged place in our discourse that only $100 billion a year can buy, the campaign has succeeded. Only in this attenuated sense is consumerism what the people want.

What do ads do? Do they provide us with useful information about products, or . . . something else? Usually, something else. Advertisers, as we saw, have concluded that the cellar door to the consumer's will is often open—nonrational appeals work. And so, through the magic of advertising, products were not just products. They were (among other things) salves for the wounds inflicted by their own production process—the loss of autonomy, of intimacy, of nature. Products were icons of the American Way, and so they were badges of belonging for a nation of strangers.

Along the way, ads gently escort women and blacks to "their place" in a sexist, segregated society. Along the way, ads have helped to debase our sense of self, our language, and our politics.

In the end, advertising has given us "capitalist realism"—a prescribed way of thinking about the Good Life that has become *our* way of thinking.

References

1. William Leiss, Stephen Kline, and Sut Jhally, *Social Communication in Advertising*, (Scarborough, Ontario: Nelson Canada, 1990): 1. Reprinted by permission of Nelson Canada.
2. John Micklethwait, "The Proof of the Pudding: A Survey of the Advertising Industry," *The Economist*, (vol. 315, June 9, 1990).
3. Michael Schudson, *Advertising: The Uneasy Persuasion*, (New York: Basic Books, 1984): 175.
4. William Leiss, Stephen Kline, and Sut Jhally, *Social Communication in Advertising:* 128.
5. John Micklethwait, "The Proof of the Pudding: A Survey of the Advertising Industry."
6. Erik Barnouw, *The Sponsor*, (New York: Oxford University Press, 1978): 81–82.
7. Philip Gold, *Advertising, Politics, and American Culture*, (New York: Paragon, 1987): 31.
8. David Ogilvy, "What's Wrong With Advertising?" *Advertising in Society*, edited by Roxanne Hovland and Gary B. Wilcox, (Lincolnwood, Ill.: NTC Business Books, 1989): 478.
9. Stuart Ewen, *Captains of Consciousness*, (New York: McGraw-Hill, 1977): 58.

10. Philip Gold, *Advertising, Politics, and American Culture:* 15.
11. Max Weber, *The Protestant Ethic and the Spirit of Capitalism,* translated by Talcott Parsons, (New York: Charles Scribner's Sons, 1958): 166.
12. Milton M. Gordon, *Assimilation in American Life,* (New York: Oxford University Press, 1964): 73.
13. Michael Novak, *The Rise of the Unmeltable Ethnics,* (New York: MacMillan, 1971): 114.
14. Paul John Kleppner, *The Politics of Change in the Midwest,* (unpublished Ph.D. dissertation, University of Pittsburgh, 1967): 110.
15. Max Weber, *The Protestant Ethic and the Spirit of Capitalism:* 80.
16. Oscar Handlin, *The Uprooted,* (Boston: Little, Brown, 1952): 79–80.
17. See Herbert G. Gutman, "Work, Culture, and Society in Industrializing America," *American Historical Review,* vol. 78, 3, (1973); Stuart Ewen, *Captains of Consciousness;* E. P. Thompson, "Time, Work-Discipline, and Industrial Capitalism," *Past and Present,* (vol. 38, December 1967); Leo Marx, *The Machine in the Garden,* (New York: Oxford University Press, 1964).
18. Philip Gold, *Advertising, Politics, and American Culture:* 17–18.
19. Stuart Ewen, *Captains of Consciousness:* 87– 88.
20. Philip Gold, *Advertising, Politics, and American Culture:* 18.
21. Ibid.: 17.
22. William Leiss, Stephen Kline, and Sut Jhally, *Social Communication in Advertising:* 267.
23. Ibid.: 230–31.
24. Philip Gold, *Advertising, Politics, and American Culture:* 51.
25. Roland Marchand, *Advertising the American Dream,* (Berkeley: University of California Press, 1985).
26. Martin Mayer, *Madison Avenue U.S.A.,* (New York: Harper and Bros., 1958): 53.
27. Michael Schudson, *Advertising: The Uneasy Persuasion:* 62.
28. Ibid.: 50.
29. John Micklethwait, "The Proof of the Pudding: A Survey of the Advertising Industry": 5.
30. Michael Schudson, *Advertising: The Uneasy Persuasion:* 50.
31. Raymond Williams, *Television: Technology and Cultural Form,* (Fontana, Great Britain: Colins, 1960): 27.
32. In Roland Marchand, *Advertising the American Dream:* 211.
33. Philip Gold, *Advertising, Politics, and American Culture:* 101.
34. Leo Marx, *The Machine in the Garden.*
35. Stuart Ewen, *Captains of Consciousness:* 80.
36. Roland Marchand, *Advertising the American Dream:* 224–28.
37. Erik Barnouw, *The Sponsor:* 156.
38. Bill Walker, "Green Like Me," *Greenpeace,* (May–June 1991): 9.
39. Diane Barthel, *Putting on Appearances,* (Philadelphia: Temple University Press, 1988): 172–79.
40. Richard Sennett and Jonathan Cobb, *The Hidden Injuries of Class,* (New York: Vintage, 1972): 164.
41. Michael Schudson, *Discovering the News:* 141.
42. George Creel, *How We Advertised America,* (New York: Arno Press, 1972): 156.
43. Philip Gold, *Advertising, Politics, and American Culture:* 9.
44. Michael Schudson, *Advertising: The Uneasy Persuasion:* 219.

45. Philip Gold, *Advertising, Politics, and American Culture:* 96.
46. *Economist,* "America's Corporate Flag Waving: Rednecks Redux," (vol. 316, July 1990): 68–69.
47. Randall Rothenberg, "GE Shows Bright Side of East Bloc," *New York Times,* (April 6, 1990): D7.
48. *Economist,* "America's Corporate Flag Waving: Rednecks Redux": 69.
49. Emily Listfield, "A Light Goes on in Budapest," *American Way,* (October 1, 1991): 32.
50. Michele Barrett, *Women's Oppression Today,* (London: Verso, 1980).
51. Lydia Sargent, *Women and Revolution,* (Boston: South End Press, 1981).
52. Thomas W. Whipple and Alice E. Courtney, "Female Role Portrayals in Advertising and Communication Effectiveness: A Review," *Journal of Advertising,* (vol. 14, 1985): 3.
53. Summary of Erving Goffman, *Gender Advertisements,* (Cambridge: Harvard University Press, 1979) in William Leiss, Stephen Kline, and Sut Jhally, *Social Communication in Advertising:* 217.
54. Ronald Berman, *Advertising and Social Change,* (Beverly Hills, Calif.: Sage, 1981): 52.
55. Diane Barthel, *Putting on Appearances:* 10.
56. Elizabeth Monk-Turner, "Comparing Advertisements in British and American Women's Magazines: 1988–1989," *Sociology and Social Research,* (vol. 75, October 1990): 53–56.
57. Diane Barthel, *Putting on Appearances:* 39.
58. Ibid.: 60–61.
59. A version of this argument can be found in Stephen Fox, *The Mirror Makers,* (New York: Vintage, 1984): chapter 7.
60. Diane Barthel, *Putting on Appearances:* chapter 8.
61. See Anne Koedt, Ellen Levine, and Anita Rapone, *Radical Feminism,* (New York: Quadrangle, 1973); Hester Eisenstein, *Contemporary Feminist Thought,* (Boston: G. K. Hall, 1983).
62. Michael Schudson, *Advertising: The Uneasy Persuasion:* chapter 7.
63. Ronald Humphrey and Howard Schuman, "The Portrayal of Blacks in Magazine Advertisements: 1950–1982," *Public Opinion Quarterly,* (vol. 48, 1984): 551–63.
64. Philip Gold, *Advertising, Politics, and American Culture:* 20.
65. Diane Barthel, *Putting on Appearances:* 92.
66. John Berger, *Ways of Seeing,* (London: British Broadcasting Company, 1972): 132–33.
67. Jerry Della-Famina, in Philip Gold, *Advertising, Politics, and American Culture:* 119.
68. Varda Leymore, *Hidden Myth,* (New York: Basic Books, 1975): 156.
69. Marshall McLuhan, *The Mechanical Bride,* (Boston: Beacon, 1951): v.
70. William Leiss, Stephen Kline, and Sut Jhally, *Social Communication in Advertising:* 188.
71. Ibid.: 186; Douglas C. McGill, "Star Wars in Cola Advertising," *New York Times,* (March 27, 1989): D1, 16.
72. Richard Pollay, "The Distorted Mirror: Reflections on the Unintended Consequences of Advertising," *Advertising in Society,* edited by Roxanne Hovland and Gary B. Wilcox, (Lincolnwood, Ill.: NTC Business Books, 1989): 443.
73. Ben Bagdikian, *The Media Monopoly,* (Boston: Beacon, 1987): 143–48.
74. Erik Barnouw, *The Sponsor:* 157.

75. Michael Schudson, *Advertising: The Uneasy Persuasion:* 226–27.
76. Erik Barnouw, *The Sponsor:* 91.
77. Philip Gold, *Advertising, Politics, and American Culture:* 21.
78. Stuart Ewen, *Captains of Consciousness:* chapters 2 and 3.
79. Ibid.: 47.
80. S. I. Hayakawa, *Language in Thought and Action,* (New York: Harcourt, 1964): 268–69.
81. Philip Gold, *Advertising, Politics, and American Culture:* 90.
82. Murray Edelman, *Political Language,* (New York: Academic Press, 1977).
83. Frank Sorauf, *Party Politics in America,* (Boston: Little-Brown, 1980): 379.
84. See Calvin F. Exoo, *Democracy Upside Down,* (New York: Praeger, 1987): chapter 2; Thomas Byrne Edsall, *The New Politics of Inequality,* (New York: W. W. Norton, 1984); and Francis Fox Piven and Richard Cloward, *Why Americans Don't Vote,* (New York: Pantheon, 1988).
85. Montague Kern, *30-Second Politics,* (New York: Praeger, 1989): 23.
86. James D. Barber, *The Pulse of Politics,* (New York: W. W. Norton, 1980): 314.
87. Joe McGinnis, *The Selling of the President,* (New York: Penguin, 1988): 193–94.
88. Kathleen Hall Jamieson, "The Evolution of Political Advertising in America," *New Perspectives on Political Advertising,* edited by Lynda Lee Kaid, Dan Nimmo, and Keith R. Sanders, (Carbondale, Ill.: Southern Illinois University Press, 1986): 13.
89. Ibid.
90. Thomas E. Patterson and Robert D. McClure, *The Unseeing Eye,* (New York: Praeger, 1976): 101, 103.
91. Ibid.: 102.
92. Benjamin I. Page, *Choices and Echoes in Presidential Elections,* (Chicago: University of Chicago Press, 1978): 103.
93. Thomas E. Patterson and Robert D. McClure, "Television and Voters' Issue Awareness," *The Party Symbol,* edited by William Crotty, (San Francisco: W. H. Freeman, 1980): 329.
94. See Richard A. Joslyn, "The Content of Political Spot Ads," *Journalism Quarterly,* (vol. 57, 1980): 96; Montague Kern, *30-Second Politics:* 52.
95. Nicholas Lemann, "Implications: What Americans Wanted," *The Elections of 1984,* edited by Michael Nelson, (Washington, D.C.: CQ Press, 1985): 266.
96. Theodore J. Lowi, "An Aligning Election, A Presidential Plebiscite," *The Elections of 1984,* edited by Michael Nelson, (Washington, D.C.: CQ Press, 1985): 289.
97. Montague Kern, *30-Second Politics:* 30.
98. Ibid.: 94.
99. Ibid.: 99.
100. Hanna F. Pitkin, *Wittgenstein and Justice,* (Berkeley: University of California Press, 1972): chapter 3.
101. M. Brewster Smith, Jerome Bruner, and Ralph White, *Opinions and Personality,* (New York: Wiley, 1964).
102. Seymour M. Lipset and William Schneider, *The Confidence Gap,* (New York: The Free Press, 1983).
103. Montague Kern, *30-Second Politics:* 26.
104. See Seymour M. Lipset and William Schneider, *The Confidence Gap;* Steven J. Rosenstone and John M. Hanson, *Mobilization, Participation, and Democracy in America,* (New York: MacMillan, 1993): 144.
105. David B. Hill and Norman R. Luttbeg, *Trends in American Electoral Behavior,* (Itasca, Ill.: F. E. Peacock, 1983): 129.

106. See John F. Zipp, "Perceived Representativeness and Voting: An Assessment of the impact of Choices vs. Echoes," *American Political Science Review*, (vol. 79): 50–61; Kim Ezra Shienbaum, *Beyond the Electoral Connection*, (Philadelphia: University of Pennsylvania Press, 1984): 29.
107. Thomas Byrne Edsall, *The New Politics of Inequality:* 117.
108. Jeffrey M. Berry, *The Interest Group Society*, (Boston: Little Brown, 1984): 140.
109. Ronald Berkman and Laura W. Kitch, *Politics in the Media Age*, (New York: McGraw-Hill, 1986): 283.
110. William G. Domhoff, *The Powers That Be*, (New York: Random House, 1978): 184.
111. Ronald Berkman and Laura W. Kitch, *Politics in the Media Age:* 241.
112. Ibid.: 292.
113. Erik Barnouw, *The Sponsor:* 144.
114. Ibid.
115. Steven D. Lydenberg, *Bankrolling Ballots Update 1980*, (New York: The Council on Economic Priorities, 1981).
116. Robert G. Meadow, "Political Advertising as Grassroots Lobbying," *The Social Science Journal*, (vol. 20, 1983): 54.
117. Ibid.
118. Dwight L. Teeter, Jr., Gary B. Wilcox, and Roxanne Hovland, "Commercial Speech and the First Amendment," *Advertising in Society*, edited by Gary B. Wilcox and Roxanne Hovland: 211.

One alternative to the passive consumption of mass media is political action.

Alternatives

At the end of his allegory, Plato asks us to picture one of his prisoners set free, ascending from the cave and out into the sunlight.

But how? If our own cave wall show is the one produced by the mass media, how might we emerge from it to see another reality?

Alternative Media

Let's begin by talking about the alternatives. These are the movies not playing at a theatre near you, the periodicals that are not on your supermarket shelf, the television not jumping out at you from full-page ads in *TV Guide* These are the media the culture has asked to stand in the back. These media are "alternative" in two senses. First, their overriding purpose is not profit. This means, in turn, that they are not subject to all the mass media's rules for maximizing audience and profit: No LOP, no LCD; no "make it wiggle," no "down the middle"; no horse race and hooplah, no soap opera; no pseudo-events, photo ops, or sound bites; no titillate and terminate; no spinoffs, copies, or recombinants; no dummy-down, belly-up, high-concept, low-brow, make-em-laugh, shoot-em-up shadow show. So what's left? Plenty.

The Alternative Press

Take the news, for example. For the past 15 years, communications professor Carl Jensen has annually assembled a panel of experts to choose the top ten "censored" stories of the year. These are the most important stories that the mainstream media somehow missed. In the vast majority of cases, however, they *were* covered—by the alternative press.

A sampling of these stories includes such headlines as, "Truth is First Casualty in Gulf War"; "CIA Involvement in the S&L Crisis"; "NASA Space Shuttle Destroys the Ozone Layer"; "What *Really* Happened in the Panama Invasion"; "America's Coming Banking Crisis," and "The Pentagon's Secret Billion-Dollar Stash."

For those of us who never heard of some of these important stories, maybe we should consider the alternatives.

Here's how a few of them were described in the *Utne Reader's* Annual Alternative Press Awards:

Mother Jones: *Mother Jones* has returned to its distinguished tradition of investigative reporting. Recent triumphs include breakthrough reporting on the breast implant controversy and some of the very best reporting and analysis of the Persian Gulf War.

The New Internationalist: The unjust relationship between the powerful and the powerless in both rich and poor nations is the focus of *The New Internationalist*, which is truly global in its coverage. This monthly looks at world development not only through politics and big news stories, but also by reporting how real people actually live their lives. Excellent use of charts, photographs, maps, and cartoons helps readers grasp the meaning of often intricate issues.

In These Times: This weekly leftist newspaper offers an indispensable alternative to the likes of *Time* and *Newsweek* in its thorough coverage of international affairs, politics, the environment, women, minorities, workers, and cultural issues. In addition to strong coverage of Europe, Central America, and

Washington, D.C., *ITT* offers fresh investigative reports, cartoons, feature stories, and personality profiles. This was the publication that kept the October Surprise scandal alive through George Bush's term. It's not *all* serious, though; the back page consistently casts a wry eye on the foibles and fables of modern life.

The Village Voice: This oldest of the alternative newsweeklies continues to be required reading for those who want to stay on top of the comings and goings of American culture. The *Voice* consistently provides outstanding cultural coverage, with passionate and outspoken writers including advertising critic Leslie Savan, media columnists Doug Ireland and James Ledbetter, and cultural essayist C. Carr, as well as excellent photographers. In addition, every month it includes *The Voice Literary Supplement,* a good publication in its own right.

Earth Island Journal: This quarterly magazine of the Earth Island Institute lives up to its masthead, providing "local news from around the world" and "international environmental news" like no one else. This is a magazine modest in design but grand in scope—thoroughly covering an impressive array of topics from the turtle apocalypse of Mexico to the ecological impact of military action on Middle Eastern deserts.

Adbusters: If you don't like the messages you see in TV and magazine advertising, change them. That's the philosophy of *Adbusters,* a quarterly from Vancouver that is an indispensable tool for media activists and anyone else concerned with sexism, stereotypes, and propaganda in the popular media. Over the past year, *Adbusters* has been especially commendable for its coverage of media boycotts and for its tips on getting homemade alternative "counter-ads" on the air.

Ms.: *Ms.* has changed its format, but not its dedication to providing a space for feminist voices to unite. Now advertising-free, the new *Ms.* has traded its glossy, full-color pages and lower subscription rates for complete editorial freedom. The result is a refreshingly frank magazine that is a challenging and engrossing resource for both women and men.

Z Magazine: Whoever said humor and politics don't mix needs to read *Z Magazine.* While best known for its international reporting and unabashed leftist opinions, *Z* also features some hilarious, scathing social commentary and ironic humor. To its credit, *Z Magazine* consistently goes beyond establishment-bashing to offer realistic solutions and thoughtful protest techniques.

The Nation: America's oldest weekly magazine remains a vital voice in any discussion of politics or culture. Probing investigative reports, incisive international coverage, a stable of top-notch writers, and wide-ranging writing on many aspects of American society keep *The Nation* consistently in the forefront of the best of the alternative press.[1]

Such journals are testimony that sensational pictures and establishment spokesmen are not "all the news that's fit to print."

Alternative Television and Film

It has been more difficult to create alternatives on television. In this medium, the number of broadcast outlets is limited, and the bidding for these enormously profitable stations is high. Increasingly, as we have seen, the highest bidders have been heavily capitalized conglomerates.

But the growth of cable has opened another door to alternative TV. In 1971, the FCC began requiring cable companies to provide a "public access channel" as part of its service. Though the agency has since repealed that requirement, some local governments have required their cable systems to continue providing public access. In a handful of cities across the country, video activists have walked through the door of public access to provide an alternative to the politics-as-usual of mainstream TV.

In Austin, Texas, for example, a group calling itself "Austin Community Television" set up shop in 1970, providing "weekly anti-nuclear programs, black and Chicano series, gay programs, . . . feminist programs, and a weekly left news magazine, 'Alternative Views.' " Its guests have included Helen Caldecott, Daniel Ellsberg, David Dellinger, Benjamin Spock, Stokley Carmichael, feminist, gay, and union activists, representatives from the Sandinista and Allende governments, from the democratic front in El Salvador and "many other Third World countries and revolutionary movements."[2] "Oprah" it's not.

Another way of providing alternatives to TV's usual message is counter-advertising. For example, the nonprofit Media Foundation argues in its journal, *Adbusters,* that television and its advertising are socially and environmentally destructive. Lately, it has taken its message to the airwaves, in "a series of paid TV spots called 'Tubehead,' in which people struggle to wrench TV sets off their heads. 'Don't spend your life in the tube,' the voiceover warns." [3]

Movie-making, as we saw in Chapter 3, is also hard for those who would work outside the studios and their formulae. Nevertheless, alternative films are made.

Pick up any recent issue of *Jump Cut, Cineaste,* or *Afterimage.* There you might read an article about African and Black Diaspora films, like the work of Isaac Julien, a black, working-class British director whose movies take on issues of racism, sexism, and the decline of industrial society.

There too you can read about Barbara Kopple's *American Dream,* a documentary about the hardship of workers staging a strike against the Hormel meatpacking company, and, in these hard times for workers, finding themselves divided from their fellow workers and from their own union.

Or try John Sayles' *City of Hope,* which looks at the reemergence of ethnic tribalism in a time when national leaders' implicit message is, "It's everybody for themselves."

In these alternative-film journals, you'll find an account of the Film Institute of El Salvador, a project of the FMLN to "record their own revolution." You'll find an interview with Hector Babenco, whose *At Play in the Fields of the Lord* narrates what he calls "the failure of the white approach to the native" in the Amazon rainforest.

The distinctiveness of such films is striking. Their purposes, their subjects, their perspectives, even their styles are different from Hollywood's; so different that they tempt comparison with the difference between seeing shadows and seeing objects.

Alternative Lives

Alternative media are not the only exit from the mass media's subterranean theatre. Another is simply to spend less time on any sort of media.

That would seem an obvious point. But it is one that seems lost on most Americans. We have already reviewed the numbers: The seven hours of television the average family watches each day; the 1 million advertisements the average American sees by age 40; the $150 million spent to see the latest blockbuster movie. The consumption of media is consuming us.

Suppose we were to turn off the TV, put the magazine down, and pass by the movie theatre. Whatever would be left to do then? Once again, the answer is, "Plenty."

The truth is, our addiction to the media has kept us from making a number of important acquaintances—with ourselves. The several selves inside each of us might include an artistic self, a political self, a religious, athletic, scientific, literary, artisan, or exploratory self. I am not speaking here only of those few people who may be literary geniuses or athletic marvels. I am talking about all of us, each one of us full of capacities for creativity and expression. It is these dimensions of ourselves, these abilities to act and to make, that go untended as we while away the hours in passive oblation to mass media.

The idea that we might be a more active people is not a utopian fantasy. *We used to be* a more active people. In the nineteenth century, with no mass media to amuse them, Americans entertained themselves. Coteries gathered in parlors to hear and see one another recite poetry, sing and play music, stage plays, and dance.

> *There were of course circuses, music halls, concert halls and touring theater companies, but leisure time in America under the influence of the Protestant work ethic was thought best spent in self-improvement. Even relatively small communities were apt to have someone who could give young people instruction in elocution and public speaking—who could teach drawing and painting, singing and piano, the dances and deportment of the ballroom. There were "uplifting" activities like the church choir, the Shakespeare Club, debating societies, the Reading Room Association, where recreation and the acquisition of "culture" were aggressively intermixed.[4]*

Politics, in those days, was also something to *do*, not just watch. At election time, in every town and ward in the country, legions of voters joined up in their party's campaign army. Some formed campaign clubs, rented a headquarters, drafted constitutions, held weekly open meetings to hear speeches, and organized the drive. Others joined the uniformed marching companies that led torchlight parades down the campaign trail. Workmen built floats for these parades displaying their crafts—and their fealty to the party. Others joined the party's glee clubs or brass bands.

Estimates are that these activities attracted millions of votes. "During the campaign of 1880," for example, "New Haven, a city of 62,000 people living in thirteen wards produced 42 clubs and 68 companies for the two major parties. Perhaps 5,000 out of 16,000 eligible voters signed club constitutions or marched in the city's campaign army." And New Haven was not unique: "More than a fifth of Northern voters probably played an active part" in the campaigns of the latter 19th century.[5]

Then there were the millions more who flocked to the parades and rallies staged by these activists.

> *In cities the appearance of a party hero from another state, with an escort of local marching companies, filled halls and "opera houses." Unable to find seats inside, thousands of people often stood in the streets to hear orators speak from make-shift platforms. Away from the cities, all-day rallies highlighted the campaign. In the morning, farmers formed their wagons in procession and drove to the county seat to watch a parade, perhaps eat a free lunch, listen to an afternoon of speeches from visiting party leaders, and then applaud a torchlight parade at night.[6]*

Finally, on election day, about 75 percent of the eligible electorate would go to the polls—a figure 50 percent higher than the turnouts of our day.

I am not suggesting that it is time to bring back the torchlight parade. I am suggesting that even without the torchlights, there is still plenty to do in politics. There are still marches to march, wards to heel, legislators to write to, pieces to be said at the meetings that meet in our town halls and schools and churches and workplaces. The fact that lately most of us have opted just to *watch* politics instead of *doing something* about it has not produced conspicuously successful results. Perhaps it's time, to paraphrase an old slogan, for us to "tune out, turn off, rise up."

Environmentalist Bill McKibben suggests one more dimension of life that has been lost to the media. And he suggests a way to recapture it: take a hike. His compelling book is an account of two very different "days" in his life. On one of these days, McKibben "collected on videotape nearly every minute of television that came across the enormous [93 channel] Fairfax, [Virginia], cable system from one morning to the next." Then he watched it.

On the other day, he hiked up a small mountain near his home in the Adirondacks, took a swim in its pond, made supper there, and watched the stars till he fell asleep.

His TV day begins this way:

> *"If you have a cold, you do not need to worry about reinfecting yourself with your lip balm." That's Beverly, who leads Christian calisthenics on Channel 116, Family Net. "If you used someone else's lip balm, I could see that. But not your own."* So much

happens *between seven and eight in the morning on the ninety-three stations of the Fairfax, Virginia, cable system, until recently the largest in the world.* On Good Morning America, *Joel, the movie critic, says, "I learned something about England. For sore throats, the actors of Shakespeare's time used to take a live frog and lower the frog by its foot into their mouths. They figured that would keep the juices going. That's where the expression 'a frog in your throat' comes from."* Since seaweed grows "in the nutrient-rich ocean," *it comes as no surprise to anyone in the Annushka cosmetics organization that it attacks and destroys cellulite. An Amtrak train has gone off the rails in Iowa, according to CNN, and American companies will now be allowed to sell laptop computers in Eastern Europe. Kevin Johnson of the Phoenix Suns, so racked with the flu he had to be fed intravenously, nonetheless tallied 29 points and 12 assists in last night's game. Meanwhile, a robot surgeon has successfully replaced a dog's arthritic hip with an artificial joint. On the Fox affiliate, a cartoon Mr. Wilson is sure that's Dennis (the Menace) in the gorilla suit, so he uses a pair of pliers on the snout; entertainingly, however, it's an actual gorilla escaped from the zoo. The Infiniti Q-45 goes 0–60 in 6.9 seconds—" 'Wow' is an involuntary response of pure pleasure."* [7]

His day on the mountain yields no such information. Instead, it is mostly rumination. It ends this way:

Nights are as different, one from another, as days. Tonight, to the southwest, banks of clouds close in one corner of the sky—instead of seeing, as the cosmologists insist, toward the start of time and the edge of the universe, you could see just a rounded edge of black. But the rest of the sky was lit up—moon enough to run a trail of rippling white across the pond, and when it set the million stars were joined by a billion others. Even then sight didn't altogether fail me: on all but the inkiest nights you can feel your way through the darkness, picking out patterns like the gaps in trees that demarcate trails. And the noise—we think of the woodland creatures bedding down for the night, but of course many of them are just rising. Several coyote howled somewhere far in the distance; a mouse rustled across the nylon on the tent flap; on the pond a fish jumped now and again, slipping back into the water with a liquid plonk that died as soon as it had sounded. And a mosquito sawed in my ear, of course. [8]

The conclusion McKibben draws from his experiment is, like the rest of his book, modest:

> *I'm not interested in deciding which of these ways of spending time is "better." Both are caricatures, and neither strikes me as a model for a full and happy life. But caricatures have their uses—they draw attention to what is important about the familiar. Our society is moving steadily from natural sources of information toward electronic ones, from the mountain and the field toward the television; this great transition is very nearly complete. And so we need to understand the two extremes. One is the target of our drift. The other an anchor that might tug us gently back, a source of information that once spoke clearly to us and now hardly even whispers.*[9]

This point might be extended. We are moving away not only from the mountain and the field in the media age, but from the meeting hall, the concert hall, the block club, the corner pub, the church, and the parlor full of poetry, drama, and dance.

The sweep of this movement toward a media-centered life is powerful. Once again Plato's myth is prescient, and suggests just how powerful the pull of the cave can be. In the end, his escaped prisoner, returning to tell his fellow prisoners of another reality, is derided. "They laugh and say that he has gone up only to come back with his sight ruined; it is worth no one's while even to attempt the ascent. If they could lay hands on the man who was trying to set them free and lead them up, they would kill him."

This, as I say, is revealing. As endings go, though, it is also not very satisfying. Perhaps we can come to a more hopeful conclusion. At the same time, let's not be cloudy-headed about the possibility. After all, the task at hand is not only to see beyond the shadow show. Once we've done that, we'll have to address the less-than-picture-perfect reality that confronts us. That reality, as I argued in Chapter 1, is one where wars are not glorious; where everyday life is not much like the Huxtables'; where the good guys don't always win. Instead, it is a reality too often marked by excess and need, rapacity and poverty, inequality and injustice, concentrated power and widespread suffering. It is a firmly entrenched reality, partly because it is so effectively ignored, denied, or justified by the shadow show going on beneath it. How can we begin to challenge it?

If Plato's myth is, in the end, too bleak an answer to that question, let's try another. I suggest that we challenge the way things are in the spirit of Sysiphus. Sysiphus himself, Greek mythology tells us, issued a challenge to the status quo. Out of the underworld on a weekend pass from his fate, he went AWOL. The best threats of the powers that used to be could not bring him back to camp. His punishment, although terrible, must have seemed familiar to a man who would not be resigned to the way things are.

> *The gods . . . condemned Sysiphus to ceaselessly rolling a rock to the top of a mountain, whence the stone would fall back of its own weight. They had thought with some reason that there is no more dreadful punishment than futile and hopeless labor.*[10]

Our ending is not, you may be thinking, off to a particularly hopeful start. Nor should it be. This book has been about some of what we are up against in the hard rock of hegemony. In all the media industries, we have seen increases in the concentrations of ownership, in the devotion to profit, and in the rigidity of the unwritten rules that govern media content.

All this is good cause for what Gramsci called "pessimism of the intellect." It was part of his motto. But for Gramsci, there was also a more important part: "optimism of the will."

Sysiphus, too, is a pessimist of the intellect, but an optimist of the will. His modern-day interpreter, Albert Camus, asks us to picture him as he descends the mountain to begin his task again.

> *Sysiphus, proletarian of the gods, powerless and rebellious, knows the whole extent of his wretched condition; it is what he thinks of during his descent. The lucidity that was to constitute his torture at the same time crowns his victory. There is no fate that cannot be surmounted by scorn. . . . "I conclude that all is well," says Oedipus, and that remark is sacred. It echoes in the wild and limited universe of man. It teaches that all is not, has not been, exhausted. It drives out of this world a god . . . with a preference for futile sufferings. It makes of fate a human matter, which must be settled among men.*

Now picture the men and women of the counterculture, nearing the end of such a descent: drawing a last deep breath, rolling up shirtsleeves, choosing the rock, relishing its challenge. They are there, as we have seen, at work in the alternative media, challenging the shadow show's reality with another. And they are there in other spheres as well, working for change in the factories, the schools, and the churches; in legislative hallways, backyards, storefronts, suburban malls, town halls, farm fields, and city streets.

The change they hope for will not come tomorrow. These descendants of Sysiphus know that. Still, their work goes on. And in the end, this much can be said with certainty of Sysiphus' stone:

it will be moved. Those struggling, failing, persisting resistances going on all around us will grow. Probably, the movement of the stone will not be rapid. Probably it will not happen without reversals. Quite likely, somewhere near the top, years of struggle will fall down in failure. And then, just as surely, it will begin again.

> *I leave Sysiphus at the foot of the mountain! One always finds one's burden again. But Sysiphus teaches the higher fidelity that negates the gods and raises rocks. He too concludes that all is well. This universe henceforth without a master seems to him neither sterile nor futile. Each atom of that stone, each mineral flake of that night-filled mountain, in itself forms a world. The struggle itself toward the heights is enough to fill a man's heart. One must imagine Sysiphus happy.*

References

1. *Utne Reader*, "Fourth Annual Alternative Press Awards," (July–August 1992): 96–97; *Utne Reader*, "Third Annual Alternative Press Awards," (July–August 1991): 59–60. Reprinted with permission from *Utne Reader*, July/Aug. 1991 and July/Aug. 1992.
2. Douglas Kellner, "Public Access Television: Alternative Views," *American Media and Mass Culture*, edited by Donald Lazere, (Berkeley: University of California Press, 1987): 610–18.
3. Leslie Savan, "Op-ads," *Utne Reader*, (January–February 1992): 72.
4. Malcolm McCormick, *A Brief History of Home Entertainment*, (Canton, N.Y.: Village Historian's Office, 1992): 3.
5. Michael E. McGerr, *The Decline of Popular Politics*, (New York: Oxford University Press, 1986): 26.
6. Ibid.: 27.
7. Bill McKibben, *The Age of Missing Information*, (New York: Random House, 1992): 3–4. From *The Age of Missing Information* by Bill McKibben. Copyright © 1992 by Bill McKibben. Reprinted by permission of Random House, Inc.
8. Ibid.: 221–22.
9. Ibid.: 10.
10. Indented quotations are from Albert Camus, *The Myth of Sisyphus and Other Essays*, translated by Justin O'Brien. (New York: Alfred A. Knopf, 1955): 88–91. From *The Myth of Sisyphus and Other Essays by Albert Camus, translated by Justin O'Brien. Copyright © 1955 by Alfred A. Knopf, Inc. Reprinted by permission of Alfred A. Knopf, Inc.*

Selected Bibliography

Abercrombie, Nicholas, Stephen Hill, and Bryan S. Turner. *The Dominant Ideology Thesis.* London: George Allen and Unwin, 1980.

Anderson, Perry. "The Antinomies of Antonio Gramsci." *New Left Review,* 100 (1976–77): 5–80.

Atkin, David, and Barry Litman. "Network TV Programming: Economics, Audiences, and the Ratings Game, 1971–1986." *Journal of Communication,* 36 (1986): 3, 32–50.

Auletta, Ken. *Three Blind Mice.* New York: Random House, 1991.

Austin, Bruce. *Immediate Seating.* Belmont, Calif.: Wadsworth, 1989.

Bagdikian, Ben H. "The Fruits of Agnewism." *Columbia Journalism Review,* January–February 1973: 9–23.

————. *The Media Monopoly.* 2d ed. Boston: Beacon, 1987.

————. "The Lords of the Global Village." *The Nation,* (June 12, 1989): 805–820.

Barnouw, Erik. *A Tower in Babel.* New York: Oxford University Press, 1966.

————. *The Image Empire.* New York: Oxford University Press, 1970.

————. *The Sponsor.* New York: Oxford University Press, 1978.

————. *Tube of Plenty.* New York: Oxford University Press, 1990.

Barthel, Diane. *Putting on Appearances.* Philadelphia: Temple University Press, 1988.

Bennett, Lance W. *News: The Politics of Illusion.* New York: Longman, 1988.

————. *The Governing Crisis.* New York: St. Martin's, 1991.

Berger, John. *Ways of Seeing.* London: British Broadcasting Co., 1972.

Berger, Peter L. *The Capitalist Revolution.* New York: Basic, 1986.

Blankenburg, William B. "Unbundling the Modern Newspaper." *The Future of News,* edited by Philip Look, Douglas Gomery, and Lawrence W. Lichty. Baltimore, Md.: Johns Hopkins University Press, 1992.

Bluestone, Barry and Bennett Harrison. *The Deindustrialization of America.* New York: Basic Books, 1982.

Blum, Richard A., and Richard D. Lindheim. *Primetime.* New York: Focal Press, 1987.

Bogart, Leo. *Press and Public: Who Reads What, When, Where, and Why in American Newspapers.* Hillsdale, N.J.: Lawrence Earlbaum Associates, 1981.

Boorstin, Daniel. *The Image: A Guide to Pseudo-Events in America.* New York: Atheneum, 1961.

Bower, Robert T. *The Changing Television Audience in America.* New York: Columbia University Press, 1985.

Breed, Warren. "Social Control in the Newsroom: A Functional Analysis." *Social Forces,* 33 (1955): 326–35.

Broder, David S. *Behind the Front Page.* New York: Simon and Schuster, 1987.

Brown, Jane D., Carl R. Bybee, Stanley T. Weardon, and Dulcie M. Straughn. "Invisible Power: Newspaper News Sources and the Limits of Diversity." *Journalism Quarterly,* 63 (1987): 45–54.

Ceplair, Larry and Steven Englund. *The Inquisition in Hollywood.* Berkeley: University of California Press, 1983.

Comstock, George, with Haejung Park. *Television and the American Child.* San Diego: Academic Press, 1991.

Comstock, George. *Television in America.* 2d ed. Beverly Hills, Calif.: Sage, 1991.

Crouse, Timothy. *The Boys on the Bus.* New York: Random House, 1973.

Dominick, Joseph R. "Business Coverage in Network Newscasts." *Media Power in Politics,* edited by Doris A. Graber. Washington, D.C.: Congressional Quarterly Press, 1984.

Donahue, Suzanne M. *American Film Distribution.* Ann Arbor, Mich.: UMI Research Press, 1987.

Donohue, G. A., P. J. Tichenor, and C. N. Olien. "Mass Media and the Knowledge Gap: A Hypothesis Reconsidered." *Communication Research,* 2 (1975): 3–23.

Dreier, Peter. "The Corporate Complaint Against the Media." *American Media and Mass Culture,* edited by Donald Lazere. Berkeley: University of California Press, 1987.

Edelman, Murray. *Political Language.* New York: Academic Press, 1977.

————. *Constructing the Political Spectacle.* Chicago: University of Chicago Press, 1988.

Edsall, Thomas B. *The New Politics of Inequality.* New York: W. W. Norton, 1984.

Edwards, Richard C., Michael Reich, and David M. Gordon. *Labor Market Segmentation.* Lexington, Mass.: D. C. Heath, 1975.

Eisenstein, Hester. *Contemporary Feminist Thought.* Boston: G. K. Hall, 1983.

Epstein, Edward Jay. *News from Nowhere.* New York: Vintage Books, 1973.

Ewen, Stuart. *Captains of Consciousness.* New York: McGraw-Hill, 1976.

Ewen, Stuart and Elizabeth Ewen. *Channels of Desire.* New York: McGraw-Hill, 1982.

Exoo, Calvin F. "Elections and the Media." *Polity,* XVI (1983): 343–53.

————, ed. *Democracy Upside Down: Public Opinion and Cultural Hegemony in the United States.* New York: Praeger, 1987.

Faludi, Susan. *Backlash: The Undeclared War Against American Women.* New York: Anchor Books, 1991.

Ferrall, Victor E., Jr. "The Impact of Television Deregulation on Private and Public Interests." *Journal of Communication,* 39, no. 1 (1989): 8–38.

Foner, Eric. "Why Is There No Socialism in the United States?" *History Workshop Journal,* 17 (1984): 57–73.

Forer, Lois. *A Chilling Effect.* New York: Norton, 1986.

Gabler, Neal. *An Empire of Their Own.* New York: Crown, 1988.

Gans, Herbert J. *Deciding What's News.* New York: Pantheon Books, 1979.
_____. "Are U.S. Journalists Dangerously Liberal?" *Columbia Journalism Review,* November–December (1985): 29–33.
Genovese, Eugene D. "On Antonio Gramsci." *Studies on the Left,* VII (1967): 284–316.
Gerbner, George, Larry Gross, Michael Morgan, and Nancy Signorielli. "Charting the Mainstream: Television's Contributions to Political Orientations." *Journal of Communication,* 32, no. 2 (1982): 100–127.
Gitlin, Todd. *The Whole World Is Watching.* Berkeley: University of California Press, 1980.
_____. *Inside Prime Time.* New York: Pantheon, 1985.
_____. "Television's Screens: Hegemony in Transition." Berkeley: University of California Press, 1987.
Goffman, Erving. *Gender Advertisements.* Cambridge: Harvard University Press, 1979.
Gold, Philip. *Advertising, Politics, and American Culture.* New York: Paragon, 1987.
Gordon, David M., Richard Edwards, and Michael Reich. *Segmented Work, Divided Workers.* Cambridge: Cambridge University Press, 1982.
Graber, Doris J. *Processing the News.* New York: Longman, 1984.
Gramsci, Antonio. *Selections from the Prison Notebooks.* Edited and translated by Quinton Hoare and Geoffrey N. Smith. New York: International Publishers, 1971.
Gustafson, Robert. "'What's Happening to Our Pix Biz?' From Warner Bros. to Warner Communications, Inc." *The American Film Industry,* edited by Tino Balio. Madison: Univeristy of Wisconsin Press, 1985.
Halberstam, David. *The Powers That Be.* New York: Alfred A. Knopf, 1979.
Hamill, Pete. "Fear and Favor at the *New York Times.*" *The Village Voice,* 30 (1985): 17–24.
Harrison, Bennett and Barry Bluestone. *The Great U-Turn.* New York: Basic Books, 1988.
Herman, Edward, and Noam Chomsky. *Manufacturing Consent.* New York: 1988.
Hertsgaard, Paul. *On Bended Knee.* New York: Schocken, 1989.
Hofstetter, C. Richard. *Bias in the News.* Columbus: Ohio State University Press, 1976.
Humphrey, Ronald and Howard Schuman. "The Portrayal of Blacks in Magazine Advertisements: 1950–1982." *Public Opinion Quarterly,* 48 (1984): 551–63.
Izod, John. *Hollywood and the Box Office, 1895–1986.* New York: Columbia University Press, 1988.
Jamieson, Kathleen Hall. "The Evolution of Political Advertising in America." *New Perspectives on Political Advertising,* edited by Lynda Lee Kaid, Dan Nimmo, and Keith R. Sanders. Carbondale, Ill.: Southern Illinois University Press, 1986.
_____. *Eloquence in an Electronic Age.* New York: Oxford University Press, 1988.

Johnstone, John W. C., Edward Slawski, and William W. Bowman. *The News People.* Urbana: University of Illinois Press, 1976.

Kellner, Douglas, "Public Access Television: Alternative Views." *American Media and Mass Culture,* edited by Donald Lazere. Berkeley: University of California Press, 1987.

Kern, Montague. *30-Second Politics.* New York: Praeger, 1989.

Koszatski, Richard. "Politics and the Movies, or: That's Democracy!" *Culturefront,* (Fall 1992): 24–29.

Krasnow, Erwin G., Lawrence D. Longley, and Herbert A. Terry. *The Politics of Broadcast Regulation.* New York: St. Martin's, 1982.

Lee, Martin A. and Norman Solomon. *Unreliable Sources.* Secaucus, N.J.: Carol Publishing, 1990.

Leiss, William, Stephen Kline, and Sut Jhally. *Social Communication in Advertising.* Scarborough, Ontario: Nelson, Canada, 1990.

Levi-Strauss, Claude. *The Raw and the Cooked: Introduction to a Science of Mythology: I.* Translated by John and Doreen Weightman. New York: Harper and Row, 1975.

Levy, Mark. "Why VCRs Aren't Pop-Up Toasters: Issues in Home Video Research." *The VCR Age,* edited by Mark Levy. Newbury Park, Calif.: Sage, 1989.

Leymore, Varda. *Hidden Myth.* New York: Basic Books, 1975.

Lichter, S. Robert, Stanley Rothman, and Linda Lichter. *The Media Elite.* New York: Adler and Adler, 1986.

Lichter, Robert and Stanley Rothman. "Media and Business Elites." *Public Opinion,* December–January 1982: 42–46.

Lippmann,Walter. *Public Opinion.* New York: Harcourt Brace, 1922.

Litwak, Mark. *Reel Power.* New York: William Morrow, 1986.

MacArthur, John R. *Second Front: Censorship and Propaganda in the Gulf War.* New York: Hill and Wang, 1992.

Maltby, Richard. "The Political Economy of Hollywood." *Cinema, Politics, and Society in America,* edited by Philip Davies and Brian Neve. New York: St. Martin's, 1981.

Marchand, Roland. *Advertising the American Dream.* Berkeley: University of California Press, 1985.

Marx, Karl. *A Contribution to the Critique of Political Economy,* edited by Maurice Dobb. New York: International Publishers, 1970.

Marx, Karl and Frederick Engels. *The German Ideology,* edited by S. Ryazanskaya. Moscow: Progress Publishers, 1964.

Mattera, Philip. *Prosperity Lost.* New York: Addison-Wesley, 1990.

McClymer, John F. "The Americanization Movement and the Education of the Foreign-Born Adult, 1914–25." *American Education and the European Immigrant: 1840–1940,* edited by Bernard J. Weiss. Urbana: University of Illinois Press, 1982: 96–116.

McGerr, Michael E., *The Decline of Popular Politics.* New York: Oxford University Press, 1986.

McKibben, Bill, *The Age of Missing Information.* New York: Random House, 1992.

Micklethwait, John. "The Proof of the Pudding: A Survey of the Advertising Industry." *The Economist*, (June 9, 1990): 1–18.

Miller, Marc C. "Prime Time: Deride and Conquer." *Watching Television*, edited by Todd Gitlin. New York: Pantheon, 1986.

_____. "Hollywood: The Ad." *The Atlantic Monthly*, (April 1990).

Mills, C. Wright. *The Sociological Imagination*. New York: Oxford University Press, 1959.

Minnow, Newton. *Equal Time: The Private Broadcaster and the Public Interest*. New York: Antheneum, 1964.

Monaco, James. *American Film Now*, rev. ed. New York: New American Library, 1984.

Newfield, Jack. "Journalism: Old, New and Corporate." *The Reporter as Artist: A Look at the New Journalism*, edited by Ronald Weber. New York: Hastings House, 1974.

Ogilvy, David. "What's Wrong With Advertising?" *Advertising in Society*, edited by Roxanne Hovland and Gary B. Wilcox, Lincolnwood, Illinois: NTC Business Books, 1989: 477–485.

Paletz, David L. and Robert M. Entman. *Media-Power-Politics*. New York: The Free Press, 1981.

Paraschos, Manny. "Europe." *Global Journalism*, edited by John C. Merrill. New York: Longman, 1991.

Parenti, Michael. *Inventing Reality*. New York: St. Martin's, 1986.

_____. *Make-Believe Media*. New York: St. Martin's, 1992.

Patterson, Thomas E. and Robert D. McClure. *The Unseeing Eye*. New York: Putnam, 1976.

Patterson, Thomas E. *The Mass Media Election*. New York: Praeger, 1980.

Peck, Abe. *Uncovering the Sixties*. New York: Pantheon, 1985.

Pitkin, Hanna F. *Wittgenstein and Justice*. Berkeley: University of California Press, 1972.

Piven, Francis Fox and Richard Cloward. *Why Americans Don't Vote*. New York: Pantheon, 1988.

Pollay, Richard. "The Distorted Mirror: Reflections on the Unintended Consequences of Advertising." *Advertising in Society*, edited by Roxanne Hovland and Gary B. Wilcox. Lincolnwood, Ill.: NTC Business Books, 1989.

Postman, Neil. *Amusing Ourselves to Death*. New York: Viking, 1985.

Randall, Richard S. "Censorship: From *The Miracle* to *Deep Throat*." *The American Film Industry*, edited by Tino Balio. Madison: University of Wisconsin Press, 1985.

Ray, Robert. *A Certain Tendency of the Hollywood Cinema*. Princeton, N.J.: Princeton University Press, 1985.

Robinson, Michael J. and Margaret A. Sheehan. *Over the Wire and on TV*. New York: Russell Sage Foundation, 1983.

Robinson, Michael J. and Austin Ranney, eds. *The Mass Media in Campaign '84*. Washington, D.C.: American Enterprise Institute.

Rusher, William A. *The Coming Battle for the Media*. New York: William Morrow, 1988.

Sabato, Larry. *Feeding Frenzy.* New York: Free Press, 1991.

Sargent, Lydia. *Women and Revolution.* Boston: South End Press, 1981.

Schatz, Thomas G. *Old Hollywood, New Hollywood; Ritual, Art, and Industry.* Ann Arbor, Mich.: UMI Research Press, 1983.

————. "St. Elsewhere and the Evolution of the Ensemble Series." *Television: The Critical View,* edited by Horace Newcomb. New York: Oxford University Press, 1987.

Schiller, Dan. *Objectivity and the News.* Philadelphia: University of Pennsylvania Press, 1981.

Schneir, Walter and Miriam Schneir. "Beyond Westmoreland: The Right's Attack on the Press." *Nation,* 30 (March 1985): 361–67.

Schram, Martin. *The Great American Video Game.* New York: William Morrow, 1987.

Schudson, Michael. *Discovering the News.* New York: Basic Books, 1978.

————. *Advertising: The Uneasy Persuasion.* New York: Basic Books, 1984.

————. "The Politics of Lou Grant." *Television: The Critical View,* edited by Horace Newcomb. New York: Oxford University Press, 1987.

Shore, Elliott. *Talkin' Socialism.* Lawrence, Kan.: University of Kansas Press, 1988.

Sigal, Leon V. *Reporters and Officials.* Lexington, Mass.: D. C. Heath, 1973.

Signorielli, Nancy. "Selective Television Viewing: A Limited Possibility." *Journal of Communication,* 36, no. 3 (1986): 64–75.

————. "Television and Conceptions About Sex Roles." *Sex Roles,* 21 (1989): 341–60.

Simon, Roger. *Gramsci's Political Thought.* London: Lawrence and Wishart, 1982.

Stein, Ben. *The View from Sunset Boulevard.* New York: Basic, 1979.

Steinfels Peter. *The Neoconservatives.* New York: Simon and Schuster, 1979.

Stille, Alexander. "Libel Law Takes on a New Look." *National Law Journal,* 1 (October 24, 1988): 32–33.

Stoler, P. *The War Against the Press.* New York: Dodd, 1986.

Surgeon General's Scientific Advisory Committee on Television and Social Behavior. "Television and Growing Up: The Impact of Televised Violence." Report to the Surgeon General, United States Public Health Service, Washington, D.C.: U.S. Government Printing Office, 1972.

Teeter, Dwight L., Jr., Gary B. Wilcox, and Roxanne Hovland. "Commercial Speech and the First Amendment." *Advertising in Society,* edited by Roxanne Hovland and Gary B. Wilcox, Lincolnwood, Ill.: NTC Business Books, 1989: 202–219.

Thompson, E. P. "Time, Work-Discipline, and Industrial Capitalism." *Past and Present,* 38 (December 1989): 56–97.

Underwood, Paul S. "Europe and the Middle East." *Global Journalism,* edited by John C. Merrill. New York: Longman, 1983.

Veblen, Thorstein. *The Theory of Business Enterprise.* New York: Charles Scribner's Sons, 1904.

Waterman, David. "The Failure of Cultural Programming on Cable TV: An Economic Interpretation." *Journal of Communication*, 36, no. 3 (1986): 92–107.

Weaver, David H., and G. Cleveland Wilhoit. *The American Journalist.* Bloomington: Indiana University Press, 1986.

Weber, Max. *The Protestant Ethic and the Spirit of Capitalism.* Translated by Talcott Parsons. New York: Charles Scribner's Sons, 1958.

Whipple, Thomas W. and Alice E. Courtney. "Female Role Portrayals in Advertising and Communication Effectiveness: A Review." *Journal of Advertising,* 14 (1985): 3.

Williams, Raymond. *Television: Technology and Cultural Form.* Fontana, Great Britain: Colins, 1960.

Wiro, Osmo. "Government and Media in Scandinavia." *Government and the Media—Comparative Dimensions,* edited by Dan Nimmo and Michael W. Mansfield. Waco, Texas: Baylor University Press, 1982.

Yule, Andrew. *Fast Fade.* New York: Delacorte, 1989.

Index

About the Author

Calvin F. Exoo is professor of government at St. Lawrence University. He is editor and principal author of *Democracy Upside Down: Public Opinion and Cultural Hegemony in the United States.* His numerous articles and essays on the politics of the media have appeared in such publications as *Polity, New Political Science, The Journal of Ethnic Studies, The Journal of Politics, The American Political Science Review, The New York Times, The Baltimore Evening Sun,* and the *Los Angeles Times* wire service.